Mitigation in the Law of Damages

Mitigation in the Law of Damages

ANDY SUMMERS

Associate Professor of Law, London School of Economics & Political Science

OXFORD
UNIVERSITY PRESS

OXFORD
UNIVERSITY PRESS

Great Clarendon Street, Oxford, OX2 6DP,
United Kingdom

Oxford University Press is a department of the University of Oxford.
It furthers the University's objective of excellence in research, scholarship,
and education by publishing worldwide. Oxford is a registered trade mark of
Oxford University Press in the UK and in certain other countries

Published in the United States of America by Oxford University Press
198 Madison Avenue, New York, NY 10016, United States of America

British Library Cataloguing in Publication Data
Data available

Library of Congress Control Number: 2024940617

ISBN 9780198825333

DOI: 10.1093/9780191864032.001.0001

Printed and bound by
CPI Group (UK) Ltd, Croydon, CR0 4YY

FSC www.fsc.org MIX Paper | Supporting responsible forestry FSC® C013604

Acknowledgements

This book has been a long time coming, and along the way I have amassed a lot of people I would like to thank. I hope that these acknowledgements also give the reader some insight into the intellectual influences that have shaped (directly or otherwise) the style and main arguments of the book.

The spur to write on mitigation originally came from the Commercial Remedies seminars I attended as a BCL student in Oxford. Sitting at the front were Professors Andrew Burrows, James Edelman, Charles Mitchell, and Ed Peel. These days, I think the technical term for this kind of teaching arrangement would be 'overstaffed'. I found it inspiring and terrifying in equal measure. The reading list contained a large tranche of cases on recovery for 'avoided loss' which, even by the panel's own excitable standards, provoked some of the most vehement disagreements of the entire course. This started the itch that eventually took me fifteen years to scratch.

James Edelman was the one who persuaded me to stay on for the MPhil. His infectious enthusiasm for private law, coupled with his misplaced optimism that I could 'solve' avoided loss within one year (presumably projecting his own rate of productivity on to me), led me to take on a research degree when otherwise I had planned to head straight to the bar. The realization that I could not, in fact, do justice to this topic in this timescale, coupled with essential financial assistance from the Arts and Humanities Research Council—without which I surely would not have carried on—prompted me to extend the project for another three years on the DPhil.

While in Oxford, I benefited hugely from discussions with DPhil compatriots from the Obligations Discussion Group, including Eli Ball, Tatiana Cutts, Andrew Lodder, Fred Wilmot-Smith, and David Winterton. Our weekly informal seminars were very formative for me. 'Progress through relentless combat' is not an academic environment that suits everyone, but now working mainly with economists, it seems I must be drawn to it. Apropos of nothing, I also remember with great fondness many discussions about the themes of this book with Rob Stevens, when we were teaching together in Commercial Remedies seminars, and afterwards in the pub.

My thesis supervisor, following James Edelman's departure for the bench in Australia, was Ed Peel. Ed's eye for detail was critical in the later stages of the DPhil, when my arguments needed refining rather than buttressing against all-out attempts at demolition. Ed also helped to shepherd the thesis over the line with judicious nudges once I had been sitting on it for too long. I am also very grateful to my examiners, Andrew Burrows and Nick McBride, for their detailed comments which have led to several improvements, and for their strong endorsement of the work that I know was critical in securing the book contract with OUP. Still, I will await with great trepidation my first citation by Lord Burrows.

I have co-authored with two outstanding scholars on damages, Adam Kramer and David McLauchlin, both of whom helped shape my thinking on mitigation. I met Adam after it emerged that we were writing parallel conference papers on the so-called 'breach date' rule of damages. It was Adam who gave me the confidence to 'go public' with my (then nascent) theory of mitigation as part of our joint article in the Law Quarterly Review in 2014. Some years later, I teamed up with David McLauchlan to write about *The New Flamenco*, finding common ground after we had written opposing case notes on the decision in the Court of Appeal. David was also a wonderful host at the University of Wellington, where I spent the best sabbatical of my career, working on the book and travelling around New Zealand.

The London School of Economics and Political Science (LSE), where I have spent the last decade, has also had an important influence on the style and scope of the book. It obviously would have been possible for me to have looked beyond the legal literature (as I do in Chapter 5) while at Oxford, but it was only after I moved to LSE that I actually thought about doing this. My foray into the empirical evidence on causation and cognition was, I think, crucial in giving the causal explanation of mitigation—which forms the book's main argument—a fresh perspective. Many LSE colleagues also gave their time to comment on ideas and drafts. Singling out just two, Charlie Webb and Emmanuel Voyiakis directly influenced my thinking and I refer to their work (hopefully without butchering it) at various points.

I am heavily indebted to three superb research assistants who worked with me sequentially in the latter stages of the book: Josiah Senu, Alex Georgiou, and Vincent LaFortune. All of them were over-qualified for the role and quite capable of making their own substantial marks on private law scholarship, as indeed they already have done in several works. We had fantastic probing discussions, and hopefully they were not too disillusioned by my too-frequent response: 'that's a really great point, someone should definitely take that up, but I really need to get this sent off soon . . . '. Their contributions leave me confident that the various loose ends and errors I have left will get resolved eventually, if not by them then by others like them.

The book's cover photo was taken by Dennis Radermacher and is entitled 'The Lone Tree'. It was taken at Lake Wanaka in New Zealand, which I visited in 2018. I chose this image for two reasons. First, it recalls the 'trunk and branches' metaphor with which I open the Introduction, and which I think captures the aims of the book. Second, to me, the tree and its reflection are like the avoidable and avoided loss rules respectively: the book's key argument is that these rules function as mirror images. I am grateful to the OUP editorial and production teams for allowing me to run with this. I would also like to especially thank Paulina dos Santos Major and Charlotte Kershaw for their support and efficiency throughout the editorial process. If I tried their patience at times, it never showed, and their encouragement was always gratefully received.

Finally, I would like to thank those closest to me. My parents for everything they did that enabled me to pursue a career in academia. My siblings for their forbearance on several family holidays. And most of all, my wife Kate, who I am sure has spent longer discussing the law of mitigation than any non-lawyer ever, and most lawyers to boot. This book is not so much 'for' her—she has her own research agenda and this book is not much use to it—but 'because of' her. She helped shape my decision to be an academic, and without her I would never have finished this book. To clear up any confusion for readers, she is also the reason why the book goes under a different name from my early articles on mitigation. Although not intended as such, I think this is a suitable measure of her part in the project.

Because of Kate, without whom I might never have finished this book.
For Ted and Lara, without whom I might have finished somewhat sooner.

Brief Contents

Detailed Contents

PART 3. RESTATEMENT

Table of Cases

AUSTRALIA

CANADA

NEW ZEALAND

UNITED KINGDOM

Introduction

1 Overview

> The reported decisions on many branches of this subject have become so numerous as to tend to obscure the general principles which underlie them. They may be compared to the leaves of a tree; when a tree is in full foliage the numbers of its leaves frequently hide from view the form and development of the trunk and branches which support them.[1]

The aim of this book is to reveal the trunk and branches of the law of mitigation. Mitigation plays a fundamental role in assessing damages for loss. It responds to the basic argument: 'although I did wrong, you made things worse'.[2] It applies to all claims for compensation, regardless of the claimant's cause of action and irrespective of the defendant's level of fault (if any). More technically, mitigation determines how a claimant's own response to a breach affects the damages they can recover.[3] But, so defined, mitigation could potentially encompass—or at least overlap with—several other areas of damages, including remoteness, intervening causation, contributory negligence, betterment, and the market rule.[4] The relation between mitigation and these other doctrines is one of the puzzles that this book seeks to resolve.

This book provides the first comprehensive theoretical and doctrinal treatment of mitigation in any common law jurisdiction. The existing gap is remarkable for two main reasons. First, mitigation is a strong contender for the (ignominious) title of 'most-appealed' doctrine in all of private law. Over the past decade, it has spawned over fifteen Court of Appeal decisions and has been at the centre of six disputes reaching the Supreme Court.[5] The extensive chapters on mitigation in the

[1] Mackenzie Chalmers, *The Sale of Goods: Including the Factors Act 1889* (Clowes 1890) iii.

[2] As I will show, the same rules of mitigation also govern the converse argument: 'although I did wrong, everything turned out fine'.

[3] Throughout this book, 'damages' is used as shorthand for 'compensatory damages' (excluding eg restitutionary, negotiating, or disgorgement damages), unless other otherwise indicated.

[4] For further discussion of the scope of mitigation, see further text to n 45 below, and Chapter 10.

[5] In the Supreme Court: *Bunge SA v Nidera BV* [2015] UKSC 43, [2015] 3 All ER 1082; *Energy Solutions EU Ltd v Nuclear Decommissioning Authority* [2017] UKSC 34, [2017] 1 WLR 1373; *Swynson Ltd v Lowick Rose LLP* [2017] UKSC 32, [2018] AC 313; *Fulton Shipping Inc of Panama v Globalia Business Travel SAU (The New Flamenco)* [2017] UKSC 43, [2017] 1 WLR 2581; *Sainsbury's Supermarkets Ltd v Visa Europe Services LLC* [2020] UKSC 24, [2020] 4 All ER 807; *Stanford*

Mitigation in the Law of Damages. Andrew Summers, Oxford University Press. © Andy Summers 2025.
DOI: 10.1093/9780191864032.001.0001

leading practitioner texts on damages provide little in the way of concrete guidance to judges or parties, concluding either that the existing cases cannot be reconciled or that that the application of the rules raises a 'question of fact' for which no further guidance is possible. These seem like counsels of despair that legal scholars should be hesitant to accept.

Second, mitigation also has important theoretical implications. Although judges have typically explained mitigation as an aspect of causation, legal scholars have more often favoured instrumental explanations, such as the promotion of self-reliance, economic efficiency or (relatedly) the prevention of waste.[6] Mitigation has thus come to be regarded by legal scholars as an anomalous policy tool, cut loose from general theories of damages and largely overlooked by private law theorists.[7] The doctrine remains, as Bridge noted thirty years ago, 'theoretically undernourished'.[8] I attempt to rectify this deficit, and in so doing show that mitigation has fundamental implications for our understanding of loss and causation, as well as for existing theoretical debates about the availability of damages for the infringement of rights.

Before sketching the main arguments of the book, it may help to outline two cases that illustrate the law of mitigation in action; we will return to each of these cases later. First, in *Schering Agrochemicals v Resibel*,[9] the defendant supplied defective machinery for use in the claimant's factory. The defective machines caused the goods on the claimant's production line to become dangerously overheated. Upon discovering the defect, the claimant decided to keep the machines running anyway, resulting in an explosion that destroyed the factory. The court held that the claimant could not recover for the costs incurred in the explosion, but instead awarded damages for the sums that would have been expended repairing the machines.

Second, in *Hussey v Eels*,[10] the claimants were induced to buy a house by the defendant's negligent misrepresentation that the property was free from subsidence. Upon discovering the subsidence, the claimants decided not to resell the house immediately; instead, they kept it and sought planning permission to develop a second house on the same site. Two years later, the claimants resold the site with the planning permission, for substantially more than they had paid for it. The

International Bank Ltd (In Liquidation) v HSBC Bank PLC [2022] UKSC 34, [2023] 2 WLR 79. A Westlaw search conducted in September 2023 reveals that, over the past decade, there have been more than fifteen Court of Appeal decisions raising issues of mitigation.

[6] See further Chapter 4.

[7] A notable exception is George Letsas and Prince Saprai, 'Mitigation, Fairness and Contract Law' in *Philosophical Foundations of Contract Law* (OUP, 2016).

[8] Michael Bridge, 'Mitigation of Damages in Contract and the Meaning of Avoidable Loss' (1989) 105 Law Quarterly Review 398, 399.

[9] *Schering Agrochemicals Ltd v Resibel NV SA* (CA, 26 November 1992).

[10] *Hussey v Eels* [1990] 2 QB 227 (CA).

court held that this resale must be ignored in assessing damages, instead awarding the difference between the price paid by the claimants, and the market value of the property (based on a single subsiding house) at the date of purchase.

The leading texts on damages cite these two cases as applications of the 'avoidable' and 'avoided' loss rules of mitigation, respectively. These rules are conventionally expressed as follows. First, the avoidable loss rule states that the claimant cannot recover damages for losses that it could have avoided by acting reasonably. *Schering* is said to exemplify this rule.[11] Second, the avoided loss rule states that the claimant cannot recover damages for losses that it has in fact avoided, *except* where the benefit did not 'arise out of the consequences of the breach'.[12] *Hussey* is said to exemplify this exception.[13] Although well-established in the cases, the effect of the exception to the avoided loss rule often puzzles judges and legal scholars, because it seems inconsistent with the idea of compensation for loss.

In Part One of this book, I highlight several deficiencies of the orthodox account of mitigation just described. First, the leading texts on damages present the application of the avoidable loss rule as a question of fact for which 'no fixed rules can be laid down'.[14] But this cannot be right: there are many cases in which the trial judge's decision on the (un)reasonableness of the claimant's conduct has been successfully appealed. I argue that the issue of 'reasonableness' must raise at least some questions of law. Second, it is conventionally thought that the avoidable loss rule acts as a 'guillotine' to chop off liability for part of the harm actually suffered by the claimant. Again, this cannot be right: if it was, then in cases like *Schering* the claimant would have recovered nothing at all. I show that the effect of the avoidable loss rule on damages is more sophisticated than this guillotine heuristic allows.

In relation to the avoided loss rule, I also highlight two main deficiencies. First, the leading texts on damages have struggled to articulate when a benefit will be held not to have 'arisen out of the consequences' of the breach, instead concluding that 'the authorities are in a bit of a jumble'[15] and that 'the current law is in a dreadful muddle'.[16] This amounts to saying that there is no way of knowing when the rule

[11] Note 9.

[12] This phrase derives from the leading case on mitigation, *British Westinghouse Electric & Manufacturing Co Ltd v Underground Electric Railways Co of London Ltd (No 2)* [1912] AC 673 (HL) 690 (Viscount Haldane).

[13] Note 10.

[14] Andrew Tettenborn, *The Law of Damages* (2nd edn, LexisNexis 2010) [5.79]. See also James Edelman (ed), *McGregor on Damages* (21st edn, Sweet & Maxwell 2022) [9-083]–[9-101], offering a list of 'illustrative decisions' in lieu of legal principles.

[15] Harvey McGregor, 'The Role of Mitigation in the Assessment of Damages' in Djakhongir Saidov and Ralph Cunnington (eds), *Contract Damages: Domestic and International Perspectives* (Hart 2008) 336.

[16] David McLauchlan, 'Expectation Damages: Avoided Loss, Offsetting Gains and Subsequent Events' in Djakhongir Saidov and Ralph Cunnington (eds), *Contract Damages: Domestic and International Perspectives* (Hart 2008) 384. See also, judicially, *Fulton Shipping Inc of Panama v Globalia Business Travel SAU (The New Flamenco)* [2015] EWCA Civ 1299, [2016] 1 Lloyd's Rep 383 [20] and [39] (Longmore LJ).

properly applies. Second, in cases like *Hussey*, the effect of ignoring the benefit obtained by the claimant is to put them in a better position than if the breach had not occurred. Although such awards are often stated as being for 'avoided loss', this terminology reflects a deeper confusion: what (conceptually) is the 'loss' that has been avoided, for which the claimant can recover? And how exactly are such losses assessed? The orthodox account of mitigation provides no answers to these questions.

In Part Two of the book, I develop the foundations for a new account of mitigation. Existing scholarship has become overwhelmed by the sheer volume of cases in this area: the leaves of the tree have come to hide the trunk and branches that support them. I argue that the 'trunk' of mitigation can be stated quite simply: it is an aspect of causation. Judges have been right all along to insist on this explanation, and legal scholars have been wrong to resist it. However, to see why, I argue that we need to move beyond the 'but for' concept of causation, and instead investigate how ordinary people use causal principles to attribute responsibility outside the law. The book's main thesis is that the twin principles of choice and abnormality that underlie 'commonsense' causal reasoning, also explain how judges approach questions of mitigation.

Part Three of the book restates the 'branches' of the law of mitigation. I show that mitigation applies where the claimant made a choice to respond abnormally to the breach. Two norms are relevant here. The first is a *legal* norm: it is expected that the claimant will seek to replicate the position that it would have been in but for the breach (its 'no-breach position'), as nearly as possible.[17] The second is a *descriptive* (i.e., statistical) norm: it is expected that the claimant will seek to replicate the no-breach position in a way that is usual or unexceptional in the circumstances. Claimants are not obliged to follow either of these norms; they are free to respond (or not respond) to the breach however they like. But, if a claimant does choose an abnormal response, damages are still assessed as if the relevant norm had been followed: this is the doctrine of mitigation.

The effect of mitigation is to hold claimants legally responsible for the consequences of their choice to respond abnormally to the breach, for better or worse. Whereas the orthodox account regards the avoidable and avoided loss rules as entirely distinct, I show that they function as mirror images. Where the claimant's choice turned out to aggravate the harm suffered, it will still be able to recover the sum that it would have lost if it had acted normally. Likewise, where the claimant's choice turned out to reduce or eliminate a harm that it would otherwise have suffered (if acting normally), damages will still be awarded for this 'avoided loss' even though the relevant harm did not in fact eventuate. In other words, mitigation

[17] This norm derives from the 'compensatory principle'. For an overview of this principle, see further Chapter 1.

applies in the same way regardless of whether the claimant's choice turned out to be harmful or beneficial.

We can now re-examine the two cases above. In *Schering*, the claimant could have tried to repair the machines as soon as it discovered the defect; instead, it chose to continue production. Mitigation holds the claimant legally responsible for the consequences of this choice, for better or worse. Things turned out 'for worse', because the factory exploded. I argue that the reason why the claimant could not recover damages for the cost of the explosion was not because its decision to continue production was 'unreasonable' in any conventional sense: indeed, the decision may have been entirely sensible from a commercial point-of-view. What matters is that the claimant made a *choice* not to replicate its no-breach position (as nearly as possible) by repairing the machines; consequently, damages were assessed as if it had undertaken the repair, even though in fact it did not.

In *Hussey*, if the claimants had known about the subsidence, they would never have bought the property. Having discovered the misrepresentation, they chose to not to resell immediately, and instead sought new planning permission. This decision might have turned out badly: for example, permission might have been refused and in the meantime the market might have slumped; in these circumstances, it is clear that the claimants could not have recovered for any additional costs. But as things turned out, their decision worked out well: they sold the site at a profit, despite the subsidence. I argue that the reason why this profit was ignored is again that the claimants made a choice not to replicate their no-breach position (as nearly as possible), by reselling the property as it was; consequently, damages were assessed as if they had put the property straight back on the market, even though in fact they did not.

This new understanding of mitigation has several further implications for the law of damages. First, the so-called 'market rule' of damages applies where the claimant could have replicated its no-breach position as nearly as possible by resorting to the *market* to obtain substitute performance; in these circumstances, damages are assessed as if it had resorted to the market, even though it did not. Expressed in these terms, the market rule is just rule of thumb that reflects a specific application of the more general mitigation doctrine. Second, the doctrine of intervening (or 'supervening') acts by the claimant applies where the claimant made a choice to act abnormally *other than* in the course of replicating its no-breach position. Third, the doctrine of 'betterment' involves a choice by the claimant to put itself in a *better* position than if the breach had not occurred.

I also identify several other doctrines that are distinct from the law of mitigation, despite some overlaps in their practical application. These include the doctrines of remoteness and contributory negligence. Although, like mitigation, both of these doctrines can apply to the claimant's post-breach conduct, they have different explanations and effects. In particular, unlike mitigation, remoteness and contributory negligence both function as true 'limitations' on damages, with asymmetrical effect: they can only ever cut back recovery of the claimant's loss. The scope, application, and effects of these doctrines also differ from mitigation in important respects. My new account of mitigation helps to pinpoint these differences, and also to resolve the issues that arise where the doctrines apply concurrently with mitigation.

Finally, my analysis of mitigation also contributes a new perspective on three foundational concepts in private law: causation, choice, and loss.

On causation, I revive the 'commonsense' theory originally developed by Hart and Honoré in *Causation in the Law*.[18] I argue that their explanation of how judges decide questions of causation deserves renewed attention in light of new experimental research into how ordinary people make causal judgements outside the law. By applying these insights to the law of mitigation, I provide a concrete example of how experimental evidence can, in the context of causation, generate useful new hypotheses about the principles affecting judicial decisions. Although I do not presuppose any determinative link between judicial reasoning and commonsense reasoning, I argue that this methodological approach can be informative where judges themselves have stated that their causal judgments are based on common sense, as in mitigation.

The concept of choice plays an important role in my account of mitigation. In particular, the voluntariness of the claimant's action or inaction serves as a precondition of their responsibility for the consequences of not replicating the no-breach position (or doing so in an unusual way). I discuss the boundaries of what amounts to a 'choice' in this context, for example when the claimant is acting under some of kind of constraint. The law of mitigation also squarely raises the fundamental question of whether it is *making* a choice, or the fact of *having* a choice, that matters for the attribution of responsibility. This question has divided moral philosophers and already been the subject of major work in private law.[19] I do not attempt to resolve the debate writ large, but I show how the remaining doctrinal uncertainties in the scope of mitigation appear to map this moral distinction.

Perhaps most significantly, my account of mitigation provides grounds for fundamentally rethinking the legal concept of loss. In the law of damages, the definition of 'loss' is prescribed by the compensatory principle. This principle entails a comparison between the position that the claimant is in as a result of the breach ('breach position'), and the position that it would have been in if the breach had not occurred ('no-breach position'). It is well-known that the no-breach position rests on a counterfactual assessment. However, my account of mitigation shows how the claimant's breach position can rely on a counterfactual assessment as well.

[18] HLA Hart and Tony Honoré, *Causation in the Law* (2nd edn, Clarendon 1985).

[19] See eg Thomas Scanlon, *What We Owe to Each Other* (HUP 1998); Serena Olsaretti, 'Scanlon on Responsibility and the Value of Choice (2013) 10 Journal of Moral Philosophy 465–83; Emmanuel Voyiakis, *Private Law and the Value of Choice* (Hart Publishing 2017).

Specifically, where mitigation applies, the claimant's loss is assessed as if they had taken steps to replicate the no-breach position in the usual way, even though in fact they did not. Accordingly, I develop the argument that mitigation is integral to the legal concept of loss, rather than taking effect as a subsequent limitation on damages.

2 Aims

Despite the explicit attention paid to aims and methodology in other areas of the law, and elsewhere in the social sciences, the aims of private law scholarship are often assumed rather than stated explicitly.[20] It can sometimes seem as though private lawyers just 'do' private law. This is mostly (though not always) an illusion; informally, private law scholars engage extensively in debates about the types of claim they are making and the criteria that their accounts should be judged against. However, these assumptions often do not feature in the final draft.[21] This practice is unfortunate, because it inhibits direct comparisons with other works and wider schools of thought. In stating one's aims, it can be tempting to seek refuge in terms that can mean almost anything, and so, nothing: for example, 'discussing', 'analysing', or 'examining' an area of the law. Another common device involves recourse to metaphor: 'illuminating', 'revealing', or 'painting the best picture' of the law.

So far in this Introduction, I have relied mainly on the second device. I started by stating my aim to reveal the 'trunk' and 'branches' of the law of mitigation. I think that this metaphor captures an approach that is likely to be instinctively familiar to many private law scholars working in common law jurisdictions. It situates the book within a long tradition of 'doctrinal' private law scholarship.[22] But it is incumbent on me to state more explicitly (if imprecisely) what I think this approach entails: to break down the tree metaphor. In this section I try to highlight the main premises on which the aims of the book rest. I certainly do not claim that my aims are ones that every private law scholar has, or should have, but I hope that the following exposition will help to clarify the relationship of this book to other works on the law of damages: to indicate where there is scope for direct contestation and where there is a risk of talking at cross purposes.

In this book I have two main aims: to *restate* and to *explain* the law of mitigation. Both aims can be termed 'descriptive' (in contrast to 'evaluative' or 'normative'),[23]

[20] For two notable exceptions, adopting different approaches, see eg Stephen Smith, *Contract Theory* (OUP 2004) ch 1; Charlie Webb, *Reason and Restitution: A Theory of Unjust Enrichment* (OUP 2016) ch 1.

[21] As Burrows notes, 'we rarely find doctrinal scholars analysing the precise methodological approach that they are adopting': Andrew Burrows, *Remedies for Torts, Breach of Contract, and Equitable Wrongs* (4th edn, OUP 2019) 21.

[22] The metaphor is borrowed from a private law treatise dated 1890: n 1.

[23] A claim is 'evaluative' if it includes evaluative predicates or concepts, such as *good* or *bad*, *better* or *worse*, *desirable* or *undesirable*. A claim is 'normative' if it includes deontic operators, such as *ought*,

but they each have different objects of description. In the senses that I use here, 'restating' the law involves describing legal rules abstracted from the body of decided cases, whereas 'explaining' the law involves describing the principles that the judges endorsed in their development of the law.[24] Neither aim depends on evaluation. So, a restatement of mitigation can be correct even if it reveals a flawed set of rules, or not the rules that we should have. Similarly, an explanation of mitigation can be correct even if it reveals flawed principles, or not the principles that judges should have endorsed. In other words, my approach rests on the premise that it is perfectly possible to restate and explain an area of the law without proclaiming that it is justified. As I outline below, this is a premise that some private law theorists dispute.

In any case, a risk with labelling my aims as 'descriptive' is that description tends to have a bad reputation amongst private law scholars. For example, Stephen Smith summarizes that 'Descriptive accounts, as the name suggests, aim to describe the law as it is now';[25] however, 'A purely descriptive account would be entirely useless, if not impossible. It would amount to little more than a randomly collected list of data'.[26] Although this view is widely held, I think that it is mistaken, because it confuses the aim of describing *the law* with the more rudimentary task of describing legal *sources*. In the common law, the individual cases provide the sources from which the law can be identified, but no legal theorist would regard these sources (individually) as the law itself. I understand the common law as a set of rules *abstracted* from the body of decided cases. Reprising the metaphor, the individual cases are each just leaves on the tree; my aim is to describe the 'trunk and branches' underneath.

Restating rules of the common law (akin to the branches of the tree) involves mirroring how judges decide what the existing cases require.[27] Abstract expositions of these judicial practices are the domain of jurisprudence, specifically theories of adjudication.[28] But private law scholars have a good practical grasp of techniques such as 'distinguishing', determining the 'ratio' of a decision, assessing its degree of authority, and so on. A restatement of the law, as I understand it, must be assessed according to its consistency or 'fit' with the cases. But in assessing this fit, it is necessary to take account not only of the outcomes of individual cases (together with

permissible, *obligatory*, *right*, or *wrong*. A claim is descriptive (or 'positive') if it has no evaluative or normative content.

[24] Explanation is thus a second-order form of description: it involves describing the reasons why X, instead of X itself.

[25] Smith (n 20) 5.

[26] ibid 6.

[27] As Smith puts it, 'traditional or doctrinal legal scholarship . . . [aims] to examine the law using language, concepts and techniques that are similar to those employed by (and in) the courts': Stephen Smith, 'Taking Law Seriously' (2000) 50 University of Toronto Law Journal 241, 241.

[28] eg Joseph Raz, *The Authority of Law: Essays on Law and Morality* (Clarendon 1979) ch 10.

their material facts), but also the judicial reasoning deployed, and the differing degrees of authority of each case. That is because all of these elements form part of the judicial practice of determining what is required by the law as it currently stands, or in other words, part of applying the doctrine of precedent.[29]

Explaining rules of the common law involves identifying the reason(s) why the law is as it is (akin to the trunk of the tree). There are different types of reason with which an explanatory account of the law might be concerned. In this book, I am concerned specifically with identifying the normative principles endorsed in the judicial decisions from which the relevant legal rules are derived. However, it is important to emphasize that by 'normative principles' I merely mean propositions of a normative kind, whether or not they turn out to be true. This stipulation separates my attempt to explain the law of mitigation from either a causal history (which may rest on non-normative facts) or a justification of the rules (which must rest on principles that are true). A more detailed exposition of the type of explanatory approach that I have in mind, along with the criteria against which such a theory should be assessed, is provided in Chapter 4.

This approach to restating and explaining the law rests on two important premises: first, that the existence and content of the law does not depend on its merits;[30] and second, that it is possible to describe the law without evaluating its merits.[31] These positions are associated with substantive and methodological legal positivism, respectively.[32] Both premises are incompatible with Dworkin's interpretive jurisprudence. Dworkin took the view that 'the flat distinction between description and evaluation' has 'enfeebled legal theory'.[33] Instead, for Dworkin, justification is integral to legal analysis. He argued that both judges and legal scholars must aim to 'achieve equilibrium between legal practice as they find it and the best justification of that practice'.[34] On this view, it is impossible to restate or explain an area of the law in the way that I have proposed, separately from the task of (normatively) justifying it.[35]

[29] Compare eg Rupert Cross and James Harris, *Precedent in English Law* (4th edn, Clarendon 1991) 72 (focusing on judicial reasoning); and Arthur Goodhart, 'Determining the *Ratio Decidendi* of a Case' in Arthur Goodhart (ed), *Essays in Jurisprudence and the Common Law* (CUP 1931) 10 (focusing on identifying material facts).

[30] For detailed clarification of this proposition, see John Gardner, 'Legal Positivism: 5 1/2 Myths' (2001) 46 American Journal of Jurisprudence 199.

[31] HLA Hart, *The Concept of Law* (3rd edn, OUP 2012) vi, 240, 242–44. See further Brian Leiter, 'Beyond the Hart/Dworkin Debate: The Methodology Problem in Jurisprudence' (2003) 48 The American Journal of Jurisprudence 17, 30–43; Nicola Lacey, 'Analytical Jurisprudence Versus Descriptive Sociology Revisited' (2005) 84 Texas Law Review 944, 953–60.

[32] These terms are taken from Stephen Perry, 'Hart's Methodological Positivism' (1998) 4 Legal Theory 427.

[33] Ronald Dworkin, *A Matter of Principle* (Clarendon 1986) 148. See also Ronald Dworkin, *Taking Rights Seriously* (Duckworth 1978); Ronald Dworkin, *Law's Empire* (Hart 1998).

[34] Dworkin, *Law's Empire* (n 33) 90.

[35] For Dworkin, his interpretive approach applied not only to general theories of law, but also to theories about any specific area of the law; it is 'relentlessly interpretive': ibid 226.

Notwithstanding this disavowal of Dworkinian interpretivism, my approach to restating and explaining the law of mitigation might nevertheless be interpretive in the sense (or senses) sometimes used by private law scholars. This is because, within private law, invocation of the 'interpretive' imprint often does not stem from, or at least is not strictly faithful to, Dworkin's interpretive jurisprudence.[36] Instead, claims to be doing interpretive analysis seem to reflect a variety of intellectual influences, which vary between scholars,[37] such that it has become difficult to rely on this label to indicate any particular methodological perspective. Insofar as there is a dominant understanding, it is probably Stephen Smith's influential exposition in *Contract Theory*,[38] which proposes criteria for assessing interpretive accounts of private law.[39] Consequently, it may be helpful briefly to state how my aims relate to Smith's approach.

Smith's 'interpretive' analysis seems closer to what I have called 'explanation' than it does to Dworkinian interpretivism. Smith expressly rejects the suggestion that an interpretive theory is better if it shows the law to be justified,[40] arguing that this would conflate 'accounts of what the law should be (the goal of a prescriptive theory) with accounts of what the law is (the goal of an interpretive theory).'[41] This sharp dichotomy between what the law is and what it should be, runs directly contrary to Dworkin's notion of law as integrity.[42] Smith argues instead that 'a good [interpretive] theory should explain the law in a way that shows how the law might be thought to be justified *even if it is not justified*.'[43] This proposition seems entirely consistent with my descriptive (i.e. non-evaluative) approach to explanation, which in effect seeks to identify the principles that judges thought justified their decisions,[44] even if it turns out that they did not.

Notwithstanding departures from Dworkin, it is easy to see why many private law scholars may prefer to label their approaches as 'interpretive'. First, it can seem to underplay the complexity of much private law scholarship to refer to these works as merely 'descriptive'. However, complexity need not arise from the integration of description and evaluation: it can arise because the relevant objects of description (the rules of the common law) are complex. Second, private law scholarship may

[36] See further text to n 42. For an approach that does appear to follow Dworkin, see Ernest Weinrib, *The Idea of Private Law* (Harvard University Press 1995) ch1.

[37] Compare eg Smith, *Contract Theory* (n 20) ch 1; Robert Stevens, *Torts and Rights* (OUP 2007) vii, 306; Allan Beever, *Rediscovering the Law of Negligence* (Hart 2007) (n 20) 21; Donal Nolan and Andrew Robertson (eds), *Rights and Private Law* (Hart 2012) 5; Burrows (n 21) 21.

[38] Smith, *Contract Theory* (n 20) ch 1.

[39] eg David Winterton, *Money Awards in Contract Law* (Hart 2015) (n 37) 16–20.

[40] Smith, *Contract Theory* (n 20) 17.

[41] ibid (n 20) 18. See also Allan Beever and Charles Rickett, 'Interpretive Legal Theory and the Academic Lawyer' (2005) 68 MLR 320, 322 fn 14: 'interpretive legal theorists do not produce their accounts . . . by examining prescriptive theories'.

[42] Note 34.

[43] Smith, *Contract Theory* (n 20) 18 (emphasis added). See also Beever and Rickett (n 40) 328: 'While the interpretive method is in part normative, its "oughts" are internal to the law.'

[44] This reflects Hart's notion of the 'internal point of view': Hart (n 31).

be thought to rely on 'interpretation' in the sense that scholars must often 'read between the lines' of individual judgments and the whole body of decided cases, rather than merely recite judges' express reasons. However, the techniques that this sense of 'interpretation' seeks to capture, which are clearly evident throughout this book, need not entail the Dworkinian aim of achieving equilibrium between (descriptive) fit and (normative) justification.

Finally, although I do not offer a fully-fledged justification of the law of mitigation in this book, this omission should not be read as a concession that the current law is *not* normatively justified. In Chapter 6, I sketch how one *might* justify the law of mitigation, as I have restated and explained it. My aim here as a spur to further research, by suggesting the form that I think a successful justification is most likely to take. There are two main reasons why I do not embark on this task myself. First, the book is long enough already, and I prefer to discharge my main aims comprehensively rather than spreading myself too thinly. Second, and more importantly, I am not sure that I am best-placed to deliver a thorough justification of the law of mitigation since—if I am right about the general direction—this would involve delving deeply into areas of philosophy and psychology where others have much more expertise.

3 Scope

The substantive scope of this book is the law of mitigation. Accordingly, my analysis focuses on the decided cases in which judges have expressed their reasoning in terms of 'mitigation', together with the other cases relied upon in those decisions. In Chapters 10 and 11, I venture further by examining various other doctrines that have occasionally been alleged to have some overlap with mitigation. I conclude that the so-called 'market rule' or damages, 'intervening acts by the claimant' and 'betterment' are all subsumed by the law of mitigation, properly understood. By contrast, the doctrines of remoteness and contributory negligence (amongst others) are not. It is important to clarify how and why I made this move, from explaining and restating the law of mitigation as conventionally expressed, to drawing conclusions about other—nominally distinct—doctrines.

There exists no universally agreed definition of 'mitigation' in the law of damages; the scope of the doctrine is one of the issues that calls to be resolved. Anyone who wishes to study mitigation must therefore make a decision at the outset about which cases to analyse. This necessity poses a methodological challenge for any descriptive account of the law; there is a risk that the scholar's own normative commitments will affect the choices that they make about what to include within, or exclude from, the scope of their enquiry.[45] In the leading texts on damages, this

[45] John Finnis, *Natural Law and Natural Rights* (2nd edn, OUP 2011) ch 1; Julie Dickson, *Evaluation and Legal Theory* (Hart 2001) ch 3. See further Leiter (n 31) 30–43; Webb (n 20) 9–10.

methodological pitfall may help to explain the omission of many of the 'avoided loss' cases from the orthodox account of mitigation, reflecting the normative preference of some authors that claimants *should not* recover damages for costs that were not actually incurred.

To minimize this risk of presupposing the scope of mitigation, I have adopted the internal point of view to determine which cases to analyse. In particular, the scope of my enquiry sought to reflect the judges' own viewpoint about which cases concerned mitigation, rather than my own (or any other) external view about how far the doctrine of mitigation *should* extend.[46] In practice, this involved focusing on two main types of case: first, cases in which the judges themselves had expressed their reasoning in terms of 'mitigation'; and second, other cases that had been cited by the judges in support of their decisions in the first type of case, whether or not those other decisions were themselves expressed in terms of mitigation. In this way, I aimed to reflect the judges' own perspectives without resorting to linguistic formalism. Together, these two types of case formed the core of my enquiry into the law of mitigation.

Having developed an explanation and restatement of the law of mitigation based on these 'core' cases, I proceeded to examine cases on related doctrines. Here, by 'related' I mean merely that the doctrine has conventionally been *thought to be* related to mitigation, either by judges or legal scholars. The issue to be resolved was whether any of these putatively related doctrines are governed by the same rules and explained (in the sense described above) by the same principles as the law of mitigation. In my view the 'market rule', 'intervening acts by the claimant', and 'betterment' do share a common basis with mitigation; indeed, it can be said that each of these rules or doctrines are not merely *related to* but more specifically are *part of* the (same) law of mitigation. By contrast, the doctrines of remoteness and contributory negligence—amongst others—differ from mitigation in important respects, despite that they each have some superficial resemblance to mitigation and may arise in similar factual circumstances.

The jurisdictional scope of the book is the *English* law of mitigation. In particular, the sources from which I draw my explanation and restatement of mitigation are exclusively decisions of the courts of England and Wales.[47] I exclude foreign cases from my analysis on the basis that they cannot be a (direct) source of English law. This point is not entirely settled; foreign cases are sometimes referred to as being of 'persuasive authority' in the English courts.[48] Nevertheless,

[46] cf Edelman (n 14) [9-002]: 'The principal, and proper, meaning of the term "mitigation" . . . concerns avoiding of the consequences of a wrong.' This definition, which would include conduct by third parties, defendants, and natural events, fails to reflect the judges' internal viewpoint: *Swynson* (n 5) [46] (Lord Sumption); see further Chapter 9.

[47] However, occasional reference is made to appeals from other jurisdictions heard by the English courts: for example, decisions of the Privy Council and Scottish appeals in the House of Lords.

[48] See further Neil Duxbury, 'The Law of the Land' (2015) 78 Modern Law Review 26.

I take the view that foreign cases are merely 'informative' in the English courts and cannot be binding.[49] In any event, a major objection to relying on foreign cases to develop arguments on the English law of mitigation is that any such reliance would necessarily be partial, since such cases are so numerous. Consequently, at the risk of cherry-picking, I abstained altogether from relying on foreign cases to develop my arguments.[50]

Notwithstanding this jurisdictional focus on England and Wales, I intend the book to have international significance. In several other common law jurisdictions, the law of mitigation developed directly out of the English cases, at a time when decisions of the English courts were still authoritative; in most of these jurisdictions, it appears that the doctrine has remained substantially based on English law notwithstanding the subsequent possibility of divergence. Consequently, I hope that the book will help judges and legal scholars abroad to re-examine their own domestic law of mitigation. To this end, as an aid to navigation of the book for readers in Australia, Canada, and New Zealand in particular, I have included footnote references to the leading domestic cases from each of these jurisdictions. However, it is important to reiterate that these footnoted cases are not claimed as support for the book's arguments on the English law of mitigation, which are developed independently.

The only common law jurisdiction that appears to have diverged significantly from the English law of mitigation is the United States. As with other common law jurisdictions, the early US law of mitigation appears to have started out broadly in alignment with English law. However, judging from the Restatements of mitigation produced by the American Legal Institute,[51] the US approach now differs from the English law of mitigation as I describe it in this book.[52] The most likely reason for this divergence is the dominance of economic analyses of mitigation within American private law scholarship,[53] which appear to have shaped the Restatements in a way that cuts the US law of mitigation loose from the causal principles that (I argue) underpin mitigation in English law and in the law of most other common law jurisdictions. Consequently, for American legal scholars, this book is likely to be mainly of comparative interest: the account that I put forward here represents 'the path not taken'.

[49] ibid 34: 'Genuinely foreign precedents, whether we label them persuasive or secondary or some other type of authority, are but information in the hands of a national court.'

[50] The only exception is where the foreign decision has been cited in an English decision, and then only to the extent of the citation.

[51] American Legal Institute, *Restatement (Second) of Torts* (1979) §918–20; American Legal Institute, *Restatement (Second) of Contracts* (1981) §350; American Legal Institute, *Restatement (Third) of Torts: Apportionment of Liability* (2000) §4. However, these Restatements are not infallible because they are not themselves a source of law; just like the restatement in this book, they attempt to describe rules abstracted from the decided cases, which remain the only authoritative sources.

[52] See eg American Legal Institute, *Restatement (Second) of Torts* §918(2), §920; American Legal Institute, *Restatement (Second) of Contracts* §350 Comment (f).

[53] See further Chapter 4.

4 Structure

The book is divided into three main parts. Part One ('Orthodoxy') outlines and critiques the orthodox account of mitigation put forward by the leading texts on damages. Within this part, Chapter 1 provides a brief history of the law of mitigation, sets the doctrine in context within the law of damages, and traces the development of the orthodox account. Chapters 2 and 3 expose various deficiencies with the orthodox accounts of the avoidable and avoided loss rules respectively; the aim is to show how these descriptions of the law of mitigation are either incomplete or inconsistent with the cases, in various respects. Chapter 4 critiques several explanations of mitigation that have been put forward in the leading texts; the aim in this chapter is to show that none of the theories so far developed offer a plausible explanation of the law of mitigation as we currently find it.

Part Two ('Explanation') develops the book's main argument that mitigation is an aspect of causation. Within this part, Chapter 5 outlines a new theoretical framework for developing the causal explanation of mitigation, drawing upon two 'commonsense' principles of causal reasoning that are evident outside the law. Chapter 6 applies these two principles to the law of mitigation. This chapter forms the crux of the book: it establishes a new account of mitigation that explains and restates the existing law in terms of causation; in this chapter I also sketch the argument that the law of mitigation, so understood, may be normatively justified. Chapter 7 shows how this new account successfully resolves several puzzles faced by the orthodox account, including the insight that there is no 'duty' to mitigate, and the fact that mitigation applies universally within the law of damages, but only to conduct after breach.

Part Three ('Restatement') develops the new account of mitigation in more detail. Within this part, Chapters 8 and 9 show how the law of mitigation (as restated) applies to the cases on avoidable and avoided loss respectively, and Chapter 10 does the same for the so-called 'market rule' of damages. The aim is to show that my new account is more consistent with the reasoning and results of the decided cases than the orthodox account; in other words, that it provides a better descriptive account of the law as it is. Chapter 11 considers the relationship between mitigation (as restated) and several other doctrines within the law of damages that are nominally distinct. I argue that two of these doctrines—specifically 'intervening acts by the claimant' and betterment'—share the same explanation as mitigation and can properly be assimilated within the same set of rules, whereas the others are genuinely distinct.

The remainder of this section provides some suggestions to readers about how to go about using this book. First, I should emphasize that the book aims to develop a single thesis from beginning to end. Each chapter is intended to play a part in the thesis. Readers might be tempted to proceed directly to the new account of mitigation presented in Parts Two and Three, since these chapters contain the book's most distinctive arguments. However, Part One is also integral to the overall argument and aims to do more than merely replicate the conventional view of mitigation already familiar from the leading texts. In demonstrating the (descriptive) deficiencies of the orthodox account, Part One directly motivates Parts Two and Three of the book; it also helps to specify how my restatement of the law of mitigation departs from and improves upon the orthodox understanding. To assess this new account in context, ideally the reader should start from the beginning.

Nevertheless, for readers seeking a shortcut, it may help to pinpoint which sections to prioritize. The opening section of this Introduction summarizes the book's main arguments in a few paragraphs; however, this brief overview inevitably contains some simplifications. Chapter 6 provides a more comprehensive overview of the main thesis. There, I start by outlining the explanation of mitigation as causation, drawing on the theoretical framework developed in Chapter 5. Then, I summarize the restatement of the law of mitigation developed in detail in Part Three, and I compare this with the orthodox account critiqued in Part One. Finally, I sketch a justification of the law of mitigation as it is. The arguments in Chapter 6 are not entirely self-standing; they rely on analyses substantiated elsewhere in the book. However, my aim in this chapter is to provide something as close as possible to a 'one-stop shop' for readers who do not wish to read the book from start to finish.

For private law theorists, Chapters 4 and 5 should also be of interest, along with—most of all—the Conclusion. Chapter 4 critiques the various existing theories that legal scholars have invoked to explain mitigation; I argue that none of these theories (besides causation) offers a plausible explanation of the law, either individually or in combination. Chapter 5 develops the theoretical framework on which the new causal theory of mitigation relies: I refine Hart and Honoré's pathbreaking work on 'commonsense' causation,[54] drawing on contemporary empirical research into how ordinary people make causal judgements outside the law. The Conclusion draws out some further implications of the book's main arguments, organized around the key concepts of causation, choice, rights, and loss. My aim here is to emphasize how and why mitigation matters for private law theory generally, and to open up an agenda for future research.

For practitioners, the chapters likely to be of most interest are Chapters 1 to 3 (critiquing the orthodox account) and Chapters 8 to 11 (restating the law of mitigation). Chapters 2 and 3 should provide reassurance to practitioners who have puzzled over how the avoidable and avoided loss rules applies; I argue that the main ambiguities are embedded in and have been exacerbated by the leading texts. In Chapters 8 to 11, I aim to provide an accessible and practitioner-friendly restatement of the law of mitigation. To this end, these chapters are structured using the

[54] Hart and Honoré (n 5).

familiar terminology of avoidable and avoided loss, the market rule, intervening causation, and betterment. However, within each section, the aim is to restate the law in terms of choice and abnormality, using the theoretical framework developed in Part Two. As a primer for this new terminology, it is advisable to read the summary in Chapter 6 ('Restating Mitigation') before searching Part Three for answers to specific legal problems.

PART 1
ORTHODOXY

1
The Orthodox Account of Mitigation

1 Introduction

This chapter outlines the orthodox account of mitigation. Given the stated aims of the book to explain and restate the law of mitigation,[1] it is important to clarify from the outset what I mean by the 'orthodox account of mitigation'. I use this term to refer to the conventional view regarding the correct description of the law of mitigation as it currently stands. This view is represented, and indeed consecrated as the orthodoxy, by the descriptions of mitigation put forward in the leading texts on damages. Although there is no definitive list of 'leading texts', for present purposes I take the orthodoxy to be represented by those texts most frequently cited by judges and legal scholars on issues of mitigation.[2] Of course, not all of these texts offer precisely the same descriptions of mitigation; however, in outlining the orthodox account in this chapter, I aim to capture the main features of the doctrine, upon which these texts mostly agree.

The fact that a particular description of the law has become established as the orthodoxy does not necessarily mean that it is correct: a descriptive account of the law may be orthodox but wrong. Here, when I say that the orthodox account is 'wrong' (or 'deficient', or 'problematic'), I do not intend any evaluation of the law itself.[3] Instead, my claim is that the conventional view about what the law is, is mistaken. In other words, I aim to critique the orthodox account by showing that although it purports to describe the law it currently stands, it is in fact inconsistent with the reasoning and results of the decided cases in various respects. Ultimately, a description of the common law can only be abstracted from the cases themselves, which are the relevant source of law. Although the leading texts attempt to perform this abstraction correctly, they may sometimes get things wrong. For example, in *Johnson v Agnew*, Lord Wilberforce famously warned of:

[1] See further Introduction, Section 2.

[2] See eg James Edelman (ed), *McGregor on Damages* (21st edn, Sweet & Maxwell 2022); Hugh Beale (ed), *Chitty on Contracts* (34th edn, Sweet & Maxwell 2022); Edwin Peel (ed), *Treitel on The Law of Contract* (15th edn, Sweet & Maxwell 2020); Andrew Tettenborn (ed), *Clerk & Lindsell on Torts* (23rd edn, Sweet & Maxwell 2022); Andrew Tettenborn, *The Law of Damages* (2nd edn, LexisNexis 2010); Andrew Burrows, *Remedies for Torts, Breach of Contract, and Equitable Wrongs* (4th edn, OUP 2019). More recently, to this list may be added Adam Kramer, *The Law of Contract Damages* (3rd edn, Hart 2022); however, Kramer's description of mitigation differs in key respects from the orthodoxy as represented collectively by the other texts.

[3] In other words, I am not making any claim about whether the law is good or bad or should be changed.

Mitigation in the Law of Damages. Andrew Summers, Oxford University Press. © Andy Summers 2025.
DOI: 10.1093/9780191864032.003.0001

> the dangers, well perceived by our predecessors but tending to be neglected in modern times, of placing reliance on textbook authority for an analysis of judicial decisions. [In this case, the textbook] is on the face of it a jumble of unclear propositions not logically related to each other. It is 'supported' by footnote references to cases . . . which are not explained or analysed.[4]

One of the key arguments in this book is that mistakes within the leading texts on damages have seriously afflicted our current understanding of the law of mitigation. In Chapters 2 and 3, I show that the orthodox account of mitigation is deficient in various respects; in Chapters 8 and 9, I develop a rival 'restatement' of the law, which I argue is more consistent with the underlying cases. However, the relationship between the orthodox account and the correct description of the law is a complex one, because the current law of mitigation has not been formed entirely independently of the leading texts. Instead, just like any other area of the common law, the law of mitigation has undergone continual development, and each new case has brought with it scope for judicial decisions to be influenced by the contemporary leading texts. This issue of the 'reflexive effect' of the leading texts on the development of the law of mitigation, is discussed in further detail below.[5]

The remainder of this chapter is divided into three sections. The first section sets mitigation in context as part of a broader conventional understanding of the law of damages.[6] The second section briefly outlines the historical development of mitigation, tracing its evolution from the earliest authorities to the current orthodoxy. The third section describes the orthodox account of mitigation in more detail, outlining its division into three rules: the avoidable loss rule; the reasonable attempts rule; and the avoided loss rule. I argue that, within the broader conventional understanding of the law of damages, the reasonable attempts rule, and the 'first limb' of the avoided loss rule, are both redundant. The orthodox account of mitigation can therefore be expressed more concisely, without any change of substance, as comprising just two rules: the avoidable loss rule; and (the exception to) the avoided loss rule. Thereafter, Chapters 2 and 3 critique each of these two orthodox rules in more detail.

2 Mitigation in Context

This section sets mitigation in context, by outlining its role within the conventional understanding of the law of damages more broadly. The assessment

[4] *Johnson v Agnew* [1980] AC 367 (HL) 395–96.
[5] Text to n 121.
[6] In this chapter, and throughout the book, 'damages' refers to compensatory damages, unless otherwise specified.

of compensatory damages is conventionally thought to comprise two main stages: first, the court must apply the compensatory principle to determine what is often referred to as the claimant's 'factual loss'; and second, the court must apply various limitations on damages, which serve to cut down the recovery of factual loss. Mitigation is conventionally understood as one of the limitations on damages, although its relationship with the other limiting rules is unclear. The conventional understanding of damages is complicated by the existence of several 'exceptions' that sometimes allow the claimant to recover more than its factual loss; the scope of each of these exceptions and their relationship with the compensatory principle has proved controversial.

2.1 The compensatory principle

The first stage of assessing damages involves applying the compensatory principle. As Lord Bingham highlighted in *The Golden Victory*, the compensatory principle 'has been enunciated and applied times without number and is not in doubt'.[7] It has been described as the 'foundation',[8] the 'fundamental principle',[9] and the 'overriding rule' of damages.[10] In practice, the compensatory principle forms the point of departure for virtually every judicial decision on damages.[11] There are two common formulations of the principle, depending on whether the claim is in contract or tort. In relation to contract, in *Robinson v Harman*, Baron Parke held that:

> The rule of the common law is, that where a party sustains a loss by reason of a breach of contract, he is, so far as money can do it, to be placed in the same situation with respect to damages, *as if the contract had been performed.*[12]

In relation to tort, in *Livingstone v Rawyards Coal*, Lord Blackburn held that:

[7] *Golden Strait Corp v Nippon Yusen Kubishika Kaisha (The Golden Victory)* [2007] UKHL 12, [2007] 2 AC 353 [9]. See also, to similar effect, *Morris-Garner v One Step (Support) Ltd* [2018] UKSC 20, [2018] 2 WLR 1353 [32] (Lord Reed).

[8] *Ruxley Electronics & Construction Ltd v Forsyth* [1994] 1 WLR 650 (CA) 660 (Mann LJ).

[9] *The Golden Victory* (n 7) [29] (Lord Scott); *Bunge SA v Nidera BV* [2015] UKSC 43, [2015] 3 All ER 1082 [14] (Lord Sumption). See also Burrows, *Remedies* (4th edn) (n 2) 38: 'These compensatory aims are of fundamental importance. They guide the whole process of assessment.'

[10] *County Personnel (Employment Agency) Ltd v Alan R Pulver & Co* [1987] 1 WLR 916 (CA) 925 (Bingham LJ).

[11] It has also sometimes been used as a cross-check on the final award: see eg *Dodd Properties (Kent) Ltd v Canterbury City Council* [1980] 1 WLR 433 (CA) 451 (Megaw LJ).

[12] *Robinson v Harman* (1848) 1 Ex 850, 154 ER 363 855 (emphasis added). See also *British Westinghouse Electric & Manufacturing Co Ltd v Underground Electric Railways Co of London Ltd (No 2)* [1912] AC 673 (HL) 688–89 (Viscount Haldane); *Johnson* (n 4) 400 (Lord Wilberforce).

> in settling the sum of money to be given for reparation of damages you should as nearly as possible get at that sum of money which will put the party who has been injured, or who has suffered, in the *same position as he would have been in if he had not sustained the wrong.*[13]

The difference between these two formulations reflects differences in the underlying obligations in contract and tort;[14] the remedial rule itself is the same for both causes of action.[15] Consequently, the formulations are often expressed as a single principle: damages aim to put the claimant in the same position as if the breach had not occurred.[16] Of course, it is often impossible to put the claimant in *exactly* the same position as if the breach had not occurred, either where money is incapable of providing direct equivalence to the claimant's injury,[17] or where it is no longer possible to replicate the claimant's expected position exactly due to the passage of time or other events.[18] For these reasons, in his canonical formulation of the compensatory principle, Lord Blackburn clarified that the aim was to put the claimant '*as nearly as possible*' in the same position as if the breach had not occurred.[19]

The application of the compensatory principle involves a comparison between two positions.[20] First, it requires an assessment of the position that the claimant *is* in as a result of the breach, referred to in this book as the claimant's 'breach position'. Second, it requires a counterfactual assessment of the position that the claimant *would have been in* if the breach had not occurred,[21] referred to here as the claimant's 'no-breach position'.[22] These two positions have conventionally

[13] *Livingstone v The Rawyards Coal Co* (1879–80) LR 5 App Cas 25 (HL) 39 (emphasis added).

[14] *Morris-Garner* (n 7) [31] (Lord Reed). Accordingly, where the underlying obligation is the same (eg a duty to take reasonable care), the two formulations will yield the same basic measure of damages whichever cause of action is chosen: [33] (Lord Reed).

[15] Daniel Friedmann, 'The Performance Interest in Contract Damages' (1995) 111 Law Quarterly Review 628, 638–43. Contra Jane Stapleton, 'The Normal Expectancies Measure in Tort Damages' (1997) 113 Law Quarterly Review 257, 260.

[16] See also, in relation to equitable compensation: *AIB Group (UK) plc v Mark Redler & Co Solicitors* [2014] UKSC 58, [2014] 3 WLR 1367 [64] (Lord Toulson), [93] (Lord Reed), discussed in Chapter 7.

[17] For example: pain and suffering; loss of enjoyment; or loss of amenity.

[18] For example, where the stipulated time for performance has already passed, such that any substitute performance will inevitably be late.

[19] *Livingstone* (n 13) 39 (emphasis added). See also *Robinson* (n 12) 855: 'so far as money can do it'.

[20] *Parry v Cleaver* [1970] AC 1 (HL) 23 (Lord Morris); *Esso Petroleum Co v Mardon* [1976] QB 801 (CA) 821 (Lord Denning); *Jobling v Associated Dairies* [1982] AC 794 (HL) 814 (Lord Keith); *Nykredit Mortgage Bank plc v Edward Erdman Group Ltd* [1997] 1 WLR 1627 (HL) (n 24) 1631 (Lord Nicholls); *Morris-Garner* (n 7) [36] (Lord Reed).

[21] As Diplock LJ emphasized in *Lavarack v Woods of Colchester* [1967] 1 QB 278 (CA) 294, the assessment involves 'assuming that what has not occurred and never will occur has occurred or will occur'. See also *Durham Tees Valley Airport Ltd v bmibaby Ltd* [2010] EWCA Civ 485, [2011] 1 All ER (Comm) 731, [63] (Patten LJ); *Flame SA v Glory Wealth Shipping Pte Ltd* [2013] EWHC 3153 (Comm), [2013] 2 Lloyd's Rep 653 (n 20) [18] and [85] (Teare J); *Jet2.com Ltd v SC Compania Nationala de Transporturi Aeriene Romane Tarom SA* [2014] EWCA Civ 87 [45] (Christopher Clarke LJ).

[22] This terminology was first adopted in Andrew Dyson and Adam Kramer, 'There is No "Breach Date Rule": Mitigation, Difference in Value and Date of Assessment' (2014) 130 Law Quarterly Review 259, 261.

been referred to as 'the actual and the hypothetical calculations', respectively.[23] The difference between the claimant's breach and no-breach positions, expressed in monetary terms, constitutes the 'basic measure' of damages.[24] This measure also constitutes the legal conception of loss.[25] In other words, the compensatory principle prescribes that the claimant has suffered a 'loss' if and to the extent that its breach position is worse than its no-breach position.[26]

Judges and legal scholars sometimes refer to the claimant's 'factual loss' evident at the date of trial.[27] This conception of loss involves assessing the claimant's breach and no-breach positions by taking into account *all* events that have happened between breach and trial.[28] Authority for this approach is often derived from the decision in *Bwllfa and Merthyr Dare Steam Collieries v Pontypridd Waterworks*, where Lord Macnaghten asked rhetorically: 'with the light before him, why should [the judge] shut his eyes and grope in the dark?'[29] Consequently, the approach has become known as the '*Bwllfa* principle'.[30] However, there are various established exceptions to the *Bwllfa* principle, whereby certain types of post-breach event are 'ignored' in the assessment of damages;[31] in each of these circumstances, it is recognized that the claimant may recover damages greater or less than its factual loss evident at the date of trial.

I will use the term 'factual loss' throughout this book, because it has become conventional. But a more accurate term would strictly be 'single counterfactual

[23] *South Australia Asset Management Corp v York Montague Ltd ('SAAMCo')* [1997] AC 191 (HL) 210 (Lord Hoffmann). See also *Morris-Garner* (n 7) [36] (Lord Reed); Burrows, *Remedies* (4th edn) (n 2) 147. However, the term 'actual' can be misleading, because—as I argue in this book—the breach position sometimes also involves a counterfactual assessment.

[24] *Nykredit* 1631 (Lord Nicholls); *Tiuta International Ltd v De Villiers Surveyors Ltd* [2017] UKSC 77, [2017] 1 WLR 4627 [6] (Lord Sumption).

[25] *Alfred McAlpine Construction Ltd v Panatown Ltd* [2001] 1 AC 518 (HL) 580. See also *The Golden Victory* (n 7) [57] (Lord Carswell); *Parry* (n 20) 32 (Lord Morris); *Kuwait Airways Corp v Iraqi Airways Co (No 6)* [2002] UKHL 19, [2002] 2 AC 883 [67] (Lord Nicholls); *Ruxley Electronics & Construction Ltd v Forsyth* [1996] AC 344 (HL) 357 (Lord Jauncey); *Morris-Garner* (n 7) [95] (Lord Reed). See also Burrows, *Remedies* (4th edn) (n 2) 35.

[26] See eg *Nykredit* (n 20) 1631 (Lord Nicholls); *Morris-Garner* (n 7) [36] (Lord Reed).

[27] This term appears to derive originally from *Parry* (n 20) 17, where Lord Pearce held that 'in claiming that he has lost something a plaintiff must prove a genuine factual loss'.

[28] Various other terms are also used in this context: see eg ibid (n 21) 7, 10, and 22 (Lord Morris) ('actual loss'); *Smith New Court Securities Ltd v Citibank NA* [1997] AC 254 (HL) 268 (Lord Browne-Wilkinson) (the 'loss actually suffered'); *Koufos v C Czarnikow Ltd (The Heron II)* [1969] 1 AC 350 (HL) 395 (Lord Reid) (the loss 'in fact suffered').

[29] *Bwllfa and Merthyr Dare Steam Collieries (1891) Ltd v Pontypridd Waterworks Co* [1903] AC 426 (HL) 431. See also 432 (Lord Robertson): 'estimate and conjecture are superseded by facts'. See also *The Kingsway* [1918] P 344 (CA) 362 (Scrutton LJ); *Carslogie Steamship Co Ltd v Royal Norwegian Government (The Carslogie)* [1952] AC 292 (HL) 300 (Viscount Jowitt); *Curwen v James* [1963] 1 WLR 748 (CA) 753 (Harman LJ); *Kennedy v Van Emden & Co* [1996] PNLR 409 (CA) 419 (Schiemann LJ); *Dudarec v Andrews* [2006] EWCA Civ 256, [2006] 1 WLR 3002 [50] (Waller LJ); *Bunge* (n 9) [86] (Lord Toulson).

[30] See eg *The Golden Victory* (n 7) [12] (Lord Bingham), [65] (Lord Carswell), [78] (Lord Brown); *Whitehead v Searle* [2008] EWCA Civ 285, [2009] 1 WLR 549 [80] (Rimer LJ); *Secretary of State for Defence v Duncan* [2009] EWCA Civ 1043 [48] (Elias LJ).

[31] See further text to n 56 below.

loss',[32] because even (so-called) factual loss still involves a counterfactual assessment of the claimant's no-breach position. The risk with describing the application of the compensatory principle, in conjunction with the *Bwllfa* principle, as an assessment of the claimant's 'factual loss', is that it can mislead one into thinking that this conception—unlike other conceptions of loss—has a special extra-legal quality. However, Fuller and Perdue were correct, despite other serious flaws in their argument,[33] to point out that 'the loss which the plaintiff suffers . . . is not a datum of nature but the reflection of a normative order'.[34] Although often referred to as factual loss, the conception of loss on which the conventional understanding of damages rests, still involves the application of a *legal norm* to assess the position as if the breach had not occurred.[35]

2.2 Mitigation as a limitation on damages

After applying the compensatory principle, the second stage of assessing damages involves applying various limiting rules. The effect of each of these rules is to 'cut down' the recovery of damages for the claimant's factual loss.[36] Mitigation is conventionally thought to function in this way.[37] It serves to 'reduce the damages that full adherence to the compensatory aims would dictate'.[38] As a limiting rule, mitigation is regarded as distinct from, and indeed somewhat in conflict with, the compensatory principle. By extension, the doctrine is also regarded as distinct from the legal conception of loss: first the court assesses the claimant's (factual) loss; then it applies mitigation to cut down recovery. Katy Barnett succinctly summarizes the orthodox view when she says: 'Mitigation explicitly enters into contract law as a *separate stand-alone doctrine* used to limit the availability of damages in particular circumstances.'[39]

[32] On this approach, 'compound counterfactual loss' would describe the application of additional counterfactual processes in the assessment of the breach and/or no-breach positions.

[33] See further Friedmann, 'The Performance Interest in Contract Damages' (n 15).

[34] Lon Fuller and William Perdue, 'The Reliance Interest in Contract Damages' (1936) 46 Yale Law Journal 52. See also Andrew Tettenborn, 'What is a Loss?' in Jason Neyers, Erika Chamberlain, and Stephen Pitel (eds), *Emerging Issues in Tort Law* (Hart 2007) 456.

[35] This point is highly significant to the law of mitigation: see further Chapter 6.

[36] Edelman (n 2) [2-005]; Andrew Burrows, *A Restatement of the English Law of Contract* (OUP 2016) 128.

[37] See eg Edelman (n 2) [2-005]; Beale (n 2) [29-096]; Burrows, *Remedies* (4th edn) (n 2) 84. See also Iain Field, 'Contributory Negligence and the Rule of Avoidable Losses' (2018) 38 Oxford Journal of Legal Studies 475, 481.

[38] Burrows, *Remedies* (4th edn) (n 2) 83. See also Kramer, *Contract Damages* (3rd edn) (n 2) [15-05], noting that mitigation 'may seem to interfere with the basic compensatory principle'.

[39] Katy Barnett, 'A Critical Consideration of Substitutive Awards in Contract Law' (2018) 81 Modern Law Review 1064, 1077 (emphasis added). See also David Winterton, *Money Awards in Contract Law* (Hart 2015) 227.

The scope of mitigation is conventionally thought to concern how the claimant's own response to breach affects the assessment of damages. *McGregor on Damages* defines the doctrine more broadly, proposing that 'The principal, and proper, meaning of the term "mitigation" . . . concerns avoiding of the consequences of a wrong'.[40] However, in all of the other leading texts on damages, mitigation is defined as concerning the *claimant's* conduct in particular,[41] and this narrower definition seems more consistent with the use of the term 'mitigation' by the courts.[42] More specifically, mitigation is also conventionally understood to apply only to the claimant's *post-breach* conduct (ie actions or omissions after the breach has occurred), although it is sometimes suggested that the doctrine may apply by analogy in other circumstances prior to there being any actual breach.[43] These issues of scope are addressed in more detail in Chapter 7.

Besides mitigation, at least four other doctrines are also conventionally classified as limitations on damages:[44] remoteness; contributory negligence; intervening causation; and the 'SAMMCo principle'.[45] On the orthodox account of mitigation, the relationship between mitigation and each of these other doctrines is unclear. In particular, the rules of remoteness, intervening causation, and contributory negligence are also understood to cover the claimant's post-breach conduct where the conduct was unforeseeable, unusual, or negligent. Consequently, as *McGregor on Damages* puts it, 'difficulties arise in distinguishing among themselves the various limits set by the courts upon the recovery of damages'.[46] In his seminal article on mitigation, Michael Bridge similarly noted that '[a]n injured plaintiff's failure to recover on the ground of his intervening behaviour may be variously put down to lack of factual causation, remoteness, contributory negligence and mitigation'.[47]

One practical difficulty arising from the interrelationship between mitigation and the other limitations on damages concerns the order in which these doctrines

[40] Edelman (n 2) [9-002].

[41] Beale (n 2) [29-096]; Tettenborn, *Clerk & Lindsell on Torts* (23rd edn) (n 2) [27-09]; Peel, *Treitel on Contract* (15th edn) (n 2) [20-104]; Burrows, *Remedies* (4th edn) (n 2) 127; Tettenborn, *Damages* (2nd edn) (n 2) [5.61] fn 1.

[42] See eg *Swynson Ltd v Lowick Rose LLP* [2017] UKSC 32, [2018] AC 313 [13] (Lord Sumption), [45] (Lord Mance), [97] (Lord Neuberger).

[43] See eg Peel, *Treitel on Contract* (15th edn) (n 2) [2-105]; Jonathan Morgan, 'Smuggling Mitigation into White & Carter v McGregor: Time to Come Clean?' [2015] Lloyd's Maritime and Commercial Law Quarterly 575.

[44] The list of 'limitations' is also sometimes said to include: betterment; the rule restricting the availability of 'cost of cure' damages; and the rule in contract law restricting recovery of non-pecuniary losses. The claimant's 'impecuniosity' has also previously been included, but this rule was abolished by the House of Lords in *Lagden v O'Connor (sub nom Burdis v Livsey)* [2003] UKHL 64, [2004] 1 AC 1067; see further Burrows, *Remedies* (4th edn) (n 2) 144–46.

[45] Burrows, *Remedies* (4th edn) (n 2) ch 7. See also Peel, *Treitel on Contract* (15th edn) (n 2) [20-099]–[20-134] ('Methods of Limiting Damages'), which adopts a similar list but excludes the SAAMCo rule: [20-131].

[46] Edelman (n 2) [6-010]. See also Burrows, *Remedies* (4th edn) (n 2) 84–85; Field (n 37).

[47] Michael Bridge, 'Mitigation of Damages in Contract and the Meaning of Avoidable Loss' (1989) 105 Law Quarterly Review 398, 403.

are to be applied, in circumstances where more than one appears to be concurrently applicable, and where each has different legal effects.[48] The leading texts on damages currently offer remarkably little guidance on this problem; only *McGregor on Damages* offers a direct resolution to the issue.[49] This reticence reflects a deeper theoretical uncertainty about why the courts recognize each of these limitations on damages. In this regard, there appears to be no 'orthodox' view that is reflected consistently across the leading texts. It is sometimes suggested that mitigation shares a common explanation with some or all of the other limitations on damages; however, it is also often pointed out that mitigation differs from these other doctrines in scope, application, and effect. The place of mitigation within the law of damages as a whole therefore remains profoundly unclear.

2.3 Recovery greater than factual loss

The claimant's factual loss is sometimes treated, at least presumptively, as an upper limit on the award of compensatory damages.[50] This understanding is commonly (although not always consistently) invoked by the leading texts. Here, I will refer to it as the 'factual loss cap'. Awards exceeding the factual loss cap have been said to 'offend the compensatory principle',[51] because their effect is to put the claimant in a better position than if the breach had not occurred.[52] One of the most commonly-cited authorities for this view is *Wertheim v Chicoutimi Pulp*, where Lord Atkinson held that it would be 'against all justice' for the claimant to 'be compensated for a loss he never suffered, and be put, as far as money can do it, not in the same position in which he would have been if the contract had been performed, but in a much better position'.[53] On the same basis, several legal scholars have argued that recovery of damages greater than the claimant's factual loss amounts to 'overcompensation'.[54]

[48] See further Chapter 11.

[49] Edelman (n 2) [6-013], proposing that the limiting rules be applied in the order of contributory negligence, remoteness, then mitigation.

[50] See eg *Cerberus Software Ltd v Rowley* [2001] EWCA Civ 78, [2001] ICR 376 [27] (Sedley LJ): 'The principle that a claimant's damages should not exceed his real losses is a bedrock of our law.' See also Burrows, *Restatement of Contract* (n 37) 121.

[51] *The Golden Victory* (n 7) [38] (Lord Scott); see also [83] (Lord Brown).

[52] Burrows, *Remedies* (4th edn) (n 2) 147 and 196; David McLauchlan, 'Expectation Damages: Avoided Loss, Offsetting Gains and Subsequent Events' in Djakhongir Saidov and Ralph Cunnington (eds), *Contract Damages: Domestic and International Perspectives* (Hart 2008) 384.

[53] *Wertheim v Chicoutimi Pulp Co* [1911] AC 301 (PC), 308. See also *Elbinger AG v Armstrong* (1874) LR 9 QB 473 (QB) 479 (Blackburn J); *Bence Graphics International Ltd v Fasson UK Ltd* [1998] QB 87 (CA) 102 (Auld LJ); *Bacciottini v Gotelee & Goldsmith* [2016] EWCA Civ 170, [2016] 4 WLR 98 [39] (Davis LJ).

[54] See eg Burrows, *Remedies* (4th edn) (n 2) 190–92; McLauchlan (n 52) 364–65; Samuel Beswick, '"Losses in Any Event" in the Case of Damage to Property' (2015) 35 Oxford Journal of Legal Studies 755, 773.

There are nevertheless three main exceptions to the factual loss cap that are conventionally recognized as forming part of the law of compensatory damages (and not some other type of money award),[55] even though they can result in a sum greater than the claimant's factual loss. First, there are two well-established exceptions for insurance payments and benevolent donations by third parties.[56] The insurance rule provides that 'where a plaintiff recovers under an insurance policy for which he has paid the premiums, the insurance moneys are not deductible from damages'.[57] The benevolence rule similarly provides that 'when the plaintiff receives money from the benevolence of third parties . . . the amount received is again to be disregarded'.[58] Both rules have been affirmed as part of the assessment of compensatory damages by the House of Lords on several occasions,[59] despite that their effect is to award 'a net gain to the plaintiff resulting from his injury' and thereby to allow 'double recovery'.[60]

Second, it is widely recognized that the claimant may recover more than its factual loss through the application of the 'market rule' of damages.[61] Several cases have awarded the *prima facie* measure of damages under the Sale of Goods Act 1979,[62] despite this award exceeding the claimant's factual loss.[63] At common law, such awards preceded the first Sale of Goods Act,[64] and have also been applied in relation to shares and land outside the statutory regime.[65] Furthermore, damages have sometimes been awarded for 'diminution in value' or 'direct loss' measured by the market cost of repairs,[66] even where it is known that the claimant did not in fact

[55] For example, 'negotiating' or 'disgorgement' damages. In relation to 'substitutionary' damages (which are distinct from these), see further Winterton (n 39) 87–95.

[56] *British Transport Commission v Gourley* [1956] AC 185 (HL) 197–98 (Earl Jowitt); *Hussain v New Taplow Paper Mills Ltd* [1988] AC 514 (HL) 527 (Lord Bridge); *Swynson* (n 42) [11] (Lord Sumption), [47] (Lord Mance), [98] (Lord Neuberger).

[57] *Hussain* (n 57) 527 (Lord Bridge); see also *Bradburn v The Great Western Railway Co* (1874–75) LR 10 Ex 1 (Ex Ch). The rule also extends to other benefits earned by the claimant: see eg *Smoker v London Fire and Civil Defence Authority* [1991] 2 AC 502 (HL) (contractual disablement pension); *Parry* (n 20) (incapacity pension); *Hopkins v Norcros plc* [1994] ICR 11 (CA) (retirement pension).

[58] *Hussain* (n 57) 527 (Lord Bridge); see also *Redpath v Belfast & County Down Railway* [1947] NI 167 (HCNI). The rule also extends to benefits in kind and services: see eg *Liffen v Watson* [1940] 1 KB 556 (CA) (board and lodging); *Donnelly v Joyce* [1974] QB 454 (CA) 462 (Megaw LJ) (personal care), although see criticism of this decision in *Hunt v Severs* [1994] 2 AC 350 (HL) 361 and 363 (Lord Bridge).

[59] In relation to insurance, see: *Parry* (n 20) 14 (Lord Reid); *Hussain* (n 57) 527 (Lord Bridge); *Hodgson v Trapp* [1989] AC 807 (HL) 819 (Lord Bridge). In relation to benevolence, see *Parry* (n 20) 13 (Lord Reid); *Hunt* (n 58) 358 (Lord Bridge).

[60] *Hussain* (n 57) 527–28 (Lord Bridge).

[61] See further Chapter 10. See also Dyson and Kramer, 'There is No "Breach Date Rule"' (n 22).

[62] ss 50(3) (non-acceptance), 51(3) (non-delivery), and 53(3) (breach of warranty).

[63] See eg *Williams Bros v Ed T Agius Ltd* [1914] AC 510 (HL); *Slater v Hoyle & Smith Ltd* [1920] 2 KB 11 (CA); *Campbell Mostyn (Provisions) Ltd v Barnett Trading Co* [1954] 1 Lloyd's Rep 65 (CA).

[64] See eg *Jones v Just* (1867–68) LR 3 QB 197 (QB); *Rodocanachi, Sons & Co v Milburn Bros* (1887) LR 18 QBD 67 (CA). The preamble to the first Sale of Goods Act 1893 describes it as 'an Act for codifying the Law relating to the Sale of Goods'.

[65] See eg *AKAS Jamal v Moolla Dawood Sons & Co* [1916] 1 AC 175 (PC) (shares); *Blue Circle Industries plc v Ministry of Defence* [1999] Ch 289 (CA) (n 20) (land). In *Smith New Court* (n 28) 279, Lord Steyn held that 'the same legal principle must govern sales of shares, goods, a business or land'.

[66] *Coles v Hetherton* [2013] EWCA Civ 1704, [2015] 1 WLR 160 [27], [33] (Aikens LJ).

pay for the repairs,[67] or paid less than the market rate.[68] These decisions appear inconsistent with the factual loss cap on damages, and have accordingly sometimes attracted criticism from the leading texts as 'contrary to the avowed compensatory goal'.[69]

Third, and most importantly for present purposes, there is a further exception to the factual loss cap, often referred to as the 'avoided loss rule'[70] or 'mitigation in fact'.[71] This rule is held to apply where the claimant's own post-breach conduct resulted in receipt of a benefit that 'arose independently from the circumstances giving rise to the loss'.[72] Where applicable, the effect of the avoided loss rule is that the benefit is ignored in the assessment of damages, such that the claimant may recover damages greater than its factual loss.[73] Although the rule is most commonly associated with the law of mitigation, it has no settled home in the leading texts, sometimes appearing under various other headings including 'compensating advantages',[74] 'collateral benefits',[75] and 'avoided loss'.[76] Some legal scholars have argued that most or all of the cases purporting to apply this rule are wrongly decided;[77] others have relied on these cases to challenge the conventional 'loss-based' understanding of damages altogether.[78]

3 A Brief History of Mitigation

This section briefly outlines the historical development of the law of mitigation, tracing its evolution from the earliest authorities to the current orthodoxy. The history of what is now referred to as the 'mitigation' doctrine can be divided into three main parts. First, the earliest authorities established rules for determining the effect of the claimant's post-breach conduct without using the terminology of

[67] See eg *The Endeavour* (1890) 6 Asp MC 511 (PD); *The Glenfinlas* [1918] P 363 (PD); *The London Corporation* [1935] P 70 (CA); *Burdis v Livsey (sub nom Lagden v O'Connor)* [2002] EWCA Civ 510, [2003] QB 36; *Mueller Europe Ltd v Central Roofing (South Wales) Ltd* [2013] EWHC 237 (TCC), 147 Con LR 32.

[68] *Jones v Stroud DC* [1986] 1 WLR 1141 (CA); *Coles* (n 66). See also, in relation to car hire at less than the market rate: *Bee v Jenson* [2007] EWCA Civ 923, [2007] 4 All ER 791.

[69] Burrows, *Remedies* (4th edn) (n 2) 196. See also McLauchlan (n 52) 377–78.

[70] See eg Edelman (n 2) ch 9; Tettenborn, *Damages* (2nd edn) (n 2) ch 5.

[71] See eg Peel, *Treitel on Contract* (15th edn) (n 2) [20-110]; Harvey McGregor, 'The Role of Mitigation in the Assessment of Damages' in Djakhongir Saidov and Ralph Cunnington (eds), *Contract Damages: Domestic and International Perspectives* (Hart 2008) 337.

[72] Peel, *Treitel on Contract* (15th edn) (n 2) [20-111], citing *Swynson* (n 42) [11] (Lord Sumption).

[73] See eg *Primavera v Allied Dunbar Assurance plc* [2002] EWCA Civ 1327, [2003] Lloyd's Rep PN 14 [38] (Mance LJ).

[74] See eg Burrows, *Remedies* (4th edn) (n 2) ch 8.

[75] See eg Law Commission, *Damages for Personal Injury: Medical, Nursing and Other Expenses; Collateral Benefits* (Law Com No 262, 1999), Section B.

[76] See eg Edelman (n 2) ch 9; Tettenborn, *Damages* (2nd edn) (n 2) ch 5.

[77] See eg McLauchlan (n 52); Burrows, *Remedies* (4th edn) (n 2) 148–52.

[78] See eg Robert Stevens, *Torts and Rights* (OUP 2007); Winterton (n 39).

mitigation specifically. Second, the landmark House of Lords decision in *British Westinghouse v Underground Electric Railways of London* developed out of these early authorities to establish two main rules of mitigation.[79] Third, the current orthodoxy of mitigation has been shaped significantly by *McGregor on Damages*,[80] which has been without doubt the most influential text on the law of mitigation from the mid-twentieth century to the present day.[81]

3.1 Early authorities

The rules that are now considered part of the doctrine of mitigation can be traced back to at least the seventeenth century, although the terminology of mitigation was not then in use. One of the earliest reported cases is *Vertue v Bird*, decided in 1676.[82] The claimant agreed to deliver corn to the defendant in Ipswich, but the defendant failed to appoint a specific place for unloading. The claimant contended that this failure had 'caused four of the plaintiff's horses to catch diseases and die', but the court rejected the claim on the basis that 'the plaintiff might have taken his horses out of the cart, or have laid down the corn anywhere in Ipswich'.[83] It is instructive that in this case the court's decision was framed in terms of causation.

A series of cases in the early nineteenth century also proceeded without reference to 'mitigation'.[84] In *Ansett v Marshall*, the defendants wrongfully prevented the claimant from travelling aboard a voyage from England to Australia, thinking that he had not paid the full fare.[85] Upon realizing their mistake, the defendants offered the claimant free passage on another ship sailing a few days later. The claimant refused and instead stayed in England to pursue his claim. Crompton J held that 'the damages could not legally include the expenses of the plaintiff's keep up to the time of trial, for he might have gone to Australia in a very few days after he was removed from the vessel'; the test was 'whether it was reasonable' that the claimant should have remained in England.[86] This appears to be the earliest instance of the 'reasonableness' test.

79 *British Westinghouse* (n 12).
80 For the current edition, see Edelman (n 2).
81 The chapter on mitigation underwent a major re-write in Harvey McGregor's inaugural edition: Harvey McGregor (ed), *Mayne and McGregor on Damages* (12th edn, Sweet & Maxwell 1961).
82 *Vertue v Bird* (1676) 3 Keb 766, 84 ER 1000.
83 ibid.
84 See eg *Boyce v Bayliffe* (1807) 1 Camp 58, 170 ER 875; *Harries v Edmonds* (1845) 1 Car & K 686, 174 ER 991; *Beckham v Drake* (1849) 2 HL Cas 579, 9 ER 1213; *Ansett v Marshall* (1853) 22 LJQB 118; *Borries v Hutchinson* (1865) 18 CB (NS) 445, 144 ER 518 (CP); *Anderson (Commander of the Flying Fish) v Hoen (The Flying Fish)* (1865) 3 Moo PC NS 77, 16 ER 29 (PC).
85 *Ansett* (n 84).
86 Available at http://solo.bodleian.ox.ac.uk/OXVU1:oxfaleph013186467, 226.

The first general statement of what would now conventionally be referred to as the avoidable loss rule was provided in *Dunkirk Colliery v Lever*, where James LJ held that:

> What the Plaintiffs are entitled to is the full amount of the damage which they have really sustained by a breach of the contract; the person who has broken the contract not being exposed to additional cost by reason of the Plaintiffs not doing what they ought to have done as reasonable men, and the Plaintiffs not being under any obligation to do anything otherwise than in the ordinary course of business.[87]

Three points about this judicial statement are worthy of note. First, the term 'mitigation' is entirely absent from the decision in *Dunkirk Colliery*; this terminology developed later. Second, the rule is said to apply where the claimant has not done what they ought to have done as a 'reasonable man', but this test (which has since become known as the 'reasonableness test')[88] is explained in terms of 'the ordinary course of business'.[89] Third, where the rule applies, James LJ did not appear to envisage a *reduction* in damages; instead he regards the effect of the rule as being to assess 'the full amount of the damage which they have really sustained'.[90] In other words, rather than serving as a distinct limitation on the claimant's factual loss, the rule was expressed as part of the assessment of loss itself.

It was not until the late nineteenth century that the rules for determining the effect of the claimant's post-breach conduct on damages started to become known as 'mitigation'. Previously, although 'mitigation' appeared in the cases on damages, the term was used to describe the reduction of damages on several different legal grounds.[91] *Frost v Knight*, decided in 1871, appears to be the earliest authority in which mitigation was used to refer to the *claimant's conduct* specifically, rather than to the effect on damages generally.[92] In that case, Cockburn CJ held that the claimant would be entitled to damages subject to 'abatement in respect of any circumstances which may have afforded him the means of *mitigating his loss*'.[93]

[87] *Dunkirk Colliery Co v Lever* (1878) 9 Ch D 20 (CA) 25.

[88] See further Chapter 2.

[89] *Dunkirk Colliery* (n 87) (emphasis added).

[90] James LJ envisages an '*additional* cost' attributable to the claimant's failure to act as a reasonable man: n 87.

[91] See eg *Bonham Kight v Lord Sturton* (1554) 1 Dyer 105, 73 ER 230 (justification of slander); *Barker v Holder* (1685) 1 Vern 316, 23 ER 493 (delay in bringing a claim); *Michell v Reynolds* (1711) 10 Mod 27, 88 ER 610 (no reduction in recovery of debt); *Crake v Northfolke* (1719) Lil 41, 170 ER 21, 24 (prevention of double recovery); *Mondel v Steel* (1841) 8 M & W 858, 151 ER 1288 (counterclaim for breach of warranty).

[92] *Frost v Knight* (1871–72) LR 7 Ex 111 (Ex Ch) 113. See also *Brown v Muller* (1871–72) LR 7 Ex 319 (Ex Ch) 323 (Kelly CB).

[93] *Frost* (n 92) 113 (emphasis added). In *Roper v Johnson* (1873) LR 8 CP 167 (CP) 183, Grove J refers to Cockburn CJ's judgment but reverts to using mitigation to describe the effect on assessment of damages.

3.2 The decision in *British Westinghouse*

The landmark decision in *British Westinghouse v London Underground* marks the beginning of the modern law of mitigation.[94] The case concerned the supply of eight steam turbines by the defendant for use by the claimant in supplying power to its London Underground lines. The turbines were less efficient than specified and therefore consumed additional coal at the claimant's expense. The claimant replaced the defendants' turbines with new machines from Parsons. The replacement turbines were significantly more efficient than the defendant's turbines would have been even if they had met the contractual specification. In a claim to recover the cost of replacing the defendants' turbines, the issue was whether the additional efficiency of the Parsons turbines was to be taken into account in the assessment of damages.

In the House of Lords, Viscount Haldane expressed what has since become known as the 'classic statement of mitigation'[95] or 'the avoidable loss rule'.[96] The rule 'imposes on a plaintiff *the duty of taking all reasonable steps to mitigate the loss* consequent on the breach, and debars him from claiming any part of the damage which is due to his neglect to take such steps'.[97] This statement appears to be the very first judicial expression of a 'duty . . . to mitigate'.[98] Citing the formulation of James LJ in *Dunkirk Colliery*, Viscount Haldane emphasized that the rule 'does not impose on the plaintiff an obligation to take any step which a reasonable and prudent man would not ordinarily take in the course of his business'.[99] The effect of the rule, which 'debarred' the claimant from recovering part of the damage, was described as a 'qualification' of the compensatory principle.[100]

Viscount Haldane also expressed another rule, which has since become known as 'mitigation in fact'[101] or the 'avoided loss rule'.[102] Here Viscount Haldane's judgment is frequently misunderstood and needs to be examined carefully.[103] His formulation consisted of two (related) limbs. The first limb was that 'when in the

[94] *British Westinghouse* (n 12). For a more detailed analysis of this decision, see Andrew Dyson, 'British Westinghouse Revisited' [2012] Lloyd's Maritime and Commercial Law Quarterly 412.

[95] *Pilkington v Wood* [1953] Ch 770 (Ch) 775 (Harman J); *Koch Marine Inc v d'Amica Societa di Navigazione arl (The Elena d'Amico)* [1980] 1 Lloyd's Rep 75 (QB), 88 (Robert Goff J); *Burdis* (n 68) [89] (Aldous LJ); *Fulton Shipping Inc of Panama v Globalia Business Travel SAU (The New Flamenco)* [2015] EWCA Civ 1299, [2016] 1 Lloyd's Rep 383 [21] (Longmore LJ).

[96] Edelman (n 2) [9-004].

[97] *British Westinghouse* (n 12) 689 (emphasis added). See also *Jamal* (n 65) 179 (Lord Wrenbury).

[98] However it was not the first time that 'duty' had been used in relation to the claimant's post-breach conduct: see eg *Harries* (n 84); *Beckham* (n 84).

[99] *British Westinghouse* (n 12) 689, citing *Dunkirk Colliery* (n 87) 25 (James LJ), quoted at n 88.

[100] *British Westinghouse* (n 12) 689. In this regard, Viscount Haldane's understanding of the rule differed from that of James LJ. See text to n 91.

[101] See eg Peel, *Treitel on Contract* (15th edn) (n 2) [20-110]; McGregor, 'The Role of Mitigation' (n 71) 337.

[102] See eg Edelman (n 2) [9-006].

[103] See further Chapter 3.

course of his business [the claimant] has taken action arising out of the transaction, which action has diminished his loss, the effect in actual diminution of the loss he has suffered may be taken into account even though there was no duty on him to act.'[104] In these circumstances, the court 'may properly look at the whole of the facts and ascertain the result in estimating the quantum of damage.'[105] In other words, where the first limb applied, the assessment of factual loss prescribed by the compensatory principle was not displaced: the claimant recovered its factual loss and no more.

The second limb of Viscount Haldane's formulation served as an exception to the first limb. He held that 'the subsequent transaction, if to be taken into account, must be one arising out of the consequences of the breach and in the ordinary course of business.'[106] By contrast, if the claimant's conduct was 'an independent or disconnected transaction', or in other words was *not* 'part of a continuous dealing with the situation in which they found themselves',[107] then it would be regarded as '*res inter alios acta*',[108] meaning that it would not be 'taken into account' in the assessment of damages.[109] The effect of this exception to the first limb of the avoided loss rule was thus also (like the avoidable loss rule) to qualify the compensatory principle;[110] however, rather than limiting recovery of the claimant's factual loss, it could result in an award of damages *greater* than the factual loss evident at the date of trial.

On the facts of *British Westinghouse*, Viscount Haldane held that 'The transaction was not *res inter alios acta*, but one in which the person whose contract was broken took a reasonable and prudent course quite naturally arising out of the circumstances in which he was placed by the breach.'[111] The claimant's conduct in purchasing the Parsons turbines was 'a natural and prudent course';[112] in particular, 'men of business would be doing the only thing they could properly do in replacing [the turbines] with new and up-to-date machines.'[113] Consequently, Viscount Haldane held that both the costs *and* benefits of the replacement turbines must be taken into account in the assessment of damages.[114] On this basis, the claimants had suffered no net loss, because the benefit of operating these turbines

[104] *British Westinghouse* (n 12) 689.
[105] ibid 690.
[106] ibid 690.
[107] ibid 692.
[108] ibid 691.
[109] ibid 690.
[110] In this respect, it mirrored the classic statement of mitigation: text to n 98.
[111] *British Westinghouse* (n 12) 691.
[112] ibid 691.
[113] ibid 691. As Leggatt J observed in a more recent decision: 'It is clear that in the *British Westinghouse* case the House of Lords considered that London Underground would have been acting unreasonably if they had continued to use the British Westinghouse turbines': *Thai Airways International Public Co Ltd v KI Holdings Co Ltd* [2015] EWHC 1250 (Comm), [2016] 1 All ER (Comm) 675 [41].
[114] *British Westinghouse* (n 12) 691: 'I think the principle which applies here is that which makes it right for the jury or arbitrator to look at what actually happened, and to balance loss and gain.'

(compared with the defendant's turbines, even at their contractual specification) outweighed the cost of purchasing them.[115]

3.3 The influence of McGregor on Damages

Perhaps more than any other doctrine in the law of damages, the orthodox account of mitigation has been shaped by a single text. *McGregor on Damages*, which was authored by Harvey McGregor for eight editions from 1961 to 2014,[116] stands above all others for its influence on the conventional understanding of mitigation. With one recent exception,[117] all of the other leading texts on damages have modelled their descriptions of the law of mitigation on the exposition first put forward by McGregor in 1961, in what was then the twelfth edition of *Mayne's Treatise on Damages*.[118] Not all of these texts have adopted McGregor's tripartite structure (discussed further below),[119] but the basic distinction that they draw between the avoidable and avoided loss rules nevertheless bears the clear imprint of McGregor's approach. Although the most recent edition of *McGregor on Damages* is now under the new editorship of James Edelman, for now, the chapter on mitigation remains in McGregor's image.

It is important to understand the influence of *McGregor on Damages* on the current orthodoxy of mitigation, not just as an exercise in legal historiography, but because legal scholarship can often have a 'reflexive effect' on the development of the common law itself. This effect is a specific instance of a wider phenomenon; as sociologist Anthony Giddens has highlighted, 'The concepts of the social sciences are not produced about an independently constituted subject-matter, which continues regardless of what these concepts are. The "findings" of the social sciences very often enter constitutively into the world they describe.'[120] This process is evident, at least to some extent, in the modern law of mitigation. In several cases, whole passages from *McGregor on Damages* have been cited by courts verbatim,[121]

[115] The case was sent back to the arbitrator for a final assessment, but this was the inevitable conclusion: ibid 692.

[116] McGregor, *Mayne and McGregor on Damages* (12th edn) (n 81); Harvey McGregor (ed), *McGregor on Damages* (19th edn, Sweet & Maxwell 2014).

[117] Kramer, *Contract Damages* (3rd edn) (n 2).

[118] McGregor, *Mayne and McGregor on Damages* (12th edn) (n 81). The series began with John Mayne, *A Treatise on the Law of Damages* (Sweet 1856). This was the second ever treatise on the English law of damages: the first was Joseph Sayer, *The Law of Damages* (London 1770). John Mayne continued to edit the series (jointly with Lumley Smith) up to and including the seventh edition in 1903, after which the series had different editors for each of the next four editions from 1909 to 1946. McGregor took over in 1961.

[119] Text to n 140.

[120] Anthony Giddens, *Social Theory and Modern Sociology* (Polity 1987).

[121] See eg *Bellingham v Dhillon* [1973] QB 304 (QB) 307 (Forbes J); *Moore v DER Ltd* [1971] 1 WLR 1476 (CA) 1479 (Davies LJ), 1481 (Karminski LJ); *Linklaters Business Services v Sir Robert McAlpine Ltd* [2010] EWHC 2931 (TCC) [159] (Akenhead J); *Manton Hire and Sales Ltd v Ash Manor Cheese Co Ltd* [2013] EWCA Civ 548 [32] (Tomlinson LJ) and further at n 138.

sometimes directly as authority instead of citing judicial precedents.[122] McGregor himself reported several occasions on which the courts had expressly adopted the position that he had taken in earlier editions of his text.[123]

It is very difficult to tell precisely how much influence *McGregor on Damages* has had on the *law* of mitigation itself, as distinct from merely the orthodox account of the law conveyed by the other leading texts. At the margins, where the application of the rules of mitigation based on past decisions has seemed (to varying degrees) unclear, it seems plausible that McGregor's exposition will have had some influence on judicial decisions. To the extent that it has influenced the reasons given by the court, or even the outcome of some cases, then *McGregor on Damages* will have developed or changed the law.[124] McGregor's account will, as Giddens would put it, have entered constitutively into the world it described. On the other hand, as the following chapters show, there remains a large number of cases (including those decided after 1961) that are inconsistent with McGregor's exposition. To this extent, the law of mitigation appears to have maintained its independence from McGregor's description of it.

The influence of *McGregor on Damages* is most evident from the distinction that is now conventionally drawn between the 'avoidable' and 'avoided' loss rules. This distinction was McGregor's invention. When he took over *Mayne's Treatise on Damages* in 1961,[125] the previous edition was then fifteen years old and it was widely agreed that a thorough re-editing was 'badly needed'.[126] To this end, McGregor rewrote the chapter on mitigation completely.[127] In the new edition, he proposed the subdivision of mitigation into 'three different, although closely interrelated, rules': the 'avoidable loss rule'; the 'reasonable attempts rule'; and the 'avoided loss rule'.[128] Previous editions of *Mayne's Treatise*,[129] in common with other contemporaneous texts,[130] had not drawn this distinction. As McGregor himself proclaimed, 'this analysis into three rules, although clearly implicit in the cases, is one which had not, at the first time of writing in the late 1950s, been given

[122] See eg *Downs v Chappell* [1997] 1 WLR 426 (CA) 437 (Hobhouse LJ); *Gardner v Marsh & Parsons* [1997] 1 WLR 489 (CA) 507–08 (Gibson LJ); *Lagden* (n 44) [78] (Lord Scott); *Borealis AB v Geogas Trading SA* [2010] EWHC 2789 (Comm), [2011] 1 Lloyd's Rep 482 [50] (Gross J); *Sayce v TNT (UK) Ltd* [2011] EWCA Civ 1583, [2012] 1 WLR 1261 [29] (Moore-Bick LJ).

[123] See eg McGregor, *McGregor on Damages* (19th edn) (n 116) [9-098]–[9-099], [9-121] fn 484.

[124] For the jurisprudential premises that underpin this understanding of the common law, see further Introduction and Chapter 4, Section 2.

[125] McGregor, *Mayne and McGregor on Damages* (12th edn) (n 81).

[126] Harry Street, *Principles of the Law of Damages* (Sweet & Maxwell 1962) v.

[127] McGregor, *Mayne and McGregor on Damages* (12th edn) (n 81) ch 7; cf WG Earengey (ed), *Mayne's Treatise on Damages* (11th edn, Sweet & Maxwell 1946) ch 7.

[128] McGregor, *Mayne and McGregor on Damages* (12th edn) (n 81) [144].

[129] In particular, the (modern) 'avoidable' and 'avoided' loss rules were intermixed in the chapter on mitigation: Earengey (n 127) ch 7.

[130] See eg John Burke and Peter Allsop (eds), *Chitty on Contracts* (21st edn, Sweet & Maxwell 1955) 433–35; Guenter Treitel, *The Law of Contract* (1st edn, Stevens 1962) 610–11.

explicit statement in English law. It is submitted that such a division lends clarity to a difficult topic.'[131]

The tripartite exposition proposed by McGregor has subsequently been replicated in many (but not all)[132] of the other leading texts on damages. Starting with its 1968 edition, *Chitty on Contracts* transposed McGregor's three rules in full.[133] Others, such as Tettenborn's *The Law of Damages*, have adopted the division between the avoidable and avoided loss rules but not the reasonable attempts rule.[134] Starting with the judgment of Robert Goff J in *The Elena D'Amico*,[135] several judicial decisions have quoted McGregor's tripartite exposition directly from the text.[136] Recently, even decisions that have raised doubts about certain aspects of McGregor's analysis have nevertheless begun their exposition of mitigation by quoting from his three rules.[137] In this way, the tripartite exposition of mitigation now not only constitutes the orthodox account of mitigation expressed by the leading texts, but it also appears to have had at least *some* impact on judicial decisions, and so, on the development of the law.

4 Mitigation: The Current Orthodoxy

The orthodox account of mitigation is currently most-often presented as three rules: the 'avoidable loss rule'; the 'reasonable attempts rule'; and the 'avoided loss rule'.[138] This tripartite exposition was first put forward by McGregor in 1961,[139] and has since become generally accepted.[140] This section begins by outlining briefly the content of each of the three rules, as expressed by the leading texts. However, it is also necessary to consider the tripartite exposition in the context of the broader conventional understanding of the law of damages outlined above.[141]

131 McGregor, *McGregor on Damages* (19th edn) (n 116) [9-003].

132 See eg Burrows, *Remedies* (4th edn) (n 2); Peel, *Treitel on Contract* (15th edn) (n 2). See also Kramer *Contract Damages* (3rd edn) (n 2), which expressly rejects McGregor's exposition: [15-44] fn 52.

133 Anthony Guest (ed), *Chitty on Contracts* (23rd edn, Sweet & Maxwell 1968) [1482]–[1489]; Beale (n 2) [26-087].

134 Tettenborn, *Damages* (2nd edn) (n 2) ch 5. See also Bridge (n 47) 398.

135 *The Elena d'Amico* (n 95) 88.

136 See eg *Gardner* (n 122) 505 (Gibson LJ); *Standard Chartered Bank v Pakistan National Shipping Corp* [1999] 1 Lloyd's Rep 747 (QB) 775 (Toulson J); *Sembawang Corp Ltd v Pacific Ocean Shipping Corporation* [2004] EWHC 2743 (Comm) [19] (Gross J); *The New Flamenco (CA)* (n 96) [14] (Longmore LJ).

137 *Fulton Shipping Inc of Panama v Globalia Business Travel SAU (The New Flamenco)* [2014] EWHC 1547 (Comm), [2015] 1 All ER (Comm) 1205 [18] (Popplewell J); *Thai Airways* (n 113) [32] (Leggatt J), who also expressed reservations about the exposition at [33].

138 See Edelman (n 2) [9-003].

139 Text to n 133.

140 Winterton (n 39) 248: 'It appears to be generally accepted that a reference to "mitigation" is intended to describe an overarching principle or doctrine comprising three inter-related rules.' However, Winterton himself departs from this view, instead contending that the third (avoided loss) rule 'is not really part of any broader "mitigation" principle': 249.

141 Text to n 27.

In this context, the reasonable attempts rule and the 'first limb' of the avoided loss rule are both redundant,[142] because they merely reiterate the first stage of assessing the claimant's factual loss. Accordingly, the orthodox account of mitigation can be expressed more concisely, without any change of substance, as comprising just two rules: the avoidable loss rule and (the exception to) the avoided loss rule.

4.1 The tripartite exposition

4.1.1 Avoidable loss rule

The conventional exposition of the avoidable loss rule is that 'the claimant must take all reasonable steps to mitigate the loss to him consequent upon the defendant's wrong and cannot recover damages for any such loss which he could thus have avoided but has failed, through unreasonable action or inaction, to avoid'.[143] In summary, as *McGregor on Damages* puts it, 'the claimant cannot recover for avoidable loss'.[144] This rule is said to derive from Viscount Haldane's classic statement of mitigation in *British Westinghouse*.[145] Following its invention by McGregor, the terminology of avoidable loss has now been adopted judicially. For example, in *Sayce v TNT*, Moore-Bick LJ referred to 'the established rule that avoidable loss (that is, loss that the claimant could and should reasonably have avoided) is not recoverable'.[146]

Although the leading texts on damages note that there is not really any 'duty' to mitigate, they nevertheless tend to express the rule in prescriptive terms, ie that the claimant 'must' or 'should' act reasonably.[147] All of the leading texts emphasize that the reasonableness of the claimant's conduct is a question of fact.[148] Accordingly, the application of the reasonableness test tends to be 'illustrated', rather than explained in detail. Readers are provided with a catalogue of previous decisions, subdivided by context rather than by legal principle.[149] As Andrew Tettenborn puts it, 'no fixed rules can be laid down'.[150] Where the claimant acted unreasonably, it is said to be unable to recover for the avoidable loss. The legal effect of the rule is thus

[142] For the distinction between the 'first' and 'second' limbs of the avoided loss rule, see further text to n 104.

[143] Edelman (n 2) [9-004].

[144] ibid [9-004]. See also Peel, *Treitel on Contract* (15th edn) (n 2) [20-104]: '[T]he claimant cannot recover damages for a loss that he ought to have avoided.'

[145] *British Westinghouse* (n 12) 689; Edelman (n 2) [9-014].

[146] *Sayce* (n 123) [27]. See also *Standard Chartered Bank v Pakistan National Shipping Corp (No 2)* [2002] UKHL 43, [2003] 1 AC 959 [41] (Potter LJ); *Uzinterimpex JSC v Standard Bank plc* [2008] EWCA Civ 819, [2008] 2 CLC 80 [49] (Moore-Bick LJ).

[147] See further Chapter 7, Section 2.

[148] See further Chapter 2, Section 2.2.

[149] See eg Edelman (n 2) [9-047]–[9-078], [9-083]–[9-100]; Burrows, *Remedies* (4th edn) (n 2) 127–29.

[150] Tettenborn, *Damages* (2nd edn) (n 2) [5.79].

sometimes described as 'all-or-nothing', but it is more often understood to involve 'cutting back' the award of damages.[151]

It is well established that the avoidable loss rule applies equally in relation to both torts and breaches of contract, as well as other forms of civil wrong; it also applies in the same way irrespective of the defendant's level of fault (if any).[152] However, the temporal scope of the rule is constrained in that the duty to mitigate only arises once the claimant becomes aware of the breach, or once it accepts the defendant's anticipatory breach of contract.[153] On the orthodox account, the relationship between the avoidable loss rule and the other limitations on damages is uncertain.[154] The leading texts suggest that there is an overlap with the rules of remoteness and intervening (or 'supervening') acts by the claimant; there also appears to be a further overlap with the doctrine of betterment and the market rule of damages.

4.1.2 Reasonable attempts rule

The reasonable attempts rule provides that 'where the claimant does take reasonable steps to mitigate the loss to him consequent upon the defendant's wrong, he can recover for loss incurred in so doing'.[155] The apparent significance of this rule is that 'this is so even though the resulting damage is in the event greater than it would have been had the mitigating steps not been taken'.[156] *McGregor on Damages* summarizes that 'the claimant can recover for loss incurred in reasonable attempts to avoid loss'.[157] The rule is said to be a 'corollary' of the avoidable loss rule.[158] *McGregor* claims that '[a]t the date of this book's initial compilation and publication in 1961, this principle boasted no clear illustration in English law'.[159] This claim is not strictly correct,[160] but it is right to point out that McGregor was the first to express it as a distinct rule.

The effect of the reasonable attempts rule has been affirmed several times by the appellate courts. In *Lagden v O'Connor*, Lord Scott held that '[i]f the mitigating steps do not succeed in reducing the loss but were, nonetheless, reasonable steps in all the circumstances for the injured party to take . . . the injured party can add to his damages claim the cost of taking the steps in question'.[161] The rule has been

[151] See further Chapter 2, Section 3.
[152] See further Chapter 7, Section 3.1.
[153] See further Chapter 7, Section 3.2.
[154] See further text to n 49, and Chapter 11.
[155] Edelman (n 2) [9-005].
[156] ibid [9-005].
[157] ibid [9-005].
[158] ibid [9-005], [9-101].
[159] ibid [9-103].
[160] See eg *Borries* (n 85) 525 (Erle CJ); *Wilson v United Counties Bank Ltd* [1920] AC 102 (HL) 125 (Lord Atkinson); *Melachrino v Nickoll & Knight* [1920] 1 KB 693 (KB) 697 (Bailhache J); *Harling v Eddy* [1951] 2 KB 739 (CA); *Jones v Watney Combe Reid & Co* (1912) 28 TLR 399 (KB); *Bloor v Liverpool Derricking & Carrying Co Ltd* [1936] 3 All ER 399 (CA) 402 (Greer LJ, obiter).
[161] *Lagden* (n 44) [78]. See also *Downs* (n 122) 437 (Hobhouse LJ).

applied in various contexts.[162] If the claimant reasonably enters into a substitute transaction, the costs of so doing are recoverable even if (with hindsight) it would have been better not to have entered into the substitute at that time, or at all.[163] If the claimant reasonably attempts to repair defective goods, the cost is recoverable even if the repairs are ultimately unsuccessful.[164] Similarly, the costs of reasonable medical treatments are recoverable even if they exacerbate the claimant's injury.[165]

4.1.3 Avoided loss rule

The conventional exposition of the avoided loss rule is that 'where the claimant does take steps to mitigate the loss to him consequent upon the defendant's wrong and these steps are successful, the defendant is entitled to the benefit accruing from the claimant's action'.[166] *McGregor on Damages* further specifies, in common with the other leading texts, that 'this is so even though the claimant would not have been debarred under the first rule from recovering the whole loss'[167] had it not taken the relevant steps; this understanding is said to have been derived from the first limb of Viscount Haldane's formulation in *British Westinghouse*.[168] *McGregor* summarizes that 'the claimant cannot [generally] recover for avoided loss'.[169] This summary is adopted by most of the leading texts on damages and has also been recited in several judicial decisions.[170]

In *McGregor on Damages*, the main summary of the avoided loss rule fails to mention the exception that Viscount Haldane identified (the second limb of his formulation).[171] However, in a later section McGregor identifies that the problem of ascertaining 'what subsequent transactions of the claimant are to be regarded as arising out of the consequences of the wrong . . . represents the core of the problem

[162] See further: *Lloyds and Scottish Finance Ltd v Modern Cars and Caravans (Kingston) Ltd* [1966] 1 QB 764 (QB) 782–83 (Edmund-Davies J); *Nigerian National Shipping Lines Ltd v Mutual Ltd (The Windfall)* [1998] 2 Lloyd's Rep 664 (QB) 671–72 (Rix J); *Humber Oil Terminal Trustee Ltd v Owners of the Sivand (The Sivand)* [1998] CLC 751 (CA) 107–08 (Hobhouse LJ); *Vinmar International Ltd v Theresa Navigation SA* [2001] 2 Lloyd's Rep 1 (QB) 15 (Tomlinson J).

[163] See eg *Melachrino* (n 160) 697 (Bailhache J); *Esso* 821 (Lord Denning MR), 829 (Ormrod LJ), 833 (Shaw LJ); *Gebruder Metelmann GmbH & Co KG v NBR (London) Ltd* [1984] 1 Lloyd's Rep 614 (CA) 364 (Browne-Wilkinson LJ); *Choil Trading SA v Sahara Energy Resources Ltd* [2010] EWHC 374 (Comm) [156]–[161] (Christopher Clarke J).

[164] See eg *Harling* (n 160); *Hoffberger v Ascot International Bloodstock Bureau* (1976) 120 SJ 130 (CA).

[165] See eg *Jones v Watney* (n 160); *Bloor* (n 160) 402 (Greer LJ, obiter).

[166] Edelman (n 2) [9-006].

[167] ibid [9-006].

[168] *British Westinghouse* (n 12) 689; Edelman (n 2) [9-110]. See further text to n 104. In Chapter 3, I argue that McGregor's reading of Viscount Haldane's formulation is incorrect.

[169] McGregor, *McGregor on Damages* (19th edn) [9-006]. In the 20th edition, under the new editorship of James Edelman, the word 'generally' was added, and has been retained in the latest (21st) edition: Edelman (n 2) [9-006].

[170] See eg Beale, *Chitty on Contracts* (34th edn) (n 2) [29-112]; Tettenborn, *Damages* (2nd edn) (n 2) [5-01]; *Dimond v Lovell* [2002] 1 AC 384 (HL) 406 (Lord Hobhouse), cited in *Pankhania v Hackney LBC* [2004] EWHC 323 (Ch), [2004] 1 EGLR 135 [33] (Vos QC); *Coles v Hetherton* [2012] EWHC 1599 (Comm), [2013] 1 All ER (Comm) 453 [22] (Cooke J).

[171] Edelman (n 2) [9-006]. See further text to n 107.

of mitigation by way of avoided loss'.[172] On this key issue, McGregor resolved that 'the authorities are in a bit of a jumble'.[173] This view is widely shared within the leading texts on damages; other scholars have similarly lamented that 'the current law is in a dreadful muddle'.[174] The application of the avoided loss rule is conventionally regarded as an exceptional departure from the compensatory principle. Several legal scholars have sought to reject as wrongly decided most (if not all) of the cases that have applied the rule.[175]

4.2 Three rules or two?

In light of the broader conventional understanding of damages outlined above, the orthodox account of mitigation can be expressed more concisely, without any change in substance, as comprising just two rules. Recall that the assessment of damages is conventionally divided into two main stages: first, apply the compensatory principle to assess the claimant's factual loss; and second, apply limitations on damages. Also recall that 'factual loss' is understood to take into account all events up to the date of trial.[176] Applying these conventional understandings, both the reasonable attempts rule and the *first limb* of the avoided loss rule are redundant, because they merely reiterate the first stage of assessing the claimant's factual loss. On this (still entirely orthodox) view, the only rules of mitigation that play a distinctive role in the assessment of damages are the avoidable loss rule and the *exception to* the avoided loss rule.

The reasonable attempts rule is redundant because it does not add anything to the conventional understanding of the law of damages that, unless a limitation on damages applies, the claimant will recover damages for the full amount of its factual loss.[177] Where the claimant acted reasonably in response to the breach, the avoidable loss rule is inapplicable and there is thus no need to displace the award of damages for factual loss.[178] In *Thai Airways v KI Holdings*, Leggatt J accordingly described the reasonable attempts rule as 'simply the non-application of any rule'.[179] For this reason, some of the leading texts on damages do not include

[172] ibid [9-110].
[173] McGregor, 'The Role of Mitigation' (n 71) 336.
[174] McLauchlan (n 52) 384.
[175] See eg McLauchlan (n 52), which expressly concludes that all of the following cases were wrongly decided: *Williams Bros* (n 63); *Slater* (n 63); *Rodocanachi* (n 64); *Campbell Mostyn* (n 63); *Gardner* (n 122); *Primavera* (n 73). See also Burrows, *Remedies* (4th edn) (n 2) 190.
[176] Text to n 27.
[177] In *Wells v Wells* [1999] 1 AC 345 (HL) 382–83, Lord Steyn described this approach as the '100% principle'. See also Peter Cane and James Goudkamp, *Atiyah's Accidents, Compensation and the Law* (9th edn, CUP 2018) 143–45; Burrows, *Remedies* (4th edn) (n 2) 83 fn 2. This approach is also a corollary of the 'Bwllfa principle': see further text to n 30.
[178] Unless one of the other limiting rules (such as remoteness) applies.
[179] *Thai Airways* (n 113) [33], citing Adam Kramer, *The Law of Contract Damages* (1st edn, Hart 2014) 348 fn 47 with approval.

McGregor's reasonable attempts rule in their exposition of mitigation.[180] For example, Burrows points out that 'it is simpler to view [the reasonable attempts rule] as a natural consequence of there being no relevant restriction limiting the compensatory principle'.[181]

The *first limb* of the avoided loss rule is similarly redundant.[182] This part of the rule holds (according to *McGregor on Damages*) that 'the claimant cannot recover for avoided loss',[183] or to use Viscount Haldane's formulation, 'the effect in actual diminution of the loss he has suffered may be taken into account even though there was no duty on him to act'.[184] But to the extent that the claimant has successfully 'avoided' harm, this means that they have not suffered any factual loss. The first limb of the avoided loss rule is therefore simply a consequence of the conventional understanding as to how the compensatory principle applies at the first stage of assessing damages; there is no need to state this proposition as a separate limitation on damages at the second (or any other) stage. Indeed, McGregor's terminology of 'avoided loss' is alien to the conventional understanding of damages, because by definition there is no (factual) loss evident at the date of trial.[185]

The orthodox account of mitigation can thus be expressed more concisely in terms of just two rules: the avoidable loss rule and the *exception to* the avoided loss rule.[186] The avoidable loss rule 'imposes on a plaintiff the duty of taking all reasonable steps to mitigate the loss consequent on the breach, and debars him from claiming any part of the damage which is due to his neglect to take such steps'.[187] It takes effect as a limitation on damages;[188] it can result in an award *less than* the claimant's factual loss. The *exception to* the avoided loss rule (hereafter referred to simply as 'the avoided loss rule'), holds that the claimant's conduct, 'if to be taken into account, must be one arising out of the consequences of the breach and in the ordinary course of business'.[189] It takes effect as an exception to the 'factual loss cap' on damages;[190] it can result in an award *greater than* the claimant's factual loss. On this analysis, both rules of mitigation function as departures from the compensatory principle, albeit in opposite directions.

180 See eg Burrows, *Remedies* (4th edn) (n 2) ch 7; Tettenborn, *Damages* (2nd edn) (n 2) ch 5.

181 Burrows, *Remedies* (4th edn) (n 2) 127 fn 229.

182 See *Thai Airways* (n 113) [33] (Leggatt J), describing it as the 'non-application of any rule'.

183 Edelman, *McGregor on Damages* (20th edn) (n 2) [9-006].

184 *British Westinghouse* (n 12) 689.

185 See further Chapter 3.

186 Although the 'tripartite' exposition formally consists of three rules, the third (avoided loss) rule itself consists of two limbs; thus the modern orthodoxy is effectively in four parts (two of which are redundant). In this book, references to the 'avoided loss rule' should be understood as references to the exception comprised in the second limb of Viscount Haldane's formulation, unless otherwise specified.

187 *British Westinghouse* (n 12) 689 (emphasis added). See also *Jamal* (n 65) 179 (Lord Wrenbury).

188 See eg *Smith New Court* (n 28) 285 (Lord Steyn): 'The third limiting principle is the duty to mitigate.'

189 *British Westinghouse* (n 12) 690. See further text to n 107.

190 See further text to n 51.

Some of the leading texts on damages have adopted this two-rule structure of mitigation in preference to following McGregor's tripartite exposition.[191] The question of whether the orthodox account of mitigation currently comprises three rules or two thus depends on which of the leading texts are consulted. However, this apparent variation between the accounts offered by the leading texts is not substantively important. All of these texts agree on the effect of the (so-called) reasonable attempts rule; they differ merely as to whether this rule requires distinctive expression in the chapter on mitigation. More importantly, all of the leading texts adopt very similar expositions of the avoidable loss rule and the avoided loss rule, which can collectively be said to constitute the orthodox account of mitigation. The following two chapters address each of these rules in more detail.

[191] See eg Tettenborn, *Damages* (2nd edn) (n 2) ch 5; Tettenborn, *Clerk & Lindsell on Torts* (23rd edn) (n 2) [27-09]–[27-11]; Burrows, *Remedies* (4th edn) (n 2) 127–32, 148–51.

2
The Avoidable Loss Rule

1 Introduction

The previous chapter described the evolution and main features of the orthodox account of the law of mitigation. In this and the next chapter, I aim to critique that account. In particular, I highlight several problems with the descriptions of the avoidable and avoided loss rules currently put forward by the leading texts on damages. As already foreshadowed, a descriptive account of the law may be orthodox but wrong, and so it is with mitigation. First, I show that the expositions of the avoidable and avoided loss rules put forward by the leading texts are in various respects inconsistent with the reasoning and results of the decided cases on mitigation. Second, these expositions are also incomplete, because at crucial junctures they fail even to *attempt* to describe any legal rules abstracted from the decided cases; instead, they fall back inadequately on a 'case-by-case' approach or conclude (incorrectly) that the law is uncertain.

This chapter is in two sections. The first section examines when the rule applies. The rule is conventionally thought to be triggered where the claimant failed to act 'reasonably' in response to the breach. However, the leading texts fail to specify how this reasonableness criterion applies; instead, they suggest ambiguously that its application is a question of fact, effectively relying on a 'case-by-case' approach. The second section examines the effect on damages where the avoidable loss rule applies. The leading texts have sometimes described mitigation as an all-or-nothing rule, or they have adopted the 'guillotine heuristic', which assumes that mitigation simply chops off recovery for part of the harm actually suffered by the claimant. I show that the avoidable loss rule instead results in a counterfactual assessment of the claimant's conduct.

2 Application

The application of the avoidable loss rule is usually said to depend on whether or not the claimant acted 'reasonably' in response to the breach. More specifically, it is claimed that the rule applies only where the claimant acted 'unreasonably'.[1] The main problem with this orthodox account is its failure to specify *how*

[1] *Wilding v British Telecommunications plc* [2002] EWCA Civ 349, [2002] ICR 1079 [55] (Potter LJ).

Mitigation in the Law of Damages. Andrew Summers, Oxford University Press. © Andy Summers 2025.
DOI: 10.1093/9780191864032.003.0002

the reasonableness test is applied; instead, the leading texts rely on the ambiguous claim that reasonableness is a question of fact. This claim is either banal, if it means merely that the reasonableness test is fact-sensitive, or incorrect, if it means that the trial judge's application of the test cannot be appealed. In this respect, the orthodox account of the avoidable loss rule provides at best an incomplete description of the law: instead of attempting to specify legal criteria for determining when the rule applies, the leading texts effectively fall back on a 'case-by-case' approach.

2.1 The reasonableness test

All of the leading texts on damages express the avoidable loss rule in terms of reasonableness.[2] *McGregor on Damages* summarizes that 'the claimant must take all reasonable steps to mitigate his or her loss consequent upon the defendant's wrong and cannot recover damages for any such loss which he or she failed, through unreasonable action or inaction, to avoid'.[3] However, this formulation leaves open the question of when conduct will (or will not) be regarded as unreasonable. The criterion of reasonableness itself is not specified. True, the leading texts often state that the standard is 'not high'; this is often justified on the basis that the defendant is an admitted wrongdoer.[4] Some texts also specify that the application of the avoidable loss rule involves 'balancing' the interests of the claimant and defendant. However, neither of these propositions adequately specifies how the reasonableness test applies; I will address each proposition in turn.

First, the proposition that the standard is 'not high' is meaningless without specifying a relevant metric; it is like saying that the standard is 'sixty per cent', without saying sixty per cent *of what*. The underlying assumption, although not explicitly stated in any of the leading texts, appears to be that the standard is fault-based and concerns the blameworthiness of the claimant's conduct. This understanding would explain why the reasonableness standard is often characterized as though on a *vertical* scale (ie from high to low fault, or better to worse conduct) and also why writers have invoked the defendant's comparative fault to justify there being a low standard. If fault was indeed the relevant metric applied by the courts, this would at least give some content to the claim that the standard of reasonableness

[2] See eg James Edelman (ed), *McGregor on Damages* (21st edn, Sweet & Maxwell 2022) [9-004]; Hugh Beale (ed), *Chitty on Contracts* (34th edn, Sweet & Maxwell 2022) [29-096]; Andrew Tettenborn (ed), *Clerk & Lindsell on Torts* (23rd edn, Sweet & Maxwell 2022) [27-09]; Andrew Burrows, *Remedies for Torts, Breach of Contract, and Equitable Wrongs* (4th edn, OUP 2019) 127; Andrew Tettenborn, *The Law of Damages* (2nd edn, LexisNexis 2010) [5.79].

[3] Edelman (n 2) [9-004].

[4] ibid [9-079] (emphasis added). See also Beale (n 2) [29-099]; Tettenborn (n 2) [5.79]. This proposition has occasionally been picked up by the courts: see eg *Walker v Geo H Medlicott & Son* [1999] 1 WLR 727 (CA) 743 (Simon Brown LJ), citing Harvey McGregor (ed), *McGregor on Damages* (16th edn, Sweet & Maxwell 1997) 211.

was 'not high', albeit that difficult problems would remain in quantifying the relevant degree of blameworthiness.

However, it is clear from the cases on mitigation that the reasonableness standard is not fault-based.[5] First, judges have frequently emphasized that the claimant is not under any 'duty' to mitigate, and indeed is 'completely free to act as he judges to be in his best interests' following the breach.[6] Second, one might expect that a fault-based standard of reasonableness would be lowered where the defendant was an intentional wrongdoer. However, as the leading texts have acknowledged,[7] this is not the law.[8] Instead, it is well-established that the reasonableness test applies in exactly the same way regardless of the defendant's fault. Indeed, the test is the same even where the basis for the defendant's liability was strict,[9] such that the defendant was not an 'admitted wrongdoer' at all.[10] Both of these features of the avoidable loss rule are discussed in more detail in Chapter 7; for now, it is enough to observe that they are inconsistent with a fault-based standard of reasonableness.

The leading texts have also expressed the view that the reasonableness test involves balancing the interests of the claimant and defendant. For example, *McGregor on Damages* suggests that 'in assessing reasonableness, while it has been said that the claimant is "not bound to nurse the interests" of the defendant, it has also, and for long, been said that the claimant must act with the defendant's as well as his own interests in mind.'[11] There is some limited support for this proposition in the cases on mitigation,[12] but actually applying a balancing approach would not be straightforward. First, it is unclear what are the relevant interests to be balanced. Second, there is the difficulty of balancing interests that are incommensurable. Third, even if the relevant interests can be compared—for example, where the claimant's and defendant's interests were both financial—it is uncertain where (ie, in what proportion) the balance is to be struck.

One response to these difficulties might be that the reasonableness test does not require any further specification; 'reasonableness' is a term for which the definition is self-evident. However, the issue cannot be dismissed so easily, because judges have frequently emphasized that in mitigation, 'reasonableness' has a special

[5] Although judges have occasionally implied the adoption of a fault-based standard: see eg *Lodge Holes Colliery Co Ltd v Wednesbury Corp* [1908] AC 323 (HL) 325 (Lord Loreburn CJ); *Borealis AB v Geogas Trading SA* [2010] EWHC 2789 (Comm), [2011] 1 Lloyd's Rep 482 [137] (Gross LJ).

[6] *Sotiros Shipping Inc v Sameiet Solholt (The Solholt)* [1983] 1 Lloyd's Rep 605 (CA) 608 (Sir John Donaldson MR).

[7] Edelman (n 2) [9-080].

[8] *Smith New Court Securities Ltd v Citibank NA* [1997] AC 254 (HL) 285 (Lord Steyn); *Standard Chartered Bank v Pakistan National Shipping Corp* [1999] 1 Lloyd's Rep 747 (QB) 760 (Toulson J).

[9] *Elliott Steam Tug Co Ltd v Shipping Controller* [1922] 1 KB 127 (CA); *Welford v EDF Energy Networks (LPN) plc* [2007] EWCA Civ 293, [2007] 2 P & CR 15.

[10] Note 4.

[11] Edelman (n 2) [9-081]. See also Beale (n 2) [26-100].

[12] See eg *Darbishire v Warran* [1963] 1 WLR 1067 (CA) 1072 (Harman LJ), 1076 (Pearson LJ).

meaning.[13] As the courts have put it, the test 'is not simply one of general rationality',[14] and does not depend 'upon [the claimant's] reason for acting as they did'.[15] In particular, 'the claimant may have acted in a way which was reasonable from the point of view of its own business interests or personal objectives and yet not have adopted what the law regards as a "reasonable" response'.[16] In *The Elena D'Amico*, Goff J summarized that '[i]t does not matter . . . that [the claimant's] decision was a reasonable one, or was a sensible business decision'.[17] So, whatever reasonableness means in this context, it is clearly not just its literal or dictionary definition.[18]

The distinction between the usual definition of reasonableness and the application of the avoidable loss rule is illustrated by the House of Lords' decision in *Dimond v Lovell*.[19] Following a car accident, the claimant hired a replacement vehicle from a credit hire company. This service cost more than the standard hire rate because it provided additional convenience and no up-front charges. In considering (obiter) the recoverability of the credit hire costs, Lord Hoffmann held that 'I would accept the judge's finding that Mrs Dimond acted reasonably ... I am sure that any of your Lordships in her position would have done the same . . . But that does not necessarily mean that she can recover the full amount'.[20] Lord Hobhouse concluded that '[i]t was reasonable for her to pay the additional sum in order to obtain the additional benefits ... But she cannot claim the whole cost as the cost of mitigating the loss'.[21]

This distinction can be demonstrated more generally using a simple hypothetical example.[22] Suppose again that the claimant's car is negligently damaged by the

[13] As Kramer puts it, 'a special sense of "reasonable" is meant': Adam Kramer, *The Law of Contract Damages* (3rd edn, Hart 2022) [16-52]; see also [15-67].

[14] *Thai Airways International Public Co Ltd v KI Holdings Co Ltd* [2015] EWHC 1250 (Comm), [2016] 1 All ER (Comm) 675 [34] (Leggatt J).

[15] *Deutsche Bank AG v Total Global Steel Ltd* [2012] EWHC 1201 (Comm) [159] (Andrew Smith J). See also *Riyad Bank v Ahli United Bank (UK) plc* [2005] EWHC 279 (Comm), [2005] 2 Lloyd's Rep 409 [171] (Moore-Bick J).

[16] *Thai Airways* (n 14) [37] (Leggatt J). See also, in the application of the market rule: *Habton Farms v Nimmo* [2003] EWCA Civ 68, [2004] QB 1 [66], [100] (Clarke LJ); *Campbell Mostyn (Provisions) Ltd v Barnett Trading Co* [1954] 1 Lloyd's Rep 65 (CA) 71 (Romer LJ); *Downs v Chappell* [1997] 1 WLR 426 (CA) 437 (Hobhouse LJ); *Blue Circle Industries plc v Ministry of Defence* [1999] Ch 289 (CA) 306 (Aldous LJ); 321 (Simon Brown LJ).

[17] *Koch Marine Inc v d'Amica Societa di Navigazione arl (The Elena d'Amico)* [1980] 1 Lloyd's Rep 75 (QB) 89. This part of Goff J's judgment was repeated in *Glory Wealth Shipping Pte Ltd v Korea Line Corp (The Wren)* [2011] EWHC 1819 (Comm), [2012] 1 All ER (Comm) 402 [16] (Blair J) and *Fulton Shipping Inc of Panama v Globalia Business Travel SAU (The New Flamenco)* [2014] EWHC 1547 (Comm), [2015] 1 All ER (Comm) 1205 [64] (Popplewell J). See also *Fulton Shipping Inc of Panama v Globalia Business Travel SAU (The New Flamenco)* [2017] UKSC 43, [2017] 1 WLR 2581 [16](5) (Lord Clarke).

[18] See eg, *Oxford Dictionary of English* (3rd edn, OUP 2010), which defines unreasonableness as 'not guided by or based on good sense'.

[19] *Dimond v Lovell* [2002] 1 AC 384 (HL). This decision raised an issue of 'betterment', although the House of Lords also referred to mitigation.

[20] ibid 401.

[21] ibid 407. Instead, the majority (Lord Nicholls dissenting) held that the claimant would only have been entitled to recover the standard hire rate.

[22] This will be referred to as the 'car accident example'.

defendant. Now suppose that instead of repairing the car, the claimant decided (at greater expense) to buy a new car.[23] This may be an eminently 'reasonable' decision, on the usual understanding of this term: maybe she decided that it would be more convenient to have a bigger car; or maybe the new car was available at a temporary discount. Suppose alternatively that the claimant decided to buy a bicycle (at lesser expense). Again, this may be eminently 'reasonable': maybe she concluded she really did not need a car anyway and would be better-off cycling to work. The point is that none of these *reasons* make any difference to the application of the avoidable loss rule, which in this example will apply to any choice (for whatever reason) not to repair the car.

In Chapter 6, I argue that the concepts of choice and abnormality better describe the judicial application of mitigation than does the conventional terminology of 'reasonableness'. In particular, the reasoning and results of the decided cases are more consistent with the view that mitigation applies whenever the claimant made a choice to depart from the 'normal' response to breach.[24] This restatement of the law differs from the description of the reasonableness test put forward by most of the leading texts on damages; however, it has an affinity with the original formulation of mitigation established in *British Westinghouse v London Underground*, where Viscount Haldane referred to steps that the claimant 'would not ordinarily take'.[25] I discuss how my account applies to the familiar cases on avoidable and avoided loss, in Chapters 8 and 9 respectively.

2.2 Reasonableness as a 'question of fact'

In the absence of more specific criteria, the reasonableness of the claimant's conduct is often said to be a 'question of fact'.[26] This claim is made by all of the leading texts on damages.[27] Historically, the designation of an issue as a question of fact would have meant that it was put to the jury to decide.[28] However, in the modern

[23] These were essentially the facts of *Moore v DER Ltd* [1971] 1 WLR 1476 (CA). Davies LJ held that 'It seems to me a sensible and businesslike course to put in for a new Rover' but thought it obvious that this cost could not be recovered by the claimant: 1479–80.

[24] In Chapter 6, I argue that there are two relevant norms. First, a *legal* norm that the claimant will take steps to replicate the no-breach position as nearly as possible. Second, a *descriptive* norm that the claimant will do so in a usual (ie not exceptional) way.

[25] *British Westinghouse Electric & Manufacturing Co Ltd v Underground Electric Railways Co of London Ltd (No 2)* [1912] AC 673 (HL) 689. See also the addition to *McGregor on Damages* under Edelman's editorship, noting that the claimant's actions 'will generally be reasonable where they are ordinary': Edelman (n 2) [9-082].

[26] See eg Michael Bridge, 'Mitigation of Damages in Contract and the Meaning of Avoidable Loss' (1989) 105 Law Quarterly Review 398, 400: 'The extent to which there should have been mitigation is a question of fact and the plaintiff must take steps consistent with the demands of reasonable and prudent action.'

[27] See eg Edelman (n 2) [9-016] and [52-031]; Beale (n 2) [29-099]; Burrows, *Remedies* (4th edn) (n 2) 127; Tettenborn (n 2) [5.79].

[28] Edelman (n 2) [52-029].

English legal system, where civil juries have become all but extinct, the implications of this proposition for the law of mitigation are ambiguous.[29] First, it might mean merely that the issue of reasonableness is 'fact-sensitive', or in other words, that the application of the reasonableness test depends on a close examination of the facts of the case. Second, it might mean that the reasonableness of the claimant's conduct raises an issue of 'primary fact' that cannot be appealed. The first of these two understandings is accurate but essentially banal; the second is incorrect.

McGregor on Damages asserts that 'Whether the claimant has acted reasonably is in every case a question of fact, not of law',[30] adding elsewhere that this proposition 'has never been doubted' and 'tends to be regarded as trite law.'[31] In support, *McGregor* cites the decision in *Payzu v Saunders* as the earliest and leading authority.[32] In that case, Bankes LJ held that the issue of whether the claimant had acted reasonably 'must be one of fact in the circumstances of each particular case'.[33] However, it is important to view this judicial statement in context; it was intended to rebut counsel's argument that it would *always* (ie whatever the circumstances) be reasonable for a claimant to reject an offer by the defendant following breach.[34] Against this background, the Court of Appeal's decision in *Payzu* merely served to emphasize that the application of the reasonableness test was *fact-sensitive* ie that its application requires a close examination of the all of the circumstances.

More recent decisions have similarly emphasized that the application of the reasonableness test in mitigation is 'heavily fact sensitive',[35] and must 'be decided in the light of all the circumstances'.[36] But this point is essentially banal; the application of most legal tests is a 'question of fact' in this sense. The problem is that fact-sensitivity cannot provide any guidance on its own; other principles are needed to determine *which* facts the court must be sensitive to. In this respect, the proposition that reasonableness is a 'question of fact' is uninformative, because as Lord

[29] See further George Letsas and Prince Saprai, 'Mitigation, Fairness and Contract Law' in Gregory Klass, George Letsas, and Prince Saprai (eds), *Philosophical Foundations of Contract Law* (OUP 2014) 330.

[30] Edelman (n 2) [9-079].

[31] ibid [9-016].

[32] *Payzu v Saunders* [1919] 2 KB 581 (CA), also citing *The Solholt* (n 6) 77–78 (Sir John Donaldson MR).

[33] ibid 589. See also 589 (Scrutton LJ). This proposition has subsequently been cited in *Moore* (n 23) 1479 (Davies LJ); *The Solholt* (n 6) 608 (Sir John Donaldson MR); and *Gul Bottlers (PVT) Ltd v Nichols plc* [2014] EWHC 2173 (Comm) [22] (Cooke J).

[34] *Payzu* (n 32) 588–89. In particular, the claimant argued that 'in considering what steps should be taken to mitigate the damage all contractual relations with the party in default must be excluded': 589 (Scrutton LJ).

[35] *LSREF III Wight Ltd v Gateley LLP* [2016] EWCA Civ 359, [2016] PNLR 21 [39] (Briggs LJ). See also Andrew Burrows, *A Restatement of the English Law of Contract* (OUP 2016) 132: 'what should reasonably have been avoided is fact-specific'.

[36] *Secretary of State for Health v Servier Laboratories Ltd* [2016] EWHC 2381 (Ch), [2016] 5 CMLR 25 [42] (Henderson J). See also *Barings plc v Coopers & Lybrand (No8)* [2003] EWHC 2371 (Ch) [838] (Evans-Lombe J); *Burdis v Livsey (sub nom Lagden v O'Connor)* [2002] EWCA Civ 510, [2003] QB 36 [147]–[148] (Aldous LJ); *Borealis* (n 5) [47] (Gross LJ).

Hoffmann highlighted, 'unless you know the question, you will not be able to get the right answer'.[37] To put the point another way, judges and scholars should heed Diplock LJ's warning that 'the law is nearly always most obscure in those fields in which judges say the principle is plain, but the difficulty lies in its application to particular facts'.[38]

A second possible understanding is that the reasonableness of the claimant's conduct raises issues of 'primary fact', which cannot (or can only rarely) be appealed. This proposition contains within it a further ambiguity as between its 'narrow' and 'wide' versions. The narrow version holds merely that it is necessary to make certain findings of primary fact before the reasonableness of the claimant's conduct can be assessed; in other words, the application of the reasonableness test relies on prior findings of primary fact. This is of course accurate, but again, essentially banal; it is true of just about every legal test. By contrast, the wide meaning is that the trial judge's decision on the reasonableness of the claimant's conduct is *itself* a finding of primary fact. This proposition is incorrect; it is plainly inconsistent with numerous cases on mitigation, both in reasoning and outcomes.

As regards the narrow version, the application of the avoidable loss rule must obviously rely on certain prior findings of primary fact concerning the claimant's circumstances: for example, the reliability of any offers made to the claimant by the defendant or third parties, or the question of whether alternative responses (besides the one actually taken) were available to the claimant.[39] The appellate courts have emphasized that it will rarely be appropriate to interfere with such findings.[40] For example, in *Fyfe v Fife Coal* the House of Lords rejected the appellant's argument that the claimant had given too much weight to the advice of his own doctor instead of other doctors.[41] Viscount Dunedin held that this issue as to the reliability of advice received by the claimant (from the claimant's perspective), raised 'a pure question of fact' that was better determined by the arbitrator, who had heard directly from the witnesses.[42] This conclusion is entirely correct, but is hardly a special feature of the law of mitigation.

[37] Lord Hoffmann, 'Common Sense and Causing Loss' (Chancery Bar Association Lecture, 15 June 1999) 3.

[38] *Ilkiw v Samuels* [1963] 1 WLR 991 (CA) 1004. cf Harvey McGregor, 'The Role of Mitigation in the Assessment of Damages' in Djakhongir Saidov and Ralph Cunnington (eds), *Contract Damages: Domestic and International Perspectives* (Hart 2008) 334: 'Illustrations of circumstances raising the issue of whether loss from breach of contract should have been avoided abound ... English law on such issues being fairly straightforward, I leave these on one side.'

[39] See eg *The Solholt* (n 6) 610 (Sir John Donaldson MR); *Uzinterimpex JSC v Standard Bank plc* [2008] EWCA Civ 819, [2008] 2 CLC 80 [50] (Moore-Bick LJ); *Welford* (n 9) [36] (Thomas LJ).

[40] See eg *Standard Chartered Bank v Pakistan National Shipping Corp* [2001] EWCA Civ 55, [2001] 1 All ER (Comm) 822 [47] (Potter LJ).

[41] *Fyfe v Fife Coal Co Ltd* (1927) SC (HL) 103 (HL) 106 (Viscount Dunedin). See also, on very similar facts: *Steele v Robert George & Co* [1942] AC 497 (HL) 501 (Viscount Simon), 502 (Lord Wright).

[42] *Fyfe v Fife* (n 41) 107.

As regards the wide version, the leading texts on damages have sometimes implied that the trial judge's decision on the reasonableness of the claimant's conduct is *itself* a finding of primary fact that cannot (or can only rarely) be interfered with on appeal. For example, *McGregor on Damages* states that 'once a court of first instance has decided that there has been, or has not been, a failure to mitigate, it is difficult to persuade an appellate court to come to a different view'.[43] This proposition is wider than the one established in cases like *Fyfe*, because it concerns the outcome of the reasonableness test, not merely the findings to which the test is applied. In support of this proposition, *McGregor* cites *Standard Chartered Bank v Pakistan National Shipping*, where Potter LJ held that because 'mitigation of damage is a question of fact . . . it is therefore rarely appropriate to interfere with the conclusions of the trial judge based as they are on the evidence'.[44]

The decision in *Standard Chartered* is not an appropriate authority for the wide version that *McGregor on Damages* endorses. In that case, the appellant's arguments concerned the initial findings of primary fact to which the reasonableness test then applied, rather than the application of the test itself. In particular, counsel's argument was that the trial judge should not have rejected the evidence provided by the defendant's expert at trial, as to the price for which damaged cargo could have been resold.[45] In further support of the wide version, *McGregor* cites two other cases in which the trial judge's decision on reasonableness was subsequently upheld on appeal.[46] However, neither of these cases demonstrate a reluctance to interfere on appeal, because they are equally explicable on the basis that the appellate court considered that the trial judge had applied the reasonableness test correctly as a matter of law.

Looking at the whole body of cases on mitigation, it is clear that the trial judge's decision on the reasonableness of the claimant's conduct has frequently been overturned on appeal, often with no hesitation or reluctance.[47] Perhaps the most striking example is *Moore v DER*, which concerned the reasonableness of the claimant's conduct in hiring a replacement car for eighteen weeks following a car accident.[48] The trial judge held that the claimant's conduct was unreasonable and therefore reduced the damages to the equivalent of three weeks' hire. On appeal, both Davies LJ and Karminski LJ endorsed the proposition that the application of

[43] Edelman (n 2) [9-016]. But see also [9-007] and [52-031] fn 147, both of which appear to contradict this position.

[44] *Standard Chartered (CA)* (n 40) [47] (Potter LJ).

[45] ibid [43]–[44] (Potter LJ).

[46] Edelman (n 2) [9-016], citing *The Solholt* (n 6) and *Uzinterimpex* (n 39).

[47] See eg *Richardson v Redpath Brown & Co* [1944] AC 62 (HL) 72–73 (Viscount Simon), 74 (Lord Russell); *Darbishire* (n 12) 1072 (Harman LJ); *Moore* (n 23) 1480 (Davies LJ), 1481 (Karminski LJ), 1481 (Stamp LJ); *Fyfe v Scientific Furnishings Ltd* [1989] ICR 648 (EAT) 655–56 (Wood J, on appeal from an industrial tribunal); *Wilding* (n 1) [36] (Potter LJ); *Copley v Lawn* [2009] EWCA Civ 580, [2010] 1 All ER (Comm) 890 [23]–[24] (Longmore LJ); *Sayce v TNT (UK) Ltd* [2011] EWCA Civ 1583, [2012] 1 WLR 1261 [21]–[22] (Moore-Bick LJ); *LSREF* (n 35) [44]–[52] (Briggs LJ).

[48] *Moore* (n 23).

the reasonableness test was a 'question of fact', relying on the authority in *Payzu v Saunders*.[49] Despite this proposition, they unanimously overturned the trial judge's decision on this issue and entered judgment for the cost of all eighteen weeks of hire.[50]

The wide version of the proposition that the reasonableness test raises issues of primary fact was expressly considered and rejected by the Court of Appeal in *Wilding v BT*.[51] In that case, Potter LJ (who, it will be recalled, also delivered the judgment in *Standard Chartered*)[52] dismissed the respondent's submission that the court was precluded from re-examining the Tribunal's application of the reasonableness test. Instead, he emphasized that:

> The primary argument on this appeal is whether the Tribunal properly applied the correct legal test or . . . asked itself the right question in coming to its conclusion. If it did not do so, or if in applying the legal test it took into account irrelevant factors, or left out of account relevant factors or, if having made its findings of primary fact, it drew a wrong inference or inferences or gave wholly inappropriate weight to a particular factor or factors, the Tribunal may be treated as having erred in law in coming to its decision.[53]

This reasoning shows that the application of the reasonableness test itself was regarded as raising a question (or questions) of law. In particular, the test involved the application of legal rules to determine the *relevant* factors to take into consideration and the appropriate inferences to draw from them. Although these rules were not specified by the Court of Appeal, Potter LJ was clearly of the opinion that such rules existed (thereby constituting 'the correct legal test') and hence that a trial judge's conclusion on the reasonableness of the claimant's conduct could be overturned if they had erred in law by misapplying the rules.

A series of recent cases reinforce this view. In *Copley v Lawn*, the respondents argued that the lower courts' decisions on reasonableness were '"findings of fact" and should not be interfered with by this court'.[54] Longmore LJ rejected that submission on the basis that 'there is no question of any interference with any finding of primary fact'.[55] In particular, he held that 'questions of mitigation are however, questions of evaluation and judgment and there is no reason why this court should

[49] *Payzu* (n 32). See further text to n 32.

[50] *Moore* (n 23) 1480 (Davies LJ), 1481 (Karminski LJ), 1481 (Stamp LJ). The most likely explanation for this approach is that Davies LJ and Karminski LJ had in mind the proposition that the reasonableness test was fact-sensitive ie the first understanding outlined at text to n 35.

[51] Note 1.

[52] Text to n 44.

[53] *Wilding* (n 1) [36] (Potter LJ). Potter LJ considered the appellant's grounds of appeal on this basis, but concluded that there had been no error in the Employment Appeal Tribunal's approach.

[54] *Copley* [23] (Longmore LJ).

[55] ibid [23].

not interfere, if the judge's conclusions are, in its considered opinion, wrong'.[56] Longmore LJ considered the facts of the two cases subject to the appeal, and allowed both appeals on the issue of reasonableness, on the basis that the trial judges had erred in concluding that the claimants had acted unreasonably by refusing the defendants' offers.[57]

The Court of Appeal affirmed Longmore LJ's approach in *Sayce v TNT*.[58] Moore-Bick LJ sought to clarify that 'Longmore LJ was merely pointing out that since the question whether the claimant failed to act reasonably in mitigation involves an evaluation of the primary facts, it is a decision with which the court can more readily interfere'.[59] In particular, the trial judge had erred in 'brushing aside' the precedent set by Longmore LJ in *Copley* as to the proper approach for determining whether the claimant's conduct had been unreasonable.[60] Moore-Bick LJ was clear that the principle established by Longmore LJ formed part of the ratio of *Copley*,[61] and therefore bound the trial judge in his subsequent decision. To have had this binding effect, the relevant principle must plainly have settled a question of law not fact.

Most recently, in *LSREF III Wight v Gately*, the Court of Appeal again rejected the respondent's submission that it could not interfere with the trial judge's decision on reasonableness.[62] Briggs LJ accepted that 'mitigation issues are heavily fact sensitive, multifactorial questions'.[63] However he concluded that 'the question at the end of the day is whether there has been an unreasonable failure to mitigate, and the application of a reasonableness test does, in the final analysis, require . . . something more than just fact-finding'.[64] Briggs LJ went on to consider each of the seven reasons that the trial judge had given for deciding that the claimant's conduct had been reasonable, and rejected all seven.[65] He therefore allowed the appeal on the basis that '[i]n my judgment, none of the judge's reasons, singularly or in the aggregate, justify the conclusion that the claimant had not unreasonably failed to mitigate its loss'.[66]

56 ibid [23].
57 ibid [24].
58 *Sayce*. See also *Beechwood Birmingham Ltd v Hoyer Group UK Ltd* [2010] EWCA Civ 647, [2011] QB 357 [27] (Potter LJ).
59 *Sayce* (n 58) [18].
60 ibid [18]–[23].
61 ibid [21]–[22] (Moore-Bick LJ): 'I think it is clear, therefore, that [Longmore LJ] did adopt and apply the principle that a claimant does not act unreasonably for the purposes of mitigation in rejecting an offer from the defendant unless he is aware that by doing so he will increase the ultimate burden on the defendant, regardless of the effect on his own position . . . If, as I think, that is the ratio of *Copley v Lawn*, the judge was bound to apply it.'
62 *LSREF* (n 35).
63 ibid [39].
64 ibid [39]. Briggs LJ observed that 'No part of the judge's careful findings of primary fact is challenged': ibid [12].
65 ibid [44]–[52].
66 ibid [53].

2.3 The case-by-case approach

I have argued that the leading texts on mitigation effectively leave the criterion of reasonableness unspecified. Tettenborn is the most candid about this, noting simply that 'no fixed rules can be laid down'.[67] Other texts superficially offer guiding principles, but these turn out to be indeterminate.[68] It is tempting to conclude that judicial references to reasonableness must therefore reflect what John Gardner terms a 'legally deregulated' zone, ie 'a zone of legally licensed adjudicative discretion'.[69] But, whilst this analysis may correctly describe the effect of reasonableness tests in some areas of the law, in mitigation this conclusion cannot be sustained. As I have emphasized, the issue of what amounts to (un)reasonable conduct by the claimant clearly *does* raise questions of law, which may be the subject of successful appeal. The problem is that the orthodox account of mitigation fails to state what the relevant legal rules are.

In lieu of specifying legal rules that govern the application of the reasonableness test, the leading texts offer a catalogue of decided cases. For example, the exposition of the avoidable loss rule in *McGregor on Damages* comprises four paragraphs on 'the criterion of reasonableness and the standard of reasonableness',[70] bookended by fifty paragraphs of 'illustrative decisions'.[71] These decisions are loosely organized under sub-headings that do not purport to have any legal significance: for example, according to their commercial context, or whether liability was in contract or tort.[72] Similarly, Kramer acknowledges that his account of mitigation 'does not seek to formulate a general principle or set of factors that govern all of these cases';[73] instead, he argues that 'it is best to look at the decisions in the cases similar to the one at hand'.[74] I refer to this tendency as the 'case-by-case' approach.

The case-by-case approach does not qualify as a description of the law. The aim of a restatement of the law is to describe rules abstracted from the decided cases, yet in relation to the reasonableness test, the leading texts effectively disclaim this task: instead, they just report the cases themselves.[75] In this respect, the orthodox account of the avoidable loss rule is not so much wrong as incomplete. The problem

[67] Tettenborn (n 2) [5.79].

[68] See further text to n 4 and n 11 above.

[69] John Gardner, 'The Many Faces of the Reasonable Person' (2015) 131 Law Quarterly Review 563, 582. See also John Gardner, 'The Reasonable Person Standard' in Hugh LaFolette (ed), *The International Encyclopedia of Ethics* (2nd edn, Wiley-Blackwell 2020).

[70] Edelman (n 2) [9-079]–[9-082]. For analysis of the principles offered in this section, see further text to nn 4 and 11.

[71] ibid [9-047]–[9-078] and [9-083]–[9-100]. See also Burrows, *Remedies* (4th edn) (n 2) 127–29.

[72] For example, 'goods', 'employment', 'land', etc; again, there is no suggestion that any of these different categories are legally significant.

[73] Kramer (n 13) [16-01].

[74] ibid [15-22]. See also Burrows, *Remedies* (4th edn) (n 2) 127.

[75] In other words, they describe legal sources, but not the law. For further discussion of this distinction, see Introduction.

with invoking a case-by-case approach is well-known: as Hart put it, 'until it is established what resemblance and differences are relevant, [the proposition] "Treat like cases alike" must remain an empty form'.[76] In other words, without stating the relevant rules or principles to be applied, the case-by-case approach is incapable of providing any legal guidance. Michael Bridge has acknowledged this problem, concluding that 'the constant emphasis on fact and reasonableness, so characteristic of a common law that is concerned with the need for retaining flexibility, has served the law badly in this section of mitigation'.[77]

3 Effect on Damages

The orthodox account of mitigation equivocates over the legal effect of the avoidable loss rule. The leading texts each offer subtly different accounts.[78] For many years, the two most common expositions were the 'all-or-nothing' view, and what I call (following Adam Kramer) the 'guillotine heuristic'. The all-or-nothing view has recently diminished in prominence; it is wrong in all but the very simplest of cases. The guillotine heuristic offers a somewhat more plausible account of the law, but nevertheless breaks down in more complex cases. More recently it has come to be accepted by the leading texts—correctly—that the effect of mitigation is to assess damages on a counterfactual basis as if the claimant had acted reasonably. I discuss the application of this counterfactual assessment in more detail in Chapter 8.

3.1 The all-or-nothing view

The avoidable loss rule has sometimes been expressed as having an 'all-or-nothing' effect on damages: if the claimant acted reasonably, it can recover its loss in full; but if it acted unreasonably, it can recover nothing at all. Andrew Burrows adopted the all-or-nothing view in his earlier writings on mitigation,[79] stating that 'the consequence of [a failure to mitigate] is simply that no damages are given for the avoidable loss';[80] on this basis, he described the doctrine as a 'total defence'.[81] Burrows

[76] HLA Hart, *The Concept of Law* (3rd edn, OUP 2012) 159.

[77] Bridge (n 26) 423.

[78] *McGregor on Damages* even appears to offer three different accounts within the same chapter: compare the formulations in Edelman (n 2) at [9-004] (the all-or-nothing view), [9-007] (counterfactual assessment), and [9-014] (the guillotine heuristic). See also Beale (n 2) [29-098].

[79] Andrew Burrows, 'Contributory Negligence in Contract: Ammunition for the Law Commission' (1993) 109 Law Quarterly Review 175, 177, referring to the 'all or nothing concepts of causation and duty to mitigate'. On all-or-nothing rules generally (excluding mitigation), see Tony Weir, 'All or Nothing?' (2004) 78 Tulane Law Review 511.

[80] Andrew Burrows, *Remedies for Torts and Breach of Contract* (3rd edn, OUP 2004) 122. See also 143.

[81] ibid 75–76.

has subsequently disavowed this view,[82] but several other leading texts have persisted with similar propositions. For example, *Chitty on Contracts* states that '[a]ny loss which is directly caused by a failure to [mitigate] is not recoverable from the defendant'.[83] The idea that mitigation forms a total defence to a claim for damages is often expressed in contrast to the partial effect of contributory negligence.[84]

Where the type of harm (or 'head of damage') actually suffered by the claimant would not have been suffered at all but for the claimant's unreasonable conduct, the all-or-nothing view can appear plausible.[85] But outside this simple paradigm, this description of the law is obviously untenable. For example, suppose that the claimant unreasonably spends £5,000 repairing their car following the defendant's negligent collision, even though a suitable repair could have been obtained for £2,000. The all-or-nothing view would hold that the claimant can recover nothing in these circumstances, whereas the cases clearly establish that the claimant would be entitled to damages of £2,000.[86] The expositions in the leading texts may be flexible enough to accommodate this conclusion, but their ambiguity leaves open the all-or-nothing (mis)interpretation.

3.2 The 'guillotine' heuristic

A somewhat more plausible understanding, also evident in the leading texts, is what Adam Kramer has termed the 'guillotine' approach.[87] On this view, the avoidable loss rule 'chops off' any harm that could have been avoided if the claimant had acted reasonably. It therefore permits partial recovery, rather than necessitating an all-or-nothing approach. For example, *McGregor on Damages* summarizes that 'the law requires [the claimant] to take all reasonable steps to mitigate the loss . . . and refuses to allow him damages *in respect of any part of the loss* which is due to his neglect to take such steps'.[88] *Treitel on Contract* makes the same point

[82] Burrows, *Remedies* (4th edn) (n 2) 83–86.

[83] Beale (n 2) [29-098]. See also Edelman (n 2) [9-004]: 'the claimant must take all reasonable steps to mitigate the loss . . . and cannot recover damages for any such loss which he could thus have avoided'.

[84] See eg Iain Field, 'Contributory Negligence and the Rule of Avoidable Losses' (2018) 38 Oxford Journal of Legal Studies 475, 476; Edelman (n 2) [6-013].

[85] See eg *Stacey v Autosleeper Group Ltd* [2014] EWCA Civ 1551 [25] (Floyd LJ), refusing damages for the costs of a mediation that would not have been necessary if the claimant had acted reasonably.

[86] *The Pactolus* (1856) Sw 173, 166 ER 1079, 1081 (Dr Lushington); *Lodge Holes* (n 5) 325 (Lord Loreburn LC); *Owners of the Georgidore v Owners of the Pacific Concord (The Pacific Concord)* [1961] 1 WLR 873 (PD) 884 (Lord Merriman); *Sunlife Europe Properties Ltd v Tiger Aspect Holdings Ltd* [2013] EWHC 463 (TCC), 147 Con LR 105 [37], [43], [46] (Eduards Stuart J), affirmed *Sunlife Europe Properties Ltd v Tiger Aspect Holdings Ltd* [2013] EWCA Civ 1656, [2014] 1 EGLR 30 [14] (Lewison LJ); *Coles v Hetherton* [2013] EWCA Civ 1704, [2015] 1 WLR 160 [45] (Aikens LJ).

[87] Kramer (n 13) [15-65]. Kramer himself rejects the guillotine heuristic: see text to n 100.

[88] Edelman (n 2) [9-014] (emphasis added).

the other way around: 'If the claimant fails to take reasonable steps to minimize his loss, he cannot recover anything *in respect of extra loss* due to that failure.'[89]

This view fits with the conventional understanding of the avoidable loss rule as a limitation on damages: the court starts by making an assessment of the claimant's factual loss; then it proceeds via mitigation and other doctrines to determine how much of that loss is recoverable in damages.[90] Viscount Haldane's judgment in *British Westinghouse* could be read in this way.[91] There, he held that mitigation 'debarred' the claimant 'from claiming *any part of the damage* which is due to his neglect to take [reasonable] steps'.[92] Other formulations reflecting the notion of cutting back recovery have been adopted in subsequent cases.[93] The essence of these expositions, whether judicial or academic, is that they treat the award of damages as being carved out from (or a subset of) the harm actually suffered by the claimant.

I call this understanding the guillotine *heuristic* because it functions like a mental shortcut. The shortcut works adequately where two conditions hold. First, the harm actually suffered by the claimant must be quantitatively divisible, or in other words, capable of occurring to a greater or lesser extent, rather than either occurring (in full) or not.[94] Second, it must be the case that the same *type* of harm would still have been suffered if the claimant had acted reasonably. One example where these conditions are satisfied is with the excess cost of repairing the car, as outlined above.[95] Another is where the claimant suffered a loss of profits, but the total amount of profits lost could have been reduced by reasonable action.[96] In such cases, the avoidable loss rule appears simply to chop off some divisible part of the harm that was actually suffered by the claimant, leaving a smaller amount recoverable in damages.

However, the guillotine heuristic breaks down in more complex cases, most often where the harm that would have been suffered if the claimant had acted

[89] Edwin Peel (ed), *Treitel on The Law of Contract* (15th edn, Sweet & Maxwell 2022) (n 2) [20-106]. See also David Allen, Robyn Martin, and John Hartshorne, *Damages in Tort* (Sweet & Maxwell 2000) [4-067].

[90] See eg Bridge (n 26) 399: 'mitigation operates pro tanto as a conditional bar to the recovery of damages'.

[91] *British Westinghouse* (n 25) 689 (Viscount Haldane). On the other hand, Viscount Haldane also cited with approval the formulation of James LJ in *Dunkirk Colliery v Lever*, which referred to the *reduced* sum (after mitigation had been applied) as 'the full amount of the damage which they have really sustained': *Dunkirk Colliery Co v Lever* (1878) 9 Ch D 20 (CA) 25.

[92] *British Westinghouse* (n 25) 689 (emphasis added).

[93] See eg *Compania Financiera Soleada SA v Hamoor Tanker Corp Inc (The Borag)* [1981] 1 WLR 274 (CA) 284 (Templeman LJ), 279–80 (Lord Denning MR); *Minchburn v Peck* (1988) 20 HLR 392 (CA) 398; *Dimond* (n 19) 403 (Lord Hoffmann); *Lagden v O'Connor (sub nom Burdis v Livsey)* [2003] UKHL 64, [2004] 1 AC 1067 [27] (Lord Hope); *Joyce v Bowman Law Ltd* [2010] EWHC 251 (Ch), [2010] PNLR 22 [118]-[119] (Vos J); *Copley* (n 54) [30] (Longmore LJ); *Coles* (n 86) [45] (Aikens LJ).

[94] In practice, this distinction can be difficult to draw and depends on precisely how the relevant type of harm is defined. The difficulty is resolved by the recognition of a counterfactual assessment: see further Chapter 8.

[95] Text to n 86.

[96] See eg *Joyce* (n 93).

reasonably was of a different type altogether from the harm actually suffered. For example, suppose that a claimant unreasonably decided not to repair their car at all following an accident involving the defendant; then, as a result of the ongoing defect, suppose the claimant had another accident, this time resulting in personal injury. Here, the mental shortcut of denying recovery for some divisible part of the harm actually suffered (the personal injury) no longer works, because that harm would not have been suffered at all but for the claimant's unreasonable conduct. Instead, if the claimant had acted reasonably, they would have suffered a different type of harm altogether (the cost of repairs). In such cases, applying the guillotine heuristic effectively leads back to an all-or-nothing approach.[97]

3.3 Counterfactual assessment

Realizing the pitfalls of the all-or-nothing approach and guillotine heuristic, in the third edition of his textbook Burrows speculated that 'although there appears to be no case in point, the principle of *Cory v Thames Ironworks* may apply by analogy: i.e. even though the actual expenses were unreasonably incurred, a lesser amount, equivalent to what would have been reasonable expenses, may be recoverable'.[98] More recently, *McGregor* proclaimed that the 2012 decision of Newey J in *Herrmann v Withers* was 'the first decision where damages have been claimed and allowed for expenditure which has not been incurred at all'.[99] Kramer correctly emphasizes that mitigation 'does not merely act as a guillotine to a benefit or harm, but deems to have been incurred a harm (cost) that was in fact not incurred'.[100] Consequently, it has now become widely accepted that where mitigation applies, damages are assessed on a *counterfactual* basis as if the claimant had acted reasonably.[101]

In truth, this is not a new insight.[102] In *Payzu v Saunders*, referring to the avoidable loss rule, Scrutton LJ held that the claimant 'can recover no more than he

[97] See eg Bridge (n 26) 404, noting that 'at present it might be easier to limit the effect of a failure to mitigate where the plaintiff's injury is a divisible one', compared with 'where the injury is an indivisible whole'. See also Field (n 84) 14: 'neither the rule of avoidable losses nor the intervening act rule are of much use when subsequent claimant negligence contributes to a single indivisible damage'.

[98] Burrows, *Remedies* (3rd edn) (n 80) 126 fn 6, citing *Cory v Thames Ironworks & Shipbuilding Co Ltd* (1867–68) LR 3 QB 181 (QB), which concerns the assessment of damages where the remoteness rule applies.

[99] Edelman (n 2) [9-108], citing *Herrmann v Withers LLP* [2012] EWHC 1492 (Ch), [2012] PNLR 28.

[100] Kramer (n 13) [15-36] and [15-70].

[101] See also Burrows, *Remedies* (4th edn) (n 2) 131–32; Beale (n 2) [29-098].

[102] See eg Harry Street, *Principles of the Law of Damages* (Sweet & Maxwell 1962) 42: 'Where the defendant proves that the plaintiff has failed to mitigate his loss, damages are assessed on the assumption that he had so mitigated.' See also Dan Dobbs, *Law of Remedies: Damages, Equity, Restitution* (2nd edn, West Pub Co 1993) 381; Law Commission, *Contributory Negligence as a Defence in Contract* (No 219, 1993) [3.21].

would have suffered if he had acted reasonably.'[103] In *McAuley v London Transport Executive*, where the claimant unreasonably refused an operation that would have helped to treat his personal injury, Jenkins LJ held that 'damages ought to be assessed as they would properly have been assessable if he had, in fact, undergone the operation'.[104] In *Lavarack v Colchester*, Lord Denning MR held that 'If [the claimant] has not acted reasonably, the court must calculate the sums which he might reasonably have been expected to receive if he had acted reasonably.'[105]

A neat example is provided by *Schering Agrochemicals v Resibel*,[106] which concerned a claim by the purchaser of defective machinery parts against the supplier of those parts. The claimants used the parts in their factory despite knowing of the risk that they were defective, ultimately leading to an explosion that destroyed the factory. Hobhouse J rejected the claim for the value of the damaged property, but correctly held that 'The Plaintiffs are [nevertheless] entitled to recover the cost of bringing the alarm and safety system up to specification and the loss of profit etc that would result from the line being out of production meanwhile.'[107] Hobhouse J's conclusion on this point was not challenged on appeal.[108]

It is remarkable that the leading texts took so long to acknowledge the counterfactual effect of mitigation, given that such awards are routine.[109] Further examples include the counterfactual costs of moving house;[110] sub-letting;[111] borrowing money;[112] repairing property;[113] pursuing legal proceedings;[114] and re-negotiating leases.[115] Yet more examples could be given.[116] There is now also direct authority

[103] *Payzu* (n 32) 589. Similarly in Australia: *Hardi Finance Corporation Pty Ltd v Ahern (No 3)* [2010] WASC 403, [764].

[104] *McAuley v London Transport Executive* [1957] 2 Lloyd's Rep 500 (CA) 505.

[105] *Lavarack v Woods of Colchester* [1967] 1 QB 278 (CA) 287.

[106] *Schering Agrochemicals Ltd v Resibel NV SA* (QB, 4 May 1991).

[107] ibid (n 101). It appears that this aspect of Hobhouse J's decision was initially overlooked by Burrows, who criticized *Schering* on the basis that it 'meant that no damages at all should be awarded for the loss caused by the fire': Burrows, *Remedies* (3rd edn) (n 80) 142. See also Burrows, 'Contributory Negligence in Contract' (n 79) 177.

[108] *Schering Agrochemicals Ltd v Resibel NV SA* (CA, 26 November 1992) 2 (Purchas LJ).

[109] For two isolated counterexamples, see *Beoco Ltd v Alfa Laval Co Ltd* [1995] QB 137 (CA); *Watts v Morrow* [1991] 1 WLR 1421 (CA) 1436 (Gibson LJ). Given the weight of contrary authority, these two cases can confidently be treated as wrongly decided on this point.

[110] *Patel v Hooper & Jackson* [1999] 1 All ER 992 (CA) 1801 (Nourse LJ).

[111] *Marionette Ltd v Visible Information Packaged Systems Ltd* [2002] EWHC 2546 (Ch) [78] (Warren QC).

[112] *Equitas Ltd v Walsham Bros & Co Ltd* [2013] EWHC 3264 (Comm), [2014] Lloyd's Rep IR 398 [123] (Males J). See also *Parabola Investments Ltd v Browallia Cal Ltd* [2010] EWCA Civ 486, [2011] QB 477 [58] (Toulson LJ) (obiter).

[113] *McGlinn v Waltham Contractors Ltd* [2007] EWHC 149 (TCC), [2008] Bus LR 233 [875]–[880] (Coulson QC).

[114] *Symrise AG v Baker & McKenzie* [2015] EWHC 912 (Comm), [2016] 1 All ER (Comm) 603 [66] (Burton J).

[115] *Jolliffe v Charles Coleman & Co* (1971) 219 EG 1608 (QB) (Brown J).

[116] See eg *Stephenson Blake (Holdings) Ltd v Streets Heaver Ltd* [2001] Lloyd's Rep PN 44 (QB) [159] (Hicks QC); *Golden Strait Corp v Nippon Yusen Kubishika Kaisha (The Golden Victory)* [2007] UKHL 12, [2007] 2 AC 353 [10] (Lord Bingham); *MSC Mediterranean Shipping Co SA v Cottonex Anstalt* [2015] EWHC 283 (Comm), [2015] 1 Lloyd's Rep 359 [59] (Leggatt J); *Thai Airways* (n 14) [33] (Leggatt J).

on this point in the recent Supreme Court decision in *Stanford International v HSBC*.[117] There, Lord Leggatt stated in relation to loss or damage to goods that 'damages are assessed as if the claimant entered the market and obtained . . . a substitute at the earliest reasonable opportunity whether or not the claimant in fact did so'.[118] This is the correct approach and no longer seriously in dispute.

117 *Stanford International Bank Ltd v HSBC Bank PLC* [2022] UKSC 34, [2023] 2 WLR 79.
118 ibid [43].

3
The Avoided Loss Rule

1 Introduction

This chapter critiques the orthodox account of the rule of mitigation known as the 'avoided loss rule'. It follows a similar structure and line of argument to the preceding chapter. Again, just as with the avoidable loss rule, the application of this rule is conventionally acknowledged to be uncertain. Instead of describing how the relevant test is applied by the courts, the leading texts on damages conclude that no further rules can be stated, and so fall back once more on a 'case-by-case' approach. The effect of the rule is also misunderstood. Whereas the orthodox account of the avoidable loss rule relies on the 'guillotine' heuristic, in relation to the avoided loss rule the leading texts rely on an 'ignoring' heuristic instead. Just as with the avoidable loss rule, the adoption of this mental shortcut hides the counterfactual process by which the claimant's damages are assessed when the rule applies.

2 Application

This section considers the orthodox account of when the avoided loss rule applies. I begin by assessing the summary of the rule developed by Harvey McGregor, whose exposition has had a significant influence on the other leading texts on damages. I argue that McGregor's summary is misleading in two key respects; consequently, it is necessary to re-examine Viscount Haldane's original formulation in *British Westinghouse v London Underground* in some detail, so as to unpick the confusion that has subsequently taken root in the orthodox account. Viscount Haldane's formulation is conventionally characterized as a 'directness' test; however, the leading texts fail to specify how this criterion of directness has been applied by the courts. Instead, just as with the avoidable loss rule, the orthodox account falls back on the ambiguous proposition that the application of the directness test is a question of fact, effectively relying on the 'case-by-case' approach to determine when the avoided loss rule applies.

Mitigation in the Law of Damages. Andrew Summers, Oxford University Press. © Andy Summers 2025.
DOI: 10.1093/9780191864032.003.0003

2.1 McGregor's summary

The orthodox account of the avoided loss rule can be traced to an influential summary of the rule developed by McGregor in his inaugural edition as editor of (what is now) *McGregor on Damages*. There, McGregor summarized the rule as follows:

> The third [avoided loss] rule is that were the plaintiff does take steps to mitigate the loss to him consequent upon the defendant's wrong and these steps are successful, the defendant is entitled to the benefit accruing from the plaintiff's action and is liable only for the loss as lessened; this is so even although the plaintiff would not have been debarred under the first [avoidable loss] rule from recovering the whole loss, which would have accrued in the absence of his successful mitigating steps, by reason of these steps not being ones which were required of him under the first rule. Put shortly, the plaintiff cannot recover for avoided loss.[1]

The terminology of 'avoided loss' was entirely McGregor's own invention;[2] it is not found in any of the cases or texts prior to 1961. His summary of the avoided loss rule has remained essentially unchanged over successive editions of *McGregor on Damages*, including in the current edition.[3] It has also subsequently been adopted by most of the other leading texts on damages, and so has come to constitute the conventional understanding of the avoided loss rule.[4] As a description of the law, McGregor's summary is misleading in two key respects: first, it omits the crucial 'second limb' of Viscount Haldane's formulation in *British Westinghouse*; and second, it adds an unwarranted inference from the 'first limb' of that formulation,[5] concerning the effect on damages of conduct that may be said to be 'better-than-reasonable'. In the remainder of this section I address each of these issues in turn.

First, in his summary of the avoided loss rule, McGregor omitted entirely the *second limb* of Viscount Haldane's formulation in *British Westinghouse*.[6] He derived from Viscount Haldane's first limb that 'the defendant is entitled to the benefit

[1] Harvey McGregor (ed), *Mayne and McGregor on Damages* (12th edn, Sweet & Maxwell 1961) [144].

[2] Harvey McGregor, 'The Role of Mitigation in the Assessment of Damages' in Djakhongir Saidov and Ralph Cunnington (eds), *Contract Damages: Domestic and International Perspectives* (Hart 2008) 330: 'The terms which I use here—which indeed I coined when I first wrote my book on damages—are therefore avoidable loss and avoided loss.'

[3] James Edelman (ed), *McGregor on Damages* (21st edn, Sweet & Maxwell 2022) [9-006]. Two subtle changes have been introduced under the new editorship of James Edelman: first, a reference to 'reasonably necessary' steps in the first sentence of the summary; and second, the addition of the qualifier 'generally' in the final sentence.

[4] Text to n 12.

[5] For a summary of each of these two limbs of Viscount Haldane's formulation, see further Chapter 1, Section 3.2.

[6] *British Westinghouse Electric & Manufacturing Co Ltd v Underground Electric Railways Co of London Ltd (No 2)* [1912] AC 673 (HL) 689–90.

accruing from the plaintiff's action and is liable only for the loss as lessened',[7] but did not include the second limb that 'the subsequent transaction, if to be taken into account, must be one arising out of the consequences of the breach and in the ordinary course of business'.[8] This marked an important departure from previous editions of *Mayne's Treatise on Damages*, which had given significant emphasis to Viscount Haldane's second limb.[9] Under McGregor's editorship, although this limb was still discussed later in the text,[10] it was left out of his main summary of the rule. This approach continues in the current edition of *McGregor on Damages*.[11]

McGregor's summary of the avoided loss rule was subsequently transposed into several of the other leading texts on damages. The summary in *Chitty on Contracts* now states, also without qualification, that 'if the claimant in fact avoids or mitigates his loss consequent upon the defendant's breach, he cannot recover for such avoided loss'.[12] Similarly, in *Clerk & Lindsell on Torts*, the main text states only that '[d]amages are not recoverable for such losses as the claimant has avoided by taking action subsequent to the tort: the general principle of compensation implies that he can claim only for losses actually sustained';[13] previous editions had cited the second limb of Viscount Haldane's formulation in the footnotes but this has now been removed.[14] Of the leading texts on damages, only Burrows, Treitel, and (more recently) Kramer eschew the terminology of 'avoided loss' in favour of their own expositions;[15] these texts also correctly emphasize the central importance of Viscount Haldane's second limb.

It appears that McGregor's marginalization of Viscount Haldane's second limb has had some reflexive effect on judicial attempts to summarize the law.[16] For example, in *The World Beauty*, Wilmer LJ stated without qualification that 'Where the plaintiffs have taken action arising out of the casualty, which has avoided or diminished their loss, they cannot recover in respect of such avoidance or diminution.

[7] McGregor, *Mayne and McGregor on Damages* (12th edn) (n 1) [144]. On McGregor's interpretation of this first limb, see further text to n 23.

[8] *British Westinghouse* (n 6) 690. This qualification is raised only later in the text: McGregor, *Mayne and McGregor on Damages* (12th edn) (n 1) [162].

[9] WG Earengey (ed), *Mayne's Treatise on Damages* (11th edn, Sweet & Maxwell 1946) 148–49, and 151–52 subheaded 'Collateral matter not admissible to reduce damages'. See also John Burke and Peter Allsop (eds), *Chitty on Contracts* (21st edn, Sweet & Maxwell 1955) [843].

[10] See further text to n 50.

[11] Edelman (n 3) [9-006].

[12] Hugh Beale (ed), *Chitty on Contracts* (34th edn, Sweet & Maxwell 2022) [29-096]. See also the subsection headed 'Loss which is avoided cannot be recovered': [29-112]. See further Andrew Tettenborn, *The Law of Damages* (2nd edn, LexisNexis 2010) [5.01].

[13] Andrew Tettenborn (ed), *Clerk & Lindsell on Torts* (23rd edn, Sweet & Maxwell 2022) [27-09].

[14] Michael Jones (ed), *Clerk & Lindsell on Torts* (21st edn, Sweet & Maxwell 2014) [28-09], fnn 52 and 53.

[15] Andrew Burrows, *Remedies for Torts, Breach of Contract, and Equitable Wrongs* (4th edn, OUP 2019) 147–51; Edwin Peel (ed), *Treitel on The Law of Contract* (15th edn, Sweet & Maxwell 2022) [20-110]; Adam Kramer, *The Law of Contract Damages* (3rd edn, Hart 2022) ch 16.

[16] On the phenomenon of 'reflexive effect' in law (and social science generally), see further Chapter 1, text to n 120.

Put more shortly, they cannot recover for avoided loss.'[17] Although Wilmer LJ cited *British Westinghouse* in support of this proposition,[18] his phrasing bears a striking resemblance to McGregor's formulation.[19] Other more recent judgments have repeated this formulation.[20] The summary has accordingly become to some extent embedded in judicial decisions. However, it appears to have had much less impact on the *ratio* of judicial reasoning and the *outcomes* of cases; in practice, the claimant's post-breach conduct is frequently held to be 'collateral', often resulting in recovery greater than the claimant's factual loss.[21]

The second issue arising from McGregor's summary concerns an unwarranted inference drawn from the *first limb* of Viscount Haldane's formulation in *British Westinghouse*. To recap, Viscount Haldane's formulation proposed that:

> when in the course of his business [the claimant] has taken action arising out of the transaction, which action has diminished his loss, the effect in actual diminution of the loss he has suffered may be taken into account *even though there was no duty on him to act.*[22]

Based (it would appear, exclusively) on that passage, McGregor inferred that:

> the defendant is entitled to the benefit accruing from the plaintiff's action and is liable only for the loss as lessened; this is so *even although the plaintiff would not have been debarred under the first [avoidable loss] rule from recovering the whole loss, which would have accrued in the absence of his successful mitigating steps, by reason of these steps not being ones which were required of him under the first rule.*[23]

Notice the difference between the two italicized phrases here. In Viscount Haldane's judgment, the italicized phrase is straightforwardly compatible with the proposition that the claimant is not *obliged* to act reasonably, but that if the claimant *does* act reasonably then the consequences of those steps will be taken

[17] *Owners of the Andros Springs v Owners of the World Beauty (The World Beauty)* [1969] P 12 (CA) 19.

[18] ibid, citing *British Westinghouse* (n 6).

[19] See text to n 1.

[20] See eg *Dimond v Lovell* [2002] 1 AC 384 (HL) 406 (Lord Hobhouse): 'compensation is not paid for an avoided loss'. See also *IM Properties plc v Cape & Dalgleish* [1999] QB 297 (CA) 307 (Hobhouse LJ); *Lagden v O'Connor (sub nom Burdis v Livsey)* [2003] UKHL 64, [2004] 1 AC 1067 [78] (Lord Scott); *Pankhania v Hackney LBC* [2004] EWHC 323 (Ch), [2004] 1 EGLR 135 [33] (Vos QC); *Omak Maritime Ltd v Mamola Challenger Shipping Co Ltd (The Mamola Challenger)* [2010] EWHC 2026 (Comm), [2011] Bus LR 212 [65] (Teare J); *Coles v Hetherton* [2012] EWHC 1599 (Comm), [2013] 1 All ER (Comm) 453 [22] (Cooke J); *Swynson Ltd v Lowick Rose LLP* [2017] UKSC 32, [2018] AC 313 [11] (Lord Sumption), [93] (Lord Neuberger).

[21] See further Chapter 9.

[22] *British Westinghouse* (n 6) 689 (emphasis added).

[23] McGregor, *Mayne and McGregor on Damages* (12th edn) (n 1) [144] (emphasis added).

into account in the assessment of damages, for better or worse. In other words, it is consistent with a simple dichotomy between *two* categories of conduct: 'reasonable' steps, which are taken into account in the assessment of damages; and 'collateral' steps, which are not. On this view, the first limb of Viscount Haldane's formulation is just a mirror image of what McGregor elsewhere called the 'reasonable attempts rule'.[24] That rule holds that the *costs* of the claimant's reasonable steps are taken into account in the assessment of damages; the first limb simply applies the same approach to any *benefits* received.

By contrast, the italicized phrase in McGregor's formulation seems to infer a novel *third* category of conduct: one that is neither reasonable nor collateral, but instead is 'better-than-reasonable'. McGregor thus departed from a simple dichotomy between two alternative standards of conduct, instead proposing an intermediate standard. In particular, he seemed to envisage the following *three* categories of conduct: reasonable steps that the claimant had a 'duty' to take under the avoidable loss rule (which are taken into account in the assessment of damages); collateral steps that are 'independent' from the breach (which are not taken into account); *and* (McGregor's third category) *better-than-reasonable steps* where the claimant 'by sound action [has] avoided more consequences than the dictates of the law required of them'[25] (which must also be taken into account in the assessment of damages). The key issue is whether this inference of a third category of conduct was warranted, based on Viscount Haldane's judgment.

Initially, other legal scholars expressed scepticism about McGregor's interpretation. Two other major works of scholarship on damages were published in the year after McGregor's 1961 edition. In *The Principles of the Law of Damages* (published in 1962), Harry Street specially emphasized that '[t]here is no authority for the proposition that where a claimant is under no duty to mitigate his loss by acting in a certain general way the gain which accrues to him from so acting is to be set off'.[26] This clarification appears to have been delivered in direct contradiction to McGregor's inference of a third category of better-than-reasonable conduct, given that McGregor's 1961 edition was the first time that this interpretation of Viscount Haldane's judgment had been suggested.[27] Likewise, in his 1962 edition of *The Law of Contract*, Guenter Treitel responded sceptically to McGregor's understanding,

[24] See further Chapter 1, Section 4.1.2.

[25] McGregor, *Mayne and McGregor on Damages* (12th edn) (n 1) [162]: 'Frequently a plaintiff will have taken the required reasonable steps of mitigation and thereby have avoided such part of the loss as was avoidable. No difficulty arises in these circumstances. But the plaintiff may have gone further and by sound action have avoided more consequences than the dictates of the law required of him.' This text remains substantially unchanged in the current edition: Edelman (n 3) [9-110]. See also McGregor, 'The Role of Mitigation' (n 2) 338; Katy Barnett, 'Substitutive Damages and Mitigation in Contract Law' (2016) 28 Singapore Academy of Law Journal 795, 810.

[26] Harry Street, *Principles of the Law of Damages* (Sweet & Maxwell 1962) 182.

[27] The inference adopted by McGregor was not present in any of the previous editions of *Mayne's Treatise on Damages*, and nor does it appear in any judicial decisions on mitigation prior to 1961.

asking, 'Why should A benefit from subsequent acts on B's part, which B was not bound to do?'.[28]

These two opposing analyses, of McGregor on the one hand, and Street and Treitel on the other, marked an important crossroads in the development of the orthodox account of mitigation. *Chitty* soon adopted McGregor's interpretation,[29] and other leading texts followed. Street and Treitel's contrary view became buried; indeed remarkably, within a few editions, even Treitel's own exposition of the avoided loss rule seems to have shifted closer to McGregor's.[30] McGregor's interpretation now forms the conventional understanding of the avoided loss rule amongst legal scholars; his reformulation of Viscount Haldane's first limb is still reflected in the current edition of *McGregor on Damages*,[31] as well as in several of the other leading texts on damages.[32] McGregor's understanding is also evident in some subsequent judicial decisions (including through direct citation),[33] although for the most part judges have not followed his interpretation in practice, and in some cases have expressly cast doubt on it.[34]

There is a well-recognized danger in reading passages from legal judgments as though they were statutory provisions.[35] Nevertheless, a careful re-examination of Viscount Haldane's judgment is now required, not for its own sake, but to isolate the error in McGregor's interpretation and thus to unpick the confusion that has subsequently taken root in the orthodox account of the avoided loss rule. To this end, it is important to read the relevant part of Viscount Haldane's judgment carefully, and in context:

> [The principle of mitigation] does not impose on the plaintiff an obligation to take any step which a reasonable and prudent man would not ordinarily take in the course of his business. *But when in the course of his business he has taken action arising out of the transaction, which action has diminished his loss, the effect in actual diminution of the loss he has suffered may be taken into account even though there was no duty on him to act.*[36]

[28] Guenter Treitel, *The Law of Contract* (1st edn, Stevens 1962) 611. Although framed as a normative criticism, in context it seems that Treitel also intended to cast doubt on McGregor's description of the law following *British Westinghouse*.

[29] Anthony Guest (ed), *Chitty on Contracts* (23rd edn, Sweet & Maxwell 1968) [1482].

[30] Guenter Treitel, *The Law of Contract* (4th edn, Stevens 1975) 654: 'there is a further group of cases in which the plaintiff benefits from something that he was *not bound* to do in performance of his duty to mitigate; and such benefits are sometimes taken into account.'

[31] Edelman (n 3) [9-006].

[32] eg Beale (n 12) [26-095]; Tettenborn, *Damages* (n 12) [5.07].

[33] eg *Gardner v Marsh & Parsons* [1997] 1 WLR 489 (CA) 506 (Peter Gibson LJ, dissenting); *Bacciottini v Gotelee & Goldsmith* [2016] EWCA Civ 170, [2016] 4 WLR 98 [60] (Davis LJ).

[34] eg *Thai Airways International Public Co Ltd v KI Holdings Co Ltd* [2015] EWHC 1250 (Comm), [2016] 1 All ER (Comm) 675 [45] (Leggatt J): 'There is thus no need to invoke McGregor's "avoided loss" rule in order to explain the decision [in *British Westinghouse*].'

[35] *Makdessi v Cavendish Square Holdings BV* [2015] UKSC 67, [2015] 3 WLR 1373 [22] (Lord Neuberger and Lord Sumption).

[36] *British Westinghouse* (n 6) 689 (emphasis added).

McGregor's inference was drawn from the second (italicized) sentence of this passage. However, in context, it is clear that this sentence does not refer to a distinct standard of 'better-than-reasonable' conduct; instead, it refers directly to the reasonableness standard that Viscount Haldane had set out in the preceding sentence.[37] This view is reinforced by Viscount Haldane's subsequent reference to conduct that 'a reasonable and prudent person might in the ordinary conduct of business properly have taken, and in fact did take whether bound to or not'.[38] Fortunately, in most subsequent judicial decisions, judges have tended correctly to treat Viscount Haldane's passage as referring to reasonable (rather than 'better-than-reasonable') conduct. For example, in *Dimond v Lovell*, Lord Hoffmann held that *British Westinghouse* established 'the rule that requires additional benefits obtained as a result of taking reasonable steps to mitigate loss to be brought into account in the calculation of damages'.[39]

There is no indication elsewhere in Viscount Haldane's judgment of any third category of better-than-reasonable conduct, distinct from collateral conduct. Nor is there any suggestion of such a standard in any of Viscount Haldane's subsequent decisions on mitigation,[40] or in any of the other contemporaneous cases prior to McGregor's 1961 edition.[41] In particular, just two years after *British Westinghouse*, Viscount Haldane gave judgment again in *Williams Bros v Agius*, where the House of Lords upheld an award of damages greater than the claimant's factual loss on the basis of the claimant's collateral conduct. In that case, Viscount Haldane specifically noted that 'This decision is quite in harmony with what was recently said in this House in *British Westinghouse*.'[42] Nowhere here does Viscount Haldane refer to the possibility of conduct by the claimant that is 'better-than-reasonable', yet not collateral.

It follows that McGregor's inference about 'better-than-reasonable' conduct had no judicial basis in any of the cases prior to 1961, either in *British Westinghouse* or in other contemporaneous decisions. Instead, the first limb of Viscount Haldane's formulation was merely intended to clarify that where the claimant acted reasonably ('in the course of his business'), the consequences must be taken into account for better or worse: that is, including both the costs incurred by the claimant and any benefits received. The operative part of Viscount Haldane's formulation was

[37] The two sentences are clearly linked together by the phrase 'in the course of his business'.

[38] *British Westinghouse* (n 6) 690.

[39] *Dimond* (n 20) 401–02. See also, in support of this view: *Hussey v Eels* [1990] 2 QB 227 (CA) 236 (Mustill LJ); *Famosa Shipping Co Ltd v Armada Bulk Carriers Ltd (The Fanis)* [1994] 1 Lloyd's Rep 633 (QB) 635–36 (Mance J); *Gardner* (n 33) 498 (Hirst LJ), 514 (Pill LJ); *Thai Airways* (n 34) [45] (Leggatt J).

[40] *Williams Bros v Ed T Agius Ltd* [1914] AC 510 (HL); *AKAS Jamal v Moolla Dawood Sons & Co* [1916] 1 AC 175 (PC); *Hill v Showell* (1918) 87 LJKB 1106 (HL).

[41] See eg *Jamal* (n 40); *Williams Bros* (n 40); *Slater v Hoyle & Smith Ltd* [1920] 2 KB 11 (CA); *Jewelowski v Propp* [1944] KB 510 (KB). In all of these cases, the claimant was awarded damages greater than its factual loss. Viscount Haldane gave judgment in *Jamal* and *Williams*.

[42] *Williams Bros* (n 40) 520.

thus his *second limb*, concerning conduct that is *not* taken into account in the assessment of damages. However, this was ironically the aspect of Viscount Haldane's judgment that McGregor chose to omit from his summary of the avoided loss rule. In this respect, McGregor's summary, which has come to represent the orthodox account of the avoided loss rule, is doubly misleading and in need of correction.

2.2 The directness test

The key issue for the application of the avoided loss rule concerns the circumstances in which the claimant's conduct will be treated as 'collateral' to the breach. Despite omitting the second limb of Viscount Haldane's formulation from the summary of the rule, even *McGregor on Damages* acknowledges that this issue forms 'the core of the problem of mitigation by way of avoided loss'.[43] Both the cases and the leading texts have tended to stick closely to Viscount Haldane's original formulation that 'the subsequent transaction, if to be taken into account, must be one arising out of the consequences of the breach and in the ordinary course of business'.[44] This formulation is conventionally characterized as a 'directness' test. The problem is that the leading texts again fail to specify how this test is applied by the courts; instead, just as with the avoidable loss rule,[45] they fall back on a 'case-by-case' approach. At best, these accounts are therefore incomplete.

In applying the avoided loss rule, most of the cases since *British Westinghouse* have tended to follow Viscount Haldane's formulation, asking whether or not the relevant benefit 'arose out of the consequences of the breach'.[46] More recently, in *The New Flamenco*, Lord Clarke held that '[t]he essential question is whether there is a sufficiently close link' between the breach and the benefit received by the claimant, adding that 'The relevant link is causation.'[47] Similarly, in *Swynson v Lowick Rose*, Lord Sumption summarized that '[b]roadly speaking, collateral benefits are those whose receipt arose independently of the circumstances giving rise to the loss', in contrast to benefits that were 'derived from steps taken by the Claimant in consequence of the breach'.[48] And in *Quilter v Hodson*, Floyd LJ asked

[43] Edelman (n 3) [9-110].

[44] *British Westinghouse* (n 6) 690. See also 692, where Viscount Haldane distinguished between conduct that 'formed part of a continuous dealing with the situation in which they found themselves' and conduct that amounted to 'an independent or disconnected transaction'.

[45] See further Chapter 2, Section 2.3.

[46] eg *Primavera v Allied Dunbar Assurance plc* [2002] EWCA Civ 1327, [2003] Lloyd's Rep PN 14 [20] (Simon Brown LJ), [38] (Mance LJ); *Hussey* (n 39) 241 (Mustill LJ); *Gardner* (n 33) 503 (Hirst LJ); *Fulton Shipping Inc of Panama v Globalia Business Travel SAU (The New Flamenco)* [2015] EWCA Civ 1299, [2016] 1 Lloyd's Rep 383 [23] (Longmore LJ), [47] (Christopher Clarke LJ); *Bacciottini* (n 33) [62] (Davis LJ). cf *The Fanis* (n 38) 636, where Mance J opposed the use of 'precise verbal formulae'.

[47] *Fulton Shipping Inc of Panama v Globalia Business Travel SAU (The New Flamenco)* [2017] UKSC 43, [2017] 1 WLR 2581 [30]. On the causal explanation of mitigation, see further Chapter 5.

[48] *Swynson* (n 20) [11].

whether or not 'the subsequent transaction is all part and parcel of the transaction which gave rise to the wrong'.[49]

Citing Viscount Haldane's formulation, McGregor originally proposed that 'the basic rule is that the benefit to the plaintiff, if it is to be taken into account in mitigation of damage, must *arise out of the act of mitigation itself*.'[50] Burrows expressly approves of this exposition,[51] summarizing that 'indirect compensating advantages are not deducted',[52] and adding that the test is 'whether the compensating advantage was derived from actions taken by the claimant *to avoid* the consequences of the wrong'.[53] Elsewhere, Burrows also suggests that the test is whether the benefit was 'too far removed from' or 'completely collateral to' the breach.[54] Tettenborn proposes that 'Another formulation . . . is that there must be a direct causal link between the matters reducing the claimant's loss and the defendant's original wrongdoing.'[55] The conventional understanding, represented across the leading texts, is thus that the application of the avoided loss rule turns on a form of 'directness' test.

The main problem with the orthodox account is that the leading texts have effectively given up on any attempt to specify how this directness test is applied. McGregor himself concluded that 'Moving to avoided loss we come upon a topic of great difficulty. It needs to be handled with great care because the authorities are in a bit of a jumble.'[56] The current edition of *McGregor on Damages* concedes that 'the line between those avoided consequences which are collateral and those which are not is an exceedingly difficult one to draw'.[57] McLauchlan similarly concludes that 'the current law is in a dreadful muddle',[58] describing the application of the avoided loss rule as 'One of the most intractable areas of the law relating to the assessment of damages', because 'The cases are difficult and replete with fine distinctions, and many of them are irreconcilable'.[59] Winterton concurs that 'the relevant cases are notoriously difficult to reconcile'.[60]

[49] *Quilter v Hodson Developments Ltd* [2016] EWCA Civ 1125, [2017] PNLR 7 [34].

[50] McGregor, *Mayne and McGregor on Damages* (12th edn) (n 1) [169] (emphasis added). See also McGregor, 'The Role of Mitigation' (n 2) 338. However, the current edition of *McGregor on Damages* (under Edelman's editorship) now suggests that 'a better expression would be whether the claimant's action is reasonably necessary': Edelman (n 3) [9-120].

[51] Burrows, *Remedies* (4th edn) (n 15) 148 fn 6.

[52] ibid 148.

[53] ibid 148 (emphasis in original).

[54] Andrew Burrows, *A Restatement of the English Law of Contract* (OUP 2016) 121.

[55] Tettenborn, *Damages* (n 12) [5.40]. See also [5.15].

[56] McGregor, 'The Role of Mitigation' (n 2) 366.

[57] Edelman (n 3) [9-111]. See also the judicial comments in *Hussain v New Taplow Paper Mills Ltd* [1988] AC 514 (HL) 528 (Bridge LJ); *Burdis v Livsey* [2001] 1 WLR 1751 (QB) 1757 (Gray J); *The New Flamenco (CA)* (n 47) [20] and [39] (Longmore LJ).

[58] David McLauchlan, 'Expectation Damages: Avoided Loss, Offsetting Gains and Subsequent Events' in Djakhongir Saidov and Ralph Cunnington (eds), *Contract Damages: Domestic and International Perspectives* (Hart 2008) 384.

[59] ibid 360.

[60] David Winterton, *Money Awards in Contract Law* (Hart 2015) 88. See also 249.

Faced with this seemingly intractable puzzle, the orthodox account again falls back on a case-by-case approach. In other words, just as with the avoidable loss rule, the leading texts simply present a catalogue of 'illustrative' decisions, loosely organized under subheadings that do not purport to have any legal significance.[61] This approach does not qualify as a description of the law, because it makes no attempt to describe rules abstracted from the body of decided cases. Attempts to restate the law must not only report the cases, but also identify the relevant similarities or differences between them. The orthodox account of the avoided loss rule does not do this. For example, in *McGregor on Damages*, one section refers to 'a growing miscellany of similar cases', but the only similarity identified is just a reiteration of the conclusion that 'the benefit would appear to have arisen out of the consequences of the breach';[62] another section is entitled simply 'Situations where the position is unclear'.[63]

The case-by-case approach of the orthodox account is also indicated by the tendency to identify the application of the directness test as a 'question of fact'.[64] Superficially, there is some judicial support for this proposition,[65] but the proposition is ambiguous.[66] It is correct (albeit banal) to note that the directness test is 'fact-sensitive' or, in other words, that its application requires a close examination of the facts of the case.[67] However, it is clearly *incorrect* to suggest that the trial judge's application of the directness test raises an issue of primary fact that cannot be appealed.[68] Just as with the reasonableness test under the avoidable loss rule, there are numerous examples where the trial judge's application of the directness test has been overturned on appeal.[69] It is therefore clear that the test *does* raise questions of law; the problem is just that the leading texts have been unable to identify what they are.

[61] eg Edelman (n 3) [9-121]–[9-153]. Elsewhere, it is acknowledged that the rule applies equally in contract and tort: [9-114].

[62] ibid [9-131].

[63] ibid [9-153].

[64] See eg David Allen, Robyn Martin, and John Hartshorne, *Damages in Tort* (Sweet & Maxwell 2000) [4-082]; McLauchlan (n 57) 384; Elizabeth Blackburn, 'Damaging Revelations: Compensation and Giving Credit Where Credit is Due' [2017] Lloyd's Maritime and Commercial Law Quarterly 482, 503 fn 79.

[65] See eg *The Oropesa* [1943] P 32 (CA) 39 (Lord Wright); *Gardner* (n 33) 503 (Hirst LJ), 510 (Peter Gibson LJ), and 511 (Pill LJ); *Hussey* (n 39) 236 (Mustill LJ); *Wapshott v Davis Donovan & Co* [1996] PNLR 361 (CA) 361 (Hobhouse LJ); *Needler Financial Services Ltd v Taber* [2002] 3 All ER 501 (Ch) [24] (Sir Andrew Morritt V-C); *Farmer v Wood* (CA, 7 July 2000) [57] (Robert Walker LJ).

[66] See further Chapter 2, Section 2.2.

[67] This appears to be the meaning that Davis LJ had in mind in *Bacciottini* (n 33) [65].

[68] cf *R Pagnan & Fratelli v Corbisa Industrial Agropacuaria Ltd* [1970] 1 WLR 1306 (CA) 1315 (Salmon LJ); *The Fanis* (n 38) 637 (Mance J).

[69] See eg *Hussey* (n 39) 234–36 (Mustill LJ); *Gregory v Shepherds* [2000] Lloyd's Rep PN 724 (CA) [46] (Morritt LJ); *Burdis v Livsey (sub nom Lagden v O'Connor)* [2002] EWCA Civ 510, [2003] QB 36 [105] (Aldous LJ); *The New Flamenco (UKSC)* (n 47) [36] (Lord Clarke).

3 The Effect on Damages

There are two main problems with the orthodox understanding of the legal effect of the avoided loss rule. First, when Viscount Haldane's second limb applies, it may result in an award of damages greater than the claimant's factual loss. Although this result is well-established in the cases, it results in an apparent tension between the avoided loss rule and the conventional 'loss-based' understanding of the law of damages. The orthodox account of mitigation makes no attempt to explain this tension. Second, the orthodox account relies upon an 'ignoring heuristic' to explain the effect of the avoided loss rule on damages. However, this heuristic misdescribes the application of the law, which involves a counterfactual assessment of what would have happened if the 'ignored' events had not occurred.

3.1 Recovery greater than factual loss

As I outlined in Chapter 1, the orthodox account of damages consists of two main stages. First, one must identify the claimant's factual loss in order to apply the compensatory principle; this stage involves taking into account all events up to the date of trial. Second, one must apply limitations on damages; this stage involves the application of legal rules that reduce (but cannot extend) recovery of the claimant's factual loss.[70] It follows from this orthodox understanding that the claimant cannot, other than in exceptional circumstances,[71] recover more than its factual loss. I referred to this as the 'factual loss cap'. Damages exceeding the factual loss cap are said to involve 'overcompensation'[72] or 'double recovery'[73] because they put the claimant in a better position than if the breach had not occurred.

The legal effect of the avoided loss rule is in tension with this conventional 'loss-based' understanding. In cases where Viscount Haldane's second limb applies, the claimant's conduct is regarded as 'res inter alios acta',[74] meaning that is not 'taken into account' in the assessment of damages.[75] By ignoring the benefit obtained by the claimant between breach and trial, the avoided loss rule may result in an award of damages greater than the claimant's factual loss. Burrows acknowledges the challenge that this poses to the orthodox account of damages:

[70] See eg Qiao Liu, 'The Date for Assessing Damages for Loss of Prospective Performance Under a Contract' [2007] Lloyd's Maritime and Commercial Law Quarterly 273, 275: 'the mitigation principle, even when applied, cannot be employed in such a way as to derogate from the compensatory principle or enable the innocent party to claim damages in excess of its actual loss'.

[71] See further Chapter 1, Section 2.3.

[72] See eg (n 15) 191; McLauchlan (n 57) 364–65. Samuel Beswick, '"Losses in Any Event" in the Case of Damage to Property' (2015) 35 Oxford Journal of Legal Studies 755, 773.

[73] See eg *Gardner* (n 33) 511 (Pill LJ).

[74] *British Westinghouse* (n 6) 691 (Viscount Haldane).

[75] ibid 690 (Viscount Haldane).

> Where the claimant's actual position has been, or will be improved by benefits acquired subsequent to and as a result of the tort or breach of contract, one might expect (in accordance with the compensatory aims) that such benefits would be taken into account . . . But in fact compensating advantages are often not deducted.[76]

This tension between the effect of the avoided loss rule and the 'compensatory aims' explains why the orthodox account of mitigation has sought to marginalize Viscount Haldane's second limb.[77] In his analysis of the avoided loss rule, McLauchlan argues that 'A court should never compensate the plaintiff for a loss which it knows has not been suffered. To award more than the "real" loss is, by definition, to allow an unjustifiable windfall.'[78] McLauchlan's conclusion is that all of the cases applying Viscount Haldane's second limb are 'wrongly decided'.[79] The other leading texts on damages adopt a similar approach. Burrows also criticizes the decisions that have awarded damages exceeding the claimant's factual loss;[80] McGregor adopts many of these criticisms but accepts that some of the cases are correctly decided.[81]

The criticism that the cases applying Viscount Haldane's second limb are all 'wrongly decided' is ambiguous. As an evaluation of the law, one might argue that it is never justified for claimants to recover more than their factual loss.[82] This is a tenable viewpoint, although proponents of the orthodox account of mitigation do not offer any normative arguments to support it. By contrast, as a description of the law, the criticism is not tenable. Of course, one may conclude that certain outlying decisions are wrongly decided because they are inconsistent with the rules abstracted from the remaining body of precedents. However, there comes a point at which so many cases must be regarded as 'wrongly decided' that one must instead recognize the need to adjust the account.[83] The orthodox account of the avoided loss rule crosses this threshold.

[76] Burrows, *Remedies* (4th edn) (n 15) 147.

[77] See eg Beale (n 12) [29-112]: 'The claimant is entitled to damages only for his actual loss.'

[78] McLauchlan (n 57) 367.

[79] ibid 360–88, criticizing *Jebsen v East & West India Dock Co* (1874–75) LR 10 CP 300 (CP); *Williams Bros* (n 39); *Jamal* (n 39); *Rodocanachi, Sons & Co v Milburn Bros* (1887) LR 18 QBD 67 (CA); *Slater* (n 41); *Campbell Mostyn (Provisions) Ltd v Barnett Trading Co* [1954] 1 Lloyd's Rep 65 (CA); *Gardner* (n 33); *Primavera* (n 46); *Needler* (n 64); *Bear Stearns Bank plc v Forum Global Equity Ltd* [2007] EWHC 1576 (Comm); *Oxus Gold plc v Templeton Insurance Ltd* [2007] EWHC 770 (Comm).

[80] Burrows, *Remedies* (4th edn) (n 15) 150–52, 191–96, criticizing *Hussey* (n 39); *The New Flamenco (UKSC)* (n 47); *Williams Bros* (n 39); *Slater* (n 41); and *Campbell Mostyn* (n 79).

[81] Edelman (n 3) [9-133]–[9-184], criticizing *Needler* (n 64); *Hussey* (n 39); *Gardner* (n 33); *Slater* (n 41); *Williams Bros* (n 39); *Rodocanachi* (n 78), but approving *Jamal* (n 39); *Campbell Mostyn* (n 79); *Primavera* (n 46).

[82] See eg Burrows, *Remedies* (4th edn) (n 15) 196, criticizing *Campbell Mostyn* (n 79) on the basis that it 'runs contrary to the avowed compensatory goal.' See also McLauchlan (n 57) 377–78.

[83] McLauchlan analyses a total of sixteen English decisions on 'avoided loss' and concludes that eleven of them were wrongly decided: McLauchlan (n 57) 360–88.

Judicial reasoning also sometimes invokes the factual loss cap. In *Gardner*, Peter Gibson LJ dissented on the basis that 'The law does not permit the plaintiff to recover more than is seen to be his actual loss and the rules of mitigation may deprive the plaintiff of all or part of the damages for loss which otherwise he might have recovered.'[84] Davis LJ relied on this proposition as dispositive in *Bacciottini*,[85] holding that Peter Gibson LJ's comment was 'surely uncontroversial as a general proposition'.[86] In *The New Flamenco*, Longmore LJ alluded to similar reasoning in suggesting that when applying Viscount Haldane's second limb, 'an arbitrator in my view is entitled to remind himself . . . of Baron Parke B's even more fundamental principle' that a claimant is to be put in same position (and by implication, no better position) than if the contract had been performed.[87]

The problem with this absolutist approach is that the factual loss cap is already subject to numerous exceptions, acknowledged even by proponents of the conventional 'loss-based' account of damages. These exceptions include the insurance and benevolence rules as well as the market rule.[88] It is plainly inaccurate to assert that a claimant can *never* recover more than its factual loss in damages. As Scrutton LJ recognized in *Slater v Hoyle*, 'The rules of English law do not always give exact indemnity'.[89] In *Smiley v Townshend*, Denning LJ similarly acknowledged 'many cases in which a thing that happens after a breach of contract or after a wrong done cannot be prayed in aid by the man who breaks his contract or by the tortfeasor in diminution of damages, because it is res inter alios acta'.[90] As a matter of description, the factual loss cap is evidently not dispositive in every case. The aim should therefore be to describe and explain the scope of the exceptions, rather than denying them altogether; the orthodox account of mitigation makes no attempt to do this.

3.2 The 'ignoring' heuristic

In the previous chapter, I argued that the orthodox account of the avoidable loss rule suffers from overreliance on the 'guillotine heuristic'. This heuristic involves the simplistic mental shortcut of 'chopping off' recovery of the claimant's factual loss, which works well enough in simple cases but breaks down in complex cases

[84] *Gardner* (n 33) 505. See also *Blue Circle Industries plc v Ministry of Defence* [1999] Ch 289 (CA) 317 (Chadwick LJ); *Campbell Mostyn* (n 79) 69 (Birkett LJ). In both of these cases, the court nevertheless unanimously awarded damages exceeding the factual loss.

[85] *Bacciottini* (n 33) [56]. See also *Swynson Ltd v Lowick Rose LLP* [2015] EWCA Civ 629, [2015] PNLR 28 [31] (Davis LJ, dissenting).

[86] *Bacciottini* (n 33) [45].

[87] *The New Flamenco (CA)* (n 47) [39].

[88] See further Chapter 1, Section 2.3 and Chapter 9, Section 4.1.

[89] *Slater* (n 41) 25. See also *Joyner v Weeks* [1891] 2 QB 31 (CA) 34 (Wright J).

[90] *Smiley v Townshend* [1950] 2 KB 311 (CA). See also *Gardner* (n 33) 512; *British Transport Commission v Gourley* [1956] AC 185 (HL) 212 (Lord Reid).

because it obscures the underlying counterfactual effect of the rule. Precisely the same problem arises in relation to the avoided loss rule. This time, the heuristic involves 'ignoring' benefits obtained by the claimant; this heuristic is also captured by the Latin phrase 'res inter alios acta'.[91] Again, the mental shortcut works satisfactorily in simple cases, but in others creates difficulties by hiding the counterfactual assessment involved in applying Viscount Haldane's second limb.

The orthodox account of mitigation adopts a variety of phrases to describe the effect of the avoided loss rule. McGregor summarizes that 'matter completely collateral and merely *res inter alios acta* cannot be used in mitigation of damage'.[92] McGregor similarly proposes that 'the benefit to the claimant, if it is to be taken into account in mitigation of damage, must arise out of the act of mitigation itself'.[93] This reflects the proposition in *British Westinghouse* that 'the subsequent transaction, if to be taken into account, must be one arising out of the consequences of the breach';[94] Viscount Haldane also referred to such benefits as 'res inter alios acta'.[95] Burrows similarly asks 'when are compensating advantages ignored?'[96]

The notion of 'ignoring' or not 'taking into account' benefits is a heuristic device. It relies on a metaphorical ledger or balance sheet that is used to total up every harm and benefit that would not have occurred but-for the defendant's breach. This ledger includes all of the harms and benefits incurred up to the date of trial.[97] The balance on the ledger is the claimant's 'loss', and in circumstances where every harm and benefit is taken into account we would refer to this as the claimant's 'factual loss'. The effect of the avoided loss rule is metaphorically to 'strike out' certain benefits from the ledger; in this way one appears to be 'ignoring' benefits in the assessment of damages. This mental shortcut works tolerably well in cases where the harm suffered by the claimant was followed by a discrete benefit. However, it breaks down in more complex cases for two main reasons.

First, what is 'ignored' is not really the benefit itself, but rather the *event* through which the benefit was obtained. This is the simple reason why the claim in *British Westinghouse* was bound to fail.[98] The claimants had argued that the benefit of the increased efficiency of the replacement turbines should be ignored, but that the

[91] The resort to Latin ought to serve as a warning. As Stevens notes, 'When English lawyers do not know how to classify a rule, they ... use other languages, usually French (eg tort) or Latin (eg res ipsa loquitur)': Robert Stevens, *Torts and Rights* (OUP 2007) 299.

[92] Edelman (n 3) [9-111].

[93] ibid (n 3) [9-120]. See also Beale (n 12) [26-098].

[94] *British Westinghouse* (n 6) 690 (Viscount Haldane).

[95] ibid 691. See also *Slater* (n 41) 23 (Scrutton LJ); *Gardner* (n 33) 503 (Hirst LJ); *Dimond* (n 20) 398–99 (Lord Hoffmann); *Burdis* (n 69) [91] (Aldous LJ).

[96] Burrows, *Remedies* (4th edn) (n 15) 147. See also, in relation to insurance and benevolence: *Hunt v Severs* [1994] 2 AC 350 (HL) 358; *Hussain* (n 57) 527 (Lord Bridge): 'the amount received is again to be disregarded'.

[97] It also includes the harms and benefits that will be incurred after trial, though these need not concern us for present purposes.

[98] *Hussey* (n 39) 236 (Mustill LJ).

cost of purchasing the replacement should be taken into account. As Tettenborn puts it, 'the plaintiff cannot, so to speak, take plums but leave the duff'.[99] Viscount Haldane held that effect of the second limb would be to ignore the '*subsequent transaction*' altogether (and not merely the benefits of the transaction).[100] However, on the facts, the second limb did not apply;[101] in these circumstances the court was correct to 'look at what actually happened, and to balance loss and gain'.[102] It is never appropriate to include the harms but ignore the benefits in respect of the same event.[103]

In their original pleadings, the claimants in *British Westinghouse* had alternatively claimed damages based on the cost of excess coal consumption over the lifetime of the defective turbines.[104] This claim was at least internally consistent in that it involved ignoring both the costs and benefits of the claimants' subsequent transaction. If successful, this claim would have involved an award for 'avoided loss' because the excess coal consumption was not in fact suffered. However, this claim was also bound to fail because, as Viscount Haldane held, the purchase of the replacement turbines was 'a reasonable and prudent course quite naturally arising out of the circumstances in which he was placed by the breach'.[105] Although pleaded, the claim was not pursued in any of the proceedings, presumably because the claimants realized that it had little chance of success.

Second, the 'ignoring heuristic' does not provide any guidance on how courts approach the assessment of damages once the relevant event has been ignored. Two examples illustrate this point. In *Primavera v Allied Dunbar Insurance*, the claimant was induced to enter into a pension scheme by the defendant's misrepresentation about its tax implications.[106] After discovering the correct tax position, the claimant nevertheless chose to remain in the scheme. Applying the avoided loss rule, the Court of Appeal held that the increase in value of the pension scheme between breach and trial should be ignored.[107] Instead, it awarded damages equal to the tax charge that the claimant would have incurred if he had closed the fund as soon as he discovered the misrepresentation.[108] The damages were thus assessed by reference to an expense (the tax charge) that was not in fact incurred.

[99] Andrew Tettenborn, 'What is a Loss?' in Jason Neyers, Erika Chamberlain, and Stephen Pitel (eds), *Emerging Issues in Tort Law* (Hart 2007) 450.
[100] *British Westinghouse* (n 6) 690 (emphasis added).
[101] See further Chapter 1, Section 3.2.
[102] *British Westinghouse* (n 6) 691 (Viscount Haldane).
[103] This is the simple explanation for the various decisions listed in Edelman (n 3) [9-130]–[9-132], eg *Nadreph Ltd v Willmett & Co* [1978] 1 WLR 1537 (Ch); *Port of Sheerness Ltd v Brachers* [1997] IRLR 214 (QB); *Fyffes Group Ltd v Reefer Express Lines Pty Ltd (The Kriti Rex)* [1996] 2 Lloyd's Rep 171 (QB).
[104] See further Andrew Dyson, 'British Westinghouse Revisited' [2012] Lloyd's Maritime and Commercial Law Quarterly 412, 415–16.
[105] *British Westinghouse* (n 6) 691.
[106] *Primavera* (n 45).
[107] ibid [43] (Mance LJ), [49] (Latham LJ).
[108] Simon Brown LJ referred to this as 'the capitalised loss resulting from having to take a higher proportion of the fund in the form of a taxable annuity': ibid [6].

In *The New Flamenco*, a contract for the hire of a vessel was repudiated early by the hirers.[109] The owners subsequently decided to sell the vessel. Applying the avoided loss rule, the Supreme Court held that this sale should be ignored in the assessment of damages: Lord Clarke referred to it as 'irrelevant'.[110] Instead, he held that damages should be assessed by reference to 'the difference between the contract rate and what was or ought reasonably to have been earned from employment of the vessel under shorter charterparties, as for example on the spot market'.[111] In other words, having ignored the actual sale of the vessel, the Supreme Court based its award on a counterfactual assessment of the claimant's breach position, as if the vessel had instead been redeployed by the owners for spot hire, and compared this to the no-breach position in which the owners would have received the contractual rate of hire from the defendants.

In both of these cases, merely stating that the court 'ignored' the events that actually occurred does not provide any guidance as to the alternative basis on which damages were assessed. More precisely, as well as ignoring what actually happened, the court substituted other events in their place. Just as with the avoidable loss rule outlined in the previous chapter, the application of the avoided loss rule thus results in a counterfactual assessment of claimant's breach position, assessing damages as if the claimant took steps which it did not in fact take. The ignoring heuristic unhelpfully obscures this process. In Chapter 9, I explain in more detail how the counterfactual assessment works when the avoided loss rule applies.

[109] *The New Flamenco (UKSC)* (n 47). For a detailed analysis of this decision, see further David McLauchlan and Andrew Summers, 'Mitigation and Causation of Benefits' [2018] Lloyd's Maritime and Commercial Law Quarterly 171.

[110] *The New Flamenco (UKSC)* (n 47) [29].

[111] ibid [34].

4
Flawed Explanations of Mitigation

1 Introduction

'The principle of mitigation is to a surprising degree theoretically undernourished and underwritten'.[1] Bridge wrote this over thirty years ago, yet the doctrine continues to receive relatively little attention from private law theorists.[2] Many of the leading texts on damages do not offer any affirmative explanation of mitigation at all.[3] Amongst scholars who have addressed the point, most have tended to explain mitigation as seeking to promote various policy objectives, although they differ on the specific objective. The prevailing judicial approach has been to treat mitigation as an aspect of causation, yet legal scholars have tended firmly to resist this explanation.[4] Accordingly, although a number of possible explanations for mitigation have been floated, none have so far attracted widespread academic support.

In his 1989 article, Bridge canvassed three main explanations of mitigation:[5] first, that the doctrine aims to prevent economic waste; second, that it aims to promote self-help by the claimant; and third, that it is an aspect of other remedial rules such as causation, remoteness, or contributory negligence.[6] In addition to these theories, I consider others that have been raised subsequently in the legal scholarship, for example the explanation that mitigation aims to promote co-operation between the parties, or that it responds to demands of fairness. Ultimately, I reject all of the existing theories of mitigation except for the causal explanation, which I go on to endorse and develop in Chapter 5.

[1] Michael Bridge, 'Mitigation of Damages in Contract and the Meaning of Avoidable Loss' (1989) 105 Law Quarterly Review 398, 399.

[2] Consider by comparison the doctrine of remoteness, the remedy of negotiating damages, and the rule against penalties, all of which have provoked extensive theoretical debates spanning decades.

[3] See eg James Edelman (ed), *McGregor on Damages* (21st edn, Sweet & Maxwell 2022); Andrew Tettenborn (ed), *Clerk & Lindsell on Torts* (23rd edn, Sweet & Maxwell 2017); Andrew Tettenborn, *The Law of Damages* (2nd edn, LexisNexis 2010).

[4] See further Chapter 5, Sections 2 and 3.

[5] Bridge (n 1) 399–411.

[6] Bridge also considered various other explanations, including that mitigation mollifies the strictness of contractual obligations (headed 'promises and expectations'), that it seeks to prevent one-way speculation at the defendant's expense, and that it achieves simplicity. However, none of these explanations have received any substantial take-up from legal scholars.

Mitigation in the Law of Damages. Andrew Summers, Oxford University Press. © Andy Summers 2025.
DOI: 10.1093/9780191864032.003.0004

2 What is an 'Explanation'?

Before turning to specific explanations of mitigation, in this section I clarify what I mean by an 'explanation' of a legal doctrine and seek to distinguish it from other kinds of theory. The aim of an explanation, as I use the term here, is to identify reasons why the law is as it is. My interest is in explaining the current law, rather than the law as it ought to be, if different. The type of explanatory reasons (or 'principles') that I am looking for have two key features: (1) they purport to justify (ie count in favour of) the legal rules in question; *and* (2) they are endorsed by the judicial decisions from which those rules are determined. My explanatory focus is therefore on the 'normative' or 'rational' principles that the judges endorsed rather than the wider array of influences that might be identified as part of a causal history of the law.[7]

Two aspects of the first feature require particular emphasis. First, the law could be explained by principles that turn out not to justify the rule, either all-things-considered or even pro tanto, provided that the principle is at least of a normative kind ie it *purports* to count in favour of the rule. For example, 'the promotion of self-reliance' could conceivably *explain* the law of mitigation even if we concluded that the law ought not to promote self-reliance (ie the promotion of self-reliance could not *justify* the law). By contrast, the non-normative fact that 'all of the cases in which the claimant recovered damages were decided after lunch', could not constitute an explanation of the law in the sense that I am aiming at, even if one could show that this factor played some causal role in judicial decision-making.

Second, beyond the exclusion of non-normative facts, I take a broad view of the kinds of proposition that may purport to count in favour of a legal rule, and hence qualify as a potential explanation of it. Some legal scholars insist that private law rules can only ever be justified by principles that also count in favour of individuals having a personal obligation of that kind;[8] others hold that such rules may be justified by consequentialist considerations about the effects of the rule, even if these considerations do not ground personal obligations on the part of individuals.[9] I accept both of these (amongst other) types of purported justification as potential explanations of the law ie I do not exclude any particular types of normative proposition a priori, provided that they purport to count in favour of the rule in some way.

In relation to the second feature of explanation, two further clarifications are in order. First, I am seeking the principles that were *in fact* endorsed in the judicial decisions from which the legal rules in question are determined, not any other

[7] See further text to n 18.

[8] See eg Ernest Weinrib, *The Idea of Private Law* (Harvard University Press 1995). This view also entails some assumptions about the background connection between moral obligations and legal rules.

[9] For example, those who believe that legal systems ought to incentivize efficiency maximization but that individuals do not have any personal moral duty to act efficiently.

reasons that *could* have guided these decisions but did not.[10] These principles need not correspond precisely with the judges' express reasoning, although they often will. An explanation could consist in a principle to which judges implicitly committed themselves, even though they did not frame their judgments in quite those terms. Still, one must strive to identify the principles that were actually endorsed by the relevant decisions, for as Webb notes: 'it's doubtful what use there is in an account which explains a body of law by reference to considerations which no [judge] either does or ought to endorse.'[11]

Second, my focus is on explaining the rules of a particular legal system. Specifically, in this chapter, I aim to assess how well various principles may explain the English rules of mitigation,[12] rather than how well they can explain the 'concept' or general 'idea' of mitigation, or the rules of mitigation in another legal system. This means that I am concerned with the English rules of mitigation specifically (the explanandum), and with the principles that were endorsed in the decisions of the English courts from which those rules are determined (the explanation). It is for this reason that the case law of other jurisdictions is only of limited relevance to my enquiry; such decisions may be relevant where and to the extent that they have 'cross-fertilised' into English law through citation to and by English judges, but not otherwise.

What makes a *good* explanation? The primary criterion is 'fit' with the legal rules in question. How well do the prescriptions of the principle match up with the key features and other contours of the rules as they are? More formally, the principles offered by the theory should entail the rules that one in fact finds in the system. This follows from the fact that an explanation of the law is a theory of the law 'as it is'. It remains possible that some cases can be discarded as being 'wrongly decided', especially when this is supported by further contingent facts about the legal system (notably the rules of precedent). But although the boundary is difficult to identify precisely, there comes a point at which so much of the law has been discarded that the explanation of what remains is no longer an explanation of the actual law of the system in question.

Another important criterion is the extent to which the explanation fits with the reasoning expressed by individual law-makers (whether judges or legislators).[13] As noted above, this is because explanations aim to identify the principles that were in fact endorsed by the judges when they developed and applied the rules in question, rather than all possible reasons that could be given in favour of a set of rules that

[10] Here I am seeking to draw on Raz's distinction between 'explanatory' and 'guiding' reasons (I am interested in the former): Joseph Raz, *Practical Reason and Norms* (OUP 1999) 15–20. This distinction is helpfully elaborated in Charlie Webb, 'Contract as Fact and as Reason' in Gregory Klass, George Letsas, and Prince Saprai (eds), *Philosophical Foundations of Contract Law* (OUP 2014) 139–41.

[11] Webb (n 10) 141.

[12] More precisely, the law of mitigation in England and Wales.

[13] At least, when acting in their law-making capacity.

have the same content. The express reasoning of the judges will often play an important role in determining the plausibility of an explanation of the law, although it is not decisive. Occasionally, the principle as stated by the judge may not in fact entail the rule ie their express reasoning suffers from a non-sequitur. Where there is a conflict, I favour consistency with the result rather than the judge's express reasoning, reflecting the insight (widely accepted in the field of psychology)[14] that people often err when self-reflecting on their reasons for a decision.[15]

This foregoing understanding of an 'explanation' should be distinguished from at least three distinct kinds of theory: 'prescriptions', 'justifications', and 'histories' of law.

'Prescriptive' theories differ most sharply from explanations of the law. These theories proceed by identifying the normative considerations to which an area of law responds and then determining what is, all things considered, the correct set of legal rules (if any) to adopt in those circumstances. In this respect, unlike explanations of the law, prescriptive theories have no necessary relation with the legal rules as they are; what is prescribed may look quite unlike the actual existing law. Moreover, unlike explanations, prescriptive theories are exclusively concerned with true normative principles; consequently, it is essential to provide arguments for the truth of the normative propositions on which the theory rests.

'Justifications' of an area of law are closer to explanations in that they share a focus on the law 'as it is'. However, there are two key differences. First, this type of theory does not share the agnosticism of an explanatory theory about whether the principles are normatively true: the truth of the normative principles is an essential feature of a justificatory theory, and so must be argued for.[16] Second, unlike explanations, it does not matter for a justification of the law whether or not the principle was in fact endorsed in the judicial decisions from which the relevant legal rules are determined. As Webb puts it, 'There may be good reasons for a practice which differ from the reasons which in fact guided those engaged in it.'[17] Consequently, although the theory must fit the rules (in order to be a justification *of* those rules), there is no requirement that it should be consistent with the judges' reasoning, whether express or implicit.

'Histories' of the law, just like explanations, attempt to identify the reasons why the law is as it is. However, they are concerned with a broader set of reasons. An explanation of the law is focused on 'principles' as normative propositions; this

[14] See eg Jonathan Heidt, 'The Emotional Dog and its Rational Tail: A Social Intuitionist Approach to Moral Judgment' (2001) 108 Psychological Review 814, which provides a meta-analysis of the studies on moral reasoning.

[15] I am grateful to Alex Georgiou for this point.

[16] However, such theories are not necessarily committed to the proposition that, all things considered, a particular legal system ought to have the set of rules in question; theories of this kind can admit the possibility that there are further genuine reasons, which the law has overlooked, which show that different rules would be preferable.

[17] Webb (n 10) 139.

type of reason at least purports to count in favour of the legal rule that is being explained. In contrast, histories of the law may be concerned with identifying any and all influences on the actions of the lawmakers (judges or legislators). These can be but *need not be* normative principles: they could also be non-normative facts, including—infamously—'what the judge had for breakfast'.[18] The goal of such theories is to identify the complex set of causal factors which have, ultimately, led to the law to take the form it presently does. Thus, theories of this kind are closely associated with so-called American legal realism.

My attention to 'explanation' in this book—rather than the other types of theory outlined above—is motivated by two main factors. First, explanatory theories seem most akin to the way in which participants in a legal system themselves reason about the development of the law, at least below the level of the apex court where arguments about the normative truth of a principle may assume more importance. The task of assessing which explanations of the law are more or less plausible reflects a methodology that is broadly similar to that found in judgments involving a novel point of law, or in the submissions that a barrister might make to the court. Second, and relatedly, the skills required to develop a theory of this type fall most distinctively within the expertise of lawyers, again given the similarities with judicial reasoning. By contrast, the question of whether or not a particular principle is normatively true necessarily draws more heavily on claims of a philosophical nature.[19]

Finally, before turning to assess some possible explanations of the law of mitigation, it may help to start with a 'trial run'. Take for example the obviously implausible claim that mitigation is explained by 'the policy of punishing claimants for acting unreasonably'. This claim at least qualifies as an explanatory theory in that it offers a normative principle that purports to count in favour of the mitigation rule. What makes this a bad explanation of the law is not that the normative principle is false (although it almost certainly is) ie that the law ought not to punish claimants for acting unreasonably. That would rule the theory out as a justification, but not as an explanation. Instead, what makes this a bad explanation of mitigation is that the principle does not fit with the key features of the mitigation rule—such as the circumstances when it applies and its effects on the assessment of damages—or with any aspect of judicial reasoning in the cases on mitigation, whether express or implicit.

[18] There is some dispute about the etymology of this phrase: see further Brian Leiter, *Naturalizing Jurisprudence: Essays on American Legal Realism and Naturalism in Legal Philosophy* (OUP 2007) 62.

[19] Of course, some lawyers also make excellent philosophers, and I do not mean to claim that all lawyers should steer clear of making philosophical claims. My point is merely that lawyers *as a class* do not have *distinctive* expertise in this domain.

3 Economic Efficiency

Efficiency theories of private law doctrines come in a number of varieties, some of which clearly do not aim at explaining the law as it is.[20] Many analyses of the mitigation doctrine by scholars working in the 'law and economics' tradition are primarily or exclusively *prescriptive*, positing that this area of law ought to strive for efficient outcomes, whether or not the existing rules achieve (or fit with) this objective. This mode of scholarship has been used to criticize the existing rules of mitigation as inefficient.[21] It has also been used to make detailed prescriptions about how these rules ought to apply in particular circumstances,[22] whilst acknowledging the 'puzzling divergence' between the relevant efficiency criterion and the content of the mitigation rules as they have actually evolved.[23]

One strand of law and economics scholarship does, however, appear to aim at providing explanations of private law doctrines. The most prominent example is the early work of Richard Posner,[24] who (in the words of Richard Craswell) claimed 'not so much that it was good for the common law to be efficient, but simply that, as a descriptive matter, it happened to be the case that the common law was efficient'.[25] There are relatively few examples where this type of explanatory theory has been applied to the law of mitigation specifically,[26] and even fewer where the explanation has been developed in detail.[27] Before addressing the main difficulties with efficiency explanations of mitigation, it is important to note a key distinction between two quite different concepts of efficiency that have been relied upon in this context.

The editors of *Chitty* claim that '[t]he purpose of the rules on mitigation is to prevent the waste of resources in society, since they are obviously limited'.[28] Treitel

[20] For an overview of different types of economic analysis of law, their purposes and deficiencies, see further Eric Posner, 'Economic Analysis of Contract Law After Three Decades: Success or Failure?' (2002–2003) 112 Yale Law Journal 829 and Richard Craswell, 'In That Case, What Is the Question? Economics and the Demands of Contract Theory' (2003) 112 The Yale Law Journal 903.

[21] Paul Fenn, 'Mitigation and the Correct Measure of Damages' (1981) 1 International Review of Law and Economics 223.

[22] Charles Goetz and Robert Scott, 'The Mitigation Principle: Toward a General Theory of Contractual Obligation' (1983) 69 Virginia Law Review 967.

[23] ibid 1023.

[24] Richard Posner, *Economic Analysis of Law* (Little Brown 1972).

[25] Craswell (n 20) 904. Craswell also notes (at 904–905) that this movement has since fallen out of favour, and that Richard Posner himself later retreated from it. For his later position, see Richard Posner, *The Problems of Jurisprudence* (Harvard University Press 1990) 353–74.

[26] Although Eric Posner's work on limitations on damages could perhaps be read in an explanatory spirit, his analysis is better understood as an attempt to *justify* the general principle of mitigation in terms of efficiency, whilst recognizing that some of the doctrine's more specific features sit uneasily with this goal: Eric Posner, 'Contract Remedies: Foreseeability, Precaution, Causation and Mitigation' in Boudewijn Bouckaert and Gerrit De Geest (eds), *Encycopaedia of Law and Economics* (Edward Elgar 2000) 169–72.

[27] The leading example is Jeffrey MacIntosh and David Frydenlund, 'An Investment Approach to a Theory of Contract Mitigation' (1987) 37 University of Toronto Law Journal 113.

[28] Hugh Beale (ed), *Chitty on Contracts* (34th edn, Sweet & Maxwell 2022) [29-097]. See also Bridge (n 1) 404–05.

adopts a similar position.[29] This explanation reflects the idea that mitigation helps to maximize the resources of society as a whole.[30] We can think of this objective as somewhat akin to the economic aim of maximizing social welfare.[31] By contrast, the US scholarship on mitigation emphasizes the narrower aim of achieving efficiency between the parties. For example, although MacIntosh and Frydenlund also explain mitigation in terms of the prevention of waste, their theory is concerned exclusively with the 'joint welfare of the contracting parties'.[32] Accordingly, there is no universal definition of 'economic waste' and it is necessary to consider both alternatives as potential explanations of the law of mitigation.

The aim of maximizing the resources of society as a whole does not fit the scope of the mitigation doctrine. It rests heavily on a small subset of mitigation cases in which the claimant sits back and does nothing whilst irreversible harm is suffered: for example, by failing to call the fire services to put out a burning building.[33] However, outside these paradigm instances of unreasonable conduct leading to physical destruction of property, the avoidable loss rule does not seem to play any role in preventing waste. For example, consider another type of mitigation case in which the claimant delays in obtaining a market substitute for performance.[34] Such delay could alter the allocation of resources as between claimant, defendant, and third-party suppliers, but it does not have any obvious implications for the resources of society as a whole.

Moreover, this explanation finds almost no support in judicial reasoning.[35] In *MSC Mediterranean Shipping Co SA v Cottonex Anstalt*, Leggatt J noted that the rules of mitigation are 'designed to encourage the efficient use of resources'.[36] However, his comment was obiter dictum in a decision on recovery of the action for the agreed sum rather than damages, and appears to be an outlier. In applying the avoidable and avoided loss rules, judges do not inquire at all into the effect of the claimant's mitigating conduct on the use of resources across society as a whole.[37] Indeed, the House of Lords has emphasized that claimants may be

[29] Edwin Peel (ed), *Treitel on The Law of Contract* (15th edn, Sweet & Maxwell 2020) [21-015]: 'the policy of the mitigation rules . . . is to prevent needless waste'.

[30] See also Charles McCormick, *Handbook on the Law of Damages* (West Pub Co 1935) 127, cited in Bridge (n 1) 404 fn 41: 'Legal rules and doctrines are designed not only to prevent and repair individual loss and injustice, but to protect and conserve the economic welfare and prosperity of the whole community.'

[31] However, there are at least two important differences. First, economists typically seek to maximize 'welfare' (or 'utility') rather than resources; and second, their concern is with the (weighted) sum of individuals' welfare rather than the welfare of 'society' as a collective concept.

[32] MacIntosh and Frydenlund (n 27) 114.

[33] Bridge (n 1) 405.

[34] ibid 405.

[35] On the general point that efficiency explanations of private law lack fit with judicial reasoning, see further Stephen Smith, *Contract Theory* (OUP 2004) 132–36 and Brian Bix, 'Contract Rights and Remedies, and the Divergence between Law and Morality' (2008) 21 Ratio Juris 194, 198.

[36] *MSC Mediterranean Shipping Co SA v Cottonex Anstalt* [2015] EWHC 283 (Comm), [2015] 1 Lloyd's Rep 359 [111].

[37] As a *prescriptive* account of mitigation, one could argue that judges ought to take such considerations into account. However, this argument would depend on asserting the institutional capacity

entitled to recover damages for a defendant's failure to perform a 'grotesque folly',[38] despite that such performance may involve an inefficient waste of resources from a societal perspective.[39]

The narrower aim of achieving efficiency between the parties can overcome some of these objections, but an important difficulty remains. The explanation relies on the idea that the avoidable loss rule incentivizes individuals to act more efficiently as soon as they are faced with a breach. However, to serve this function effectively, there would need to be widespread understanding of the existence and effect of the law of mitigation amongst potential claimants. There is no empirical evidence for this and it seems unlikely in many contexts, especially those involving non-commercial parties. Moreover, the design of the mitigation rules do not seem to fit this purpose, and judges have never expressed this aim. In particular, the 'reasonableness' criterion—at least as presently articulated by judges—is so open-textured that it is often difficult to assess whether the mitigation rule applies even *ex post*, let alone as an *ex ante* guide to claimants' conduct.

4 Self-reliance

Several scholars have claimed that the avoidable loss rule can be explained by the aim of promoting self-reliance by the claimant.[40] For example, Burrows argues that 'the policy is one of encouraging the claimant, once a wrong has occurred, to be to a reasonable extent self-reliant or, in economists' terminology, to be efficient, rather than pinning all loss on the defendant'.[41] Notwithstanding Burrows' apparent identification of self-reliance and economic efficiency, the two are not necessarily equivalent. After breach, the defendant might remain the 'cheapest cost avoider' for taking action to minimize the harm, and in these circumstances the claimant's self-reliance would be *inefficient* as between the parties.[42] Nevertheless, the key element in Burrows' account appears to be self-reliance, since he also emphasizes

and constitutional competence of the judiciary to engage in the 'polycentric task' of assessing social welfare: see further Lon Fuller, 'The Forms and Limits of Adjudication' (1978) 92 Harvard Law Review 353, 394–404.

[38] *Ruxley Electronics & Construction Ltd v Forsyth* [1996] AC 344 (HL) 361 (Lord Mustill).

[39] See ibid 361 (Lord Mustill), emphasizing that the folly 'may be so discordant with general taste that in purely economic terms the builder may be said to do the employer a favour by failing to install them'.

[40] It has never been suggested that the avoided loss rule can be explained in these terms.

[41] Andrew Burrows, *Remedies for Torts, Breach of Contract, and Equitable Wrongs* (4th edn, OUP 2019) 127. See also Bridge (n 1) 409–10; and Edelman (n 3) [9-014]: 'Even persons against whom wrongs have been committed are not entitled to sit back and suffer loss.'

[42] On the theory of cheapest cost avoidance generally, see Guido Calabresi, *The Cost of Accidents: A Legal and Economic Analysis* (Yale University Press 1970). On its application to the avoidable loss rule, see Goetz and Scott (n 22) 972–75.

that the claimant 'should not sit back and do nothing . . . but should rather use its resources to do what is reasonable'.[43]

An initial difficulty with the self-reliance explanation is that it has received virtually no judicial support, either directly or indirectly. There do not appear to be any examples from the English cases on mitigation where judges have explained the doctrine in terms of self-reliance. Nor is there much indirect judicial support for this theory: for example, any oblique references to the claimant being idle or overly demanding of the defendant. Proponents of this explanation must therefore contend that the judicial decisions on mitigation endorse the policy of encouraging claimants to be self-reliant even though judges have never articulated this reasoning themselves. As indicated above, this is not an insuperable challenge; however, it places even greater weight on showing that the content of the rules is a close fit with the principle of self-reliance.

Instead, these indications point the other way. Although the self-reliance explanation seems to fit with the avoidable loss cases where the claimant sits back and does nothing ('unreasonable inaction'),[44] it cannot explain why the same rule applies when the claimant *was* self-reliant, but thereby incurred unreasonable expenses ('unreasonable action').[45] The self-reliance theory suggests that the unreasonable action and inaction cases must have different explanations, even though the decided cases treat both forms of conduct as applications of the same rule. Moreover, one cannot accommodate the unreasonable action cases by reformulating the explanation as a policy of encouraging *reasonable* self-reliance (which might seem an obvious move). This modification renders the 'self-reliance' element entirely redundant: the explanation would then effectively be 'a policy of encouraging claimants to act reasonably'.

Although not the focus of this chapter, it is worth noting that some private law scholars have denied that the law *ought* to promote self-reliance following a breach of contract. For example, Shiffrin argues that 'It is morally distasteful to expect the promisee to do work that could be done by the promisor when the occasion for the work is the promisor's own wrongdoing'.[46] The doctrine of mitigation may therefore be regarded as *un*justified (or difficult to justify) to the extent that it requires the claimant to be self-reliant despite the defendant's promise to perform. As I outline above, it is of course possible that mitigation could be explained by a

[43] Burrows (n 41) 127. But see also, in the context of claims for the agreed sum (at 387): 'economic efficiency dictates that the claimant should be required to mitigate'.

[44] ibid 127–29. The 'unreasonable action' cases are discussed at 130–31.

[45] See eg *Darbishire v Warran* [1963] 1 WLR 1067 (CA); *Italian State Railways (The Legnano) v Owners of the SS Minnehaha* (1921) 6 Ll L Rep 12 (CA); *Compania Financiera Soleada SA v Hamoor Tanker Corp Inc (The Borag)* [1981] 1 WLR 274 (CA); *Owners of the Georgidore v Owners of the Pacific Concord (The Pacific Concord)* [1961] 1 WLR 873 (PD); *Riyad Bank v Ahli United Bank (UK) plc* [2005] EWHC 279 (Comm), [2005] 2 Lloyd's Rep 409; *Beechwood Birmingham Ltd v Hoyer Group UK Ltd* [2010] EWCA Civ 647, [2011] QB 357.

[46] Seana Shiffrin, 'The Divergence of Contract and Promise' (2007) 120 Harvard Law Review 708, 725.

principle that is not justified, but this moral uncertainty provides some reason to doubt that the promotion of self-reliance is widely endorsed in judicial decisions on mitigation.

5 Co-operation

An alternative view—the obverse of the self-reliance explanation—is that mitigation instantiates norms of co-operation between the parties. This theory has been put forward by Morgan to explain mitigation in the contractual context.[47] Morgan's analysis bears some resemblance to the efficiency explanation, in particular for the idea that mitigation aims at 'reducing unnecessary costs... [which] means lower prices'.[48] However, it is clear that Morgan's analysis is not reducible to the instrumental goal of promoting efficiency. He writes that 'there is no need to appeal to external values (whether ethical or economic)' in order to justify mitigation; instead, 'mitigation *gives effect to the contract*: what the parties may be presumed to have intended'.[49]

The most obvious difficulty with this explanation is that, as I show in Chapter 7, the rules of mitigation apply in the same way regardless of the cause of action, whenever compensatory damages are in issue. For claims in tort, there is often no underlying agreement or indeed any prior relationship between the parties. In these cases, mitigation cannot stem from an assumption of responsibility, whether contractual or otherwise. Moreover, an independent norm of co-operation also appears less plausible in this context. For example, the same rules of mitigation apply to a damages claim for the tort of deceit as apply following a breach of contract, yet in the former case it can scarcely be argued that the claimant has any obligation (whether moral or legal) to co-operate with the defendant after the wrong.

Even narrowly within the domain of contract, the co-operation explanation faces several difficulties. To take effect as an implied term, the 'duty to mitigate' would presumably need to pass the 'business efficacy' or 'officious bystander' tests, yet neither of these tests have been applied in any of the cases on mitigation.[50] The notion that parties might come under a literal 'duty' (ie a legal obligation) to mitigate has also consistently been rejected by the courts.[51] Morgan's co-operation explanation may posit instead that mitigation operates like a limitation of liability

[47] Jonathan Morgan, 'Smuggling Mitigation into White & Carter v McGregor: Time to Come Clean?' [2015] Lloyd's Maritime and Commercial Law Quarterly 575.
[48] ibid 579.
[49] ibid 594.
[50] Moreover, it is doubtful that mitigation could be disapplied by an express term that purported to exclude implied terms from the parties' contract.
[51] See further Chapter 7, Section 2.

clause. However, there is no cases suggesting that the rules of mitigation are affected by any of the legislation on unfair terms that seek to regulate such clauses.[52]

A markedly different kind of co-operation theory was developed by Fried, who argued that mitigation is 'a kind of altruistic duty... that recognizes that contractual liabilities are onerous enough that they should not be needlessly exacerbated'.[53] This theory, which aimed to justify the law of mitigation as it stands, has been disputed by Atiyah and others.[54] Leaving aside the normative dimension of Fried's claim, one difficulty with the theory (as an explanation) is that it does not appear to fit the temporal scope of the mitigation doctrine. In particular, it is hard to see why, if a duty of altruism exists, it should be confined to the claimant's post-breach conduct. Beyond this, it is hard to assess how well the theory fits the content of the rules of mitigation, or the judicial reasoning in the relevant cases, because Fried did not elaborate the circumstances in which a claimant's exacerbation of the defendant's liability would count as 'needless'.

6 Remoteness

Mitigation has sometimes been explained in terms of remoteness.[55] In contract law, there remains a debate about whether remoteness is an 'external rule' imposed upon the parties, the hallmark of which is reasonable foreseeability, or an 'internal rule' emanating from the parties' own agreement.[56] This section considers only remoteness as an external rule.[57] In the tort of negligence, this rule has sometimes been explained as following from the foreseeability element of liability.[58] Alternatively, it has been explained as an attempt to ensure a rough proportion between the degree of the defendant's fault and the burden of liability.[59] Given this contested ground, any explanation of mitigation in terms of remoteness is bound to encounter these further issues regarding the root of the doctrine.

[52] Eg the Unfair Contract Terms Act 1977 and Consumer Rights Act 2015.

[53] Charles Fried, *Contract as Promise: A Theory of Contractual Obligation* (2nd edn, OUP 2015) 131.

[54] Patrick Atiyah, *Essays on Contract* (Clarendon 1990) 124–25. See also Dori Kimel, *From Promise to Contract: Towards a Liberal Theory of Contract* (Hart 2003) 110; George Letsas and Prince Saprai, 'Mitigation, Fairness and Contract Law' in Gregory Klass, George Letsas, and Prince Saprai (eds), *Philosophical Foundations of Contract Law* (OUP 2014) 323–27.

[55] See eg Smith (n 35) 428–29. Rejecting this explanation, see Tettenborn, *Damages* (2nd edn) (n 3) [5.61]–[5.62]; Edelman (n 3) [9-106]. For further discussion of the relationship between mitigation and remoteness, see Chapter 11, Section 4.

[56] *Transfield Shipping Inc v Mercator Shipping Inc (The Achilleas)* [2008] UKHL 48, [2009] 1 AC 61 [9], [11] (Lord Hoffmann). See further Chapter 11, Section 4.1.

[57] I have already considered and rejected the theory that mitigation is explained by an implied agreement between the parties: see text to n 49.

[58] *Overseas Tankship (UK) Ltd v Morts Dock & Engineering Co (The Wagon Mound)* [1961] AC 388 (PC), 423, 426 (Viscount Simonds).

[59] See eg Tony Honoré, 'The Morality of Tort Law—Questions and Answers' in David Owen (ed), *The Philosophical Foundations of Tort Law* (Clarendon 1995) 91–92. See also Anthony Ogus, *The Law of Damages* (Butterworths 1973) 67, cited in Burrows (n 41) 75.

In *Contract Theory*, Smith argues that '[t]he mitigation rule is best explained as one aspect of the general concept of remoteness; the reason plaintiffs cannot recover for losses they could have avoided by acting reasonably is that such losses are too remote'.[60] Although this explanation does have some judicial support, it is limited and equivocal. The only direct support for the remoteness explanation refers to remoteness and causation interchangeably,[61] such that the reasoning is based on directness rather than foreseeability.[62] The remoteness rule has sometimes been invoked where the claimant's conduct was unforeseeable,[63] but this does not show that mitigation is an aspect (or 'subset') of remoteness; it merely shows that the remoteness rule may *also* apply to the claimant's conduct.[64]

Smith specifies that 'when determining which losses are reasonably foreseeable (or which "naturally flow") as a result of a breach, the background assumption is that the [claimant] will act reasonably'.[65] However, unforeseeability and unreasonableness cannot be equated in this way. The claimant's conduct can be unreasonable even though it was foreseeable. For example, in *McKew v Holland*, Lord Reid held that 'it is not at all unlikely or unforeseeable that an active man who has suffered such a disability will take some quite unreasonable risk. But if he does, he cannot hold the [defendant] liable for the consequences'.[66] Conversely, the claimant's conduct can be reasonable even though it was unforeseeable. In *Saunders v Williams*, Pill LJ rejected the argument that the claimant had failed to mitigate where delays in repairing a damaged wall were unforeseeable.[67] Although there is some overlap between mitigation and remoteness, Tettenborn is correct to highlight that the two doctrines 'differ in a number of respects'.[68]

The underlying distinction between reasonable foreseeability and mitigation is that, as Bridge puts it, 'remoteness is concerned with a hypothetical prediction ex ante of the consequences of a future breach', whereas mitigation is 'invariably concerned with a factual assessment of the quality of the plaintiff's behaviour in the

[60] Smith (n 35) 428.

[61] *Compania Naviera Maropan SA v Bowaters Lloyd Pulp & Paper Mills Ltd (The Stork)* [1955] 2 QB 68 (CA) 93 (Singleton LJ), 98–99 (Hodson LJ). For other interchangeable references to remoteness and causation, see eg: *The Borag* (n 45) 281–82 (Denning LJ); *Total Transport Corp v Arcadia Petroleum Ltd (The Eurus)* [1998] 1 Lloyd's Rep 351, [1998] CLC 90 (CA) 96 (Staughton LJ); *Spencer v Wincanton Holdings Ltd* [2009] EWCA Civ 1404, [2010] PIQR P8 [38] (Aikens LJ).

[62] For implicit support in terms of foreseeability, see *Shindler v Northern Raincoat Co* [1960] 1 WLR 1038 (Assizes) 1048 (Diplock J).

[63] See eg *County Ltd v Girozentrale Securities* [1996] 3 All ER 834 (CA) 857 (Hobhouse LJ): 'If the conduct of the plaintiffs had been so exceptional as to take it outside the contemplation of the parties, then it might have made the consequent loss too remote.' See also *Owners of Dredger Liesbosch v Owners of Steamship Edison (The Liesbosch)* [1933] AC 449 (HL), now overruled in *Lagden v O'Connor (sub nom Burdis v Livsey)* [2003] UKHL 64, [2004] 1 AC 1067.

[64] On the relation between mitigation and remoteness, see further Chapter 11, Section 4.

[65] Smith (n 35) 428.

[66] *McKew v Holland & Cubitts (Scotland) Ltd* [1969] 3 All ER 1621 (HL) 1623. See also *Simmons v British Steel plc* [2004] UKHL 20, 2004 SC (HL) 94 [67] (Lord Rodger).

[67] *Saunders v Williams* [2002] EWCA Civ 673, [2003] BLR 125 [21]–[27].

[68] Tettenborn, *Damages* (2nd edn) (n 3) [5.62].

circumstances'.[69] One consequence is that the claimant will not be held to have acted unreasonably in mitigation until after the breach was discovered,[70] whereas the reasonable foreseeability test applies either at the date of contract formation (in contract) or the date of breach (in tort).[71] In remoteness, the focus is on what the defendant could have reasonably foreseen, whereas in mitigation the test of reasonableness focuses directly on the claimant. For these reasons the rules do not appear to share a common explanation.

The avoided loss rule has sometimes been explained in terms of remoteness. Burrows suggests that '"Directness" puts a limit on the extent to which compensating advantages are deducted', adding that directness 'plays an analogous but reverse role to remoteness and intervening cause'.[72] In Chapter 5 I will argue that, as Burrows suggests, intervening causation does provide a good explanation for the avoided loss rule. However, the remoteness rule (in terms of foreseeability) does not, because as Lord Reid emphasized in *Parry v Cleaver*, 'No one has ever suggested that the defendant gets the benefit of receipts by the plaintiff after his accident if they are of a kind which he could have foreseen, but not if they are of a kind which he could not have foreseen, or vice versa.'[73] The directness explanation of the avoided loss rule is best understood in terms of causation rather than remoteness.

7 Fairness

Letsas and Saprai have argued that mitigation is explained by a 'principle of fairness', according to which 'it would be unfair if the promisee were entitled to claim losses from the promisor that he could easily have avoided, while obtaining what was promised'.[74] They are clear that this principle restricts the claim for damages, rather than constraining (or prescribing) the claimant's conduct: 'there is a moral duty not to claim losses that the promisee could easily have avoided, rather than a duty not to incur these losses'.[75] This explanation differs from the various instrumental theories of mitigation considered above (such as promotion of economic efficiency or self-reliance), which all posit that mitigation aims directly to guide the claimant's conduct. Letsas and Saprai's explanation is more consistent with judicial remarks that the claimant is not strictly under any 'duty' to mitigate.[76]

Two key issues arise for this theory. First, why does a principle of fairness yield the rule that parties cannot recover damages for losses that they could easily have

69 Bridge (n 1) 403.
70 See further Chapter 7, Section 4.1.
71 See eg *Jackson v Royal Bank of Scotland* [2005] UKHL 3, [2005] 1 WLR 377 [36] (Lord Hope).
72 Burrows (n 3) 148.
73 *Parry v Cleaver* [1970] AC 1 (HL) 15.
74 Letsas and Saprai (n 54) 327.
75 ibid 326–27.
76 See further Chapter 7, Section 2.

avoided? Letsas and Saprai answer that this is the rule that the parties would choose if they did not know whether they would be in the position of the claimant or the defendant.[77] The approach thus has some loose affinity with the implied agreement explanation offered by Morgan, but with the important difference that it does not posit any *actual* agreement between the parties. Consequently, it overcomes the objection that mitigation applies in the same way to claims in tort as well as breach of contract. Indeed, as Letsas and Saprai emphasize, 'the structure of the explanation from fairness is one that applies to all cases where there are secondary obligations arising out of the breach of a primary obligation.' In other words, this method for determining remedial rules can be applied more broadly than just to mitigation.

The second issue, which is less satisfactorily addressed by Letsas and Saprai, is how their theory translates to the particular rules of mitigation that we observe in the cases. Their argument from fairness is conclusory: it does not explain why hypothetical parties would choose these rules from behind a veil of ignorance. Letsas and Saprai indicate a possible reason: that in circumstances where the law recognizes a failure to mitigate, the claimant 'is exercising a choice rather than suffering a loss'.[78] For Letsas and Saprai, this explains why it is unfair to hold the defendant responsible. As we shall see, this line of thinking comes very close to the causal explanation that I develop in the next chapter, even though Letsas and Saprai themselves reject the idea that mitigation reflects causal principles.[79]

8 A Combination of the Above?

In my account of what it means to 'explain' a legal doctrine, I referred to explanatory principles—plural—leaving open that more than one principle could collectively explain an area of the law. In relation to mitigation, this kind of pluralistic explanation was favoured by Bridge, who concluded that 'numerous factors are at play in explaining the duty to mitigate'.[80] It is important to distinguish two different ways in which this proposition might be true. First, it might be that in particular cases, judges endorsed multiple reasons that each independently counted in favour of their decision. I will call this 'within case' explanatory pluralism. Second, it might be that different cases endorsed different reasons (even if only one reason was endorsed per case), but since rules of the common law are abstracted from the whole body of cases, this could also lead to explanatory pluralism, of what I will call the 'across case' variety.

[77] As Letsas and Saprai note, this reflects the philosophical method of contractualism adopted by John Rawls (where 'contractual' here has nothing to do with contract law): Letsas and Saprai (n 54) 327.
[78] ibid 327.
[79] ibid fn 11.
[80] Bridge (n 1) 410.

I do not rule out either type of explanatory pluralism a priori. However, neither seems compelling in the context of mitigation. In relation to 'within case' pluralism, a major difficulty is that many of the aforementioned explanatory principles pull against each other: for example, if mitigation is explained by the promotion of *both* self-reliance *and* economic efficiency, what happens where being self-reliant would be inefficient? If a particular combination of disparate reasons pervaded the cases on mitigation, one would expect to find at least some evidence of judges grappling with this kind of challenge. But instead, as I show in the following chapter, judicial reasoning on mitigation tends to be more singular in its focus on causal principles, with judges only occasionally helping themselves to other supporting reasons.

'Across case' explanatory pluralism is more difficult to negate because there are always bound to be some outlier cases in which the judge endorsed different reasons from those that predominated in the majority of cases. Nevertheless, when looking over the whole body of cases, it should be possible to identify which reasons constitute the mainstream and which are more peripheral. In the present context, there is very clearly one dominant theme in judicial reasoning: the rules of mitigation are an aspect of causation. This is not to deny that there is some support for other explanations in the cases, but simply that the extent of this support pales in comparison. In other words, although the cases on mitigation do not speak perfectly with one voice (which one could hardly expect for any common law doctrine developed over centuries), I will argue in the following chapter that causation is *the* explanation rather than one reason amongst many.

PART 2
EXPLANATION

5
Developing the Causal Explanation

1 Introduction

In the preceding chapter I assessed several theories that have been put forward to explain the law of mitigation. I argued that none of these theories provide a satisfactory explanation, either individually or in combination. Instead, my argument in this book is that mitigation is an aspect of causation. Judicial reasoning strongly supports this explanation; however, it has tended to be rejected by legal scholars on the basis that judicial references to causation are too vague and indeterminate to explain the specific rules of mitigation. In this chapter, I show how 'common-sense' principles of causation may provide an answer to this objection. This analysis lays the foundations for Chapters 6 to 11, which address how common-sense principles of causation fit with the law of mitigation (and related doctrines) as we currently find it.

This chapter is divided into four sections. Sections One and Two highlight the judicial support for the causal explanation of mitigation and the scholarly scepticism of this explanation, respectively. In Section Three, I argue that to understand judicial references to causation in mitigation, we need to move beyond the 'but for' notion of cause and seek to understand the common-sense causal principles that ordinary people use outside the law. My approach in this section draws extensively on the work of Hart and Honoré in *Causation the Law* but refines their theory using subsequent empirical research conducted in the field of experimental psychology. The final section pre-empts various criticisms of this approach, including objections from philosophical, empirical, and semantic perspectives.

2 Judicial support

One of the grounds for rejecting the various explanations canvassed in the preceding chapter was their lack of judicial support. I argued that those explanations face an uphill challenge because they have rarely, if ever, been endorsed—whether expressly or indirectly—in judicial reasoning. The same criticism cannot be made of the causal explanation.[1] Judicial support for this explanation is very strong.

[1] Contra James Edelman (ed), *McGregor on Damages* (21st edn, Sweet & Maxwell 2022) [9-019]: 'It is significant that the cases on the avoidable loss aspect of mitigation are not full of references to causation.' This assertion is wrong, as this section shows.

Mitigation in the Law of Damages. Andrew Summers, Oxford University Press. © Andy Summers 2025.
DOI: 10.1093/9780191864032.003.0005

Here, the challenge is reversed: sceptics would need to argue that causation does not explain the rules of mitigation even though most judges think that it does. One should exercise caution before reaching this bold conclusion. I argue that although the judges' references to causation are often imprecise, they contain an important insight that ought to be investigated rather than dismissed out of hand.

Judicial support for the causal explanation of mitigation predates 'mitigation' itself. The avoidable loss rule existed before anyone referred to it as mitigation, and at this time it was directly regarded as a causal rule. In the 1807 case of *Boyce v Bayliffe*, the claimant was falsely imprisoned for one night whilst travelling aboard a ship from Bombay to London.[2] The ship continued to sail for another month, after which the claimant disembarked in South Africa and paid £100 to board another ship to London. Lord Ellenborough held that 'the imprisonment was not the *causa proxima* of the transhipment . . . the plaintiff was not driven to it in order to redeem himself from any great peril or grievance'.[3] Accordingly the claim for special damage of £100 was denied.[4] We would now regard this decision as an application of the avoidable loss rule.

In the late nineteenth century, the avoidable loss rule started to become known as the law of 'mitigation'.[5] However, judges still sometimes refer directly to causation. In *SAAMCO*, Lord Hoffmann held that 'a plaintiff's reasonable attempt to cope with the consequences of the defendant's breach of duty does not negative the causal connection between that breach of duty and the ultimate loss'.[6] In *Activa Europe v Pressure Seal Solutions*, Patten LJ held that 'The defendant is only liable for such loss as can properly be regarded as caused by his breach of contract. In this context the claimant is under a duty to take reasonable steps to mitigate the loss which flows from the breach.'[7] These two examples are just the tip of the iceberg.[8]

[2] *Boyce v Bayliffe* (1807) 1 Camp 58, 170 ER 875. The Captain had ordered 'all hands on deck' because he mistakenly thought that a hostile vessel was approaching. The claimant passenger was kept in irons overnight as punishment for refusing the order.

[3] ibid 876. In relation to the 'unreasonableness' of disembarking, one probably needs to appreciate the historical context that such false imprisonment was not regarded with the same indignity as it might be today.

[4] The claimant was awarded £80 in respect of the false imprisonment.

[5] See further Chapter 1, text to n 83.

[6] *South Australia Asset Management Corp v York Montague Ltd ('SAAMCO')* [1997] AC 191 (HL) 219. See also, in relation to equitable compensation: *AIB Group (UK) plc v Mark Redler & Co Solicitors* [2014] UKSC 58, [2014] 3 WLR 1367 [87] (Lord Reed): 'rather than being a distinct principle, ["the plaintiff's responsibility not to act unreasonably"] might be regarded as following from the requirement of a direct causal connection'.

[7] *Activa DPS Europe Sarl v Pressure Seal Solutions Ltd* [2012] EWCA Civ 943, [2012] 3 CMLR 33 [36].

[8] See also *Compania Naviera Maropan SA v Bowaters Lloyd Pulp & Paper Mills Ltd (The Stork)* [1955] 2 QB 68 (CA) 99 (Hodson LJ); *Compania Financiera Soleada SA v Hamoor Tanker Corp Inc (The Borag)* [1981] 1 WLR 274 (CA) 285 (Templeman LJ); *Sotiros Shipping Inc v Sameiet Solholt (The Solholt)* [1983] 1 Lloyd's Rep 605 (CA) 608 (Sir John Donaldson MR); *Sealace Shipping Co Ltd v Oceanvoice Ltd (The Alecos M)* [1991] 1 Lloyd's Rep 120 (CA) 124 (Neill LJ); *Downs v Chappell* [1997] 1 WLR 426 (CA) 437 (Hobhouse LJ); *Burdis v Livsey (sub nom Lagden v O'Connor)* [2002] EWCA Civ 510, [2003] QB 36 [88] (Aldous LJ); *Habton Farms v Nimmo* [2003] EWCA Civ 68, [2004] QB 1 [66] (Clarke LJ); *Transfield Shipping Inc v Mercator Shipping Inc (The Achilleas)* [2007] EWCA Civ

If one includes judicial reasoning that the claimant's unreasonable conduct 'broke the chain of causation', the list is longer still.[9]

In *The Elena D'Amico*,[10] Goff J expressly explained mitigation in terms of causation. After summarizing McGregor's three rules, he concluded that 'in my judgment, these three aspects of mitigation are all really aspects of a wider principle . . . they are aspects of the principle of causation'.[11] In *Lagden v O'Connor*, Lord Walker similarly explained that mitigation was 'an aspect (or category) of the larger principle of causation'.[12] In *Standard Chartered Bank v Pakistan National Shipping Corp*, Potter LJ concluded that '[i]n truth, causation and mitigation are two sides of the same coin'.[13] More recently, in *Bunge v Nidera*, Lord Toulson has reiterated that 'the so-called duty to mitigate is not a duty . . . Rather, it is an aspect of the principle of causation that the contract breaker will not be held to have caused loss which the claimant could reasonably have avoided'.[14] Many more examples could be given.[15]

The same is true of the avoided loss rule. In *The Elena D'Amico*, Goff J held that 'what is alleged to constitute mitigation in law can only have that effect if there is a causative link between the wrong in respect of which damages are claimed and the action or inaction of the plaintiff'.[16] In *Hussey v Eels*, Mustill LJ asked, 'Did the negligence which caused the damage also cause the profit . . . ?'[17] In *Blue Circle Industries*, Aldous LJ thought that '[t]he question for consideration in this case is one of causation'.[18] And, in *Sainsbury's Supermarkets*, the Supreme Court stated

901, [2008] 1 All ER (Comm) 685 [102] (Rix LJ); *Sainsbury's Supermarkets Ltd v Visa Europe Services LLC* [2020] UKSC 24; | [2020] 4 All ER 807; *Stanford International Bank Ltd v HSBC Bank PLC* [2022] UKSC 34, [2023] 2 WLR 79 [43] (Lord Leggatt)

[9] See eg *The Oropesa* [1943] P 32 (CA) 39 (Lord Wright); *McKew v Holland & Cubitts (Scotland) Ltd* [1969] 3 All ER 1621 (HL) 25 (Lord Reid); *Vinmar International Ltd v Theresa Navigation SA* [2001] 2 Lloyd's Rep 1 (QB) [42] (Tomlinson J); *Simmons v British Steel plc* [2004] UKHL 20, 2004 SC (HL) 94 [67] (Lord Rodger); *ENE 1 Kos Ltd v Petroleo Brasileiro SA Petrobras (The Kos)* [2012] UKSC 17, [2012] 2 AC 164 [14] (Lord Sumption).

[10] *Koch Marine Inc v d'Amica Societa di Navigazione arl (The Elena d'Amico)* [1980] 1 Lloyd's Rep 75 (QB).

[11] ibid 88.

[12] *Lagden v O'Connor (sub nom Burdis v Livsey)* [2003] UKHL 64, [2004] 1 AC 1067 [100].

[13] *Standard Chartered Bank v Pakistan National Shipping Corp* [2001] EWCA Civ 55, [2001] 1 All ER (Comm) 822 [55]. See also *Standard Chartered Bank v Pakistan National Shipping Corp* [1999] 1 Lloyd's Rep 747 (QB) 758 (Toulson J): 'The orthodox view is that the rule as to avoidable loss is merely an aspect of the fundamental principle of causation'. Here Toulson J was referring to judicial orthodoxy, rather than to the contrary positions expressed in the leading texts on damages.

[14] *Bunge SA v Nidera BV* [2015] UKSC 43, [2015] 3 All ER 1082 [81].

[15] See also *County Ltd v Girozentrale Securities* [1996] 3 All ER 834 (CA) 857–58 (Hobhouse LJ); *Total Transport Corp v Arcadia Petroleum Ltd (The Eurus)* [1996] 2 Lloyd's Rep 408 (QB) 1111 (Rix J); *Southampton Container Terminals Ltd v Schiffahrisgesellsch 'Hansa Australia' MGH & Co (The Maersk Colombo)* [2001] EWCA Civ 717, [2001] 2 Lloyd's Rep 275 [28] (Clarke LJ); *British Midland Tool Ltd v Midland International Tooling Ltd* [2003] EWHC 466 (Ch), [2003] 2 BCLC 523 [188] (Hart J). See similarly in Australia: *Knott Investments Pty Ltd & Ors v Fulcher & Ors* [2013] QCA 67 [44]–[45].

[16] *The Elena d'Amico* (n 10) 88. See also 89.

[17] *Hussey v Eels* [1990] 2 QB 227 (CA) 241, cited with approval in *Primavera v Allied Dunbar Assurance plc* [2002] EWCA Civ 1327, [2003] Lloyd's Rep PN 14 [20] (Simon Brown LJ).

[18] *Blue Circle Industries plc v Ministry of Defence* [1999] Ch 289 (CA) 305.

that '[s]uch cases [of avoided losses] raise delicate questions as to whether a benefit is sufficiently causally connected with the breach of contract or (in tort) the wrong or whether the benefit was the result of an independent commercial decision by the claimant'. Again, more examples could be given.[19]

The statements that I have relied upon so far are all examples of 'direct' support for the causal explanation, ie, judicial reasoning that expressly refers to causation as the basis for the mitigation rules. However, one can also infer further 'indirect' support, since the cases are replete with causal metaphors.[20] In relation to both the avoidable and avoided loss rules, it is often said that the claimant's conduct was a 'break in the chain',[21] not part of a 'continuous transaction',[22] or eliminated 'any efficacy of the breach'.[23] Likewise the test is often regarded as one of 'directness'.[24] Judges have also reasoned that the harm was not 'due to' the defendant's breach,[25] or more ambiguously that the benefit was 'collateral' or '*res inter alios acta*'.[26]

The most important example of indirect support for the causal explanation comes from Viscount Haldane's seminal judgment in *British Westinghouse*.[27] There is no allusion in Viscount Haldane's judgment to any of the explanations canvassed in the preceding chapter, such as the promotion of economic efficiency or self-reliance, or the notion that mitigation is an aspect of remoteness or fairness. Admittedly, neither does the judgment mention causation directly. However, this objection looks at the reasoning too narrowly, because Viscount Haldane's formulations of the avoidable and avoided loss rules were reliant on causal metaphors,[28]

[19] See eg *Famosa Shipping Co Ltd v Armada Bulk Carriers Ltd (The Fanis)* [1994] 1 Lloyd's Rep 633 (QB) 637. *Mobil North Sea Ltd v PJ Pipe & Valve Co Ltd* [2001] EWCA Civ 741, [2001] 2 All ER (Comm) 289 [30] (Rix LJ); *Needler Financial Services Ltd v Taber* [2002] 3 All ER 501 (Ch) [24] (Sir Andrew Morritt VC), cited with approval in *Rubenstein v HSBC Bank plc* [2012] EWCA Civ 1184, [2012] 2 CLC 747 [135] (Rix LJ); *Thai Airways International Public Co Ltd v KI Holdings Co Ltd* [2015] EWHC 1250 (Comm), [2016] 1 All ER (Comm) 675 [46] (Leggatt J); *Fulton Shipping Inc of Panama v Globalia Business Travel SAU (The New Flamenco)* [2015] EWCA Civ 1299, [2016] 1 Lloyd's Rep 383 [38] (Longmore LJ).

[20] *Weld-Blundell v Stephens* [1920] AC 956 (HL) 986 (Lord Sumner): 'It is hard to steer clear of metaphors'.

[21] See eg *Blue Circle* (n 18) 308 (Aldous LJ), 317 (Chadwick LJ).

[22] See eg *Hussey* (n 17) 241 (Mustill LJ); *Primavera* (n 17) [20] (Simon Brown LJ), [38] (Mance LJ); *Needler* (n 19) [24] (Sir Andrew Morritt VC); *Rubenstein* (n 19) [134] (Rix LJ).

[23] See eg *Vinmar* (n 9) [42] (Tomlinson J). See also *Great Elephant Corp v Trafigura Beheer BV* [2013] EWCA Civ 905, [2013] 2 All ER (Comm) 992 [45] (Longmore LJ).

[24] See eg *Lavarack v Woods of Colchester* [1967] 1 QB 278 (CA) 290 (Denning LJ): 'the benefit from that investment was not a direct result of his dismissal'.

[25] See *British Westinghouse Electric & Manufacturing Co Ltd v Underground Electric Railways Co of London Ltd (No 2)* [1912] AC 673 (HL) 689 (Viscount Haldane); *AKAS Jamal v Moolla Dawood Sons & Co* [1916] 1 AC 175 (PC) 179 (Lord Wrenbury).

[26] See eg *British Westinghouse* (n 25) 691 (Viscount Haldane); *Burdis* (n 8) [91] (Aldous LJ); *Pankhania v Hackney LBC* [2004] EWHC 323 (Ch), [2004] 1 EGLR 135 [37] (Vos QC).

[27] *British Westinghouse* (n 25).

[28] ibid 692: 'it formed *part of a continuous dealing* with the situation in which they found themselves' (emphasis added). This reasoning is essentially the obverse of a 'break in the chain'.

and language associated with the attribution of causal responsibility.[29] In this sense, the judgment is indirectly supportive of the causal explanation of mitigation.

One striking aspect of the indirect support for the causal explanation is the extent to which it takes precisely the same form for both the avoidable and avoided loss rules. For example, in relation to the avoidable loss rule, in *The Metagama*, Viscount Dunedin held that 'if [the claimant] might reasonably have avoided any part of the damage he has suffered, to that extent the damage is not such as *arises directly from the act complained of*.'[30] This mirrors almost exactly Viscount Haldane's formulation of the avoided loss rule in *British Westinghouse*, that 'The subsequent transaction, if to be taken into account, must be one *arising out of the consequences of the breach*.'[31] Similarly, irrespective of whether the outcome was harmful or beneficial, judicial expositions of both rules have emphasized that the test is whether the claimant's conduct was 'independent' of the breach.[32]

3 Scholarly scepticism

Legal scholars have occasionally explained mitigation in terms of causation, but supporters of this explanation are few and far between. The only one of the leading texts to adopt this view of the avoidable loss rule is Kramer's *The Law of Contract Damages*.[33] As Kramer puts it, 'Mitigation is merely the name given to the principle of legal causation when applied to the actions and inactions of the claimant'.[34] Other scholarly articles and essays have occasionally explained the avoidable loss rule in terms of causal principles.[35] In relation to the avoided loss rule, the causal explanation appears to be accepted by Burrows, who expresses the rule in terms of 'directness' and suggests that it 'plays an analogous but reverse role to remoteness

[29] ibid: 'damage which is *due to* his neglect' (689); '*arising out of the consequences* of the breach' (690); 'not an *independent or disconnected* transaction' (692) (emphasis added).

[30] *Baron Vernon v SS Metagama (The Metagama)* (1928) SC (HL) 21 (HL) 27 (emphasis added).

[31] *British Westinghouse* (n 25) 690 (emphasis added). See also, using the same phrase: *R Pagnan & Fratelli v Corbisa Industrial Agropacuaria Ltd* [1970] 1 WLR 1306 (CA) 1315–16 (Salmon LJ); *The Elena d'Amico* (n 10) 88–89 (Goff J).

[32] See eg *Owners of the SS Singleton Abbey v Owners of the SS Paludina (The Paludina)* [1927] AC 16 (HL) 28 (Lord Sumner) (avoidable loss rule); *Mobil* (n 19) [30] (Rix LJ) (avoided loss rule). See also *British Westinghouse* (n 25) 692 (Viscount Haldane); *Glory Wealth Shipping Pte Ltd v Korea Line Corp (The Wren)* [2011] EWHC 1819 (Comm), [2012] 1 All ER (Comm) 402 [16] (Blair J); *Zodiac Maritime Agencies Ltd v Fortescue Metals Group Ltd (The Kildare)* [2010] EWHC 903 (Comm), [2011] 2 Lloyd's Rep 360 [65] (Steel J); *Pagnan & Fratelli* (n 31) 1315 (Salmon LJ).

[33] Adam Kramer, *The Law of Contract Damages* (3rd edn, Hart 2022).

[34] ibid [15-44].

[35] See eg Francis Reynolds, 'Discharge by Breach as a Remedy' in Paul Finn (ed), *Essays on Contract* (Law Book Co 1987) 183–84; Jane Stapleton, 'The Normal Expectancies Measure in Tort Damages' (1997) 113 Law Quarterly Review 257, 272; Robert Stevens, 'Should Contributory Negligence be Analogue or Digital?' in Andrew Dyson, James Goudkamp, and Frederick Wilmot-Smith (eds), *Defences in Tort* (Hart 2015) 251; Wayne Courtney, 'Contract Damages and the Promisee's Role in its Own Loss' (2019) 42 Melbourne University Law Review 406.

and intervening cause'.[36] Treitel's *The Law of Contract* also explains the avoided loss rule as an application of causal principles.[37]

More often, the idea that mitigation is an aspect of causation has been treated with scepticism by legal scholars. The staunchest opposition has come from McGregor,[38] who argued that 'this embracing of the principle of causation is unhelpful—even confusing'.[39] The gist of McGregor's criticism was that causation 'does not tell us very much',[40] because '[w]hat must be ascertained is whether the claimant has or has not acted, or failed to act, reasonably'.[41] McGregor also concluded that while 'causation is relevant to an understanding of the third rule of mitigation . . . it is not a conclusive test'.[42] His scepticism was shared by Bridge, who objected that 'reasoning like this is conclusive rather than demonstrative, in merely stating a result without giving a coherent explanation'.[43]

The causal explanation of mitigation has thus tended to be rejected on the basis that it is too vague and indeterminate; in other words, the concern is that this explanation fails to give specific reasons why the rules of mitigation take the form that they do.[44] Notwithstanding broad judicial support for the causal explanation, some judges do appear to share this concern. In *Uzinterimpex v Standard Bank*, Moore-Bick LJ concluded that the avoidable loss rule 'can be viewed [as causation], but I am not sure that to do so adds greatly to one's understanding of the

[36] Andrew Burrows, *Remedies for Torts, Breach of Contract, and Equitable Wrongs* (4th edn, OUP 2019) 148.

[37] Edwin Peel (ed), *Treitel on The Law of Contract* (15th edn, Sweet & Maxwell 2015) [20-105]. See also Harry Street, *Principles of the Law of Damages* (Sweet & Maxwell 1962) 108; David Allen, Robyn Martin, and John Hartshorne, *Damages in Tort* (Sweet & Maxwell 2000) 105–06; Kramer (n 33) [15-106].

[38] Edelman (n 1) ch 9. Previous editions under Mayne did not take this view: see WG Earengey (ed), *Mayne's Treatise on Damages* (11th edn, Sweet & Maxwell 1946) ch 7. For more moderate criticisms, see eg Michael Bridge, 'Mitigation of Damages in Contract and the Meaning of Avoidable Loss' (1989) 105 Law Quarterly Review 398, 400–02; Andrew Tettenborn, *The Law of Damages* (2nd edn, LexisNexis 2010) [5.62].

[39] Edelman (n 1) [9-019]. See also Harvey McGregor, 'The Role of Mitigation in the Assessment of Damages' in Djakhongir Saidov and Ralph Cunnington (eds), *Contract Damages: Domestic and International Perspectives* (Hart 2008) 331.

[40] Edelman (n 1) [9-019].

[41] ibid [9-019]. The irony in this objection is that on the account given in *McGregor on Damages*, reasonableness is a question of fact for which no guidance can be given.

[42] ibid [9-112]. In the previous edition of McGregor, also under the editorship of Edelman, it was concluded that the avoided loss rule cannot be explained by 'climbing the slippery slopes of causation': Edelman, *McGregor on Damages* (20th edn) [9-019].

[43] Bridge, 'Mitigation of Damages' (n 38) 400. Bridge concludes (at 402) that consequently 'even if only a technical explanation of mitigation were sufficient, causation would not be an adequate response'.

[44] Along similar lines, see Katy Barnett, 'Substitutive Damages and Mitigation in Contract Law' (2016) 28 Singapore Academy of Law Journal 795, 805; David Winterton, *Money Awards in Contract Law* (Hart 2015) 250. However, in more recent work, Winterton's position has shifted in favour of the causal explanation: David Winterton, 'Limiting the recovery of damages for breach of contract in Australia: some important unresolved questions' in Eldridge and Pilkinton (eds), *Australian Contract Law in the 21st Century* (The Federation Press 2021).

principles'.[45] Similarly in relation to the avoided loss rule, in *Bacciottini v Gotelee & Goldsmith* Davis LJ suggested that 'perhaps it is not particularly enlightening to talk in terms of whether the original breach "caused" the mitigating or avoiding act'.[46]

This criticism of causal reasoning is not confined to mitigation. It has a strong foothold in legal scholarship more generally.[47] Many legal scholars regard the 'but-for' test (i.e. counterfactual necessity) as the only meaningful concept of causation.[48] This test is typically referred to as the issue of 'factual causation'.[49] Although judges sometimes refer to other issues—including mitigation—in terms of causation, such references are regarded by many legal scholars as 'a disguise for the real ground of a decision'.[50] In particular, it is thought that such references disguise the role of legal policy, which turns instead on the scope and purpose of the relevant rules of law.[51] Accordingly, when judges attempt to select 'the' cause of an event from a range of 'but for' (counterfactually necessary) conditions, they are engaging in legal policymaking rather than causal reasoning.

The causal minimalist view seems to pose a compelling objection to the causal explanation of mitigation. On the one hand, where the claimant acted unreasonably, judges often claim that the defendant did not cause the subsequent harm; as Lord Toulson puts it, the defendant 'will not be held to have caused loss which the claimant could reasonably have avoided'.[52] On the other hand, in these circumstances it is still the case that the harm would not have occurred but-for the defendant's breach;[53] in this sense the defendant did still cause the harm.[54] Bridge notes that 'a degree of tension plainly exists between these two propositions'.[55] The same tension has been noted in relation to benefits under the avoided loss rule; for example in *The Fanis*, Mance J concluded that 'to apply a pure "but for" test to

[45] *Uzinterimpex JSC v Standard Bank plc* [2008] EWCA Civ 819, [2008] 2 CLC 80 [56]. See also *Six Continents Retail Ltd v Carford Catering Ltd* [2003] EWCA Civ 1790 [11] (Laws LJ): 'a formulation of that type merely begs the question what will count as stopping loss from flowing'.

[46] *Bacciottini v Gotelee & Goldsmith* [2016] EWCA Civ 170, [2016] 4 WLR 98 [62]. For similar scepticism in the Australian context: *Fazlic v Milingimbi Community Inc* (1982) 150 CLR 345 [17]–[18].

[47] For early proponents, see eg Leon Green, *Rationale of Proximate Cause* (Vernon 1927); Arthur Goodhart, 'Appeals on Questions of Fact' (1955) 71 Law Quarterly Review 402, 413.

[48] Eg Edelman (n 1) ch 8. In philosophy, this approach is traceable to David Hume (London 1739) 171. See also John Stuart Mill, *A System of Logic: Raciocentive and Inductive* (Longmans 1843) 360–61; David Lewis, *Counterfactuals* (Blackwell 1973) 558–59.

[49] See eg Arno Becht and Frank Miller, *The Test of Factual Causation in Negligence and Strict Liability Cases* (Washington University 1961). Others have argued that the but-for test is not exclusively factual: see eg Wex Malone, 'Ruminations on Cause-in-Fact' (1956–7) 9 Stanford Law Review 60.

[50] Edelman (n 1) [9-019].

[51] For a modern defence of this view, see Jane Stapleton, 'Causation in the Law' in Helen Beebee, Christopher Hitchcock, and Peter Menzies (eds), *The Oxford Handbook of Causation* (OUP 2009) 753. See also Edelman, *McGregor on Damages* (20th edn) (n 1) ch 8.

[52] *Bunge* (n 14) [81].

[53] For reasoning to this effect, see eg *Six Continents* (n 45) [21] (Laws LJ).

[54] See Kramer (n 33) [15-17]: 'the later event is never literally the "sole cause"'. Nevertheless, Kramer does accept another concept of causation besides 'but-for'.

[55] Bridge, 'Mitigation of Damages' (n 38) 399.

causation . . . would conflict with the common sense judgment which the cases call for in this field'.[56]

There are two possible responses to this tension. The response propounded in *McGregor on Damages*, and which has taken hold more broadly, is that the judges are mistaken. In other words, although judges often express their judgments on mitigation in terms of causation, the real reasons for their decision must be something else. Unfortunately, as I showed in the preceding chapter, there is no agreement on what this 'something else' is. Nevertheless, the structure of the enquiry is clear enough for those who wish to take it up. Causal minimalists argue that the judge's real reasons (although couched in terms of 'causation') depend on questions of legal policy. In particular, their decisions on mitigation are determined by the purpose of the relevant legal rules. The task is then to 'unmask' the legal policies behind the rules of mitigation, such as the promotion of economic efficiency or self-reliance.

A different approach, which I develop in this book, proceeds on the basis that we need to take another look at the concept of causation. The intransigence of the judiciary, who continue to explain mitigation as an aspect of causation despite the prominent objections of legal scholars,[57] is a phenomenon to which we should all pay heed. In my view it is a sensible presumption that the judges, who have been remarkably consistent in their support for the causal explanation of mitigation for over two centuries, are not all mistaken. The task is thus to inquire whether there could be other causal principles (beyond the 'but-for' inquiry) that might explain the specific rules of mitigation. In other words, rather than rejecting the causal explanation out of hand, we must try harder to understand what judges mean when they invoke causation.

4 Beyond 'But-For'

In this section I describe the principles that ordinary people use when making causal attributions outside the law.[58] My account draws heavily on the work of Hart and Honoré in *Causation in the Law*,[59] but further substantiates and refines the principles that they identified, using empirical research from the field of experimental psychology that has emerged subsequently. This research shows that,

[56] *The Fanis* (n 19) 363 (Mance J). See also *Parry v Cleaver* [1970] AC 1 (HL) 33–34, 30 (Lord Pearce).

[57] This is not mere rhetorical flourish: given the significant influence of McGregor's text on so many judicial decisions in mitigation, judges' refusal to abandon the causal explanation is telling.

[58] See further Andrew Summers, 'Common-Sense Causation in the Law' (2018) 38 Oxford Journal of Legal Studies 793.

[59] HLA Hart and Tony Honoré, *Causation in the Law* (1st edn, Clarendon 1959); HLA Hart and Tony Honoré, *Causation in the Law* (2nd edn, Clarendon 1985). All references in this chapter are to the second edition, unless stated otherwise.

outside the law, the principles used by ordinary people making causal attributions extend beyond 'but-for' causation. The principles can be particularized with sufficient precision to give content to the (otherwise nebulous) 'common-sense' concept of causation. This understanding provides the necessary first step to explaining the law of mitigation.

4.1 'Common-sense' causation

Judges often state that the legal concept of causation is a matter of 'common-sense'. Several House of Lords decisions in the mid-twentieth century expressly advocated a 'common-sense' approach to causation.[60] For example, in *Yorkshire Dale Steamship v Minister of War Transport*, Lord Wright held that 'This choice of the real or efficient cause from out of the whole complex of the facts must be made by applying common-sense standards. Causation is to be understood as the man in the street, and not as either the scientist or the metaphysician, would understand it'.[61] These decisions robustly rejected the 'philosophical doctrine of causation' (meaning exclusive reliance on the 'but for' test),[62] preferring instead to rely on causation as reflected in 'ordinary everyday life and thoughts and expressions'.[63]

Judicial reliance on 'common-sense' principles persisted through the late twentieth century and has continued to be invoked in more recent decisions.[64] For example, in *Galoo v Bright Grahame Murray*, Glidewell LJ asked himself, 'How does the court decide whether the breach of duty was the cause of the loss or merely the occasion for the loss?' continuing, 'The answer in the end is "By the application of the court's common sense." '[65] Most recently, in a criminal case Lord Hughes and Lord Toulson expressly approved the approach in *Galoo*, holding that 'In the case law there is a well-recognised distinction between conduct which sets the stage for an occurrence and conduct which on a common sense view is regarded as instrumental in bringing about the occurrence'.[66]

[60] See eg *Leyland Shipping Co Ltd v Norwich Union Fire Insurance Society Ltd* [1918] AC 350 (HL) 363 (Lord Dunedin); *Stapley v Gypsum Mines Ltd* [1953] AC 663 (HL) 781 (Lord Reid); *Hogan v Bentinck West Hartley Collieries* [1949] 1 All ER 588 (HL) 596 (Lord Normand).

[61] *Yorkshire Dale Steamship Co Ltd v Minister of War Transport* [1942] AC 691 (HL) 706.

[62] ibid 702 (Lord Macmillan). See also *Grant v Sun Shipping Co Ltd* [1948] AC 549 (HL) 564 (Lord Du Parcq), rejecting 'the language of logicians'; *Weld-Blundell* (n 20) 986 (Lord Sumner), rejecting 'scientific inquests'; *Monarch Steamship Co Ltd v Karlshamns Oljefabriker* [1949] AC 196 (HL) 228 (Lord Wright), rejecting 'philosophic speculation'; *Stapley* (n 60) 681 (Lord Reid), rejecting 'logical or scientific theory'.

[63] *Monarch* (n 62) 228 (Lord Wright). See also *Hogan* (n 60) 595 (Lord Normand), referring to 'ordinary practical affairs'.

[64] See eg *Alphacell Ltd v Woodward* [1972] AC 824 (HL) 834 (Lord Wilberforce), 837 (Lord Salmon); *County* (n 15) 858 (Hobhouse LJ); *Smith New Court Securities Ltd v Citibank NA* [1997] AC 254 (HL) 285 (Lord Steyn).

[65] *Galoo Ltd v Bright Grahame Murray* [1994] 1 WLR 1360 (CA) 1374–75.

[66] *R v Hughes* [2013] UKSC 56, [2013] 1 WLR 2461 [23].

The problem with all of these decisions, rightly seized upon by legal scholars of the causal minimalist school, is that the invocation of 'common-sense' formed both the beginning and the end of the judges' reasoning. Burrows fairly criticizes that 'unarticulated common sense or instinct is hardly a satisfactory basis for legal decision-making'.[67] Lord Hoffmann's conclusion was more damning: '[T]he opposition between common sense and abstract theory is a rhetorical device to divert attention from the absence of reasoning in the judgment.'[68] Unfortunately, resort to causal metaphors or Latin labels is no more enlightening. On this issue McGregor was correct: 'These familiar terms are in many ways more of a hindrance than a help because their very familiarity has blunted any precision of meaning they may have once had.'[69]

4.2 Hart and Honoré's theory

Causation in the Law developed a theory of 'common-sense' causation. However, unlike the nebulous judicial references to common-sense, for Hart and Honoré this notion marked the beginning but *not* the end of their enquiry. The first main aim of *Causation in the Law* was to clarify and particularize the common-sense concept of causation.[70] The technique that Hart and Honoré adopted for this purpose was an analysis of causation in ordinary language.[71] Based on this analysis, they concluded that 'common sense is not a matter of inexplicable or arbitrary assertions, and the causal notions which it employs, though flexible and complex and subtly influenced by context, can be shown to rest, at least in part, on statable principles'.[72]

The second main aim of *Causation in the Law* was to show that 'it is the plain man's notions of causation (and not the philosopher's or the scientist's) with which the law is concerned'.[73] In other words, Hart and Honoré claimed that the ordinary causal principles that they had identified *also* explained judges' causal reasoning in legal decisions.[74] The scope of this claim ranged across criminal law

[67] Burrows (n 36) 107.

[68] Lord Hoffmann, 'Common Sense and Causing Loss' (Chancery Bar Association Lecture, 15 June 1999) 2. See also *Six Continents* (n 45) [18] (Laws LJ).

[69] Edelman (n 1) ch 8. See also *Weld-Blundell* (n 20) 984 (Lord Sumner); *County* (n 15) 846 (Beldam LJ); *Environment Agency v Empress Car Co (Abertillery) Ltd* [1999] 2 AC 22 (HL) 29 (Lord Hoffmann).

[70] They argued that others' abandonment of this aim was 'a counsel of despair which we should hesitate to accept': Hart and Honoré (n 59) 26.

[71] See further text to n 152.

[72] Hart and Honoré (n 59) 26.

[73] ibid 1.

[74] They emphasized that this was a descriptive not evaluative claim: ibid 1–2: 'It may, of course, well be that when we thoroughly understand the common-sense notions of causation we should no longer wish our thought on any matters, let alone legal judgments of responsibility, to be dominated by them.' See also xxxiv.

and most of private law.[75] It presented a challenge to the causal minimalist view, because it rejected the conclusion that all causal references beyond but-for were merely a disguise for arbitrary decision or legal policy.[76] Hart and Honoré thought that this view was 'a blinding error'.[77] My aim in this book is not to endorse the claims of *Causation in the Law* as they pertain to all of private law,[78] but more narrowly to argue that Hart and Honoré were essentially correct as regards the law of mitigation.[79]

4.2.1 The 'central notion' of cause

Hart and Honoré's key insight into ordinary causal principles was that the 'central notion'[80] of cause is 'essentially something which interferes with or intervenes in the course of events which would normally take place'.[81] In other words, the cause is selected because it is 'a departure from the normal, ordinary, or reasonably expected course of events'.[82] More specifically, Hart and Honoré identified two key causal principles:[83] first, 'the contrast between what is abnormal and normal in relation to any given thing or subject-matter' (the 'abnormality principle');[84] and second, the contrast 'between a free deliberate human action and all other conditions' (the 'choice principle').[85] To illustrate these two principles, they gave the following example concerning the outbreak of a fire:

> In most cases where a fire has broken out . . . the plain man would refuse to say that the cause of the fire was the presence of oxygen, though no fire would have occurred without it: [he] would reserve the title of cause for something of the order of a short-circuit, the dropping of a lighted cigarette, or lightning.[86]

Here, the short-circuit and lightning strike both reflect the abnormality principle, and the dropped cigarette reflects the choice principle. It should be noted that in this example, the purpose of the causal enquiry could be either explanatory or attributive.[87] Causal *explanations* respond to the initial puzzle of why something

[75] ibid especially ch 6 (Tort), ch 11 (Contract), and ch 12 (Crime).
[76] ibid xxxv, 3–5, 88–108. They did accept that there was some role for legal policy questions; it was merely smaller than the causal minimalists supposed: ibid 304–07.
[77] ibid 3. See also 26.
[78] For implications beyond the law of mitigation, see Conclusion.
[79] However, Hart and Honoré themselves said very little about the law of mitigation specifically.
[80] See generally Hart and Honoré (n 59) 28–44. This book does not address other notions relating to 'interpersonal transactions' (see further 51–59) or 'opportunities' (see further 59–60).
[81] ibid 29. See also Tony Honoré, *Responsibility and Fault* (Hart 1999) 6.
[82] Hart and Honoré (n 59) 33.
[83] These principles may overlap because voluntary conduct can sometimes also qualify as the cause by virtue of its abnormality: see further ibid 41, 136, 182–85, 335–36.
[84] ibid 33.
[85] ibid 33.
[86] ibid 11.
[87] Although this example initially features in the discussion of explanations, the same example is repeated in relation to attributions: see ibid 71–74.

happened; they call for further facts before the cause can be identified.[88] By contrast, causal attributions arise after all of the facts are known; the problem is solely one of selecting 'the cause' from amongst the range of 'mere conditions' (such as the oxygen in the air).[89] Hart and Honoré pointed out that lawyers are usually concerned with causal attributions rather than explanations,[90] although they argued that both types of enquiry rely on the same causal principles.[91]

4.2.2 Abnormality principle

In relation to the abnormality principle, Hart and Honoré identified that 'what is abnormal . . . is what "makes the difference" between the accident and things going on as usual'.[92] They emphasized that 'what is normal and what is abnormal is, however, relative to the context of any given inquiry'.[93] To illustrate this point, they gave the example of a fire breaking out in a laboratory where special precautions were normally taken to exclude oxygen; here, one might well say that the presence of oxygen *was* the cause of the fire.[94] Hart and Honoré also emphasized that normality 'is very often an artefact of human habit, custom, or convention'.[95] In other words, what is abnormal may depend on social as well as physical factors. The cause need not be an 'event', in that it might equally consist of a negative or static condition. For example, 'the lack of rain was the cause of the failure of the corn crop; the icy condition of the road was the cause of the accident'.[96]

4.2.3 Choice principle

In relation to the choice principle, Hart and Honoré identified that 'a voluntary human action intended to bring about what in fact happens . . . has a special place in causal inquiries'.[97] In particular, 'the free deliberate and informed act or omission of a human being, intended to exploit the situation created by [an earlier event], negatives causal connection'.[98] Importantly, such action could be regarded as the cause even though it was 'both natural and probable';[99] the choice principle was accordingly distinct from the abnormality principle. Hart and Honoré rejected any causal distinction between actions and omissions.[100] For example, 'someone's

[88] ibid 23–24. See further 32–51.
[89] ibid 24. See further ch 3.
[90] ibid 24. See further text following n 163.
[91] ibid ch 3, especially 68–70, 73.
[92] ibid 35.
[93] ibid 35.
[94] ibid 35.
[95] ibid 37.
[96] ibid 31.
[97] ibid 42.
[98] ibid 136.
[99] ibid 158.
[100] ibid 139. See also Honoré, *Responsibility and Fault* (n 81) 12.

failure to wrap up is commonly and intelligibly taken to be the cause of his catching cold, and driving in the dark without lights to be the cause of an accident'.[101]

Hart and Honoré identified that human conduct only had special causal significance where it was 'free deliberate and informed'.[102] In order to count as 'free', the actor must have been able to make a '*fair* choice':

> When . . . the actor exercises a choice, his act is in one sense free, but if the choice is made under pressure from a prior wrongful act, or is not a fair choice because the alternative is serious harm, or may be said not to be a 'real' choice because the alternative is neglecting a duty, the decision to avoid the pressure, harm, or breach of duty is not treated as free either in ordinary life or in the law.[103]

It is important to note that this claim concerned the concept of choice as it was used outside the law, and not whether it would be fair to impose legal liability in such circumstances. Hart and Honoré particularized their intuitions by suggesting that choices made under pressure,[104] or constrained by legal or moral obligations,[105] would not be regarded as sufficiently free. They recognized that these considerations may 'involve a comparison of the importance of the respective interests sacrificed and preserved',[106] and admitted that in these circumstances 'the concept of a fully voluntary action incorporates judgments of value'.[107] However, this did not mean that the choice principle collapsed into a question of *legal* policy; this weighing of interests was common to ordinary causal attributions outside the law.

Hart and Honoré changed their mind over what it meant for conduct to be 'deliberate and informed'. In the first edition of *Causation in the Law*, they concluded that the relevant act would need to be 'intended to produce the consequence which is in fact produced'.[108] However, in the second edition they recanted that 'This was a mistake. It is clear that the intervening act can be voluntary in the full sense though it is not intended to produce the harm that in fact ensues.'[109] Instead, they concluded that the actor need only 'intend to exploit the situation created', or in other words 'treat it as providing the opportunity or occasion for a certain course of conduct'.[110] The conduct also needed to be 'informed', because the actor could not have intended to exploit the situation where he was 'ignorant of some

[101] Hart and Honoré (n 59) 50.
[102] ibid 136.
[103] ibid 142. See also 41, 77, 138, 146, 156.
[104] ibid 41. See also 149: 'an act done under the influence of panic or extreme fear will not negative causal connection unless the reaction is wholly abnormal'.
[105] ibid 41, 142.
[106] ibid 77.
[107] ibid 157.
[108] This extract from the first edition is quoted in the second edition at ibid 137 fn 23.
[109] ibid 137 fn 23.
[110] ibid 137 fn 23.

relevant circumstance'.[111] Beyond this, Hart and Honoré noted merely that the level of information required was 'a matter of degree'.[112]

4.3 Experimental support

Hart and Honoré's claims about ordinary causal principles were empirical claims.[113] However, they were based on Hart and Honoré's own observations about ordinary language, and some critics doubted whether the language used by two highly-skilled lawyers was really 'ordinary'.[114] Several legal scholars rejected Hart and Honoré's work as empirically unfounded.[115] At the time when *Causation in the Law* was first published in 1959, and even by the time of the second edition in 1985, there had been hardly any relevant experimental research into causal reasoning.[116] This branch of the cognitive sciences was then a nascent discipline. However, starting with two influential papers by Kahneman (with others),[117] there has since developed a huge body of scientific research into how ordinary people make causal judgements. This research can now retrospectively be used to evaluate Hart and Honoré's empirical claims.

The experimental research robustly supports Hart and Honoré's key insights. In particular, this research substantiates their two main principles regarding the causal significance of abnormal events and voluntary human conduct. It also usefully refines certain aspects of these principles that were left open by Hart and Honoré; for example, there has now been extensive research into the types of norm relevant to the abnormality principle. Some gaps in the experimental research remain, especially concerning the precise scope of the choice principle; however, this remains a rapidly developing field. More broadly, this line of research aims to explore the deep interrelationship between causal judgements, counterfactual thinking, and attributions of responsibility in ordinary people. The literature is vast, and cannot be evaluated here,[118] but here I summarize the major findings.

[111] ibid 149. See also, on the causal responsibility of children: 153–54.

[112] ibid 142.

[113] ibid 27: 'as with every other empirical notion we can hope only to find a core of relatively well-settled common usage'. See also Sally Lloyd-Bostock, 'The Ordinary Man and the Psychology of Attributing Causes and Responsibility' (1979) 42 Modern Law Review 143, 167.

[114] Peter Cane, *Responsibility in Law and Morality* (Hart 2002) 129. This criticism slightly mischaracterizes Hart and Honoré's aim, which was to describe ordinary usage rather than their own.

[115] See further text to n 158.

[116] See Lloyd-Bostock (n 113), although this focuses on Hart and Honoré's methodology rather than their specific claims. See further Harold Kelly, 'The Processes of Causal Attribution' [1973] American Psychologist 107, for an overview, although very few of these studies are relevant to Hart and Honoré's concern with selection.

[117] Daniel Kahneman and Amos Tversky, 'The Simulation Heuristic' in Daniel Kahneman, Paul Slovic, and Amos Tversky (eds), *Judgment Under Uncertainty: Heuristics and Biases* (CUP 1982); Daniel Kahneman and Dale Miller, 'Norm Theory: Comparing Reality to Its Alternatives' (1986) 93 Psychological Review 136.

[118] In relation to some possible empirical objections, see further text to n 152.

4.3.1 Abnormality principle

Psychologists Daniel Kahneman and Dale Miller coined the term 'norm theory' to describe the hypothesis that 'an event is more likely to be undone by altering exceptional than routine aspects of the causal chain that led to it'.[119] This insight followed from an earlier experiment in which participants were presented with a story where the subject 'did not drive home by his regular route' or 'left the office earlier than usual'.[120] Numerous studies have confirmed that people are more likely to attribute causal significance to descriptively abnormal events than to normal events, holding other factors constant.[121] This research convincingly supports the conclusions that Hart and Honoré drew (intuitively) from their famous example concerning the outbreak of a fire, in which the lightning strike was descriptively abnormal, whereas the oxygen in the air was not.

The experimental research goes much further than Hart and Honoré's theory in seeking to clarify the types of norms that are relevant to the abnormality principle. For example, experimental psychologists have shown that common-sense causal reasoning is affected by both descriptive and prescriptive abnormality. Whereas descriptive (or 'statistical') norms concern what usually happens, prescriptive norms concern what should happen.[122] It is possible to violate a prescriptive norm without departing from any descriptive norm, or in other words, whilst acting statistically normally. For example, downloading pirated music violates legal norms relating to copyright and moral norms relating to theft, even if most people do it.[123] To test the effect of prescriptive abnormality on causal selection, Joshua Knobe and Ben Fraser devised an experiment in which participants were presented with the following 'pen vignette':[124]

[119] Kahneman and Miller (n 117) 143.

[120] Kahneman and Tversky (n 117).

[121] Denis Hilton and Ben Slugoski, 'Knowledge-Based Causal Attribution: The Abnormal Conditions Focus Model' (1986) 93 Psychological Review 75; Jonathan Kominsky and others, 'Causal Superseding' (2015) 137 Cognition 196, 199–200, 205; Tobias Gerstenberg and Thomas Icard, 'Expectations Affect Physical Causation Judgments' (2020) 149 Journal of Experimental Psychology 599–607, 604

[122] Joseph Halpern and Christopher Hitchcock, 'Graded Causation and Defaults' (2015) 66 British Journal for the Philosophy of Science 413, 429–30.

[123] In addition to legal or moral norms, Halpern and Hitchcock also identify 'norms of proper functioning'. For example, 'there are specific ways that human hearts and car engines are "supposed" to work . . . a car engine that does not work properly is not guilty of a moral wrong, but there is nonetheless a sense in which it fails to live up to a certain kind of standard': n 122, 429–30. See also Christopher Hitchcock and Joshua Knobe, 'Cause and Norm' (2009) 106 Journal of Philosophy 587, 597. There may also be instances of 'institutional' prescriptive norms that do not have any legal or moral force: for example, 'gentlemen must wear a jacket and tie in the House of Commons'.

[124] Joshua Knobe and Ben Fraser, 'Causal Judgment and Moral Judgment: Two Experiments' in Walter Sinnott-Armstrong (ed), *Moral Psychology, Volume 2: The Cognitive Science of Morality* (MIT Press 2008) 443. See further Julia Driver, 'Attributions of Causation and Moral Responsibility' in Walter Sinnott-Armstrong (ed), *Moral Psychology, Volume 2: The Cognitive Science of Morality* (MIT Press 2008).

> The receptionist in the philosophy department keeps her desk stocked with pens. The administrative assistants are allowed to take the pens, but faculty members are supposed to buy their own. The administrative assistants typically do take the pens. Unfortunately, so do the faculty members. The receptionist has repeatedly e-mailed them reminders that only administrative assistants are allowed to take the pens. On Monday morning, one of the administrative assistants encounters Professor Smith walking past the receptionist's desk. Both take pens. Later that day, the receptionist needs to take an important message . . . but she has a problem. There are no pens left on her desk.[125]

Here, the conduct of both protagonists is descriptively normal (they both usually take pens), but only Professor Smith's conduct violates a prescriptive norm (to refrain from taking pens). Participants tended to agree strongly with the statement that Professor Smith caused the problem but disagreed that the administrative assistant caused the problem.[126] The finding that prescriptive (including moral) norm violations affect causal selection even in the absence of descriptive abnormality has been replicated in numerous other studies.[127]

There remains a debate amongst cognitive scientists about the mechanism by which prescriptive norm violations affect ordinary causal attributions. One argument is that they affect causal attributions directly because they are abnormal.[128] Another argument is that on some occasions they affect causal attributions indirectly because they induce judgements of blame against the norm violator.[129] However, proponents of 'blame theory' still accept that 'norm violations rule the

[125] Knobe and Fraser (n 124).

[126] ibid 443, fn 3: 'Each subject rated both statements on a scale ranging from −3 ("not at all") to þ3 ("fully"), with the 0 point marked "somewhat." The mean rating for the statement that the professor caused the problem was 2.2; the mean for the statement that the assistant caused the problem was 1⁄4 1.2. This difference is statistically significant, t(17) 1⁄4 5.5, p 5 .001.'

[127] Craig Roxborough and Jill Cumby, 'Folk Psychological Concepts: Causation ' (2009) 22 Philosophical Psychology 205; Jonathan Phillips, Jamie Luguri, and Joshua Knobe, 'Unifying Morality's Influence on Non-Moral Judgments: The Relevance of Alternative Possibilities' (2015) 145 Cognition 30; Kominsky and others, 'Causal Superseding' (n 121); Thomas Icard, Jonathan Kominsky, and Joshua Knobe, 'Normality and Actual Causal Strength' (2017) 161 Cognition 80; Hitchcock and Knobe, 'Cause and Norm' (n 123) 605; Jonathan Phillips and Jonathan Kominksy, 'Causation and Norms of Proper Functioning: Counterfactuals are (Still) Relevant' (Proceedings of the 39th Annual Conference of the Cognitive Science Society, 2017); Jonathan Kominsky and Jonathan Phillips, 'Immoral Professors and Malfunctioning Tools: Counterfactual Relevance Accounts Explain the Effect of Norm Violations on Causal Selection' (2019) 43 Cognitive Science.

[128] Driver, 'Attributions of Causation' (n 124) 430–31; Julia Driver, 'Kinds of Norms and Legal Causation: Reply to Knobe and Fraser and Deigh' in W Sinnott-Armstrong (ed), *Moral Psychology, Vol. 2. The Cognitive Science of Morality: Intuition and Diversity* (Boston Review 2008) 459–61; Hitchcock and Knobe, 'Cause and Norm' (n 123) 603–05; Kominsky and others, 'Causal Superseding' (n 121) 206; Kominsky and Phillips, 'Immoral Professors' (n 127) 32.

[129] Mark Alicke, 'Culpable Causation' (1992) 63 Journal of Personality and Social Psychology 368; Mark Alicke, David Rose, and Dori Bloom, 'Causation, Norm Violation and Culpable Control' (2011) 108 Journal of Philosophy 670: see especially 673, 689, 693; Samland and Waldmann, 'How Prescriptive Norms Influence Causal Inferences' (2016) 156 Cognition 164–76. This argument was foreshadowed in Hart and Honoré (n 59) 37–38.

causal roost for benign events that lack nefarious motives, undesirable or reckless actions, or harmful outcomes.'[130] This concession leaves the abnormality principle unchallenged in relation to blameless departures from norms.

In relation to descriptive norms of behaviour, Sytsma, Livengood, and Rose distinguished between 'population-level norms' (how a given population normally behaves) and 'agent-level norms' (how the relevant individual normally behaves).[131] Their experiments appeared to suggest that participants had a greater sensitivity to agent-level rather than population-level norms;[132] or in other words, to behaviour that was abnormal for the individual rather than for the wider population. An (untested) example given by Kahneman and Miller also appears to rely on an agent-level norm: they hypothesized that 'an observer who knows Marty's affection for his aunt and his propensity for emotional displays may be surprised if Marty does not cry at her funeral—even if Marty rarely cries and if no one else cries at that funeral.'[133]

4.3.2 Choice principle

Experimental research into the choice principle developed directly to test Hart and Honoré's theory. This research is less extensive than in relation to abnormality, but experiments have so far been conducted to test between human conduct and natural events; voluntary and involuntary conduct; intended and unintended consequences; and actions and omissions. The findings clearly substantiate Hart and Honoré's key claim that voluntary human conduct has a special place in causal enquiries. However, experimental attempts to specify the scope of voluntariness and the significance of intention have not yet established clear conclusions. This uncertainty does not challenge the importance of choice in causal attributions, but it does mean that the ordinary concept of choice outside the law remains difficult to pin down.

McClure, Hilton, and Sutton sought directly to test Hart and Honoré's claim that people prefer voluntary human conduct over natural events as explanations for why an outcome occurred.[134] They adopted Hart and Honoré's forest fire example as their prototype for a series of experiments that compared human and natural interventions.[135] The results showed that a person fanning the flames was regarded as more causally significant than the wind fanning the flames; similarly,

[130] Alicke, Rose, and Bloom, 'Culpable Control' (n 129) 673. See also 689.

[131] Justin Sytsma, Jonathan Livengood, and David Rose, 'Two Types of Typicality: Rethinking the Role of Statistical Typicality in Ordinary Causal Attributions' (2010) 43 Studies in History and Philosophy of Biological and Biomedical Sciences 814.

[132] ibid 817–18.

[133] Kahneman and Miller (n 117) 136.

[134] John McClure, Denis Hilton, and Robbie Sutton, 'Judgments of Voluntary and Physical Causes in Causal Chains: Probabilistic and Social Functionalist Criteria for Attributions' (2007) 37 European Journal of Social Psychology 879.

[135] ibid 883.

a person igniting the flames was seen as more causally significant than lightning igniting the flames.[136] Overall, the authors concluded that 'we find clear support for the prediction that voluntary causes are preferred to physical ones, despite the fact that both kinds of cause produce the target effect with the same probability'.[137] Other studies have replicated these findings.[138]

The results of experimental research into particular aspects of the choice principle are patchier and less developed than in relation to the abnormality principle. Various studies have shown that voluntary conduct is regarded as more causally significant than accidental (or 'involuntary') conduct.[139] The proposition that voluntary conduct must be informed derives some indirect support from a study showing that causal significance is diminished where the actor lacks mental capacity.[140] On the significance of intention as to consequences, a study by Hilton, McClure, and Sutton contradicts the view that Hart and Honoré's expressed in their first edition, that intention as to consequences is required.[141] However, there is support for their revised position that an intervening act *can* be treated as voluntary even where it was not intended to produce the harm that in fact ensued, provided that the conduct was informed.[142]

Finally, various studies show no clear distinction between the causal significance of acts and omissions.[143] In a recent study, Gerstenberg and Stephan have

[136] ibid 896.

[137] ibid 888.

[138] See eg Denis Hilton, John McClure, and Ben Slugoski, 'The Course of Events: Counterfactuals, Causal Sequences, and Explanation' in David Mandel, Denis Hitlon, and Patrizia Catellani (eds), *The Psychology of Counterfactual Thinking* (Routledge 2005) 52–55; David Lagnado and Shelley Channon, 'Judgments of Cause and Blame: The Effects of Intentionality and Foreseeability' (2008) 108 Cognition 754, 760–63; Denis Hilton, John McClure, and Robbie Sutton, 'Selecting Explanations from Causal Chains: Do Statistical Principles Explain Preferences for Voluntary Causes' (2010) 40 European Journal of Social Psychology 383.

[139] See eg Frank Fincham and Thomas Shultz, 'Intervening Causation and the Mitigation of Responsibility for Harm' (1981) 20 British Journal of Social Psychology 113, 118. See also Kominsky and others, 'Causal Superseding' (n 121) 197; Tania Lombrozo, 'Causal-Explanatory Pluralism: How Intentions, Functions, and Mechanisms Influence Causal Ascriptions' (2010) 61 Cognitive Psychology 303.

[140] Frank Fincham and Caton Roberts, 'Intervening Causation and the Mitigation of Responsibility for Harm Doing II: The Role of Limited Mental Capacities' (1985) 21 Journal of Experimental Social Psychology 178.

[141] Hilton, McClure, and Sutton, 'Selecting Explanations from Causal Chains: Do Statistical Principles Explain Preferences for Voluntary Causes' (n 138) 395.

[142] Lagnado and Channon (n 138) 760–63; Hilton, McClure, and Moir, 'Acting Knowingly: Effects of the Agent's Awareness of an Opportunity on Causal Attributions' (2016) 22 Thinking & Reasoning 461–94, 488. For further discussion of Hart and Honore's equivocation between their first and second editions, see further text to n 108.

[143] See eg CG Davis and DR Lehman, 'Counterfactual Thinking and Coping with Traumatic Life Events' in Neal Roese and James Olson (eds), *What Might Have Been: The Social Psychology of Counterfactual Thinking* (Psychology Press 1995); Randolph Clarke and others, 'Causation, Norms, and Omissions: A Study of Causal Judgments' (2015) 28 Philosophical Psychology 279, 290–2; Paul Henne and others, 'Cause by Omission and Norm: Not Watering Plants' (2017) 95 Australasian Journal of Philosophy 270, 278–9; Tobias Gerstenberg and Simon Stephan, 'A Counterfactual Simulation Model of Causation by Omission' (2021) 216 Cognition 14.

shown that omissions (or non-events) *can* be selected as causes, and that the process of selection is the same as the one which is engaged when active events are selected as causes. In both instances, 'expectations modulate what counterfactuals people consider'.[144] Thus, while abnormal events are *subtracted* from the counterfactual simulation and if that subtraction makes a difference to the outcome causal significance is attributed to the event, abnormally absent events are *added* to the counterfactual simulation and if that addition makes a difference to the outcome causal significance is attributed to the omitted event. This finding supports Hart and Honoré's prediction.

5 Pre-empting objections

Hart and Honoré's work on causation has faced criticism from several perspectives.[145] My aim is not to defend their work in its entirety, but instead to focus on three possible objections that might be thought to detract from the explanation of mitigation as an aspect of (common-sense) causation. These objections are broadly: philosophical; empirical; and semantic. In relation to all three objections (but especially the third) it is important to bear in mind that far less turns on the *language* of 'causation' than one might initially assume. Instead, the key debate is about the *cognitive principles* used by ordinary people (whatever labels may be attached to them). In particular, we want to know whether the principles that underlie judicial reasoning are specifically legal and raise only issues of legal policy, or whether they instead mirror the 'non-legal' cognitive principles that ordinary people rely upon outside the law.

5.1 Philosophical

Some causal minimalist objections to *Causation in the Law* appear to rest implicitly on the philosophical school of causal realism.[146] This school holds that causation describes bonds existing in external reality, separate from how people understand or express them.[147] As Menzies has summarized, 'though [causal realist] theories differ in detail, they all subscribe to the doctrine that causal relations depend completely on a substructure of mind-independent relations'.[148] In other words, one

[144] Gerstenberg and Stephan (n 143) 14.

[145] See eg Jane Stapleton, 'Law, Causation and Common Sense' (1988) 8 Oxford Journal of Legal Studies 111; John Mackie, *The Cement of the Universe: A Study of Causation* (OUP 1974) ch 5.

[146] See eg Richard Wright, 'Causation in Tort Law' (1985) 73 California Law Review 1735, 1746–47.

[147] See eg Mackie (n 145); Lewis (n 48). cf Hume, who insisted that causation is a psychological construct or 'feeling' rather than an external reality: Hume, *A Treatise of Human Nature* Part III, ch 14.

[148] Peter Menzies, 'Causation in Context' in Huw Price and Richard Corry (eds), *Causation, Physics, and the Constitution of Reality* (OUP 2007) 191–223.

cannot determine what causation *is* from what ordinary people *think* it is. If this philosophical concept of causation is correct, so the argument goes, then whatever it was that Hart and Honoré divined from 'common-sense' and ordinary language, was not causation.

My response to this objection is that Hart and Honoré were not, necessarily, seeking to explicate the philosophical concept of causation addressed by the likes of Lewis and Mackie.[149] They were instead interested in how ordinary people and judges used the concepts that these groups respectively *thought of* as causation.[150] In other words, what mattered was how these groups reasoned (and in particular whether they reasoned in similar ways) rather than whether it was philosophically correct to refer to their reasoning as 'causal'. Confusion may have arisen from the idea that Hart and Honoré were influenced by ordinary language *philosophers*.[151] But although Hart and Honoré may also have endorsed the further claim that the common-sense account of causation was the correct philosophical account of causation, this was not their primary target in *Causation in the Law*.

5.2 Empirical

Causation in the Law aimed to provide a 'delineation of the causal concepts which pervade ordinary thought'.[152] As Lloyd-Bostock clarifies, this involves 'questions of empirical fact about how people perceive causality'.[153] Importantly, Hart and Honoré's analysis of ordinary language was not an end in itself, but rather the tool that they chose to shed light on how people *think* about causal concepts. As Gardner puts it, 'Words play a supporting, mainly illustrative, role'.[154] Likewise, cognitive science now aims to describe ordinary people's thoughts about causal questions, and in order to achieve this, 'the usual approach is to look at how people apply the English word "cause"'.[155] But unlike *Causation in the Law*, modern empirical research benefits from experimental methods, a larger sample size,[156] and an improved awareness of the pitfalls of conversational pragmatics.[157]

[149] Note 147.

[150] Hart and Honoré (n 59) 1: 'it is the plain man's notions of causation (and not the philosopher's or the scientist's) with which the law is concerned'.

[151] For example, Wittgenstein, Austin, and Ryle: see further Lynd Forguson, 'Oxford and the "Epidemic" of Ordinary Language Philosophy' (2001) 84 The Monist 325. Hart and Honoré probably also invited confusion about their aims by starting their book with a review of philosophical theories: see Hart and Honoré (n 59) ch 1.

[152] Hart and Honoré (n 59) 2. See also 27: 'A conceptual investigation is served by the delineation of the main trends of usage, not by the compilation of a dictionary.'

[153] Lloyd-Bostock (n 113) 144–45. Whether what people perceive is the *philosophical* concept of causation, is another question: see text to n 147.

[154] John Gardner, 'A Life of HLA Hart: The Nightmare and the Noble Dream (Publication Review)' (2005) 121 Law Quarterly Review 329, 331.

[155] Knobe and Fraser (n 124) 444.

[156] In other words: not just Hart and Honoré themselves.

[157] See further text to n 161.

Against this background, empirical objections have been raised on two levels. The first level is to claim that what Hart and Honoré described as usage in ordinary language was really their own idiosyncratic (or even 'legalistic') use of language. Stapleton maintains that Hart and Honoré's linguistic analysis was 'merely an artefact derived from how lawyers used causal words, which they asserted was the same way that ordinary people used them'.[158] She adds that '[P]atterns of usage were merely asserted and illustrated. Yet counterexamples abound.'[159] Cane similarly criticizes that 'Hart and Honoré established the "ordinary usage of causal language" by assertion rather than evidence'.[160] Very little survives of this objection. There now is a vast body of experimental evidence on the use of causation in ordinary language, and it robustly substantiates Hart and Honoré's key insights.

The second (trickier) level of objection concerns the relationship between people's use of causal language and their thoughts about causal questions. There are difficulties with capturing thoughts through words, some of which are intractable even with careful experiment design. Lloyd-Bostock's review of Hart and Honoré's methodology gives a useful summary of the pitfalls of linguistic analysis.[161] It is fair to say that *Causation in the Law* lacked a detailed appreciation of these pitfalls. However, experimental psychologists are certainly now aware of them.[162] In particular, Hilton highlights the risk that suppositions about the purpose of the question can affect participants' causal attributions.[163] I do not seek to evaluate such concerns here, but I merely noted that within the scientific field of experimental psychology, research designs are scrutinized with these risks in mind.

5.3 Semantic

Another possible objection concerns the aptness of (common-sense) causal language in the contexts in which it was employed by Hart and Honoré. Suppose we ask, 'Did Bob cause the fire?' The answer may be uncertain, even if we know all of the relevant facts. For example, suppose Bob lit the match but Jim knocked it out of his hand. This situation calls for causal attribution. But one might object that ordinary people would not usually ask whether Bob 'caused' the fire in these circumstances; such questions seem unnatural to most non-lawyers. Only lawyers invoke

[158] Stapleton, 'Causation in the Law' (n 51) 756. See also Stapleton, 'Law, Causation and Common Sense' (n 145) 123; Jane Stapleton, 'Choosing What We Mean by "Causation" in the Law' (2008) 73 Missouri Law Review 433, 462.

[159] Stapleton, 'Causation in the Law' (n 51) 758.

[160] Cane, *Responsibility in Law and Morality* (n 114) 129.

[161] See Lloyd-Bostock (n 113).

[162] See eg Knobe and Fraser (n 124) 444, 446; Ari Beller and Tobias Gerstenberg, 'A counterfactual simulation model of causal language' (2023) PsyArXiv preprint.

[163] Denis Hilton, 'Conversational Processes and Causal Explanation' (1990) 107 Psychological Bulletin 65.

causation in an attributive context. One might conclude from this that ordinary people do not engage in attributive causal enquiries, even though they do make explanatory causal enquiries. Indeed, one might suggest that this calls into question the methods deployed by experimental psychologists, because when participants are asked to identify 'the cause' in an attributive context, they are faced with an alien question to which they have no natural answer.

This objection focuses too narrowly on the use of causal language. Although ordinary people (unlike judges) do not often express their attributive enquiries in causal terms, they frequently do make attributions of responsibility. The important issue is not whether the language of causation is invoked, but rather which cognitive principles are in play. More specifically, the issue here is whether ordinary people use the abnormality and choice principles when they make attributions of responsibility. The objection, if sound, would also prove too much. Attributions of responsibility outside the law are plainly affected by whether the conduct was a 'but-for cause' of the outcome, even where the language of causation is absent from the enquiry. The important question, then, is whether other causal principles (beyond but-for) are also in play in these circumstances.

Causal judgements and attributions of responsibility appear to be linked by the phenomenon of counterfactual thinking.[164] Philosophers tend to agree that there is a connection between causation and counterfactuals, although they may disagree about precisely what it is.[165] This view is shared by cognitive scientists.[166] Counterfactuals also play an important role in attributions of responsibility: 'It would not have made a difference anyway' is a popular denial of responsibility. Gerstenberg and Lagnado summarize that 'how responsible for an outcome a person is seen to be depends not only on what the person actually did but also on what would have happened if the person had acted differently'.[167] It may be that the cognitive principles identified by Hart and Honoré are not so much 'causal principles' as principles of 'counterfactual selection',[168] common to both explanatory causal judgements and attributions of responsibility.

[164] See generally Neal Roese, 'Counterfactual Thinking' (1997) 121 Psychological Bulletin 133 (n 141).

[165] Peter Menzies, 'The Role of Counterfactual Dependence in Causal Judgements' in Christoph Hoerl, Teresa McCormack, and Sarah Beck (eds), *Understanding Counterfactuals, Understanding Causation: Issues in Philosophy and Psychology* (OUP 2011) 186. See eg Lewis (n 48); Mackie (n 145).

[166] See eg Kahneman and Tversky (n 117) 202, discussed in Christopher Hitchcock, 'Counterfactual Availability and Causal Judgment' in Christoph Hoerl, Teresa McCormack, and Sarah Beck (eds), *Understanding Counterfactuals, Understanding Causation: Issues in Philosophy and Psychology* (OUP 2011) 172.

[167] Tobias Gerstenberg and David Lagnado, 'Attributing Responsibility: Actual and Counterfactual Worlds' in Joshua Knobe, Tania Lombrozo, and Shaun Nichols (eds), *Oxford Studies in Experimental Philosophy: Volume 1* (OUP 2014) 94. See further citations at 93.

[168] Also sometimes referred to as counterfactual 'availability' or 'mutability': see eg Kahneman and Miller (n 117) 144.

For whatever reason, one might agree that judges use the same cognitive principles as ordinary people when they apply the law of mitigation but disagree that these principles are really 'causal'. They might prefer for example to label them as principles of responsibility. Nothing much turns on this objection. The substantive issue is instead to what extent the principles used by judges are specifically legal. At least some causal minimalists argue that aside from a minimum causal threshold (usually 'but-for'), the attribution of legal responsibility depends solely on questions of legal policy. By contrast, Hart and Honoré argued that legal responsibility depended (at least partly)[169] on the same principles that ordinary people use in attributing responsibility outside the law. They referred to these principles as common-sense 'causal concepts', but the substantive point is that they were not specifically legal.

The key question, then, is whether the principles that explain the law of mitigation are specifically legal principles, or whether they instead reflect principles that are also relied upon by ordinary people when they make (what they consider to be) causal judgements outside the law. Having set out above the best available evidence on how ordinary people make causal judgements and identified the main principles in play, we are now in a position to see whether or not these principles are also reflected in the law of mitigation. The following chapters address this task, starting with an overview in Chapter 6, before turning to more detailed aspects of the rules of mitigation (and related doctrines) in Chapters 7 to 11.

[169] Hart and Honoré did accept that there was some residual role for legal policy questions as well as causal questions: Hart and Honoré (n 59) 304–07.

6
Mitigation as Causation

1 Introduction

We are now in a better position to understand what judges mean when they say that mitigation is an aspect of causation. Rather than dismissing their explanation as a disguise for unstated issues of legal policy, it is necessary to take seriously the idea that the judges' reasoning reflects the causal principles that people use outside the law. This was essentially the motivation behind Hart and Honoré's *Causation in the Law*, albeit that they gave very little attention specifically to the law of mitigation.[1] In Chapter 5, I corroborated and extended Hart and Honoré's theory using experimental research that similarly identifies the principles of choice and abnormality as central to commonsense causal reasoning. The remainder of this book shows how these causal principles also successfully explain the law of mitigation as we currently find it, through a detailed reanalysis of the cases on mitigation and related doctrines.

The present chapter serves to summarize my restatement of the law of mitigation as an aspect of causation. My account consists of two key rules, which I term the 'replication' and 'exceptionality' rules. I argue that these provide a better account of the results and reasoning of the decided cases on mitigation than the orthodox avoidable and avoided loss rules. Additionally, the replication and exceptionality rules subsume three closely related doctrines that have conventionally been labelled as distinct from mitigation: the market rule; intervening acts by the claimant; and betterment. Chapters 8 to 11 show how my account applies to the decided cases on the avoidable loss rule, avoided loss rule, the 'market rule' of damages, and other related doctrines, respectively. The purpose of this chapter is to provide an overview of my new account, which I develop in greater detail in these later chapters.

The chapter is divided into four sections. In Section One, I build on the theoretical framework developed in Chapter 5 to introduce the argument that the law of mitigation is explained by the commonsense principles of choice and abnormality. In Section Two, which makes up the bulk of the chapter, I describe the operation of the replication and exceptionality rules, including their effect on damages. Section Three sketches a justification for the law of mitigation as I have

[1] On the avoidable loss rule, see HLA Hart and Tony Honoré, *Causation in the Law* (2nd edn, Clarendon 1985) 230. On benefits obtained by the claimant's conduct, see ibid 86, 141, 160, and especially 137: 'voluntary conduct negatives causal connection not only with loss but with gain'.

Mitigation in the Law of Damages. Andrew Summers, Oxford University Press. © Andy Summers 2025.
DOI: 10.1093/9780191864032.003.0006

described it. Finally, in Section Four I compare my new account of mitigation with the orthodox account outlined in Chapter 1, to clarify how the replication and exceptionality rules relate to and differ from the conventional avoidable and avoided loss rules.

2 Explaining Mitigation

As I showed in Chapter 5, the causal explanation of mitigation is strongly favoured by judges, but their articulation of causal reasoning has often been vague or incomplete. Legal scholars have mostly resisted this explanation, preferring to search for undisclosed reasons of policy that they suppose must underlie judicial decisions on mitigation.[2] This approach represents the 'counsel of despair' that Hart and Honoré strived against.[3] Instead, I suggest that the reason why judges' causal reasoning has been so vague—and yet so pervasive—is precisely because it reflects a fundamental aspect of human cognition.[4] The task of articulating 'commonsense' causal reasoning is far from straightforward; however, in Chapter 5 I documented recent empirical evidence that choice and abnormality play an important role. Could these two principles provide the key to explaining the law of mitigation?

I argue that they can. In short, the law of mitigation is explained by the following principle: if the claimant makes a *choice* to depart from the *normal* response to breach, it will be held responsible for the consequences of that choice, for better or worse. This allocation of responsibility is achieved as a matter of law by assessing damages *as if* the claimant had undertaken the normal response to breach, even though in fact it did not. The reason why a so-called 'failure to mitigate' is often held by judges to have 'caused' the claimant's avoidable loss, is because it entails voluntary and abnormal conduct by the claimant. The explicit causal reasoning that characterizes many of the cases on mitigation is thus not a disguise for instrumental policies such as the encouragement of self-reliance or economic efficiency, but instead reflects how ordinary people make judgements of causal responsibility outside the law.

In the context of mitigation, there are two aspects to the normal response to breach. First, mitigation reflects a *legal* norm that the claimant will seek to put itself in the same position, as nearly as possible, as if the breach had not occurred. The

[2] For example, a policy of encouraging self-reliance or economic efficiency. See further Chapter 4.

[3] Hart and Honoré (n 1) 26.

[4] See Tony Honoré, *Responsibility and Fault* (Hart 1999) 5: 'ordinary people learn to apply the concept of cause with reasonable accuracy, just as most of us can drive a car or operate a computer without being able to give a convincing account of the way they work'.

compensatory principle prescribes that the defendant is responsible for the cost of replicating this 'no-breach' position.[5] However, a corollary of this principle—instantiated by the doctrine of mitigation—is that the defendant is not responsible for the consequences of the claimant's own choice to seek a different position. This does *not* mean that the claimant is under any legal (or moral) duty to replicate the no-breach position, but rather that the cost of taking such steps provides the legal benchmark (or 'norm') for assessing the extent of the defendant's responsibility for the breach.

Second, mitigation additionally reflects a *descriptive* (or statistical) norm that the claimant will seek to replicate the no-breach position in a usual or unexceptional way. There will often be a variety of ways in which the claimant could have replicated the no-breach position. For example, there may be multiple alternative suppliers and various different terms on which substitute performance could be procured. If the claimant's conduct is within the 'normal' range, then the costs incurred will be borne by the defendant via damages. However, the defendant is not responsible for the consequences of the claimant's own choice to replicate the no-breach position in a way that is unusual or exceptional. In particular, what matters is whether the claimant's conduct was unusual or exceptional given the claimant's own characteristics: in this respect mitigation reflects an agent-level (rather than population-level) statistical norm.[6]

The law of mitigation is therefore best regarded as consisting of two rules: the 'replication rule' and the 'exceptionality rule'. The replication rule applies where the claimant made a choice not to replicate the no-breach position. The exceptionality rule applies where the claimant sought to replicate the no-breach position but chose to do so in an unusual way. The replication and exceptionality rules differ from the orthodox account of the avoided and avoidable loss rules; these two sets of rules do not correspond. Both the replication and exceptionality rules are explained by causal principles; they each involve a choice to depart from the normal course of events. However, in the case of the replication rule the relevant norm is a legal construction, whereas the exceptionality rule reflects a departure from a purely descriptive norm.

Both rules are explained by commonsense causal principles. The requirement of 'choice' found in each rule is explained by the causal significance of voluntary human conduct. This principle is not specifically legal; it mirrors the way in which ordinary people attribute responsibility outside the law. And the content of each rule reflects the causal significance of departures from the normal (i.e., dictated by norms) course of events. However, within the law of mitigation, two different types of norm are relevant: legal and descriptive norms. The content of the legal norm

[5] See eg *Robinson v Harman* 154 ER 363, 365 (Parke B) in contract, and *Livingstone v The Rawyards Coal Company Co* (1879–80) LR 5 App Cas 25 (HL) 39 (Lord Blackburn) in torts.

[6] See further Chapter 5, text to n 131.

(relevant to the replication rule) derives from the benchmark of liability set by the compensatory principle ie the cost of replicating the no-breach position. By contrast, the content of the descriptive norm (relevant to the exceptionality rule) is not specifically legal.

The compensatory principle establishes that the defendant is responsible for the cost of putting the claimant as nearly as possible in the position as if the breach had not occurred. However, the defendant is not responsible for the outcome of the claimant's own choice not to seek this position after the breach. The claimant's own choice not to replicate the no-breach position is the cause of its new position; responsibility for the outcome of this choice (for better or worse) is attributed to the claimant rather than to the defendant. Although the departure is from a legal norm (replication of the no-breach position), its causal significance rests on ordinary causal principles. In particular, the requirement of choice is not specifically legal.

The exceptionality rule applies where the claimant did seek to replicate the no-breach position but chose to do so in an exceptional way. The application of this rule depends on an assessment of what the claimant would (in fact) normally have done in the circumstances. The test is what the individual claimant would normally have done, not what most people (or a 'reasonable person') would normally have done. The test is essentially subjective: it takes into account all of the claimant's own circumstances and characteristics. However, it does not take into account the defendant's potential liability to pay damages; this crucial feature of the exceptionality rule avoids circularity in the attribution of responsibility.[7] The relevant norm is thus the individual claimant's normal course of conduct if it was paying for replication out of its own pocket.

As I argue in Chapter 7, the causal explanation of mitigation resolves several of the puzzles faced by the orthodox account. First, it explains why the rules of mitigation have 'universal' application whenever the court is required to assess loss: this is because causal principles transcend different types of legal liability because they are intrinsic to the attribution of responsibility for outcomes. Second, it explains why the rules only apply once the claimant was aware of the breach: this is because the claimant must have made a *choice* to depart from a legal or descriptive norm in response to breach. Third, it explains to what extent mitigation raises 'questions of fact': both the issue of 'choice' as well as the exceptionality rule, are not specifically legal and so in this respect their application raises questions of fact; however, the replication rule requires careful identification of the obligation breached by the defendant, and to this extent raises a question of law.

[7] Text to n 38.

3 Restating Mitigation

This section gives an overview of the replication and exceptionality rules respectively. To reiterate, these two rules only apply where the claimant made a *choice* to depart from the relevant norm. Where the claimant had no choice, the rules do not apply and so (unless any other rule—such as remoteness or contributory negligence—applies) the claimant will be entitled to recover whatever factual loss it can show that it has suffered, evident at the date of trial.[8] The meaning of 'choice' is outlined separately below.[9] It is also important to note that both the replication and exceptionality rules apply symmetrically to both 'avoidable' and 'avoided' loss; in other words, they apply in the same way to both harms and benefits. The application of the replication and exceptionality rules to the cases on mitigation is discussed in detail in Chapters 8 and 9. For now, the aim is to outline some general features of each of the rules.

3.1 The replication rule

The replication rule applies where the claimant made a choice not to replicate the no-breach position. As outlined above, the compensatory principle prescribes that the defendant is responsible for the cost of replicating (as nearly as possible) the position that the claimant would have been in if the breach had not occurred. However, the defendant is not responsible for the outcome of the claimant's own choice to seek a different position after the breach. The judge must first assess the no-breach position by asking what would have happened if the defendant had not breached its obligation, and then ask whether the claimant made a choice not to take steps that were available to it and that would have replicated (as nearly as possible) that position.

Accordingly, the application of the replication rule involves three main stages. The first stage is to assess the claimant's no-breach position. As a cautionary note, it is worth emphasizing that it is crucial for this purpose to determine precisely the legal obligation that was breached. As Lord Toulson emphasized in *Bunge*, in relation to breach of contract, 'The fundamental compensatory principle makes it axiomatic that any method of assessment of damages must reflect the nature of the bargain which the innocent party has lost'.[10] In relation to torts, Hobhouse LJ has similarly emphasized the need 'accurately to identify the wrong in respect of which the claimant is entitled to recover damages'.[11] Particular care is required in relation

[8] For a definition of 'factual loss', see further Chapter 1, text to n 27.
[9] See text to n 41.
[10] *Bunge SA v Nidera BV* [2015] UKSC 43, [2015] 3 All ER 1082 [85].
[11] *Downs v Chappell* [1997] 1 WLR 426 (CA) 438.

to negligent advice: 'A breach of warranty does not have the same consequences as a failure to advise or warn.'[12]

In order to assess the no-breach position, it is also crucial to ask what would have happened if the defendant had fulfilled the relevant obligation. The only counterfactual element of this enquiry is the assumption that the breach did not occur; in this sense we ask what would 'actually' have happened but-for the breach.[13] In relation to negligent advice (which again raises the most difficulties) there are two main alternatives:[14] if the claimant had been advised carefully, either it would not have entered into the relevant transaction at all (a 'no transaction' case), or it would still have entered into the transaction but, potentially, on different terms (a 'different terms' case).[15] To 'put the claimant in the same position as if the breach had not occurred',[16] it is essential that these alternatives are distinguished and that appropriate factual findings are made by the trial judge.[17]

The second stage is to assess the steps that would 'replicate' the claimant's no-breach position, as nearly as possible. The compensatory principle was historically referred to as 'the principle of *restitutio in integrum*',[18] meaning roughly 'restoration of the whole'.[19] However 'restoration' is not entirely apt here since it implies going back to a state of affairs that existed in the past; instead, 'replication' more appropriately emphasizes that the target of the compensatory principle is a counterfactual rather than historical state of affairs. Much of the confusion surrounding 'mitigation of loss' stems from the tendency to overlook that the legal concept of loss is prescribed by the compensatory principle.[20] In particular, although a claimant may loosely be said to have been 'harmed' if they are worse off than they *were* before the breach occurred (an historical comparison), they have only suffered 'loss'

[12] ibid 438.

[13] The use of the word 'actual' is strained here because the assessment is counterfactual vis-à-vis the breach.

[14] A third possibility is that the claimant would have entered into the same transaction on the same terms, but in these circumstances, it is said that the claimant has simply suffered no loss.

[15] See further Adam Kramer, *The Law of Contract Damages* (3rd edn, Hart 2022) [3-04]–[3-10]. For cases distinguishing between these two no-breach alternatives, see eg *Hayes v James and Charles Dodd* [1990] 2 All ER 815 (CA) 818–19; *Downs v Chappell* (n 11) 440.

[16] As prescribed by the compensatory principle.

[17] Regrettably, this point is not always appreciated: see eg *LSREF III Wight Ltd v Gateley LLP* [2016] EWCA Civ 359, [2016] PNLR 21 [14] (Briggs LJ).

[18] See eg *Owners of the Steamship Gracie v Owners of the Steamship Argentino (The Argentino)* (1888) 13 PD 191 (CA) 196 (Lord Esher MR), 200 (Bowen LJ); *Owners of Dredger Liesbosch v Owners of Steamship Edison (The Liesbosch)* [1933] AC 449 (HL) 459 (Lord Wright); Harry Street, *Principles of the Law of Damages* (Sweet & Maxwell 1962) 3–6. For more recent adoption, see eg *Bunge* (n 10) [76] (Lord Toulson).

[19] Early variants of 'restoration' predate the classic statements of the compensatory principle: see eg *The Woodrop-Sims* (1815) 2 Dods 83, 165 ER 1422, 1423 (Sir William Scott); *The Dundee* (1827) 2 Hag Adm 137, 166 ER 194, 196 (Lord Stowell); *The Gazelle* (1844) 2 Wm Rob 279, 166 ER 759, 760 (Dr Lushington). Cf 'restitution', which has acquired a different meaning relating to gains obtained by the defendant.

[20] See Chapter 1, text to n 25. In short, mitigating 'harm' is not the same as mitigating 'loss' in the legal sense.

in the legal sense to the extent that they are worse off than they *would have been* if the breach had not occurred (a counterfactual comparison).

The steps that would replicate the no-breach position depend on the content of the legal obligation breached in each case, but some common examples can be given. If the defendant fails to deliver goods, the claimant can replicate the no-breach position by buying replacement goods. If the defendant damages the claimant's property, the claimant can replicate the no-breach position by repairing or replacing the property. If the defendant negligently advises the claimant in a 'no transaction' case,[21] then the claimant can replicate the no-breach position by 'extricating' itself from the transaction.[22] Often perfect replication is no longer possible, for example due to the passage of time or inadequacy of money as a substitute for performance.[23] In these circumstances, the compensatory principle provides that the claimant should be replicated 'as nearly as possible' to the no-breach position.[24]

The third stage is to assess whether the claimant chose not to take the steps that would have replicated the no-breach position as nearly as possible. There are several typical circumstances in which the claimant may have no choice. First, where the claimant was unaware of the breach. Second, where the claimant was impecunious and so could not afford to replicate the no-breach position. Third, where the claimant did not have a 'fair choice' because of overbearing conflicting interests; this concept of a fair choice raises some difficulties in application, but the difficulties are not specifically legal. Finally, there are other circumstances where the claimant could not replicate the no-breach position because, for example, there was no available market for substitute performance or the claimant could not access the market. The meaning of 'choice' in this context is discussed in more detail below.[25]

3.2 The exceptionality rule

The exceptionality rule applies where the claimant sought to replicate the no-breach position but chose to do so in an exceptional (ie unusual) way. Within the law of mitigation,[26] there are two main contexts in which the exceptionality of the claimant's conduct may arise. First, where the claimant chose an exceptional mode of replication.[27] For example, in some circumstances it may be exceptional for

[21] Text to n 18.

[22] By contrast, if it is a 'different terms' case, then the claimant may be able to replicate the no-breach position by renegotiating the terms. Here the cost of extrication is not relevant to restoration.

[23] See further Chapter 1, text to n 17.

[24] *Livingstone v Rawyards Coal* (n 5) 39 (Lord Blackburn).

[25] Section 1.2.3.

[26] Where the claimant's exceptional conduct arose other than in the course of restoring the no-breach position, it is generally expressed as an 'intervening act' rather than a 'failure to mitigate'.

[27] If the claimant chooses not to seek any of the available modes of replication, then the replication rule will apply.

the claimant to repair rather than replace; similarly, it may be exceptional for the claimant to resort to the market rather than accepting the defendant's offer of substitute performance. Second, the claimant may act exceptionally where it incurs excessive costs in replicating the no-breach position. For example, the claimant may conduct a repair in an exceptionally inefficient way or pay over-the-odds for replacement performance.

The early cases on mitigation drew an express connection between the concepts of reasonableness and exceptionality. In *The City of Lincoln*, Lindley LJ held that 'the ordinary course of things . . . includes at least the reasonable conduct of those who have sustained the damage'.[28] The classic statements of mitigation in *Dunkirk Colliery* and *British Westinghouse* both linked the reasonableness of the claimant's conduct and the 'ordinary course of business'.[29] In a separate decision, Viscount Haldane held that 'reasonable human conduct is part of the ordinary course of things'.[30] It follows that where the claimant acts 'unreasonably', its conduct is also likely to be exceptional (outside 'the ordinary course of things').[31] However, the test of exceptionality clarifies the application of the orthodox reasonableness test in three important respects.

First, the test of exceptionality is essentially subjective. The test is not what 'most people' or the (objective) 'reasonable person' would have done, but rather what would have been normal for the individual claimant. The relevant norm takes into account the claimant's own circumstances, characteristics, and preferences. For example, in relation to avoidable loss, the courts have taken into account the claimant's bargaining power,[32] inexperience in dealing with the breach,[33] sentimental preferences,[34] and special additional capacity.[35] The principle of symmetry, discussed below,[36] suggests that these characteristics should also be relevant to avoided loss, but curiously they are sometimes ignored. The best explanation of these 'outlying' decisions is a separate principle related to the insurance rule.[37]

[28] *The City of Lincoln* (1889) 15 PD 15 (CA) 18.

[29] See *Dunkirk Colliery Co v Lever* (1878) 9 Ch D 20 (CA) 25 (James LJ); *British Westinghouse Electric & Manufacturing Co Ltd v Underground Electric Railways Co of London Ltd (No 2)* [1912] AC 673 (HL) 689 (Viscount Haldane).

[30] *Baron Vernon v SS Metagama (The Metagama)* (1928) SC (HL) 21 (HL) 25, approved in *McKew v Holland & Cubitts (Scotland) Ltd* [1969] 3 All ER 1621 (HL) 27–28 (Lord Guest). See also *The Oropesa* [1943] P 32 (CA) 39 (Lord Wright).

[31] *McKew* (n 30) 25 (Lord Reid): 'one may say that unreasonable conduct . . . is not the natural and probable result of the original fault'.

[32] *Thai Airways International Public Co Ltd v KI Holdings Co Ltd* [2015] EWHC 1250 (Comm), [2016] 1 All ER (Comm) 675 [176] (Leggatt J); cf *Shearson Lehman Hutton Inc v Maclaine Watson & Co Ltd (No 2)* [1990] 1 Lloyd's Rep 441 (QB) 443 (Webster J).

[33] *The Hendrik* [1964] 1 Lloyd's Rep 371 (PD) 379 (Hewson J): 'I must have in mind their lack of training in damage control and the absence of effective damage control gear on board their vessel.'

[34] *O'Grady v Westminster Scaffolding Ltd* [1962] 2 Lloyd's Rep 238 (QB) 240 (Edmund Davies J).

[35] *Beechwood Birmingham Ltd v Hoyer Group UK Ltd* [2010] EWCA Civ 647, [2011] QB 357 [29] (Sir Mark Potter).

[36] Text to n 79.

[37] See further Chapter 9, Section 4.1.

Second, the test does not take into account the defendant's potential liability to pay damages for the costs of replication. The relevant norm is claimant-focused: it assesses the claimant's normal course of conduct if it was paying for replication out of its own pocket. The claimant will thus act exceptionally if it spends extravagantly in reliance on the defendant's potential liability. If it were otherwise, the attribution of responsibility would be circular: the defendant's responsibility would depend on the normality of the expenditure, but the normality of the expenditure would depend on the defendant's responsibility to pay for it.[38] To cut the circle, it is necessary to ignore the defendant's potential liability when assessing the claimant's normal course of conduct. In mitigation, this approach has been described as the 'prudent uninsured' standard.[39]

Third, the claimant's conduct may be 'exceptional' even though it resulted in a positive outcome. The test applies symmetrically to avoided as well as avoidable loss. In other words, the exceptionality rule also applies where the claimant's exceptional conduct was beneficial, in that it resulted in less harm than if the claimant had acted normally. So, where the claimant chooses to replicate the no-breach position in an exceptional way, the claimant is responsible for the outcome of this departure from the normal course of conduct, for better or worse. The reasonableness test is linguistically ill-suited to the problem of avoided loss because 'unreasonable' is naturally understood as pejorative; it would be odd—even though literally appropriate—to use 'unreasonable' to mean 'better-than-reasonable'.[40]

3.3 The significance of choice

Both the replication and exceptionality rules reflect departures from the normal response to breach.[41] However, the application of both rules further requires that the claimant's departure was voluntary; in other words, the claimant must have made a *choice* to depart from the relevant norm. This is a crucial feature of the law of mitigation.[42] Where for some reason the claimant had no choice but to depart

[38] In full: (1) *the defendant is responsible for the expenditure* because it was normal for the claimant to incur the expenditure; (2) it was normal for the claimant to incur the expenditure *because the defendant is responsible for the expenditure.*

[39] See eg *Owners of the Georgidore v Owners of the Pacific Concord (The Pacific Concord)* [1961] 1 WLR 873 (PD) 881; *The Naxos* [1972] 1 Lloyd's Rep 149 (QB) 154 (Brandon J); *The Ferdinand Retzlaff* [1972] 2 Lloyd's Rep 120 (QB) 123 (Brandon J); *Ateni Maritime Corp v Great Marine Ltd (The Great Marine) (No 2)* [1991] 1 Lloyd's Rep 421 (CA) 424 (Lloyd LJ).

[40] Cf *Baker v TE Hopkins & Son Ltd* [1959] 1 WLR 966 (CA) 976–77 (Morris LJ): 'it was said that Dr Baker had been "unreasonably" brave'. The use of scare quotes (in original) acknowledges that this usage is strained. See also *Mobil North Sea Ltd v PJ Pipe & Valve Co Ltd* [2001] EWCA Civ 741, [2001] 2 All ER (Comm) 289 [30] (Rix LJ).

[41] See further text to n 5.

[42] See eg in relation to avoidable loss, *Downs v Chappell* [1997] 1 WLR 426 (CA) 437 (Hobhouse LJ); in relation to avoided loss *Blue Circle Industries plc v Ministry of Defence* [1999] Ch 289 (CA) 315 (Chadwick LJ), 321 (Simon Brown LJ); and in relation to the market rule *Bunge SA v Nidera BV* [2015] UKSC 43, [2015] 3 All ER 1082 [80] (Lord Toulson).

from the normal response to breach, then the rules of mitigation are not engaged. In these circumstances, unless remoteness or some other rule applies, the claimant will recover damages for its factual loss, which results from a comparison between the claimant's actual position evident at the date of trial, and the position that the claimant would have been in if the breach had not occurred.[43]

The requirement of choice is explained by the causal significance of voluntary human conduct. As Hart and Honoré identified, this 'choice principle' is a feature of causal attributions outside the law; it is not a specifically legal principle. To put it another way, one does not need to be a lawyer to apply the choice principle. In this sense the principle raises a question of fact. In most cases it is obvious one way or the other whether the claimant had a choice. However, at the margins, the application of the choice principle is tricky to articulate. Hart and Honoré specified that the choice must be 'informed', must be a 'fair choice', and must be 'intended to exploit the situation created'.[44] These requirements have been corroborated by subsequent experimental research.[45] They also find reflection in the law of mitigation: the relevant authorities are outlined below.

The impecuniosity rule provides a good illustration of the choice principle. In *Dodd Properties v Canterbury*, Megaw LJ held that '[a] plaintiff who is under a duty to mitigate is not obliged, in order to reduce the damages, to do that which he cannot afford to do'.[46] This approach was affirmed decisively by the House of Lords in *Lagden*,[47] overruling apparently contradictory authority in *The Liesbosch*.[48] The reason why the replication rule does not apply where the claimant was impecunious is because in these circumstances the claimant effectively had no choice to replicate the no-breach position.[49] In *Lagden*, the House of Lords emphasized the connection between impecuniosity and the claimant's (lack of) choice; for the majority, Lord Hope summarized that '[i]t has to be shown that the claimant had a choice'.[50]

In *Lagden*, the House of Lords sought to clarify the meaning of 'choice' in the context of impecuniosity. For the majority, Lord Nicholls admitted that it was difficult to give firm guidance because 'lack of financial means is, almost always,

43 See further Chapter 1, text to n 27.

44 See further text to n 41.

45 See further Chapter 5, Section 4.3.

46 *Dodd Properties (Kent) Ltd v Canterbury City Council* [1980] 1 WLR 433 (CA) 453, affirmed in *Lagden v O'Connor (sub nom Burdis v Livsey)* [2003] UKHL 64, [2004] 1 AC 1067 [51] (Lord Hope). See also *Bacon v Cooper (Metals) Ltd* [1982] 1 All ER 397 (QB); *Alcoa Minerals of Jamaica Inc v Broderick* [2002] 1 AC 371 (PC); *Mattocks v Mann* [1993] RTR 13 (CA); *Martindale v Duncan* [1973] 1 WLR 574 (CA); *Clippens Oil Co Ltd v The Edinburgh and District Water Trustees* [1907] AC 291 (HL).

47 *Lagden* (n 45) [8] (Lord Nicholls), [12] (Lord Slynn), [62] (Lord Hope), [82] (Lord Scott), [102] (Lord Walker).

48 *The Liesbosch* (n 18) 460–61 (Lord Wright).

49 Or it had no choice to replicate the no-breach position in the usual way (the exceptionality rule).

50 *Lagden* (n 45) [34]. The issue here was whether the claimant had made a choice to supersede the no-breach position by obtaining additional non-compensable benefits; this is often referred to as 'betterment'.

a question of priorities'.[51] In a dissenting judgment, Lord Scott attempted a very broad definition of choice, arguing that 'it is very rare indeed for there to be "no other choice". There are nearly always choices'.[52] However, the majority rejected this absolute understanding. Lord Nicholls (with whom Lord Hope and Lord Slynn agreed) held that the appropriate test for impecuniosity was whether replication would require 'sacrifices the plaintiff could not reasonably be expected to make'.[53] In other words, the correct question was whether the claimant's choice was sufficiently voluntary (or a 'fair choice') having regard to its interests as a whole.[54]

Although often framed in terms of reasonableness, it would be a mistake to think that this concept of choice is uniquely legal.[55] We often implicitly note that a person's conduct was insufficiently voluntary to hold them responsible for a particular outcome. For example, we might say 'Jim had to leave the party early because his son was unwell'. Here, we would not be taken to mean that Jim was literally forced to leave the party early; instead, we would understand that Jim's decision was insufficiently voluntary in the circumstances. We all have a fairly good grasp of this concept of choice, even though we may struggle to articulate it precisely. The important point is that when faced with marginal decisions, judges do not invent their own legalistic metric of choice but instead seek to reflect the understanding of voluntariness familiar from attributions of responsibility outside the law.

The cases on mitigation illustrate the application of this commonsense meaning of choice. *Emeh v Kensington Area Health Authority* provides a clear-cut example. The claimant became pregnant following a negligent sterilization procedure performed by the defendant hospital.[56] The Court of Appeal overturned the trial judge's decision that the claimant had unreasonably failed to mitigate by not having an abortion.[57] Of course, the claimant did in an absolute sense have a 'choice' whether to have an abortion, and this step would have replicated (as nearly as possible) her no-breach position. However, almost no one would say that she had a fair choice (or any choice at all) in these circumstances; in other words, her

[51] ibid [9]. See also [41] (Lord Hope) 'incapable of precise definition'; [88] (Lord Scott) 'imprecise'; [106] (Lord Walker) 'vague'.

[52] ibid [75].

[53] ibid [9]. See also [11] (Lord Slynn), asking whether restoration would have required the claimant to take 'steps which he could not reasonably be expected to take in the light of his financial position'. See also *Opoku v Tintas* [2013] EWCA Civ 1299 [30]–[31] (Beatson LJ); *Anselm v Buckle* [2014] EWCA Civ 311 [24] (Briggs LJ).

[54] See also *Wilding v British Telecommunications plc* [2002] EWCA Civ 349, [2002] ICR 1079 [38] (Potter LJ), noting that the reasonableness test must 'inevitably be related to the individual conduct and circumstances of the particular claimant when faced with a choice'.

[55] See further Hart and Honoré (n 1) 156.

[56] *Emeh v Kensington Area Health Authority* [1985] QB 1012 (CA). See also *R v Blaue* [1975] 1 WLR 1411 (CA), where there was no intervening act in a prosecution for murder, where the victim was a Jehovah's Witness and had refused a blood transfusion.

[57] *Emeh* (n 56) 1019 (Waller LJ), 1027 (Purchas LJ), and Slade LJ (1024).

decision not to have the abortion was insufficiently voluntary to attract responsibility. One does not need to be a lawyer to reach this conclusion.[58]

Denny v Supplies and Transport provides a less clear-cut example.[59] The claimant was injured whilst unloading timber that had been dangerously stacked by the defendant. Although the claimant knew that the timber was unsafe,[60] Evershed MR concluded that the claimant's conduct was not a 'novus actus interveniens' or 'break in the chain'.[61] In an absolute sense, the claimant could have chosen not to unload the timber. However, the trial judge found that he had 'no practical alternative' but to unload.[62] The reasons for this finding are not entirely clear, but the circumstances suggest that if the claimant had refused to unload, he would not have been paid and may have lost his job.[63] Again, the issue concerns whether the claimant's choice was sufficiently voluntary in the circumstances; in particular, this is focused on the claimant's interests and does not involve weighing the defendant's interests.

The claimant will also not be regarded as making a fair choice where it was forced to decide in the 'agony of the moment'. The courts have consistently declined to hold that the claimant acted unreasonably where it was faced with an acutely difficult or pressing problem.[64] Where the claimant was deciding under extreme pressure,[65] the rules of mitigation will not apply merely because the claimant made 'an error of judgment in deciding on the best course in difficult circumstances',[66] or sometimes even where it acted negligently.[67] In these circumstances the defendant's breach is said to remain the cause of the further harm.[68] In relation to the exceptionality rule, there may be some practical overlap between the issue of choice and the question whether the claimant departed from the normal course in the circumstances.[69]

[58] In particular, the conclusion has nothing to do with balancing the claimant's interests in keeping the child against the hospital's interests in preventing expenses towards future care.

[59] *Denny v Supplies & Transport Co* [1950] 2 KB 374 (CA).

[60] ibid 377.

[61] ibid 379 (Evershed MR).

[62] ibid 381 (reported by Evershed MR).

[63] Cf *Quinn v Burch Bros (Builders) Ltd* [1966] 2 QB 370 (CA), where the claimant would still have been paid in full even if he had refused to work until a replacement step-latter had been provided: see 388 (Sellers LJ). See also, rejecting the *volenti* defence in similar circumstances: *Smith v Charles Baker & Sons* [1891] AC 325 (HL).

[64] See eg *Jones v Boyce* (1816) 1 Stark 493, 171 ER 540; *United States Shipping Board v Laird Line Ltd* [1924] AC 286 (HL); *The Oropesa* (n 33); *Sayers v Harlow UDC* [1958] 1 WLR 623 (CA).

[65] See *Symrise AG v Baker & McKenzie* [2015] EWHC 912 (Comm), [2016] 1 All ER (Comm) 603 [80] (Burton J), rejecting an argument along these lines, on the basis that 'there was no time pressure'.

[66] *The Metagama* (n 30) 26 (Viscount Haldane).

[67] *Gard Marine & Energy Ltd v China National Chartering Co Ltd (The Ocean Victory)* [2013] EWHC 2199 (Comm), [2013] 2 All ER (Comm) 1058 [174] (Teare J). The decision was overturned on a different point: *Gard Marine & Energy Ltd v China National Chartering Co Ltd (The Ocean Victory)* [2015] EWCA Civ 16, [2015] 2 All ER (Comm) 894.

[68] *Compania Naviera Maropan SA v Bowaters Lloyd Pulp & Paper Mills Ltd (The Stork)* [1955] 2 QB 68 (CA) 99 (Hodson LJ).

[69] *Wilson v Newport Dock Co* (1865-66) LR 1 Ex 177 (Ex Ch) 184 (Baron Martin): 'very often there is no "usual course of things" in the event of a breach'.

3.4 The effect on damages

Where mitigation applies, it has the effect of introducing an additional counterfactual into the assessment of damages. The default application of the compensatory principle involves a single counterfactual (the no-breach position), which is compared with the claimant's actual position evident at the date of trial (the breach position).[70] But where mitigation applies, the claimant's actual breach position is substituted by the *counterfactual* position that they would have been in if they had conformed with the relevant mitigation norm. Thus, where the replication rule applies, the claimant's breach position is assessed as if they had taken steps to replicate the no-breach position as nearly as possible, even though in fact they did not. Similarly, where the exceptionality rule applies, the claimant's breach position will be assessed as if they had replicated the no-breach position in a usual way.[71]

Where mitigation does not apply, the default application of the compensatory principle remains undisturbed. Damages are assessed as a comparison between the claimant's no-breach position and the position that they are actually in as a result of the breach, evident at the date of trial. The latter includes all of the expenses actually incurred by the claimant in seeking to replicate the no-breach position, together with any benefits obtained. Evidentially, one can think of this as a 'receipts' basis of assessment, because the claimant proves their breach position on the basis of what actually happened. By contrast, where the replication rule or exceptionality rule applies, what actually happened is essentially irrelevant for the assessment of damages—at least in respect of the consequences of the claimant's own post-breach conduct—because both the breach position and the no-breach position are assessed on a counterfactual basis.

Conceptually, this understanding of mitigation represents a major departure from the orthodoxy. As I outlined in Chapter 1, mitigation is conventionally understood as a *limitation* on damages, which applies only *after* the claimant's loss has been assessed by application of the compensatory principle. Instead, I argue that mitigation is better understood as *part of* the legal concept of loss itself. It operates integrally within the application of the compensatory principle, by modifying the assessment of the breach position. This new conceptual framework explains how mitigation can sometimes result in an award of damages that is greater than the claimant's factual loss evident at the date of trial. Specifically, this can occur whenever the claimant's counterfactual breach position—as modified by the replication rule or exceptionality rule—is worse than their actual breach position: known conventionally as 'avoided loss'.

[70] See further Chapter 1, text to n 20.

[71] The application of this procedure is discussed in further detail in Chapters 8 and 9, for avoidable loss and avoided loss respectively.

4 Justifying Mitigation

The new account of mitigation that I outline above, and develop in further detail in the following chapters, aims to describe and explain the law as it stands. My claim is that the account is a better fit with the reasoning and results of the decided cases on mitigation than the orthodox account, as originally developed by McGregor and subsequently adopted in most of the other leading texts on damages. However, on its own, this descriptive approach does not tell us that the law of mitigation *should* operate this way, or that it is the best law of mitigation that we could have. To make such further claims, it would also be necessary to show that the rules that I have identified are normatively *justified*. For reasons that I explain further below, I have not attempted a fully-fledged justification in this book. However, in this section I briefly outline the form that I think such a justification would need to take.

First, one must show why the claimant should bear *any* responsibility for taking steps to obtain performance, given that this was originally the responsibility of the defendant. The answer is that if judgments were always entered instantaneously upon breach, there would indeed be no need for a doctrine of mitigation.[72] Responsibility for the (predicted) cost of obtaining substitute performance as soon as possible would fall entirely on the defendant, subject to any other established limitations such as remoteness. But given that there is inevitably a delay between the breach and the court's assessment of damages, the law must have rules for determining who—as between claimant and defendant—is responsible for events that have affected the cost of substitute performance in the meantime. Mitigation performs this function.

Second, a valid justification of the current law of mitigation will be based on causal principles, or (more neutrally) cognitive principles used to attribute responsibility outside the law,[73] not instrumental or 'policy-based' goals. This is for the same reason as I rejected instrumental *explanations* of mitigation in Chapter 4: they are inconsistent with the scope and application of the law as we currently find it. One might argue that the law *should* seek to achieve these goals—for example, economic efficiency, or self-reliance—but that amounts to an argument for changing the law, not a justification of the law as it is. The most promising justifications of our existing law of mitigation will be ones that provide normative arguments in favour of the law adopting commonsense causal principles for the purpose of attributing legal responsibility, since these are the principles that we find reflected in the cases.

[72] This hypothetical instant judgment is sometimes referred to as the 'judge at the roadside' test: James Edelman, 'The Meaning of Loss and Enrichment' in Robert Chambers, Charles Mitchell, and James Penner (eds), *Philosophical Foundations of the Law of Unjust Enrichment* (OUP 2009).

[73] See further Chapter 5, Section 5, and Conclusion, text to n 17.

Third, why *should* the principles of choice and abnormality that I have identified from commonsense causal reasoning be carried over into the law of damages? I can think of two possible reasons, each with different argumentative structures. The first is if consistency between ordinary (ie non-legal) and legal attributions of responsibility is itself an important value. Plausibly this could be the case if, for example, it was necessary to achieve institutional or democratic 'buy-in' to the law's approach to assessing damages. In this case it would not matter—or at least would not count decisively against the law of mitigation as it stands—if commonsense causal principles were imperfect or flawed, since their utility for legal purposes would lie in naively tracking how people attribute responsibility outside the law, for better or worse.

An alternative—and likely more compelling—justification of the law, would be if we can identify normative reasons in favour of the choice and abnormality principles in their 'ordinary' usage outside the law and then further argue that the same reasons have force for the purpose of attributing legal responsibility. Hart and Honoré are often misinterpreted as having relied on this kind of argument in Causation in the Law. But in fact, they stated expressly that this was *not* their position:

> It may, of course, well be that when we thoroughly understand the commonsense notions of causation we should no longer wish our thought on any matters, let alone legal judgments of responsibility, to be dominated by them: we may think that they are vague, crude, or anthropomorphic, or all of these: they may be 'the metaphysics of the Stone Age' which should be replaced by modern notions of probability or 'risk'.[74]

In other words, Hart and Honoré thought that commonsense causal principles *explained* the judicial approach to causation but did not necessarily justify it. They left open that the reasons why ordinary people treated choice and abnormality as significant when making causal judgements may be bad reasons for them to rely upon. However, if we could establish that there are sound moral reasons for treating these factors as significant when attributing responsibility outside the law, it seems plausible that the same reasons would justify the judges' use of them within the law of mitigation.

The structure of this argument hopefully makes clear why justifying the law of mitigation based on commonsense causal principles is a task that may not be best suited to lawyers, or at least not lawyers alone. It requires going deep into the reasons how and why ordinary people make causal judgements in non-legal contexts, and then considering whether these reasons should be carried over to a legal

[74] Hart and Honoré (n 1). See also ibid 132, where the authors describe their aim as 'to understand rather than to manipulate the principles of legal responsibility'.

context. Fortunately, there is a large body of research that is already engaged in the former set of tasks, led by experimental philosophers and psychologists. My proposal for legal scholars interested in justifications of the law of mitigation is that they should mine this literature for insights and focus their own efforts on the latter part of the enquiry. This seems an altogether more promising approach than pursuing instrumental or 'policy-based' justifications of the law, which—however meritorious—are a poor fit with the law of mitigation as it stands.

5 Comparing the Orthodox Account

Finally, it is worth pinpointing the main doctrinal similarities and differences between my account and the orthodox account of mitigation. In general, my account will tend to reach the same results as the orthodox account in simple cases of 'avoidable loss', although it provides more specific guidance to judges than the prevailing orthodoxy. It is in relation to the so-called 'avoided loss' cases where my account is most distinctive, since it can result in recovery of damages exceeding the claimant's factual loss in circumstances where these would likely be denied according to a naive application of the orthodox avoided loss rule. To reiterate, however, this does not mean that my account entails any change in the underlying law; I argue that it is more consistent with the *existing* case law—properly understood—than the accounts espoused by the leading textbooks on damages.

Starting with the orthodox account of the *avoidable* loss rule, my distinction between the replication rule and the exceptionality rule roughly coincides with Burrows' distinction between 'unreasonable inaction' and 'unreasonable action' respectively.[75] This is because cases of unreasonable inaction typically involve a choice by the claimant not to replicate the no-breach position at all; by contrast, cases of what Burrows terms 'unreasonable action' can typically be understood as cases in which the claimant made an attempt to replicate the no-breach position but did so in a way that was particularly unusual. Despite this similarity, there are two reasons why my proposed formation (in terms of the claimant's choice not to replicate the no-breach position) is preferable to the 'reasonableness' test.

First, as Lord Leggatt recently noted, albeit in a different context, the language of reasonableness 'has no explanatory power' on its own.[76] My account helpfully anchors this test within a causal framework, and hence allows it to be viewed through the lens of the voluntariness and abnormality of the claimant's conduct. Second, in relation to cases covered by what I term the replication rule, the language of

[75] Andrew Burrows, *Remedies for Torts and Breach of Contract* (3rd edn, OUP 2004) 122. However, a choice not to replicate the no-breach position may not be inactive; it may involve doing something else instead.

[76] *Fearn v Board of Trustees of the Tate Gallery* [2023] UKSC 4, [2023] 2 WLR 339 [18] (Lord Leggatt).

reasonableness can be misleading if taken literally. This is because mitigation can apply without the claimant having acted 'unreasonably' in any standard sense. The relevant legal test is the claimant's *choice* not to replicate the no-breach position, rather than whether or not they acted (or chose not to act) with good reason.

A further difference between my account and the orthodox account of the avoidable loss rule concerns its implications for the so-called 'duty to mitigate'.[77] The replication and exceptionality rules are not prescriptive; they do not seek to tell claimants (prospectively) how they 'should' behave. Instead, they attribute responsibility (retrospectively) for the claimant's past conduct; these attributions are not dependent on any judgement of praise or blame. In particular, the replication rule does not say that the claimant 'should' replicate the no-breach position;[78] claimants are perfectly free to seek a different position instead. Similarly, the exceptionality rule does not say that the claimant 'should' adopt the normal method of replicating the no-breach position; claimants are perfectly free to adopt an exceptional approach, for better or worse.

Turning to the orthodox account of the *avoided* loss rule, it is important to appreciate first that the 'rule' itself (leaving aside the exception) just reflects the standard *non*-application of mitigation. The so-called *exception* to the rule is in fact the only legally operative part, and in most cases, its application reflects what I have termed the replication rule: it is precisely where the benefit arose from the claimant's own choice not to replicate the no-breach position that it will be held not to have 'arisen out of the consequences of the breach'. In such cases, the award of damages can leave the claimant in a better position—all things considered—than if the breach had not occurred, but this specifically due to the causal significance of the claimant's choice.

The most significant difference between my account and the orthodox understanding of mitigation is that, on my account, the doctrine operates indifferently to the eventual consequences of the claimant's conduct. I call this the 'principle of symmetry' because it reflects that, on a proper understanding of the law, the avoidable loss rule and the (exception to) the avoided loss rule operate as mirror images.[79] In more theoretical terms, this follows from the notion that attributions of responsibility depend on the nature of the conduct (its voluntariness and abnormality) and not its outcome (whether it resulted in harm or benefit). Put simply, if the claimant chose not to replicate the no-breach position, or to do so in an exceptional way, then it is responsible for the outcome, for better or worse.

Understood in this way, references to 'avoidable loss' and 'avoided loss' are simply labels to be applied ex post once the outcome of the claimant's conduct is

[77] See further Chapter 7, Section 2.

[78] This legal norm derives from the defendant's breach of a legal obligation, but it does not prescribe the claimant's conduct.

[79] This is acknowledged in *Thai Airways* (n 32) [33] (Leggatt J). See also [31].

known, but they have no legal significance. This is because, I argue, the application and effect of mitigation depends entirely on what the claimant did or did not do, and not what happened after. For example, if, the replication rule having been applied, it emerges that the claimant's actual position has turned out worse than it would have been if it had sought to replicate the no-breach position, it may be said that the claimant is debarred from recovering those avoidable losses. Conversely, if it turns out that the claimant has been left in a better position, it may be said that the claimant is recovering for an 'avoided loss'. But these are just labels: nothing turns on them.

The replication and exceptionality rules also explain other areas of the law of damages.[80] The 'market rule' is a straightforward instantiation of the replication rule: where the claimant made a choice not to resort to the market to obtain substitute performance (and thereby to replicate the no-breach position), damages are assessed as if it had done so. 'Betterment' is also an application of the replication rule: it applies where the claimant made a choice to put itself in a better position than if the breach had not occurred, or in other words to 'supersede' (rather than to replicate) the no-breach position. Intervening (or 'supervening') acts by the claimant are an application of the exceptionality rule: it applies to unusual conduct by the claimant other than exceptionality in the course of replicating the no-breach position.

Overall, I argue that my account is more consistent with the existing case law than the orthodox account. However, I obviously cannot claim that my account is consistent with every case—given the sheer number of cases, this would be an impossible task. There are two main (related) influences that I think explain most of the inconsistencies. First, although judicial development of the law has primarily been influenced by causal principles, some cases have evidently been influenced directly by McGregor's (contrary) orthodox account of mitigation, which strongly denied the causal explanation.[81] Second, it seems likely that the normative preference of some judges for what I termed in Chapter 1 a 'factual loss cap' on damages, may occasionally have tilted their decision against applying the replication or exceptionality rules as I have described them, where to do so would result in an award of damages greater than the claimant's factual loss. As I show in the following chapters, however, these cases are outliers in the wider of scheme of things, rather than characteristic of the judicial approach.

[80] See further Chapters 10 and 11.

[81] For an outline of 'reflexive effect' (or the 'double hermeneutic') in law, see further Chapter 1, text to n 121.

7
Puzzles Resolved

1 Introduction

The new account of mitigation that I outlined in the preceding chapter helps to resolve at least three 'puzzles' that arise under the orthodox account. In this chapter, I address each puzzle in turn. First, the conventional language of the 'duty' to mitigate, which persists despite routinely being disclaimed as inaccurate by judges. Second, the universal and homogenous application of mitigation to every assessment of loss, which is inconsistent with policy-based explanations of the doctrine such as self-reliance or prevention of waste. Third, the restricted temporal scope of mitigation—applying only after breach—which is hard to square with the focus on whether the claimant acted reasonably. In each case, the puzzle arises because the precise contours of mitigation are at odds with the explanations of the doctrine conventionally put forward by legal scholars. By contrast, when mitigation is understood as an aspect of causation, these pieces fit without difficulty.

2 No 'Duty' to Mitigate

The avoidable loss rule is often described in the leading texts on damages as 'the duty to mitigate'. The origin of this expression appears to be Viscount Haldane's classic statement in *British Westinghouse*.[1] Although judges do still occasionally refer to the 'duty to mitigate',[2] it is also often emphasized that this phrase is an inaccurate characterization of the rule. As Lord Toulson put it in *Bunge v Nidera*, 'It is well recognised that the so-called duty to mitigate is not a duty in the sense that the innocent party owes an obligation to the guilty party to do so.'[3] Several cases

[1] *British Westinghouse Electric & Manufacturing Co Ltd v Underground Electric Railways Co of London Ltd (No2)* [1912] AC 673 (HL) 689. Other references to the claimant's 'duty' can be traced to *Harries v Edmonds* (1845) 1 Car & K 686, 174 ER 991, 687 (Baron Parke).

[2] See eg, *Bunge SA v Nidera BV* [2015] UKSC 43, [2015] 3 All ER 1082 [32] (Lord Sumption); *Trebor Bassett Holdings Ltd v ADT Fire & Security plc* [2012] EWCA Civ 1158, [2012] BLR 441 [67] (Tomlinson LJ).

[3] *Bunge* (n 2) [81]. See also *Wallems Rederij v Muller & Co* [1927] 2 KB 99 (KB) 104-05 (Mackinnon J); *Darbishire v Warran* [1963] 1 WLR 1067 (CA) 1075 (Pearson LJ); *Koch Marine Inc v d'Amica Societa di Navigazione arl (The Elena d'Amico)* [1980] 1 Lloyd's Rep 75 (QB) 88 (Goff J); *Sealace Shipping Co Ltd v Oceanvoice Ltd (The Alecos M)* [1991] 1 Lloyd's Rep 120 (CA) 124 (Neill LJ).

Mitigation in the Law of Damages. Andrew Summers, Oxford University Press. © Andy Summers 2025.
DOI: 10.1093/9780191864032.003.0007

make clear that the claimant's decision not to mitigate involves 'no wrong against the defendant or anyone else',[4] and does not give rise to any cause of action.[5]

Proponents of the orthodox account of mitigation have acknowledged that the language of 'duty to mitigate' is technically inapt. For example, Tettenborn seeks to clarify that 'strictly speaking, the idea of a "duty" to mitigate loss is a misnomer'.[6] This point is routinely asserted in the leading texts.[7] Nevertheless, it is rarely explained. The basis for the clarification appears to be the Hohfeldian insight that, since the defendant has no 'claim-right' to mitigation, there can be no correlative duty on the claimant.[8] But despite these reservations, references to the 'duty to mitigate' remain commonplace.[9] Bridge concluded that the language of duty was 'entrenched and difficult to substitute'.[10] In this way, the leading texts equivocate over whether the language of duty has a place in the law of mitigation or not.

The problem is that the persistent references to 'duty' have deeper roots. They stem from the orthodox view that the avoidable loss rule aims to *prescribe* the claimant's conduct. As McBride summarizes (in another context), 'To say that someone has a legal duty to do *x* is a shorthand way of saying that the law tells, or requires, him or her to do *x*.'[11] At base, references to a 'duty' to mitigate reflect the view that the law tells claimants that they 'should' take steps to mitigate. This view is commonplace in the leading texts:[12] 'the claimant *must* take all reasonable steps to mitigate their loss';[13] 'the claimant cannot recover damages for a loss that he

[4] *Darbishire* (n 3) 1075 (Pearson LJ).

[5] *Empresa Cubana Importada de Alimentos 'Alimport' v Iasmos Shipping Co SA (The Good Friend)* [1984] 2 Lloyd's Rep 586 (QB) 597 (Staughton J). Similarly in Australia: *Hardi Finance Corporation Pty Ltd v Ahern (No 3)* [2010] WASC 403 [764]; *Karacominakis v Big Country Developments Pty Ltd & Ors* [2000] NSWCA 313 [187].

[6] Andrew Tettenborn, *The Law of Damages* (2nd edn, LexisNexis 2010) [5.63].

[7] James Edelman (ed), *McGregor on Damages* (21st edn, Sweet & Maxwell 2022) [9-018]; Andrew Burrows, *Remedies for Torts and Breach of Contract* (4th edn, OUP 2019) 127; Edwin Peel (ed), *Treitel on The Law of Contract* (15th edn, Sweet & Maxwell 2020) [20-104]; Hugh Beale (ed), *Chitty on Contracts* (34th edn, Sweet & Maxwell 2022) [29-098]; Andrew Tettenborn (ed), *Clerk & Lindsell on Torts* (23rd edn, Sweet & Maxwell 2022) [27-09] fn 49; Adam Kramer, *The Law of Contract Damages* (3rd edn, Hart 2022) [15-45]–[15-46].

[8] Wesley Newcomb Hohfeld, 'Some Fundamental Legal Conceptions as Applied in Judicial Reasoning' (1913–14) 23 Yale Law Journal 16; cf John Finnis, 'Some Professorial Fallacies About Rights' (1971–72) 4 Adelaide Law Review 377, 380. See also Harvey McGregor, 'The Role of Mitigation in the Assessment of Damages' in Djakhongir Saidov and Ralph Cunnington (eds), *Contract Damages: Domestic and International Perspectives* (Hart 2008) 331.

[9] See eg Peel (n 7) [20-104]; Tettenborn, *Damages* (2nd edn) (n 6) [5.63].

[10] Michael Bridge, 'Mitigation of Damages in Contract and the Meaning of Avoidable Loss' (1989) 105 Law Quarterly Review 398, 399.

[11] Nicholas McBride, 'Duties of Care—Do They Really Exist?' (2004) 24 Oxford Journal of Legal Studies 417, 417 fn 1. See also, to the same effect: Stephen Smith, 'Duties to Try and Duties to Succeed' in Andrew Dyson, James Goudkamp and Frederick Wilmot-Smith (eds), *Defences in Tort* (Hart 2015) 67.

[12] Although the prescriptive view has also been reflected in judicial expositions of the avoidable loss rule, it is less prevalent in the cases. See eg *Payzu v Saunders* [1919] 2 KB 581 (CA) 589 (Scrutton LJ); *Lagden v O'Connor (sub nom Burdis v Livsey)* [2003] UKHL 64, [2004] 1 AC 1067 [27] (Lord Hope).

[13] Edelman (n 7) [9-004].

ought to have avoided';[14] 'a claimant *should not* sit back and do nothing'.[15] Whilst this prescriptive language persists, references to the duty to mitigate will not be weeded out.

Contrary to the prescriptive view, judges have often emphasized that the avoidable loss rule does not seek to tell citizens how to behave. For example, in *The Solholt*, Sir John Donaldson MR emphasized that the claimant is 'completely free to act as he judges to be in his best interests'.[16] In *Darbishire v Warran*, Pearson LJ held that the claimant is 'fully entitled to be as extravagant as he pleases',[17] and 'if he wishes to adopt the more expensive method, he is at liberty to do so'.[18] Such statements appear to go further than merely denying the existence of any legal obligation to mitigate.[19] Instead, they seem to reflect the idea that, in applying the avoidable loss rule, the law is really not seeking to prescribe the claimant's conduct. Similarly, they indicate that the law does impute any culpability for the claimant's choice not to replicate the no-breach position (or for their choice to do so in an unusual way), despite loose references to the 'failure' to mitigate.

Letsas and Saprai convincingly reject the prescriptive view of mitigation.[20] They give an example in which A agrees to drive B to the airport but fails to turn up.[21] B could take another taxi, or a train, to get him to the airport on time. However, B chooses not to take any of these options and so misses his flight. In these circumstances, Letsas and Saprai point out that 'Surely, the promisee is free to decide that he no longer wishes to bring about the state of affairs promised. In our example, B may decide that he no longer wishes to travel.'[22] Indeed, 'it seems that he has a right to make these decisions. It would be odd to say that the promisee has a duty to travel, or a duty to take the cheapest means of getting to the airport'.[23] On the other hand, it is obvious that B cannot recover damages from A for the consequences of missing the flight.[24]

The answer to this apparent puzzle is that the avoidable loss rule serves to *attribute responsibility* for the claimant's conduct, rather than to guide (or prescribe)

[14] Peel (n 7) [20-104].

[15] Burrows (n 7) 127.

[16] *Sotiros Shipping Inc v Sameiet Solholt (The Solholt)* [1983] 1 Lloyd's Rep 605 (CA) 608 (Sir John Donaldson MR). See also *Sotiros Shipping Inc v Sameiet Solholt (The Solholt)* [1981] 2 Lloyd's Rep 574 (QB) 580 (Staughton J); *MSC Mediterranean Shopping SA v Cottonex Anstalt* [2015] EWHC 283 (Comm), [59] (Legatt J); and *Prince Arthur Ikpechukwu Eze v Conway* [2018] EWHC 29 (Ch), [162] (Keyser QC).

[17] *Darbishire* (n 3) 1075, adding: '... but not at the expense of the defendant'. In relation to this important qualification, see further text to n 33.

[18] ibid 1075.

[19] Text to n 7.

[20] George Letsas and Prince Saprai, 'Mitigation, Fairness and Contract Law' in Gregory Klass, George Letsas, and Prince Saprai (eds), *Philosophical Foundations of Contract Law* (OUP 2014).

[21] ibid 319.

[22] ibid 326.

[23] ibid 326.

[24] ibid 319.

it. This is an important distinction that has deep roots outside the law. We can hold a person responsible for an outcome based on their conduct, without judging whether that person should or should not have conducted themselves in that way. As Honoré puts it, outcome responsibility 'is an essential constituent of our character and identity, without which we would lack both achievements and failures'.[25] Responsibility does not necessarily entail praise or blame.[26] As Tadros puts it, 'culpability and responsibility are independent notions, even though some of the same facts make us both responsible and culpable'. On this view, responsibility depends exclusively on the strength of the agential connection between the person and their conduct and (unlike culpability) can apply even where the conduct in question is morally neutral.

A simple example illustrates the basic point. Consider two golfers on the tee.[27] Albert strikes a perfect shot but his ball lands on a sprinkler-head and bounces into the lake. Brian slices his tee-shot but the ball bounces off a tree and into the hole. Albert's shot is far more worthy of praise than Brian's, but it is Albert's double bogey and Brian's hole-in-one. The game of golf makes no sense without outcome responsibility. This basic idea extends well beyond sport.[28] Within private law, the notion of outcome responsibility has been used to explain instances of strict liability, where a person may be held responsible for the outcome of their conduct without any finding of fault. Likewise, it has been argued that outcome responsibility explains the objective standard in the tort of negligence.[29]

In mitigation, the avoidable loss rule attributes responsibility to the claimant for the outcome of its voluntary and abnormal conduct, without needing to establish that the claimant 'should' have acted any differently.[30] In Letsas and Saprai's example, the legal effect of the avoidable loss rule, which would prevent B from recovering the loss resulting from the missed flight, does not rely upon (or even imply) the proposition that B should have taken the flight.[31] Instead it reflects the basic idea that where the claimant has chosen not to take the flight (by foregoing other available options for travelling to the airport), the responsibility for

[25] Tony Honoré, 'The Morality of Tort Law—Questions and Answers' in David Owen (ed), *The Philosophical Foundations of Tort Law* (Clarendon 1995) 81. On this basis, Honoré also argues that 'outcome responsibility is . . . more fundamental than moral or legal responsibility, which are species of it': Tony Honoré, 'Responsibility and Luck: The Moral Basis of Strict Liability' in Tony Honoré (ed), *Responsibility and Fault* (Hart 1999) 40.

[26] Honoré, 'Responsibility and Luck' (n 25) 23–31; Peter Cane, *Responsibility in Law and Morality* (Hart 2002) 94–111; Joseph Raz, 'Being in the World' in Joseph Raz (ed), *From Normativity to Responsibility* (OUP 2011) 251–54.

[27] This example is loosely adapted from Honoré, 'Responsibility and Luck' (n 25) 30.

[28] See further ibid 30–31; Raz, 'Being in the World' (n 26) 237–39.

[29] Honoré, 'Responsibility and Luck' (n 25); Joseph Raz, 'Responsibility and the Negligence Standard' (2010) 30(1) Oxford Journal of Legal Studies 1–18.

[30] Of course, the prescription that 'the claimant should act reasonably' sounds unobjectionable, but it is necessary to bear in mind that reasonableness in mitigation does not bear the same meaning as in ordinary language: see further Chapter 2, text to n 13.

[31] Text to n 21.

the outcome of that decision is attributable to the claimant rather than to the defendant. Smith correctly concludes that 'the law is indifferent as to whether a victim of breach mitigates. The mitigation rule simply provides that damages will be calculated as if the [claimant] mitigated'.[32]

Returning to Pearson LJ's proposition in *Darbishire v Warran* that the claimant is 'fully entitled to be as extravagant as he pleases', he continued '. . . but not at the expense of the defendant'.[33] This exactly captures the nature of mitigation. The law is not telling the claimant that it *should* mitigate, or that it is to blame for not mitigating, let alone that it has a duty to mitigate. Instead, the law holds the claimant responsible for the consequences of their choice not to mitigate, for better or worse. This process of attributing responsibility is neutral with respect to the consequences. The idea that the law indirectly compels mitigation because it reduces the claimant's damages if they do not mitigate,[34] overlooks the flipside that mitigation can sometimes result in an award of damages that is *greater* than if the claimant had taken the usual mitigating steps. As I show in Chapter 9, the effect of mitigation can cut both ways.

3 Universal Application

The law of mitigation applies universally to every assessment of loss. In other words, it applies every time the court is required to assess loss,[35] whatever the cause of action and whatever the defendant's level of fault. Besides compensatory damages for torts and breach of contract, mitigation also applies to statutory rights to compensation (whether strict liability or fault-based), and to claims for equitable compensation for breach of trust. The rules of mitigation apply in exactly the same way regardless of the defendant's fault: they apply to the tort of conversion (a strict liability tort) just the same as to the torts of deceit and unlawful means conspiracy (which require intentional wrongdoing). This feature of mitigation is notable by comparison with remoteness, for example, which *does* vary depending on the defendant's level of fault.

On the orthodox account of mitigation, the universality of mitigation presents a puzzle. If the judges' causal reasoning is really based on questions of legal policy, particularly the 'purpose' and 'scope' of the relevant liability rules, why is mitigation

[32] Stephen Smith, *Contract Theory* (OUP 2004) 428.

[33] *Darbishire* (n 3) 1075. See also *Six Continents Retail Ltd v Carford Catering Ltd* [2003] EWCA Civ 1790 [19] (Laws LJ): 'The real question is whether on the proved or admitted facts the respondents should or should not be held responsible for the appellant's loss.'

[34] See eg Kramer (n 7) [15-46]: 'the law implicitly recognises a duty, at least in the limited sense that an omission by the claimant to act will break the chain of causation where the omission is treated as significant for the responsibility of the defendant . . .'.

[35] It does not however apply to the action for an agreed sum: *Abrahams v Performing Right Society Ltd* [1995] ICR 1028 (CA) 1041 (Hutchison LJ); *Jervis v Harris* [1996] Ch 195 (CA) 202–03 (Millett LJ).

insensitive to the source of liability? If mitigation aims to encourage self-reliance, why is the defendant's fault irrelevant to the extent of self-reliance demanded? By contrast, if the causal explanation of mitigation is accepted, its universal application is no puzzle at all. The rules of mitigation simply form part of what it means to 'cause loss'; consequently, wherever assessments of loss are required, the law of mitigation must follow. At a deeper level, the concept of loss involves an attribution of outcome responsibility,[36] and this task cannot be separated from the causal principles upon which the law of mitigation rests.

3.1 Causes of action

Some legal rules apply equally to all causes of action: the rules on the effect of underlying illegality on a claim are an example.[37] Others, however, vary with the type of cause of action—or indeed the specific causes of action—involved. For example, the rules of remoteness generally differ as between claims in contract and claims in tort,[38] and they differ within tort as between various torts.[39] The rules on mitigation fall into the former (universal) category, but the orthodox account provides no obvious reason why this is the case. In contrast, the causal explanation shows that this is due to the fact that these rules all derive from commonsense principles of causation that are common to all loss-based causes of action.

The rules of mitigation are exactly the same in both contract and tort. This has never been doubted, and is now well-established.[40] In *The Liverpool (No 2)*, Lord Merriman clarified that 'the classic statement about mitigation of loss by Viscount Haldane . . . although made in an action arising out of a breach of contract, applies equally, *mutatis mutandis*, to tort'.[41] Similarly, in *Dimond v Lovell*, Lord Hoffmann approved the application of the 'avoided loss' rule to liability in the tort of negligence, confirming that 'in principle this seems to me to be right: there can be no difference here between contract and tort'.[42] Where the defendant is concurrently

[36] For further discussion of 'outcome responsibility', see text to n 25.

[37] *Holman v Johnson* (1775) 1 Cowp 341 (KB) 343 (Lord Mansfield); *Patel v Mirza* [2016] UKSC 42, [2017] AC 467 [2] (Lord Toulson JSC).

[38] *Koufos v C Czarnikow Ltd (The Heron II)* [1969] 1 AC 350 (HL) 385–87.

[39] Contrast *Doyle v Olby (Ironmongers) Ltd* [1969] 2 QB 15 with *Overseas Tankship (UK) Ltd v Morts Dock & Engineering Co Ltd (The Wagon Mound)* [1961] AC 388.

[40] Edelman (n 7) [9-015] (avoidable loss), [9-114] (avoided loss). See also, in relation to betterment: *Voaden v Champion (The Baltic Surveyor)* [2002] EWCA Civ 89, [2002] 1 Lloyd's Rep 623 [83] (Rix LJ); *Thai Airways International Public Co Ltd v KI Holdings Co Ltd* [2015] EWHC 1250 (Comm), [2016] 1 All ER (Comm) 675 [77] (Leggatt J).

[41] *Owners of Steamship Enterprises of Panama Inc v Owners of SS Ousel (The Liverpool) (No2)* [1963] P 64 (CA) 77–78. See also *Beoco Ltd v Alfa Laval Co Ltd* [1995] QB 137 (CA) 151 (Stuart-Smith LJ); *Galoo Ltd v Bright Grahame Murray* [1994] 1 WLR 1360 (CA) 1369 (Glidewell LJ); *Sayce v TNT (UK) Ltd* [2011] EWCA Civ 1583, [2012] 1 WLR 1261 [20] (Moore-Bick LJ).

[42] *Dimond v Lovell* [2002] 1 AC 384 (HL) 402. See also *Bellingham v Dhillon* [1973] QB 304 (QB) 308 (Forbes J); *Robinson v Maund* (CA, 20 January 1993) (Steyn LJ); *Derby Resources AG v Blue Corinth Marine Co Ltd (The Athenian Harmony) (No 1)* [1998] 2 Lloyd's Rep 410 (QB) 416 (Colman J).

liable in contract and tort, it has been emphasized that as regards mitigation there is no difference between the contractual and tortious measures of damages.[43]

Mitigation also applies to statutory rights of compensation, whether against private or public bodies.[44] In *Steele v Robert George*, Viscount Simon noted that the Workmen's Compensation Act 1925 did not contain any express provision for a reduction in damages where the workman unreasonably refused medical treatment.[45] However, he reasoned that 'if the proximate cause of the continuing incapacity is the unreasonable refusal of a workman to avail himself of surgical or medical skill, it can no longer be said that the incapacity "results from the injury" within the meaning of s9 of the Act'.[46] Not only did Viscount Simon express mitigation in terms of proximate causation, his reasoning was that the rule forms an integral part of what it means for harm to 'result' from the defendant's conduct.

The position is the same where the defendant's statutory liability is strict. In *Elliot Steam Tug Co v Shipping Controller*, Scrutton LJ assessed damages under the Indemnity Act 1920 on the basis that the claimant was under a 'duty to act reasonably' after its tugboat had been requisitioned by the Admiralty.[47] Likewise, in *Welford v EDF Energy Networks*, the defendant received a statutory wayleave to run cables under the claimants' land.[48] The claimant sought compensation under the Electricity Act 1989. The Court of Appeal upheld the Tribunal's decision that the claimants had 'failed . . . to mitigate their loss by not seeking an alternative site' once it became clear that the cables were interfering with the claimants' business.[49] There was no suggestion that the standard of reasonableness was any higher because the defendant's liability was strict.[50]

The rules of mitigation also apply to equitable compensation for breaches of fiduciary duty,[51] including, notably, breaches of trust. Many now hold that equitable compensation is compensation for loss.[52] The reasoning of the Supreme Court in

[43] *Gardner v Marsh & Parsons* [1997] 1 WLR 489 (CA) 505 (Peter Gibson LJ).

[44] See eg *Energy Solutions EU Ltd v Nuclear Decommissioning Authority* [2015] EWCA Civ 1262, 163 Con LR 27 [33] (Vos LJ), involving a claim in damages against the Nuclear Decommissioning Authority under the Public Contracts Regulations 2006.

[45] *Steele v Robert George & Co* [1942] AC 497 (HL) 499. See also *Warncken v Moreland & Son Ltd* [1909] 1 KB 184 (CA) 189 (Fletcher Moulton LJ) (Workmen's Compensation Act 1906).

[46] *Steele* (n 45) 499 (Viscount Simon).

[47] *Elliott Steam Tug Co Ltd v Shipping Controller* [1922] 1 KB 127 (CA) 140–41.

[48] *Welford v EDF Energy Networks (LPN) plc* [2007] EWCA Civ 293, [2007] 2 P & CR 15.

[49] ibid [34] (Thomas LJ).

[50] Cf Lord Macmillan's reasoning in *Banco de Portugal v Waterlow & Sons Ltd* [1932] AC 452 (HL) 506.

[51] In *Bristol & West Building Society v Mothew* [1998] Ch 1 (CA) 17, Millett LJ suggested that mitigation applies 'by analogy', but nothing turns on this.

[52] *Target Holdings Ltd v Redferns* [1996] AC 421 (HL) 436, 439 (Lord Browne-Wilkinson); *Bristol & West* (n 51) 17 (Millett LJ); *AIB Group (UK) plc v Mark Redler & Co Solicitors* [2014] UKSC 58, [2014] 3 WLR 1367 [73] (Lord Toulson). But cf *Interactive Technology Corporation Ltd v Ferster* [2018] EWCA Civ 1594 and *Auden McKenzie (Pharma Division) Ltd v Patel* [2019] EWCA Civ 2291.

AIB v Redler helpfully illustrates the compensatory approach.[53] Lord Reed started with the proposition that 'compensation for the breach of an obligation generally seeks to place the claimant in the position he would have been in if the obligation had been performed. Equitable compensation for breach of trust is no different in principle'.[54] The object of equitable compensation was thus 'to restore the trust fund to the position it would have been in if the trustee had performed his obligation'.[55] Both Lord Toulson and Lord Reed clarified that any difference with the approach in contract and tort merely resulted from the different content of the underlying obligations.[56]

Having adopted these premisses, Lord Reed's reasoning was impeccable. He held that 'the concept of loss necessarily involves the concept of causation'.[57] From this it followed that 'the loss must be caused by the breach of trust, in the sense that it must flow directly from it. Losses resulting from unreasonable behaviour on the part of the claimant will be adjudged to flow from that behaviour, and not from the breach'.[58] The effect of the claimant's conduct, 'rather than being a distinct principle ... might be regarded as following from the requirement of a direct causal connection'.[59] The question was 'whether loss should be attributed ... to the conduct of the person to whom the duty was owed'.[60] These propositions revealed 'structural similarities between the assessment of equitable compensation and the assessment of common law damages'.[61] Although the label 'mitigation' was not used, it is clear that in substance these steps in Lord Reed's reasoning are a near-perfect fit with the account that I have developed.[62]

Remoteness was different. In this regard, Lord Reed held that 'it is common ground that equitable compensation and damages for tort or breach of contract may differ where different policy objectives are applicable'.[63] In the tort of negligence, 'the liability resulting from a failure to take reasonable care to guard against a reasonably foreseeable risk is limited to such consequences as are reasonably foreseeable'.[64] Conversely, for breach of trust, 'foreseeability does not enter into

[53] *AIB* (n 52).
[54] ibid [93]. See also [64] (Lord Toulson); *Target Holdings* (n 52) 432 (Lord Browne-Wilkinson).
[55] *AIB* (n 52) [134] (Lord Reed). See also [64] (Lord Toulson).
[56] ibid [76] (Lord Toulson), [137] (Lord Reed). See further Chapter 1, text to n 14.
[57] *AIB* (n 52) [136].
[58] ibid [135].
[59] ibid [87].
[60] ibid [136].
[61] ibid [136].
[62] See also *Target Holdings* (n 52) 438–39 (Lord Browne-Wilkinson), approving *Canson Enterprises Ltd v Boughton & Co* [1991] 3 SCR 534, 85 DLR (4th) 129 (SCC) 163 (McLachlin J). Although in that case McLachlin J rejected the label 'mitigation', again her reasoning is a very close fit in substance: 'losses resulting from clearly unreasonable behaviour on the part of the plaintiff will be adjudged to flow from that behaviour, and not from the breach'.
[63] ibid [133].
[64] ibid [92].

the wrongfulness of the defendant's conduct, and there is no reason why it should limit the extent of his responsibility'.[65] In other words, whereas mitigation (as an aspect of causation) applied to every assessment of loss, the remoteness rule differed depending on the purpose and scope of the underlying liability rule.

3.2 The defendant's fault

The rules of mitigation are also insensitive to the defendant's fault.[66] The same rules apply (in exactly the same way) to strict liability torts as to intentional torts. Again, judicial reasoning emphasizes that this conclusion follows ineluctably from the task of assessing loss. Nevertheless, this approach is a poor fit with the rival explanations of mitigation put forward by the leading texts, as I highlighted in Chapter 4. For example, if mitigation was based on the policy of encouraging self-reliance, one might expect that a victim of fraud would be allowed a wider margin of dependency than a claimant in a strict-liability case. The universality of the mitigation rules presents a similar puzzle for the remoteness explanation, given that remoteness depends on the defendant's fault.

In relation to strict liability torts, in *Uzinterimpex v Standard Bank*, Moore-Bick LJ held that 'a duty to avoid or minimise loss arises when goods are converted in the same way as in the case of other legal wrongs'.[67] Moore-Bick LJ reasoned that '[o]nce it is accepted that the correct measure of damages in a case of conversion is that which will provide just compensation for loss . . . it is impossible to ignore the claimant's own conduct in relation to that loss'.[68] He added that if mitigation did not apply, the defendant may be required 'to pay compensation for a loss that could not fairly be attributed to his wrongful act'.[69] In other words, the rules of mitigation were again regarded as part of attributing responsibility and were accordingly inseparable from the concept of loss.

Mitigation also applies to intentional torts. In *Standard Chartered Bank v Pakistan National Shipping*, Toulson J assessed damages for fraud in relation to bills of lading.[70] He concluded that 'once a plaintiff discovers that he is a victim of a fraud, the same rule about avoidable loss applies for the purpose of assessing damages in an action of deceit or conspiracy as would apply in any action for tort or

[65] ibid [92]. See also: *Canson* (n 62) 162 (McLachlin J), approved in *Target Holdings* (n 52) 439 (Lord Browne-Wilkinson); Steven Elliott, 'Remoteness Criteria in Equity' (2002) 65 Modern Law Review 588.

[66] Edelman (n 7) [9-080]. Tettenborn, *Damages* (2nd edn) (n 6) [5.64]; Glanville Williams, *Joint Torts and Contributory Negligence* (Stevens 1951) 283–85.

[67] *Uzinterimpex JSC v Standard Bank plc* [2008] EWCA Civ 819, [2008] 2 CLC 80 [69]. See also [63].

[68] ibid [67].

[69] ibid.

[70] *Standard Chartered Bank v Pakistan National Shipping Corp* [1999] 1 Lloyd's Rep 747 (QB).

breach of contract'.[71] In *British Midland Tool v Midland International Tooling*, the defendant directors of the claimant's company set up a rival company that poached the claimant's employees.[72] In assessing damages for unlawful means conspiracy,[73] Hart J nevertheless held that the defendant directors were not responsible for the losses attributable to the claimant's subsequent decision to continue trading.[74]

Doyle v Olby was the first decision to establish the application of mitigation in deceit.[75] Winn LJ's reasoning is instructive. He held that 'damage that [the claimant] seeks to recover must have flowed directly from the fraud perpetrated upon him'.[76] In this regard, 'no element in the consequential position can be regarded as attributable loss and damage if . . . the person deceived has not himself behaved with reasonable prudence'.[77] Mitigation was thus regarded as an integral part of determining the 'attributable loss'. This approach was confirmed in *Smith New Court*.[78] Lord Steyn held that 'it must still be shown that the entire loss suffered by [the defendant] is a direct consequence of the fraudulently induced transaction'; on this basis he clarified that mitigation 'has no special features in the context of deceit'.[79]

It is useful to compare the approaches to mitigation and remoteness in *Smith New Court*. Whereas mitigation applied equally to deceit, the House of Lords held that remoteness did not apply.[80] Lord Steyn reasoned that 'it is a rational and defensible strategy to impose wider liability on an intentional wrongdoer'.[81] In particular, the remoteness rule, 'which reflects considerations of legal policy, does not necessarily avail the intentional wrongdoer'.[82] Lord Steyn considered that this stricter approach was justified by the aims of deterring fraud and 'requiring the fraudster to bear the risk of misfortunes directly caused by his fraud'.[83] The obvious implication is that, unlike remoteness, mitigation is not subordinate to 'legal policy' aims and instead forms part of the directness enquiry itself.

[71] ibid 760.
[72] *British Midland Tool Ltd v Midland International Tooling Ltd* [2003] EWHC 466 (Ch), [2003] 2 BCLC 523.
[73] The unlawful means was a breach of fiduciary duty.
[74] *British Midland Tool* (n 72) [245].
[75] *Doyle* (n 39).
[76] ibid 168.
[77] ibid 168. See also 171 (Sachs LJ).
[78] *Smith New Court Securities Ltd v Citibank NA* [1997] AC 254 (HL) 266 (Lord Browne-Wilkinson), 285 (Lord Steyn). See further *Secretary of State for Health v Servier Laboratories Ltd* [2016] EWHC 2381 (Ch), [60] (Henderson J).
[79] *Smith New Court* (n 78) 285.
[80] ibid 265 (Lord Browne-Wilkinson), 269 (Lord Mustill), 282 (Lord Steyn). See also *Doyle* (n 39) 168 (Winn LJ).
[81] *Smith New Court* (n 78) 279.
[82] ibid 279.
[83] ibid 279–80.

In light of the above analysis, it is clear that *OMV Petrom SA v Glencore International AG* was wrongly decided.[84] There, the claimant buyer had contracted with the defendant seller for the purchase of eighty cargos of crude oil of a particular description. The seller fraudulently passed off thirty-two of the shipments as matching the contractual description when they did not. The buyers subsequently refined and sub-sold this oil without being aware of the breach. Many years later, thanks to a whistle-blower, they discovered the fraud and sued the defendants. The judge at first instance, whose decision was upheld by the Court of Appeal, held that the market rule ought to apply and that the damages were not to be reduced on account of the sub-sales actually completed by the claimant.

The decision in *OMV* was evidently heavily influenced by the egregious conduct of the defendant: the Court of Appeal expressly relied on a policy of discouraging wrongdoing and preventing the defendant from profiting from its wrong.[85] Subsequent cases have also attributed the approach in *OMV* to 'strong policy reasons why a fraudster should not have the benefit of any onward sub-sale in a claim for deceit which do not apply to ordinary contractual claims'.[86] However, this approach is inconsistent with precedent. As already noted, in *Smith New Securities*, Lord Steyn made clear that mitigation operated in exactly the same way in cases of deceit as for other causes of action.[87] This remains so even where the effect is to the claimant's disadvantage, since its underlying basis is the fundamental nature of the causation requirement, rather than a policy-motivated rule.

Giving proper effect to the normal rules of mitigation, the sub-sales should have been taken into account in *OMV* because they were made without awareness of the breach.[88] This fact matters because it meant that the claimant never had any opportunity to replicate the no-breach position by acquiring substitute oil matching the contractual specification. There is consequently no basis for damages based on this hypothetical market transaction; instead, they should have been based on the actual consequences of the sub-sale, for better or worse. If this approach seems harsh to the claimant on the facts of *OMV*, it is important to remember that it could equally have been to their advantage, if the sub-sales had turned out to have disastrous consequences. Then, the element of deceit (ie the fact that the sub-sales were concluded without awareness of the breach) would have provided grounds for recovery of any additional consequential losses suffered (eg through harm to reputation or compensation to the ultimate purchasers).

[84] *OMV Petrom SA v Glencore International AG* [2017] 3 All ER 157. For more detailed analysis, see A Summers and A Kramer, 'Deceit, Difference in Value, and Date of Assessment' (2017) 133 Law Quarterly Review 41, 42.

[85] ibid [57] and [78].

[86] *ED&F Man Capital Markets Ltd v Come Harvest Holdings Ltd* [2022] EWHC 229 (Comm) [577].

[87] Text to n 83.

[88] The facts of *OMV* are essentially on all fours—save for the element of deception—with *Bence Graphics International Ltd v Fasson UK Ltd* [1998] QB 87. See further Chapter 9, text to n 130.

4 Temporal Scope

The law of mitigation does not apply to the claimant's pre-breach conduct, nor to post-breach conduct undertaken without knowledge of the breach. In relation to anticipatory breaches of contract, mitigation only applies once the claimant has accepted the repudiation; it does not apply prior to acceptance, even where the defendant has made clear that it will not perform. These features of mitigation present another puzzle for the orthodox account. If the law of mitigation aims to encourage the claimant to be self-reliant, why is the claimant not required to be self-reliant all of the time? If the claimant is required to act reasonably to prevent economic waste and maximize community welfare, why would it matter whether or not the claimant has accepted the defendant's repudiation?

On the causal explanation of mitigation, these puzzles are resolved. The law of mitigation requires actual knowledge of the breach because both the replication and exceptionality rules reflect the causal significance of voluntary human conduct. Ordinary causal principles entail that conduct is only voluntary when it is informed.[89] This explanation also shows why it is insufficient for mitigation that the claimant 'ought' to have been aware of the breach.[90] In relation to anticipatory breaches, the requirement of acceptance follows from the fact that the rules of mitigation attribute responsibility for the consequences of the defendant's breach. Until the defendant's anticipatory breach has been accepted, there is no breach as a matter of law and so nothing to attribute responsibility for.

4.1 Actual knowledge of the breach

The law of mitigation does not apply prior to the defendant's breach. This is readily accepted by the leading texts,[91] notwithstanding that the restriction sits uneasily with the favoured explanations of self-reliance and prevention of waste. The breach requirement is so well established that it is rarely stated expressly, although some express statements can be found.[92] In *Wright v Dean*, Wynn-Parry J held that the claimant's failure to register an option in land, which would have prevented the

[89] See further Chapter 5, text to n 142.

[90] This does not preclude that other doctrines may apply, for example remoteness or contributory negligence, which have a different basis: see further Chapter 11.

[91] Edelman (n 7) [9-021]; Tettenborn, *Damages* (2nd edn) (n 6) [5.72]; Burrows (n 7) 130; Beale (n 7) [29-104].

[92] See eg *Tai Hing Cotton Mill Ltd v Kamsing Knitting Factory* [1979] AC 91 (PC) 99 (Lord Keith); *Losinjska Plovidba v Transco Overseas Ltd (The Orjula)* [1995] 2 Lloyd's Rep 395 (QB) 400 (Mance J); *UBC Chartering Ltd v Liepaya Shipping Co Ltd (The Liepaya)* [1999] 1 Lloyd's Rep 649 (QB) 671–72 (Rix LJ); *Bulkhaul Ltd v Rhodia Organique Fine Ltd* [2008] EWCA Civ 1452, [2009] 1 Lloyd's Rep 353 [24] (Smith LJ); *Scottish Power UK Plc v BP Exploration Operating Company Ltd* [2016] EWCA Civ 1043, [41] (Christopher Clarke LJ); and *Secretary of State for Health* (n 78) [25] (Henderson J).

defendant's wrongful sale to a third party, was not a 'failure to mitigate' because there was no breach until the defendant completed the sale.[93] The breach requirement can raise difficult issues about the precise timing of the breach,[94] both in relation to actual breaches and to anticipatory breaches.[95]

Even once a breach has occurred, the rules of mitigation will not apply to the claimant's conduct before it was aware of the breach.[96] This knowledge requirement is also accepted by the leading texts,[97] although its explanation and precise scope is unclear. In *Schering*, Scott LJ held that 'the duty to mitigate the consequences of a breach of contract can hardly arise until the person who is said to be the subject to the duty has become aware of the breach'.[98] More recently, after reviewing the authorities, Gross LJ concluded in *Borealis v Geogas Trading* that '[w]ith specific regard to the question of mitigation, the linkage between the knowledge of a claimant and the reasonableness (or otherwise) of its conduct is plain'.[99] The knowledge requirement often arises in fraud cases, where the claimant may not discover the breach for some time.[100]

More specifically, the requisite knowledge is knowledge of the facts that constitute the breach and 'not of the law or the legal consequences of those facts'.[101] This was established by Hobhouse J in *Schering* and was subsequently confirmed (also by Hobhouse LJ) in *County v Girozentrale*.[102] In *Borealis*, Gross LJ agreed that '[f]or the chain of causation to be broken, the claimant need not have knowledge of the legal niceties of the breach of contract'.[103] Where the claimant is a corporation, the knowledge requirement can raise difficult issues concerning attribution of

[93] *Wright v Dean* [1948] Ch 686 (Ch) 696.

[94] See eg *Anderson (Commander of the Flying Fish) v Hoen (The Flying Fish)* (1865) 3 Moo PC NS 77, 16 ER 29 (PC), discussed in Williams (n 66) 287. See also *Toepfer v Warinco AG* [1978] 2 Lloyd's Rep 569 (QB) 578 (Brandon J).

[95] On anticipatory breaches, see further text to n 128.

[96] *Sachs v Miklos* [1948] 2 KB 23 (CA) 40–41 (Lord Goddard CJ); *East Ham Corp v Bernard Sunley & Sons* [1966] AC 406 (HL) 445 (Lord Upjohn); *Youell v Bland Welch & Co Ltd (No 2) (The 'Superhulls Cover' Case)* [1990] 2 Lloyd's Rep 431 (QB) 461–62 (Phillips J); *Downs v Chappell* [1997] 1 WLR 426 (CA) 435 (Hobhouse LJ); *Smith New Court* (n 78) 266 (Lord Browne-Wilkinson); *The Liepaya* (n 101) 672 (Rix LJ); and *Stanford International Bank Ltd v HSBC Bank PLC* [2022] UKSC 34, [2023] 2 WLR 79 [43] (Lord Leggatt). See in Canadian case law: *410784 Ontario Limited v Little Zinger Inc (Corktown Esso)*, 2016 ONCA 90 [210]–[211]; *Armstrong v Roslyn Park Land Co Ltd* (1951) 4 WWR (NS), 270.

[97] Beale (n 7) [29-104]; Peel, *Treitel on Contract* (15th edn) (n 7) [20-105]; Tettenborn, *Damages* (2nd edn) (n 6) [5.75]; Kramer (n 7) [15-58]. cf Edelman (n 7) [9-051], merely noting that knowledge of the breach is 'an important fact in assessing whether there had been a failure to mitigate'.

[98] *Schering Agrochemicals Ltd v Resibel NV SA* (CA, 26 November 1992) 16.

[99] *Borealis AB v Geogas Trading SA* [2010] EWHC 2789 (Comm), [2011] 1 Lloyd's Rep 482 [100].

[100] *Twycross v Grant* (1877) 2 CPD 469 (CA); *Dobell & Co Ltd v Barber & Garratt* [1931] 1 KB 219 (CA); *Smith New Court* (n 78) 266 (Lord Brown-Wilkinson).

[101] *Schering Agrochemicals Ltd* (n 98) (Hobhouse J).

[102] *County Ltd v Girozentrale Securities* [1996] 3 All ER 834 (CA) 858 (Hobhouse LJ).

[103] *Borealis* (n 99) [46].

knowledge within the organization.[104] Where a latent breach comes to light gradually, there may also be a difficult question as to when the claimant first acquired sufficient knowledge of the facts: the relevant time appears to be at the end of the disclosures.[105]

The orthodox account of mitigation essentially regards the knowledge requirement as a corollary of the reasonableness test.[106] As Williams put it, 'The reasonable man does not spend his time nosing out possible wrongdoing' and the knowledge requirement 'merely incorporates this proposition of fact'.[107] However, the claimant might occasionally act 'unreasonably' by failing to take steps that would have enabled it to discover the breach. This reasoning has led many of the leading texts to propose that mitigation will also apply once the claimant 'ought to have discovered' the breach.[108] Kramer calls this 'constructive knowledge'.[109] Treitel suggests that 'there is no compelling reason for holding that [the duty to mitigate] can never apply where the claimant had, but failed to take, clear opportunities of discovering the breach'.[110]

There is no clear judicial authority for the proposition that constructive knowledge suffices for mitigation.[111] Instead the cases appear to require actual knowledge, although the position is somewhat uncertain.[112] In breach of contract cases, the most common judicial explanation for this approach is that the claimant is entitled to rely on the defendant's promised performance.[113] Although this reasoning might be taken to suggest that a failure to discover the breach is thus not 'unreasonable', other cases have established the requirement of actual knowledge directly. In *Schering*, Hobhouse J approved the approach of Phillips J in the *Superhulls Cover* case, which 'rejected any concept of imputed knowledge or treating a party as being in breach of his duty to mitigate because he did not inquire and so inform himself that there had been a breach'.[114]

[104] *Trebor* (n 2) [67] (Tomlinson LJ): 'identification of the natural person whose knowledge is appropriate for this purpose will depend upon questions of delegation of duty within the organisation'. See also *Schering Agrochemicals* (CA) (n 98) 4 (Purchas LJ).

[105] *4Eng Ltd v Harper* [2007] EWHC 1568 (Ch) [53] (Briggs J).

[106] Tettenborn, *Damages* (2nd edn) (n 6) [5.75]; Peel (n 7) [20-105].

[107] Williams (n 66) 290.

[108] Beale (n 7) [29-104]. See also Tettenborn, *Damages* (2nd edn) (n 6) [5.75].

[109] Kramer (n 7) [15-61].

[110] Peel (n 7) [20-105].

[111] The insufficiency of 'constructive knowledge' should not be confused with the proposition that knowledge of the facts rather than their legal implications is sufficient: text to n 101.

[112] See further Conclusion, text to n 29.

[113] *Mowbray v Merryweather* [1895] 2 QB 640 (CA) 644 (Lord Esher MR), 645 (Kay LJ), 646 (Rigby LJ); *Reardon Smith Line Ltd v Australian Wheat Board* [1956] AC 266 (PC) 282–83 (Lord Somervell); *Barclays Bank plc v Fairclough Building Ltd* [1995] QB 214 (CA) 227 (Beldam LJ); *Six Continents* (n 33) [22] (Laws LJ), [31] (Buxton LJ); *Flanagan v Greenbanks Ltd* [2013] EWCA Civ 1702 [37] (Rafferty LJ); *Stacey v Autosleeper Group Ltd* [2014] EWCA Civ 1551 [23] (Lloyd LJ).

[114] *Schering Agrochemicals* (QB) (n 98) (Hobhouse J), citing *The 'Superhulls Cover' Case* (n 96) 462 (Phillips J). See also *Trac Time Control Ltd v Moss Plastic Parts Ltd* [2004] EWHC 3298 (TCC) [182] (Grenfell J); *Pearson Education Ltd v The Charter Partnership Ltd* [2007] EWCA Civ 130 [33] (Lord Phillips).

It might be thought that *Bostock & Co Ltd v Nicholson and Sons* is inconsistent with this view, but in fact it is not.[115] In that case, the claimants purchased sulphuric acid from the defendants, which was supplied in breach of the implied term of correspondence with description (as the acid contained arsenic). Before the breach was known, but at a point when the claimants could, with ordinary care, have discovered the breach, the claimants used the acid in the manufacture of brewing sugar. The resultant sugar was rendered poisonous, exposing the claimants to claims by the brewers to whom the sugar was sold. Bruce J held that the claimants could not recover the sums payable to the brewers, as 'no liability is incurred in the ordinary case of a separate and distinct collateral contract with a third person uncommunicated to the original contractor or wrong-doer'.[116] It is important to note that this reasoning is not predicated on constructive knowledge of the breach by the claimant; instead, it emphasizes the fact that the existence of the sales to third parties had not been communicated to the defendant. The decision is accordingly best explained on grounds of remoteness rather than mitigation.

The case of *Secretary of State for Health v Servier Laboratories Ltd* is more difficult to square with the view that actual knowledge of the breach is required; however, the point was not conclusively decided.[117] There, Henderson J stated that 'the underlying principle of the law of mitigation remains whether the claimant has taken "all reasonable steps to mitigate the loss consequent on the breach" . . . Knowledge is thus a relevant factor, but its relevance is to the question of fact whether the claimant acted reasonably in all the circumstances.'[118] For this reason, Henderson J was prepared to accept that it was reasonably arguable that constructive knowledge would suffice. In the absence of a final decision on this point, *Servier* is surely of insufficient weight to challenge the established position in *Schering* and other earlier cases.

The requirement of actual knowledge presents a further puzzle for the orthodox account because the claimant may act unreasonably without awareness of the breach, or indeed even before the breach occurred. The causal explanation resolves this puzzle. Until the claimant is actually aware of the breach, it cannot exercise a choice as to whether (and how) to restore no-breach position. In *Schering*, Hobhouse J reasoned that 'a failure to mitigate involves voluntary conduct; acting under compulsion or without the relevant knowledge will not amount to a breach of the duty to mitigate';[119] in *Trebor Bassett v ADT Fire & Security*, Tomlinson LJ similarly reasoned that 'the act can only be said to be voluntary or

[115] *Bostock & Co Ltd v Nicholson & Sons Ltd* [1904] 1 KB 725.

[116] ibid 742.

[117] n 78.

[118] n 78 [41] prior to the ellipsis; [47] following the ellipsis.

[119] *Schering Agrochemicals* (QB) (n 98). See also *County* (n 102) 857 (Hobhouse LJ), holding that the claimant's conduct must be 'voluntary in the sense of being undertaken with a knowledge of its significance'; *The 'Superhulls Cover' Case* (n 96) 461 (Phillips J), emphasizing that the claimant's conduct must be 'voluntary' and 'deliberate'.

the duty to mitigate to arise if the relevant knowledge comes to the attention of the claimant'.[120] In other words, the requirement of actual knowledge follows from the choice principle.

The restricted scope of mitigation does not mean that a claimant's failure to discover the breach can have no legal consequences. As Phillips J clarified in the *Superhulls Cover* case, 'If it is not reasonably foreseeable that the plaintiff will remain in ignorance of the breach and fail to react to it so as to avoid loss, the loss may be too remote'.[121] Similarly, 'If the plaintiff negligently fails to discover the breach . . . the normal consequences of [contributory] negligence will follow including, where appropriate, the application of the 1945 Act'.[122] However, as I discuss in Chapter 11, the remoteness and contributory negligence rules each have different explanations from mitigation. The basis for the reasonable foreseeability rule of remoteness is unclear but does not appear to be causal.[123] Contributory negligence is fault-based, and it results in a percentage reduction in damages rather than a counterfactual assessment.[124]

Moreover, in *County v Girozentrale*, Hobhouse LJ suggested that although mitigation required actual knowledge of the breach, the claimant's failure to discover the breach might break the 'chain of causation' if it was reckless.[125] This recklessness standard has been reiterated (though not applied) in subsequent decisions.[126] It serves to emphasize the need for a voluntary choice to depart from the normal course of conduct in the circumstances. Accordingly, the causal significance of the claimant's reckless conduct derives from the wider exceptionality principle applicable where the claimant makes a choice to act unusually. However, there appears to be a convention that, where the claimant's unusual conduct is *not* part of an attempt to replicate the non-breach position, it is described as an 'intervening act by the claimant' rather than a 'failure to mitigate'.[127]

4.2 Acceptance of anticipatory repudiation

In claims for breach of contract, if the defendant acted in anticipatory repudiation of the contract prior to the date when performance was due, there are three

120 *Trebor* (n 2) [67] (Tomlinson LJ).

121 *The 'Superhulls Cover' Case* (n 96) 462. See also *County* (n 102) 857 (Hobhouse LJ).

122 *The 'Superhulls Cover' Case* (n 96) 462 (Phillips J), referring to the Law Reform (Contributory Negligence) Act 1945. See also Kramer (n 7) [15-53], [15-56]–[15-57]. In context, it is clear that Phillips J was referring to contributory negligence, rather than the tort of negligence.

123 As Street puts it, '*Hadley v Baxendale* lays down rules of policy which restrict causal rules': Harry Street, *Principles of the Law of Damages* (Sweet & Maxwell 1962) 2.

124 Law Reform (Contributory Negligence) Act 1945, s 1(1).

125 *County* (n 102) 857 (Hobhouse LJ).

126 *Borealis* (n 99) [46] (Gross LJ); *Trac Time Control* (n 114) [182] (Grenfell J); *Flanagan* (n 113) [38] (Rafferty LJ).

127 See further Chapter 11, Section 2.

possibilities for the timing of mitigation: first, when the defendant repudiated the contract ('anticipatory repudiation');[128] second, when the claimant accepted the repudiation ('acceptance');[129] or third, when the defendant's promised performance was due ('performance').[130] It appears that the rules of mitigation apply from the time of acceptance. In other words, mitigation does not apply until the claimant accepts the defendant's anticipatory repudiation, although this may be before the date when performance was due. This approach rests on the view that there is no actual breach of contract until the anticipatory repudiation has been accepted.[131]

Several early sale of goods cases established that the claimant was not bound immediately to resort to the market upon the defendant giving notice that it would not perform.[132] Subsequently in *Shindler v Northern Raincoat*, Diplock J held that 'on a matter of law it cannot be said that there is any duty on the part of the plaintiff to mitigate his damages before there had been any breach, which he has accepted as a breach'.[133] The acceptance requirement is generally acknowledged in the leading texts,[134] and was affirmed by the Supreme Court in *Bunge v Nidera*.[135] Liu summarizes the position as 'firmly established'.[136] The main authorities involve an available market for replacement performance, where (in accordance with the restoration rule) damages have been assessed as if the claimant resorted to the market at the date of acceptance or as soon as possible thereafter.[137]

Where the claimant did accept the defendant's anticipatory repudiation, mitigation can apply before the defendant's contractual performance was due. In *Frost v Knight*, Cockburn CJ held that the claimant 'will be entitled to such damages as would have arisen from the non-performance of the contract at the appointed time, subject, however, to abatement in respect of any circumstances which may

[128] Here 'repudiation' refers generally to conduct giving rise to a right to terminate the contract.

[129] The claimant's acceptance also has the effect of terminating the contract.

[130] This is the date when an 'actual breach' would first occur.

[131] See further text to n 148.

[132] *Leigh v Paterson* (1818) 8 Taunt 540, 129 ER 493, 494 (Dallas CJ); *Startup v Cortazzi* (1835) 2 Cr M & R 165, 150 ER 71, 73 (Alderson B); *Phillpotts v Evans* (1839) 5 M & W 475, 151 ER 200, 201 (Lord Abinger CB), 202 (Alderson B). These cases predate the establishment of the doctrine of anticipatory breach in *Hochster v De La Tour* (1853) 2 El & Bl 678, 118 ER 922.

[133] *Shindler v Northern Raincoat Co* [1960] 1 WLR 1038 (Assizes) 1048.

[134] See eg Edelman (n 7) [9-021]; Beale (n 7) [29-104]; Burrows (n 7) 132.

[135] *Bunge* (n 2) [17] (Lord Sumption), [83] (Lord Toulson). See also *Tai Hing Cotton* (n 92) 102 (Lord Keith); *The Solholt* (QB) 580 (Staughton J).

[136] Qiao Liu, *Anticipatory Breach* (Hart 2011) 171, citing *Frost v Knight* (1871–72) LR 7 Ex 111 (Ex Ch); *Roth & Co v Taysen, Townsend & Co* (1896) 1 Com Cas 306, 12 TLR 211 (CA); *Tredegar Iron and Coal Co Ltd v Hawthorn Bros & Co* (1902) 18 TLR 716 (CA); *Melachrino v Nickoll & Knight* [1920] 1 KB 693 (KB). However, in each of these cases the claimant had in fact accepted the defendant's anticipatory repudiation.

[137] *Millett v Van Heek* [1921] 2 KB 369 (CA); *Tai Hing Cotton* (n 92); *The Elena d'Amico* (n 3); *Kaines (UK) v Oesterreichische Warenhandelsgesellschaft Austrowaren GmbH* [1993] 2 Lloyd's Rep 1 (CA). See also *Gebruder Metelmann GmbH & Co KG v NBR (London) Ltd* [1984] 1 Lloyd's Rep 614 (CA) 634 (Brown-Wilkinson LJ), in which the claimant did in fact resort to the market as soon as possible after acceptance and was entitled to recover the costs incurred.

have afforded him the means of mitigating his loss'.[138] Several other cases have affirmed this approach to mitigation in principle,[139] although damages were assessed as at the date of performance on the basis that mitigation was not applicable on the facts.[140] In summary, the law is that the rules of mitigation will apply from the time of acceptance (even if performance has not yet become due), but not before.

The timing of mitigation following anticipatory repudiation presents a puzzle for some of the leading texts.[141] Burrows argues that 'the duty to mitigate should arise once there has been an anticipatory repudiation' because 'economic efficiency should override the wishes of the innocent party to hold the contract alive'.[142] The explanation that mitigation aims to prevent waste leads both Burrows and Treitel to conclude that the claimant should sometimes be compelled to 'accept the repudiation, claim damages and make substitute contracts' rather than unreasonably continue its own performance in order to earn the agreed sum.[143] Treitel appears to regard this as a descriptive claim,[144] but Burrows acknowledges its inconsistency with the 'traditional approach' that 'there is no duty to mitigate, unless the claimant chooses to accept the anticipatory repudiation'.[145] I discuss the application of mitigation in the context of unaccepted repudiations, such as in the so-called '*White & Carter*' type cases,[146] in further detail in Chapter 11.[147]

On the causal explanation of mitigation, the timing puzzle can be resolved. The rules of mitigation are attributive not prescriptive; in particular, they attribute responsibility for the consequences of the defendant's breach. It follows that the rules can have no application until a breach has occurred. In relation to anticipatory repudiations, the law appears to be that there is no breach of contract until the repudiation is accepted,[148] such that 'breach and termination of the contract are simultaneous'.[149] Most famously, in *Howard v Pickford Tool*, Asquith LJ held that '[a]n unaccepted repudiation is a thing writ in water and of no value to anybody; it

[138] *Frost* (n 136) 114. See also *Melachrino* (n 136) 699 (Bailhache J); *Bunge* (n 2) [17] (Lord Sumption).

[139] *Brown v Muller* (1871–72) LR 7 Ex 319 (Ex Ch) 323 (Kelly CB); *Roper v Johnson* (1873) LR 8 CP 167 (CP) 180–81 (Brett J), 183–84 (Grove J); *Millett* (n 147) 375 (Bankes LJ), 377 (Atkin LJ); *Garnac Grain Co Inc v HMF Faure & Fairclough Ltd* [1968] AC 1130 (HL) 1140 (Lord Pearson).

[140] cf *Tai Hing Cotton* (n 92) 104–05 (Lord Keith), where there was no fixed date for performance and damages were assessed one month after the date of acceptance (to allow time to negotiate a substitute contract).

[141] However, it is supported by Edelman (n 7) [9-021].

[142] Burrows (n 7) 132.

[143] ibid 435–40; Peel (n 7) [21-015]. cf Edelman (n 7) [9-021], describing this argument as 'misconceived'.

[144] Peel (n 7) [21-015]. This description is inconsistent with the authorities cited at n 132 and following.

[145] Burrows (n 7) 132. Burrows' claims in relation to the timing of mitigation are evaluative rather than descriptive: ibid 440.

[146] *White & Carter (Councils) Ltd v McGregor* [1962] AC 413 (HL).

[147] See further Chapter 11, Section 6.

[148] *Phillpotts v Evans* (1839) 5 M & W 475, 477 (Parke B).

[149] *Heyman v Darwins Ltd* [1942] AC 356 (HL) 382 (Lord Wright).

confers no legal rights of any sort or kind'.[150] On this view, '[a]n anticipatory breach was recognised as a wrong, but an "acceptance" was required to convert it into a fully-fledged breach'.[151] Without a breach recognized in law, there is nothing of legal significance for which to attribute responsibility.

The foregoing analysis rests on the assumption that there is no actual breach until an anticipatory repudiation has been accepted. In Chapter 11, I consider an alternative analysis if this is not the case.[152] Moreover, the acceptance requirement makes it important to determine whether, in addition to any unaccepted anticipatory repudiation, an 'actual breach' has also occurred.[153] If the defendant has already breached an obligation, and the claimant is aware of the breach, then the rules of mitigation will apply for the purpose of assessing damages for that breach. Here, mitigation does not depend on the claimant's acceptance of the breach so as to terminate the contract;[154] termination is only relevant to anticipatory repudiations where there is otherwise no breach at all. However, to be clear, even when there has been an actual breach, this does not mean that mitigation applies to all of the claimant's subsequent conduct;[155] it merely means that the replication and exceptionality rules apply for the purpose of assessing the loss or gain attributable to that particular breach.

[150] *Howard v Pickford Tool Co* [1951] 1 KB 417 (CA) 421. See also *Wilkinson v Verity* (1870-71) LR 6 CP 206 (CP) 209 (Willes J); *Johnstone v Milling* (1886) 16 QBD 460 (CA) 467 (Lord Esher MR), 472–73 (Bowen LJ). Admittedly, Asquith LJ's statement was made in the context of whether the contract will be discharged automatically by the defendant's breach; however, it is wide enough in its own terms to also encompass the proposition that no breach occurs until the repudiation is accepted.

[151] Liu, *Anticipatory Breach* (n 136) 24. Although Liu is sceptical of this understanding, he accepts that 'courts seem generally to acquiesce in the rule': 28. See further 22–25, 28–30.

[152] See further Chapter 11, text to n 214.

[153] See eg *Cerberus Software Ltd v Rowley* [2001] EWCA Civ 78, [2001] ICR 376 [15] (Ward LJ), [43] (Jonathan Parker LJ).

[154] The actual breach need not be repudiatory; mitigation also applies to the assessment of damages for breaches of warranty where there is no right to terminate.

[155] This view relies on the misconception that mitigation prescribes conduct.

PART 3
RESTATEMENT

8
Avoidable Loss

1 Introduction

This chapter restates the law of mitigation as it applies to the cases conventionally discussed under the rubric of 'avoidable loss'. First, I argue that the reasonableness test conceals two distinct rules: the replication rule and the exceptionality rule, which I introduced in Chapter 6. I show how these rules apply to the claimant's attempts at repair, replacement, extrication, and negotiations with the defendant. Second, where either the replication or exceptionality rule applies, the effect is that the claimant's breach position is assessed counterfactually as if they had taken steps to replicate their no-breach position in the usual way. In relation to so-called 'avoidable loss', this will result in an award of damages that is less than the claimant's factual loss evident at the date of trial. Finally, I address the procedural issues of burden of proof and whether (and when) mitigation raises questions of fact or law.

2 Applying the 'Reasonableness' Test

The orthodox account of mitigation provides that the avoidable loss rule applies where the claimant acted unreasonably. Chapter 2 exposed various problems with this understanding. The main problem was that the description of the reasonableness test as a question of fact hides an almost complete lack of guidance as to how the avoidable loss rule is applied. The replication and exceptionality rules enable a more detailed description of how the law of mitigation is applied. In particular, whereas the issues of choice and exceptionality are not specifically legal (and in this sense are 'questions of fact'), the replication rule raises an important question of law because it depends on a careful assessment of the claimant's no-breach position. This distinction matters for the appellate review of decisions regarding mitigation.

2.1 The replication rule

The replication rule applies where the claimant made a choice not to replicate the no-breach position as nearly as possible. It does not matter whether or not this choice was 'reasonable' in the ordinary meaning of being 'sensible'; the claimant's

Mitigation in the Law of Damages. Andrew Summers, Oxford University Press. © Andy Summers 2025.
DOI: 10.1093/9780191864032.003.0008

conduct is an intervening cause because it voluntarily departs from the legal norm of replication established by the compensatory principle.[1] The claimant is responsible for the outcome of its choice, regardless of whether the choice was blameworthy or praiseworthy, irrational or entirely sensible. Most of the cases applying the replication rule involve inaction by the claimant: for example, a choice not to repair, replace or extricate from the breach. The replication rule occasionally applies where the claimant refuses the defendant's offer of performance, or conversely presses for performance in circumstances where it is obviously futile. These sub-categories are not distinct rules; they are all applications of the same replication rule.

Attempts to replicate the no-breach position may involve repair, replacement, or extrication. Repair applies mainly to goods, land, and personal injury (i.e. medical treatment), whereas replacement also applies to services (including employment) and money (including financial products). Extrication refers generically to other modes by which a claimant may 'undo' certain consequences of a breach: for example, by reversing transactions entered into as a result of the defendant's negligent advice. Replication can most often be achieved by resorting to the market but may sometimes be achieved by dealing with the defendant or identified third parties. It is important to emphasize that whilst the sub-categories in this section provide a useful way of dividing up the cases, they do not represent distinct legal rules. The central question is always simply whether the claimant could have replicated the no-breach position but chose not to do so.

2.1.1 Repair

Where the defendant has damaged the claimant's property, or provided defective goods or services, the claimant may be able to replicate the no-breach position by repairing the damaged property; similarly, personal injuries may be treated. If the claimant makes a choice not to seek repair (and does not replace either), it will be held to have acted 'unreasonably'. Such cases are usually expressed as applications of the avoidable loss rule of mitigation, although occasionally they are instead explained in terms of intervening causation.[2] Where the claimant has chosen to delay repairs, the issue is most often characterized in terms of the 'date of assessment'.[3] Whatever the characterization, the rule is that the defendant is not responsible for the outcome of the claimant's choice not to conduct the repairs.

[1] See further Chapter 6, Section 3.1.

[2] See eg *Anderson (Commander of the Flying Fish) v Hoen (The Flying Fish)* (1865) 3 Moo PC NS 77, 16 ER 29 (PC); *Grant v Owners of the Egyptian (The Egyptian)* [1910] AC 400 (HL); *Farr v Butters Bros* [1932] 2 KB 606 (CA); *Lambert v Lewis* [1982] AC 225 (HL).

[3] See eg *Radford v De Froberville* [1977] 1 WLR 1262 (Ch) 1285–86 (Oliver J); *Dodd Properties (Kent) Ltd v Canterbury City Council* [1980] 1 WLR 433 (CA) 451 (Megaw LJ). See further Andrew Dyson and Adam Kramer, 'There is No "Breach Date Rule": Mitigation, Difference in Value and Date of Assessment' (2014) 130 Law Quarterly Review 259, 268–69.

Schering Agrochemicals v Resibel exemplifies the choice not to repair.[4] The defendants supplied defective parts to the claimants. The claimants, who were aware of the defects, nevertheless chose not to repair or replace the parts. Three weeks later, the defects resulted in an explosion and serious fire. At first instance, Hobhouse J held that the claimants 'had an opportunity to mitigate or avoid their loss which they unreasonably failed to take'.[5] In the Court of Appeal, Purchas LJ emphasized the voluntariness of the claimant's choice not to repair the defect.[6] As Tomlinson LJ subsequently summarized, 'The basis for denying recovery . . . is that continuing to operate the production line in the knowledge that the fire detection or suppression system is defective is a voluntary act which can be held to be the cause of the subsequent damage'.[7] Similarly, as Jackson LJ noted in *Howmet v Economy Devices*, 'Once the end user is alerted to the dangerous condition of a chattel, if he voluntarily continues to use it thereby causing personal injury or damage, he normally does so entirely at his own risk.'[8]

The replication rule also explains the application of mitigation where the claimant chose not to undergo available and effective medical treatment. In *McAuley v London Transport Executive*, the Court of Appeal held that the claimant had acted unreasonably where he refused an operation that would have given him a ninety per cent chance of restoring the use of his hand.[9] The rule does not seek to prescribe that the claimant *should* undergo treatment.[10] Instead, as Lord M'Laren held in *Donnelly v William Baird*, 'The question is whether . . . his suffering and consequent inability to work at his trade ought not to be attributed to his voluntary action in declining to avail himself of reasonable surgical treatment'.[11] Where the refusal of treatment is not the product of a sufficiently voluntary choice, the replication rule will not apply.[12]

The same rule applies in circumstances analogous to physical repair. In *Walker v Medlicott*, solicitors were negligent in drafting a will.[13] The Court of Appeal

[4] *Schering Agrochemicals Ltd v Resibel NV SA* (QB, 4 May 1991). See also, on almost identical facts, *Beoco Ltd v Alfa Laval Co Ltd* [1995] QB 137 (CA). See further *Tucker v Linger* (1882) 21 Ch D 18 (CA) 30 (Kay J); *Minchburn v Peck* (1988) 20 HLR 392 (CA) 397-98 (Dillon LJ), 398 (Bingham LJ); *Commercial Fibres (Ireland) Ltd v Zabaida* [1975] 1 Lloyd's Rep 27 (QB) 29–30 (Donaldson J); *Trac Time Control Ltd v Moss Plastic Parts Ltd* [2004] EWHC 3298 (TCC) [182] (Grenfell J): 'if [the claimant] becomes aware of a defect in goods, but continues to use the goods notwithstanding this knowledge, there is a break in the chain of causation from that point on'.

[5] *Schering Agrochemicals* (QB) (n 4).

[6] *Schering Agrochemicals Ltd v Resibel NV SA* (CA, 26 November 1992).

[7] *Trebor Bassett Holdings Ltd v ADT Fire & Security plc* [2012] EWCA Civ 1158, [2012] BLR 441 [67].

[8] *Howmet Ltd v Economy Devices Ltd* [2016] EWCA Civ 847 [92].

[9] *McAuley v London Transport Executive* [1957] 2 Lloyd's Rep 500 (CA) 505. See also *Marcroft v Scruttons* [1954] 1 Lloyd's Rep 395 (CA). Cf *Steele v Robert George & Co* [1942] AC 497 (HL) and *Richardson v Redpath Brown & Co* [1944] AC 62 (HL), where the refusal of medical treatment was held not to be unreasonable because it was not clear that the treatment would be effective.

[10] See further Chapter 7, Section 2.

[11] *Donnelly v William Baird & Co Ltd* (1908) 15 SLT 799 (CSIH) 801.

[12] For further discussion of the meaning of 'choice' in this context, see Chapter 6, Section 3.3.

[13] *Walker v Geo H Medlicott & Son* [1999] 1 WLR 727 (CA). The claim was brought in the tort of negligence following *White v Jones* [1995] 2 AC 207 (HL).

held that 'the courts can reasonably expect the plaintiff to mitigate his damage by bringing proceedings for rectification of the will'.[14] In *Toepfer v Warinco*, the claimant contracted to buy fine-ground meal but coarse-ground meal was delivered instead.[15] Brandon J held that the claimant had failed to mitigate because, although it knew of the error, it did not inform the defendants and so continued to receive goods of the wrong specification.[16] In *Symrise v Baker*, the defendants negligently exposed the claimants to a potential tax liability. Burton J rejected the claimants' tax recovery claim on the basis that they 'acted unreasonably in abandoning the proceedings which they had a very good chance of winning'.[17]

2.1.2 Replacement

The claimant may be able to replicate the no-breach position by seeking a replacement for performance of the defendant's obligation.[18] For example, it may be possible for the claimant to buy replacement goods, or to sell its services to another client. Again, where the claimant makes a choice not to seek a replacement it will be held to have acted 'unreasonably', although it is often stressed that reasonableness cannot be given its usual, dictionary definition in this context.[19] Where there is an available market for replacement goods, shares, or land, the issue is usually expressed as an application of the 'market rule';[20] however, in relation to the replacement of money or services, mitigation is often invoked directly. It is important to reiterate the significance of the claimant's *choice* not to replicate the no-breach position. Where the claimant had no choice, for example if it was unaware

[14] *Walker* (n 13) 739 (Sir Christopher Slade). See also 742 (Mummery LJ); 743 (Simon Brown LJ). The decision on this point was obiter because it was held that the solicitors did not owe a duty of care.

[15] *Toepfer v Warinco AG* [1978] 2 Lloyd's Rep 569 (QB).

[16] If they had done so, 'the [sellers] would immediately have stopped loading coarse-ground meal, altered the grinding to fine, and thereafter delivered only fine-ground meal': ibid 578 (Brandon J).

[17] *Symrise AG v Baker & McKenzie* [2015] EWHC 912 (Comm), [2016] 1 All ER (Comm) 603 [87]. See also *Joyce v Bowman Law Ltd* [2010] EWHC 251 (Ch), [2010] PNLR 22 [118] (Vos J); *Welford v EDF Energy Networks (LPN) plc* [2007] EWCA Civ 293, [2007] 2 P & CR 15 [34] (Thomas LJ).

[18] In relation to contractual obligations, the replacement will be of the promised performance; in relation to tortious obligations, the replacement will be of whatever goods or services the claimant would have had if the breach had not occurred.

[19] See eg *Fulton Shipping Inc of Panama v Globalia Business Travel Sau (The New Flamenco)* [2017] 1 WLR 2581 [16], Lord Clarke approvingly quoting Popplewell J at first instance: 'The fact that a mitigating step, by way of action or inaction, may be a reasonable and sensible business decision with a view to reducing the impact of the breach, does not of itself render it one which is sufficiently caused by the breach. A step taken by the innocent party which is a reasonable response to the breach and designed to reduce losses caused thereby may be triggered by a breach but not legally caused by the breach.'

[20] See further Chapter 10. For an example expressed directly in terms of mitigation, see *Bulkhaul Ltd v Rhodia Organique Fine Ltd* [2008] EWCA Civ 1452, [2009] 1 Lloyd's Rep 353 [4], [26] (Smith LJ). However, note recent judicial remarks at Supreme Court level explicitly linking the 'market rule' with mitigation: *Stanford International Bank Ltd v HSBC Bank PLC* [2022] UKSC 34, [2023] 2 WLR 79 (Lord Leggatt) [43]. See similar remarks in the Canadian case of *Wingold Construction Co Ltd v Kramp* [1960] SCR 556, 560.

of the breach or if no replacement was available, the replication (or 'market') rule has no application.[21]

The replication rule also applies where the claimant chose not to replace money. In *Sempra Metals v Inland Revenue Commissioners*, the House of Lords established that claimants may recover damages for late payment of debts, 'subject to the principles governing all claims for damages for breach of contract, such as remoteness, failure to mitigate and so forth'.[22] In quantifying damages for late payment, in *Equitas v Walsham Brothers*, Males J held that where the claimant chooses not to resort to the market to seek a loan, and subsequently seeks compensation for losses arising from its inability to make use of the money it is owed, then the claimant 'is likely to be met with the defence that . . . it has failed to mitigate by borrowing in order to replace the money lost'.[23] Males J added, consistently with the importance of choice, that mitigation would not apply where the claimant 'did not know and should not reasonably have known that the money was missing'.[24]

There are numerous cases in which mitigation has been applied to a choice not to seek a replacement for the defendant's service.[25] In *Ansett v Marshall*, the defendants wrongfully refused to carry the claimant on board its ship from England to Australia, but offered passage on another ship sailing one week later.[26] Crompton J rejected a claim for the cost of the claimant's accommodation in England after the time when the second ship departed, on the basis that the claimant could have taken the subsequent voyage to replace the first.[27]

Similarly, in *Wilson v Newport Dock*, the defendants failed to provide the claimant's ship with a safe dock.[28] The court held that it was unable to decide whether the defendants were responsible for damage to the ship, because the jury had been unable to come to a consensus as to whether the claimant could have obtained an alternative place of safety.[29] Absent a finding on this point by the jury, it was impossible for the court to determine whether the plaintiff had made the choice not to take up an opportunity to replicate the no-breach position. As Pollock CB stated in his speech, 'If there was a safe place to which the vessel might . . . have been taken, a verdict for the plaintiff would be a great act of injustice.'[30] This does

[21] See eg *Stanford International Bank Ltd* (n 20) (Lord Leggatt) [43]: 'But where the market mitigation rule does not yield this result—*as, for example, where the claimant is not aware of the defendant's breach until some time later* . . . the relevant loss will occur, and the damages will therefore be measured, at a different date.' (Emphasis added.)

[22] *Sempra Metals Ltd v Inland Revenue Commissioners* [2007] UKHL 34, [2008] 1 AC 561 [94] (Lord Nicholls). See also [16] (Lord Hope), [132] (Lord Scott).

[23] *Equitas Ltd v Walsham Bros & Co Ltd* [2013] EWHC 3264 (Comm), [2014] Lloyd's Rep IR 398 [123]. See also *Parabola Investments Ltd v Browallia Cal Ltd* [2010] EWCA Civ 486, [2011] QB 477 [58] (Toulson LJ).

[24] *Equitas* (n 23) [123].

[25] See also *Jolliffe v Charles Coleman & Co* (1971) 219 EG 1608 (QB).

[26] *Ansett v Marshall* (1853) 22 LJQB 118. See also *Jolliffe* (n 25).

[27] *Ansett* (n 26).

[28] *Wilson v Newport Dock Co* (1865–66) LR 1 Ex 177 (Ex Ch).

[29] ibid 191–92 (Pollock CB).

[30] ibid.

not mean that the availability of an alternative safe dock would have barred damages altogether: if this cost more than the defendant's dock, the claimants would have been awarded the difference.[31]

Finally, the replication rule also explains the legal approach to mitigation by employees following wrongful dismissal. It was established by Erle CJ in *Beckham v Drake* that 'it is the duty of the servant to use diligence to find another employment'.[32] Of course, the claimant is not really under any duty (legal or otherwise) to seek re-employment; it may be entirely sensible to retire instead, and no-one could blame the claimant for doing so. The proper question is whether the claimant made a choice not to replicate its no-breach position (as nearly as possible) by seeking replacement employment. Where the claimant *does* choose not to replicate their no-breach position (by declining to take up alternative employment), the proper measure of damages is the difference between their pre-breach salary, and the salary at which they could obtain alternative employment: the claimant's choice was only exercised in respect of the, lower, alternative salary; therefore, it is only in respect of this amount that they will be deemed to have mitigated.[33] More complex issues arise where the claimant refuses a specific offer of re-employment by the defendant.[34]

2.1.3 Extrication

Where the claimant would not have entered into a transaction but-for the breach, the claimant may be able to replicate the no-breach position by 'extricating' itself from that transaction. The replication rule will apply where the claimant chooses not to extricate despite being aware of the breach.[35] These cases seem to raise the most difficulty within the law of mitigation. First, the tension with the reasonableness test is often greatest in this context because it may be entirely 'sensible' for the claimant to adopt the transaction rather than extricating;[36] however, reasonableness (in this sense) is irrelevant to the claimant's responsibility for its choice not

[31] See further Section 1.3.1.

[32] *Beckham v Drake* (1849) 2 HL Cas 579, 9 ER 1213, 606–07. See also *Geys v Société Générale* [2012] UKSC 63, [2013] 1 AC 523 [79] (Lord Wilson). See similarly in Canada: *Cemco Electrical Manufacturing Co v Van Snellenberg* [1947] SCR 121, 128.

[33] The position is different if it can be proved that the claimant would, independent of the breach, have soon retired. In this case, the dismissal will have caused little to no loss.

[34] See eg *Brace v Calder* [1895] 2 QB 253 (CA) and *Wilding v British Telecommunications plc* [2002] EWCA Civ 349, [2002] ICR 1079, discussed at text to n 72.

[35] See eg *Waddell v Blockey* (1879) 4 QBD 678 (CA) 681 (Bramwell LJ); *Downs v Chappell* [1997] 1 WLR 426 (CA) 437 (Hobhouse LJ); *Bristol & West Building Society v Fancy & Jackson* [1997] 4 All ER 582 (Ch) 623 (Chadwick J); *Glencore Energy UK Ltd v Transworld Oil Ltd* [2010] EWHC 141 (Comm), [2010] 1 CLC 284 [78] (Blair J); *Cassa di Risparmio della Repubblica di San Marino SpA v Barclays Bank Ltd* [2011] EWHC 484 (Comm), [2011] 1 CLC 701 [557] (Hamblen J).

[36] Accordingly, it is inaccurate to say that the claimant 'should' have extricated: cf *Patel v Hooper & Jackson* [1999] 1 All ER 992 (CA) 1802 (Nourse LJ).

to extricate.[37] Second, the application of the compensatory principle demands a careful assessment of what exactly would have happened but-for the breach, as a precursor to assessing the steps that would replicate the no-breach position.

The claimant may be able to replicate the no-breach position by undoing any transactions that it would not have entered into but-for the breach.[38] If the claimant chooses not to take steps to extricate itself in this way, the replication rule will apply by deeming the claimant to have done so. Again, despite references to reasonableness and the proposition that the claimant 'should' take steps in extrication,[39] the prescriptive approach is plainly inappropriate here. The claimant may have good reasons for adopting the transaction in the circumstances (which may nevertheless turn out to be beneficial to it) and indeed this may be the course that most claimants would have taken. Nevertheless, the causal significance of the claimant's intervening conduct lies in its choice not to replicate the no-breach position where extrication is possible.

Downs v Chappell further illustrates the distinction between reasonableness and choice. The claimants were induced to purchase a business based on the defendant's fraudulent misrepresentations.[40] After discovering that they had been misled, the claimants rejected two offers to resell the business. The business subsequently declined further in value. Hobhouse LJ held that 'any losses which the plaintiffs suffered after [they could have sold] were not caused by the defendants' torts but by the plaintiffs' decision not to sell out'.[41] The claimants argued that they had not acted 'unreasonably' in rejecting the offers. However, Hobhouse LJ emphasized that 'Even accepting that they acted reasonably, the fact remains that it was their choice, freely made, and they cannot hold the defendants responsible if the choice has turned out to have been commercially unwise'.[42]

On this basis, the replication rule should have been applied in *Esso Petroleum v Mardon*.[43] The defendant misrepresented the sales volume of a petrol station leased to the claimant.[44] Despite the claimant's best

[37] On the other hand, if the claimant had no choice to extricate because it was 'locked in' to the transaction, then the replication rule will not apply: see eg *Smith New Court Securities Ltd v Citibank NA* [1997] AC 254 (HL); *Patel* (n 36).

[38] These are sometimes referred to as 'no transaction' cases: see eg *Hayes v James & Charles Dodd* [1990] 2 All ER 815 (CA) 818–19 (Staughton LJ); *Downs* (n 35) 440 (Hobhouse LJ); cf *South Australia Asset Management Corp v York Montague Ltd ('SAAMCO')* [1997] AC 191 (HL) 218 (Lord Hoffmann). Different considerations apply where the claimant would still have entered into the transaction, but at a reduced price: see eg *Philips v Ward* [1956] 1 WLR 471 (CA); *Perry v Sidney Phillips & Son* [1982] 1 WLR 1297 (CA).

[39] See eg *Patel* (n 36) 1802 (Nourse LJ).

[40] *Downs* (n 35).

[41] ibid 437. Notably this conclusion was unaffected by the fraudulent nature of the wrongdoing: see further Chapter 7, text to n 66.

[42] ibid 437. See also *Waddell* (n 35) 681 (Bramwell LJ): 'It was for the [claimant] to consider whether he would sell it or retain it. The retention of it was his own voluntary act'; *Cassa di Risparmio* (n 35) [557] (Hamblen J): 'Subsequent declines in value of the instrument are caused by the free choice to hold onto the asset . . . not by the misrepresentation.'

[43] *Esso Petroleum Co Ltd v Mardon* [1976] QB 801 (CA).

[44] See ibid 828 (Ormrod LJ).

efforts,[45] the business operated at a significant loss. Although the claimant had an opportunity to quit the tenancy, he decided to continue at a renegotiated rent. Lawson J denied damages for the further losses incurred after the renegotiation, on the basis that the claimant's decision to continue was 'on an entirely fresh basis'.[46] The Court of Appeal disagreed, holding that the claimant had not 'failed to mitigate'[47] because in persevering with the business he had 'acted most reasonably'.[48] Lawson J's approach was correct, because the claimant made a voluntary and informed choice not to quit the lease when he had the opportunity.[49] The Court of Appeal's decision on this issue exemplifies the dangers of treating 'reasonableness' as a free-ranging, open-ended test.[50]

The significance of the claimant's choice not to extricate itself from transactions induced by the breach is also frequently invoked in context of financial investments. For example, in *Cassa Di Risparmio v Barclays Bank*, Hamblen J held that: 'Subsequent declines in value of the instrument are caused by the free choice to hold onto the asset, or by subsequent market events, and not by the misrepresentation.'[51] The same reasoning has been adopted in cases concerning pension funds and other complex financial products.[52] By contrast, if the claimant *does* choose to extricate itself from the transaction after discovering the breach, then this cannot amount to a (so-called) failure to mitigate even if it might have been wiser to have retained the investment. In *Abdullah v Credit Suisse*, the defendant wrongfully induced the claimants to make high-risk investments in breach of the defendant's statutory duties. The claimant subsequently chose not to meet a margin call on the investment, leading to its liquidation. Baker J declined to hold that this choice was 'unreasonable', even though it amounted to 'financial suicide'.[53]

Watts v Morrow illustrates the importance of assessing the no-breach position. The defendant surveyors negligently (in tort and breach of contract) failed to warn

[45] Lord Denning noted that the claimant 'put all his work and endeavour into [the business]. No one could have done more to make it a success': ibid 816.

[46] ibid 821 (quoted by Lord Denning). See also Shaw LJ at 833.

[47] ibid 833 (Shaw LJ).

[48] ibid 821 (Lord Denning). See also 829 (Ormrod LJ), 833 (Shaw LJ).

[49] This responsibility cuts both ways: if the business had proved profitable after the renegotiation, this would not have reduced the damages. See Chapter 6, text to n 77.

[50] See eg *Fearn v Board of Trustees of the Tate Gallery* [2023] USKC 4, [2023] 2 WLR 339 [20] (Lord Leggatt): 'The risk of this form of expression [ie "reasonableness"], however, is that it might be mistaken for an actual test for determining liability, albeit one that is entirely open-ended and lacking in content . . . But the common law aspires to be more principled than this. As I will describe, there are principles, settled since the nineteenth century, which run through the cases and govern whether interference with the use and enjoyment of land is . . . unreasonable.' Although Lord Leggatt's comment was in the context of private nuisance, the same type of criticism can be made of the reasonableness test in mitigation.

[51] *Cassa di Risparmio* (n 35) [557].

[52] See eg *Primavera v Allied Dunbar Assurance plc* [2002] EWCA Civ 1327, [2003] Lloyd's Rep PN 14 [29] (Simon Brown LJ), [40] (Mance LJ); *Gestmin SGPS SA v Credit Suisse (UK) Ltd* [2013] EWHC 3560 (Comm) [186] (Leggatt J).

[53] *Abdullah v Credit Suisse (UK) Limited* [2017] EWHC 3016 (Comm) [240]–[241] (Baker J).

about repairs required to a property that the claimants were thinking of buying.[54] The trial judge awarded damages for the cost of repairs on the basis that the claimants 'acted entirely reasonably in deciding to repair the premises rather than resell'.[55] The Court of Appeal overturned the award, correctly emphasizing that the damages should 'put the plaintiff into as good a position as if the contract for the survey had been properly fulfilled'.[56] The defendants had not warranted that the property was free from defects.[57] If the survey had been performed carefully, the claimants would not have purchased the property at all.[58] In these circumstances, as Ralph Gibson LJ correctly held that:

> The fact that it is reasonable for the plaintiff to retain the property and to do the repairs seems to me to be irrelevant to determination of the question whether recovery of the cost of repairs is justified in order to put the plaintiff in the position in which he would have been if . . . the promise to make a careful report, had been performed.[59]

Thus the replication rule applied because the claimants chose not to take the steps that would have replicated the no-breach position as nearly as possible (ie reselling the property). After reiterating the compensatory principle that damages should provide the sum needed to put the claimant in the same position as if the contract had been performed, Ralph Gibson LJ added that 'a reasonable decision by [the claimant] to remain in the house and to repair it, on discovery of the defects, cannot alter that primary sum'.[60] Bingham LJ similarly emphasized that 'If, on learning of the defects . . . a purchaser decides, for whatever reason, to retain the house and not move out and sell, I would question whether any loss he thereafter suffers, at least in the ordinary case, can be laid at the door of the contract-breaker'.[61]

Accordingly, although the cost of repairs was 'reasonably' incurred and would not have been incurred but-for the breach (because the claimants would not have bought the property), the repairs were not steps taken to replicate the no-breach position. It followed that defendants were responsible for putting the claimants in the position as if they had never purchased the property but were not responsible for the consequences of the claimants' own choice not to extricate. In these circumstances, damages were correctly assessed as the difference between the price

[54] *Watts v Morrow* [1991] 1 WLR 1421 (CA).
[55] Recorded by Ralph Gibson LJ at ibid 1428. Indeed, the defendants conceded that the claimant's conduct was 'reasonable': 1432 (Ralph Gibson LJ). See also 1445 (Bingham LJ), holding that the decision to repair rather than resell was 'no doubt for good reason'.
[56] ibid 1434 (Ralph Gibson LJ).
[57] ibid 1435 (Ralph Gibson LJ).
[58] ibid 1425–26, 1435 (Ralph Gibson LJ).
[59] ibid 1435–36.
[60] ibid 1436.
[61] ibid 1445.

paid for the property and the market value of the property at the date at which the defects were discovered, since this was the earliest date on which the claimants could have taken steps to resell (with some allowance for time to put the property up for sale).

It is important to distinguish cases like *Watts v Morrow* from others in which the claimant would still have entered into the transaction but on different terms (a 'different terms' case).[62] The importance of this distinction emerges directly from the compensatory principle, which requires an assessment of the no-breach position; nevertheless, judges have occasionally overlooked this step and thus failed to find the relevant facts.[63] Whilst the replication rule will very often be applicable in a 'no transaction' case (where it was possible to extricate), it will only rarely be applicable in a 'different terms' case because the opportunity to renegotiate will usually have passed by the time the breach was discovered.

2.1.4 Refusing the defendant's offer

The leading texts have often puzzled over whether the claimant will be held to have acted unreasonably where it refuses an offer made by the defendant after the breach.[64] However, a simple application of the reasonableness test fails to draw important distinctions in this regard. It is important to disaggregate three different types of case: first, where the refusal of the defendant's offer amounts to a choice not to replicate the no-breach position at all; second, where the defendant's offer would not have succeeded in replicating the no-breach position anyway; and third, where the refusal amounts merely to a choice to adopt a different mode of replicating the no-breach position. It is only in relation to the first type of case that the replication rule will apply. Occasionally, the exceptionality rule may apply to the third type of case; these cases are discussed separately below.[65]

The first type of case is exemplified by the leading authority of *Payzu v Saunders*.[66] The defendants agreed to deliver crêpe de chine (a type of silk material) to the claimants in instalments. However, in repudiatory breach of contract the defendants subsequently refused to deliver unless the claimants paid cash on delivery. The claimants refused this offer. In the Court of Appeal, Bankes LJ and Scrutton LJ held that the claimants' refusal was a failure to mitigate.[67] The decision can be explained on the basis that, as the trial judge recorded, 'the market was so

[62] See eg *Philips* (n 38); *Perry* (n 38).

[63] See eg *Bacciottini v Gotelee & Goldsmith* [2016] EWCA Civ 170, [2016] 4 WLR 98 [29] (Davis LJ); *LSREF III Wight Ltd v Gateley LLP* [2016] EWCA Civ 359, [2016] PNLR 21 [14] (Briggs LJ).

[64] James Edelman (ed), *McGregor on Damages* (21st edn, Sweet & Maxwell 2022) [9-052]-[9-063], [9-076]–[9-078]; Michael Bridge, 'Mitigation of Damages in Contract and the Meaning of Avoidable Loss' (1989) 105 Law Quarterly Review 398 411–23; Andrew Burrows, *Remedies for Torts and Breach of Contract* (4th edn, OUP 2019) 127–28.

[65] See Section 1.2.2.1.

[66] *Payzu v Saunders* [1919] 2 KB 581 (CA).

[67] ibid 588–89 (Bankes LJ); 589 (Scrutton LJ).

bare of goods as to render purchases impracticable', whereas the claimants 'were in fact in a position to pay cash for the goods' from the defendant.[68] In these circumstances, the claimants' refusal of the defendant's offer amounted to a choice not to replicate the no-breach position at all, because it had no other way of obtaining replacement crêpe de chine.

Similarly, in *The Solholt*, the claimants agreed to buy the defendant's vessel, but the vessel was delivered late, and the claimants terminated the contract.[69] The defendants subsequently offered again to sell the ship to the claimants on the same terms. The Court of Appeal held that the claimants' refusal of this offer was an unreasonable failure to mitigate. However, importantly, Sir John Donaldson MR noted that 'If [the claimants] could have found a different but identical ship, clearly it would have been reasonable that they should have bought it and the price of that purchase would have established the measure of their loss. However, there is no suggestion that any such vessel was available'.[70] Again, in these circumstances, the claimant's refusal of the defendant's offer amounted to a choice not to replicate the no-breach position at all.

Several other 'unreasonable' refusals to deal with the defendant are also best explained in this way.[71] For example in *Wilding*, the claimant employee's refusal of the defendant's offer of re-employment was held unreasonable in circumstances where the employee 'had little prospect of obtaining other work' and 'had not applied for other jobs'.[72] In some other cases it is unclear whether there was an available market for replacement, because the judgment does not record any relevant findings.[73] However, in such cases the point remains that even if there was a market, the claimant did not attempt to avail itself of it. In these circumstances, 'it is generally reasonable to treat the [defendant], although he is in default, as one of those who constitute the market' and thereby to regard the refusal of the defendant's offer as a choice not to replicate the no-breach position at all.[74]

In the second type of case, the refusal of the defendant's offer is not unreasonable because the offer would not have succeeded in replicating the claimant's no-breach position anyway.[75] The leading example is *Strutt v Whitnell*.[76] The claimant buyer

[68] ibid 585–86 (McCardie J). See further discussion in Bridge, 'Mitigation of Damages' (n 64) 413.

[69] *Sotiros Shipping Inc v Sameiet Solholt (The Solholt)* [1983] 1 Lloyd's Rep 605 (CA).

[70] ibid 609.

[71] See eg *Ansett* (n 26); *Owners of Mitera Marigo v Owners of Fritz Thyssen (The Fritz Thyssen)* [1968] P 255 (CA); *Cometson v Merthyr Tydfil CBC* [2014] EWHC 419 (Ch) [123] (Morgan J).

[72] *Wilding* (n 34) [20] (Potter LJ).

[73] See eg *Brace* (n 34).

[74] *Sous Secretaire d'Etat au Ministere des Travaux Publiques Chargé de la Marine Marchande v Barnett* (1924) 19 Ll L Rep 120 (KB) 121 (Roche J).

[75] The claimant's refusal of the defendant's offer has also been held reasonable where the terms of the offer were unclear: *Copley v Lawn* [2009] EWCA Civ 580, [2010] 1 All ER (Comm) 890; *Manton Hire and Sales Ltd v Ash Manor Cheese Co Ltd* [2013] EWCA Civ 548. See to similar effect in Canadian case law: *Thiessen v Leduc* [1975] 4 WWR 387, 401–402.

[76] *Strutt v Whitnell* [1975] 1 WLR 870 (CA).

sought damages in relation to the sale of a house where (in breach of contract) the property was not conveyed with vacant possession. The claimant refused the defendant's offer to re-convey the property. The Court of Appeal held that this refusal was not unreasonable. The explanation for the decision is that re-conveying the house to the defendant would not have replicated the position which would have obtained if the contract had been performed;[77] instead it would have put the claimant in the position as if no contract had been entered into.

In *Activa Europe v Pressure Seal Solutions*, the defendant, having failed to pay for goods, argued that the claimant had acted unreasonably in refusing its offer to return them.[78] Patten LJ held that the decision in *Strutt* 'seems to me to have an obvious application to this case', rejecting the suggestion in *The Solholt* that *Strutt* turned on 'its own special facts'.[79] Patten LJ correctly reasoned that 'there is an obvious difference between taking what steps are available to reduce the loss under the contract caused by the breach and in effect reversing the transaction'.[80] This important distinction is entirely obscured by the general test of whether the claimant's refusal was 'unreasonable'. Patten LJ's reasoning affirms the importance of carefully assessing the no-breach position before applying mitigation. It followed, rightly, that the trial judge 'was entitled to conclude that [the defendant's offer to return the goods] lay beyond the scope of the claimant's duty to mitigate'.[81]

There are several other examples of the second type of case.[82] Such cases commonly arise in relation to contracts of employment, where the defendant employer's offer of re-employment following wrongful dismissal is at a lower grade than the employee's original employment.[83] Similar issues may arise where the employment post-breach would be qualitatively different to employment pre-breach, because the employee no longer has trust and confidence in the employer.[84] In these cases, there can be no (so-called) failure to mitigate by refusing the defendant's offer, because the offer—even if accepted—would not replicate the no-breach position as nearly as possible, at least in circumstances where other closer alternative employment opportunities were available to the claimant.

[77] On the facts, the only way to replicate the no-breach position would have been to negotiate the removal of the protected tenant.

[78] *Activa DPS Europe Sarl v Pressure Seal Solutions Ltd* [2012] EWCA Civ 943, [2012] 3 CMLR 33.

[79] ibid [36], citing *The Solholt* (n 69) 609 (Sir John Donaldson MR).

[80] *Activa* (n 78) [36].

[81] ibid.

[82] See eg *Heaven and Kesterton v Etablissements Francois Albiac* [1956] 2 Lloyd's Rep 316 (QB); *Truk (UK) Ltd v Tokmakidis GmbH* [2000] 2 All ER (Comm) 594 (QB).

[83] See eg *Yetton v Eastwood Froy Ltd* [1967] 1 WLR 104 (QB). See further Edelman (n 64) [9-061]; Adam Kramer, *The Law of Contract Damages* (3rd edn, Hart 2022) [16-118]. See in Canada: *Wells v Newfoundland* [1999] 3 SCR 199, 180 Nfld & PEIR 269 [65]; *Thiessen v Leduc* [1975] 4 WWR 387, 401–402.

[84] See eg *Whittaker v Unisys Australia Pty Ltd* [2010] VSC 9 (SC of Victoria) [174]: 'Even where re-employment is offered on substantially the same terms and status, it will not be unreasonable to refuse in circumstances where the employee no longer trusts his or her former employer or where there is friction between the two parties.'

The only significant outlier is *Houndsditch Warehouse v Waltex*.[85] In that case, the defendant delivered defective goods. The claimant buyer refused the defendant's offer to accept a return. Stable J relied on *Payzu* to hold that 'In refusing the offer, lock stock and barrel . . . [the claimants] were not acting reasonably'.[86] However, unlike in *Payzu*,[87] the defendant's offer in *Houndsditch* would not have replicated the no-breach position. This is because the obligation that was breached was to deliver goods of the contractual specification: by contrast, acceptance of the defendant's offer would merely have put the claimant in the same position as if the contract had never been entered into.[88] Again, it is necessary to take care in characterizing the no-breach position before deciding whether the defendant's offer would (if fulfilled) have achieved replication. The judge's reliance on 'reasonableness' obscured this important step and led to the wrong decision.

One further point to note is that a defendant's offer to replicate will not fall within the replication rule if there are reasonable grounds for doubting the defendant's ability to properly perform. So, a claimant who receives shoddy workmanship from a defendant may not be required, by the replication rule, to accept a new offer of performance from the same defendant. Of course, the question whether or not this is the case will be highly fact sensitive. However, the underlying question is not the reasonableness of the claimant's decision per se, but the actual likelihood that the defendant's offer would have been fulfilled if the claimant had accepted.

2.1.5 Pressing for performance

At the other end of the spectrum, the claimant may sometimes continue to press for performance from the defendant following a breach of contract. For example, the claimant may give the defendant additional time to perform,[89] or seek to compel performance through a claim for specific performance.[90] Of course, such attempts to press for performance will not usually be regarded as a choice not to replicate the no-breach position, because their express aim is to secure replication from the defendant. Where the claimant has pressed for performance, damages are often said to be assessed as at the date of trial.[91] The reason why the so-called breach date

[85] *Houndsditch Warehouse Co Ltd v Waltex Ltd* [1944] KB 579 (KB). See also *Uzinterimpex JSC v Standard Bank plc* [2008] EWCA Civ 819, [2008] 2 CLC 80. This decision may be explicable on the distinct ground that the claimant's refusal was descriptively abnormal, such that the abnormality rule applied.

[86] *Houndsditch* (n 85) 581.

[87] Text to n 66.

[88] In this respect, the decision in *Houndsditch* (n 85) is inconsistent with *Strutt* (n 76).

[89] See eg *Toprak Mahsulleri Ofisi v Finagrain Compagnie Commerciale Agricole et Financiere SA* [1979] 2 Lloyd's Rep 98 (CA); *Bear Stearns Bank plc v Forum Global Equity Ltd* [2007] EWHC 1576 (Comm); *Lakatamia Shipping Co Ltd v Su* [2014] EWHC 3611 (Comm), [2015] 1 Lloyd's Rep 216 [117] (Cooke J).

[90] See eg *Johnson v Agnew* [1980] AC 367 (HL).

[91] See eg ibid 400–01 (Lord Wilberforce). See also *Hickman v Haynes* (1874–75) LR 10 CP 598 (CP); *Wroth v Tyler* [1974] Ch 30 (Ch); *Malhotra v Choudhury* [1980] Ch 52 (CA).

rule is disapplied in these circumstances is that the replication rule has no application so there is nothing to displace the assessment of factual loss.

Occasionally the replication rule may apply where pressing for performance was futile.[92] In *Habton Farms v Nimmo*, the defendant wrongfully repudiated a contract to buy the claimant's horse.[93] Whilst the claimant was still pressing for performance, the horse died. Clarke LJ held that because 'the claimant acted reasonably in relying upon the "contract" . . . the fact that the horse was not sold during November arose out of the first defendant's breach . . . and was not independent of it'.[94] However, he recognized that 'There would of course come a time at which it could properly be held that the decision not to sell the horse was a market decision independent of the breach'.[95] In other words, once it becomes obvious that the defendant will not perform, the choice to continue pressing for performance instead of resorting to the market may amount to a choice not to replicate the no-breach position.[96]

The mere fact that the claimant's attempt to press for performance was ultimately unsuccessful does not itself evince a choice not to replicate the no-breach position. For example, in *Suleman v Shahsavari*, the claimant pressed unsuccessfully for specific performance and in the meantime did not resort to the market.[97] Park J nevertheless concluded that the claimant 'has conducted himself entirely reasonably in seeking to obtain specific performance, for all that I have concluded that he cannot have it. He . . . cannot be accused of having unreasonably failed to mitigate his damage'.[98] In order to trigger the replication rule, the claimant's decision to press for performance must have been so obviously futile that it effectively amounted to a choice not to seek replication at all. It is, therefore, essentially the obverse of the rule that a claimant need not accept a defendant's offer to replicate where there are obviously reasonable grounds for doubting the defendant's ability to perform.

2.2 The exceptionality rule

The exceptionality rule applies where the claimant made a choice to act unusually. If the unusual conduct arose in the course of replicating the no-breach position, it is usually regarded as an issue of 'mitigation'. Any other unusual conduct

[92] See further Kramer (n 83) [16-25]. See further the discussion in the Canadian case of *Asamera Oil Corporation Ltd v Sea Oil & General Corporation et al* [1979] 1 SCR 633, 667–68.

[93] *Habton Farms v Nimmo* [2003] EWCA Civ 68, [2004] QB 1.

[94] ibid [97]. See also [126]--[127] (Auld LJ). Jonathan Parker LJ dissented on the issue of damages.

[95] ibid [100]. See also [128] (Auld LJ).

[96] See also *Rahman v Rahman* [2020] EWHC 2392 (Ch) [68] (Master Clark).

[97] *Suleman v Shahsavari* [1988] 1 WLR 1181 (Ch).

[98] ibid 1183.

by the claimant is usually regarded as an 'intervening act'.[99] However, the underlying rule in each of these circumstances is exactly the same; this explains the often-noted overlap between mitigation and intervening (or 'supervening') causation.[100] There are three main circumstances in which the claimant may act unusually in replicating the no-breach position. First, where the claimant refuses the defendant's offer of replication in favour of another option. Second, where the claimant's choice of repair rather than replacement, or vice versa, is abnormal. Third, where the claimant's method of replication is excessively costly.

2.2.1 Refusing the defendant's offer

After the breach, the claimant may refuse the defendant's offer of replacement but instead seek to replicate the no-breach position in another way. This is the third type of case described above.[101] For example, the claimant may prefer to resort to the market or a third party rather than accepting the defendant's offer. Although the replication rule does not apply in these circumstances,[102] the exceptionality rule may apply if the claimant's preference for the alternative mode of replication was sufficiently exceptional. The test for exceptionality was outlined in Chapter 6.[103] There, I argued that the test is whether the claimant's rejection of the defendant's offer in favour of resorting to the market (or other alternative) was a departure from the normal course of conduct, having regard to the claimant's own circumstances but ignoring the defendant's potential liability.

The exceptionality rule will not usually apply where there is only a small difference between the market cost and the defendant's offer.[104] For example, in *Velmore Estates v Roseberry Homes*, the defendants agreed to buy property from the claimants, but later failed to complete.[105] After the claimants had terminated the original contract, the defendants made another offer to buy the property at the same price. The claimants refused the defendant's offer and instead sold the property to another buyer on the market for a reduced price. Rich J held that the claimants had not failed to mitigate.[106] Although the market sale price was around ten percent lower than the defendant's offer,[107] the claimants' conduct was not exceptional because the defendants had already shown themselves to be unreliable.

[99] Just as with any other intervening cause, if the claimant's unusual conduct would have occurred even but-for the defendant's breach, then it is irrelevant to the assessment of damages.

[100] See eg Burrows, *Remedies* (4th edn) (n 64) 85–86, 131. See further Chapter 11, Section 2.

[101] See text to n 64.

[102] cf the first type of case: text to n 66.

[103] Section 3.2.

[104] See eg *UBC Chartering Ltd v Liepaya Shipping Co Ltd (The Liepaya)* [1999] 1 Lloyd's Rep 649 (QB) 671 (Rix J); *Copley* (n 75) [6] (Longmore LJ).

[105] *Velmore Estates Ltd v Roseberry Homes Ltd* [2005] EWHC 3061 (Ch), [2006] 2 P & CR 10.

[106] Rich J relied on the authority of *Strutt* (n 76), but this case is distinguishable because there the defendant's offer would not have succeeded in replicating the no-breach position: text to n 76.

[107] The effective price difference was £120,000 rather than £300,000 because the claimants already had the defendant's deposit of £180,000.

However, where the alternative mode of replication is significantly more expensive than the defendant's offer, the refusal of the defendant's offer is more likely to be exceptional. In *Clegg v Andersson*, the claimant purchased a yacht from the defendant, but the hull was heavier than specified.[108] The defendant offered to repair the hull for free, but the claimant instead sought damages for the market cost of repair. Seymour J rejected this claim on the basis that 'it was the duty of [the claimants] to permit the manufacturers . . . to carry out remedial work'.[109] Although the judge's prescriptive reference to 'duty' was inapt, the decision is correct because—ignoring the defendant's potential liability to pay the claimant's expenses—the claimant would normally prefer a free repair rather than paying the market cost of replication. In this regard it was significant that the defendants were 'a very reputable company' and could be relied upon to complete the repair effectively.[110]

In *Copley v Lawn*, Longmore LJ suggested (obiter) that it may be unreasonable to refuse a defendant's offer of a free replacement where this would impose a greater burden on the defendant, even if the cost to the claimant was no different because it could obtain a free replacement from another source anyway.[111] This is incorrect. The exceptionality rule can serve to protect the defendant's interests, in that the test asks what the claimant would normally have done if paying out of its own pocket rather than at the defendant's expense; this limits the defendant's responsibility for extravagant expenditure. However, it does not follow from this approach that the defendant's interests are directly relevant.[112] In *Sayce v TNT*, Moore-Bick LJ (correctly) doubted Longmore LJ's suggestion, calling it 'surprising' and 'not reflected in the leading authorities'.[113]

2.2.2 Repair or replacement?

The claimant may sometimes be able to replicate the no-breach position either by repair *or* replacement. The choice to repair rather than to replace (or vice versa)

[108] *Clegg v Andersson* [2002] EWHC 943 (QB). See also *City Axis Ltd v Jackson* (1998) 64 Con LR 84 (QB) and *Woodlands Oak Ltd v Conwell* [2011] EWCA Civ 254, [2011] BLR 365 [18]–[25] (Sir Anthony May). In both of these cases it was held that the claimant had acted unreasonably by refusing the defendant builders' offer to repair 'snagging' defects; however, this may be explained on the basis of an implied term in construction contracts granting a contractual right to repair minor defects.

[109] *Clegg* (n 108) [61] (Seymour J). The decision was later overturned by the Court of Appeal on the grounds that the claimants had exercised their right to reject the yacht, so the mitigation point did not arise: *Clegg v Andersson* [2003] EWCA Civ 320, [2003] 1 All ER (Comm) 721 [68] (The Vice-Chancellor).

[110] *Clegg* (n 108) [61] (Seymour J). See similarly in Canada: *410784 Ontario Limited v Little Zinger Inc (Corktown Esso)* 2016 ONCA 90 [221].

[111] *Copley* (n 75) [17], [21], [32].

[112] Contra: Hugh Beale (ed), *Chitty on Contracts* (34th edn, Sweet & Maxwell 2022) [29-111]; Edelman (n 64) [9-081], citing *Smailes v Hans Dessen* (1906) 94 LT 492 (KB) 493 (Channel J); *Darbishire v Warran* [1963] 1 WLR 1067 (CA) 1072 (Harman LJ), 1076 (Pearson LJ).

[113] *Sayce v TNT (UK) Ltd* [2011] EWCA Civ 1583, [2012] 1 WLR 1261 [20]. See also *Manton Hire* (n 75) [38] (Tomlinson LJ) (confining *Copley* (n 75) to the car hire context); Kramer (n 83) [16-119]–[16-121].

will only be 'unreasonable' if it satisfies the test of exceptionality.[114] The relative costs may not be decisive, because the test also takes into account the claimant's circumstances and proclivities. For example, in *The Legnano*, Lord Sterndale MR summarized that a decision to repair rather than to replace 'may be shown to be reasonable if there are certain special circumstances which make the ship of such great value to him that it is better for him and reasonable to spend a very much larger sum than her repaired value'.[115]

In assessing the claimant's normal conduct, it is important to disregard the defendant's potential liability. In *Darbishire v Warran*, the claimant's car was damaged by the defendant.[116] Although the replacement value of the car (in good condition) was only £85, the claimant had the car repaired at a total cost of £192. The Court of Appeal held that the claimant 'did not show that he had any special use for which this car alone was suitable'.[117] In these circumstances the decision to spend 'more than twice the replacement market value' on repair was exceptional.[118] On the facts, the court likely considered that the claimant would not have opted for repair if paying out of his own pocket. This feature of the exceptionality test provides the best explanation for Harman LJ's reasoning that the claimant should take into account the defendant's interests.[119]

2.2.3 Incurring excessive cost

The exceptionality rule may apply where the claimant incurs excessive cost in the course of effecting repair, replacement, or extrication. It is sometimes suggested that the rule will apply unless the claimant obtains replication as cheaply as possible. For example, in *Thai Airways v KI Holdings*, Leggatt J referred to 'a general expectation that, where more than one option is reasonably available, the claimant will adopt the one which is or is likely to be the least expensive'.[120] Whilst this is appropriate as a general expectation, it is not a fixed rule. The test must take into account the claimant's circumstances, such that the normal course of conduct may not always be the cheapest, even assuming that the claimant is paying out of its own pocket.[121]

[114] The same test is now embodied by the requirement of 'disproportionality' under the Consumer Rights Act 2015, s 23(3)(b).

[115] *Italian State Railways (The Legnano) v Owners of the SS Minnehaha* (1921) 6 Ll L Rep 12 (CA) 13. The Court of Appeal nevertheless upheld (with some reluctance) the trial judge's decision that the repair had been unreasonable.

[116] *Darbishire* (n 112). See also *The Legnano* (n 115).

[117] *Darbishire* (n 112) 1072 (Harman LJ). cf *O'Grady v Westminster Scaffolding Ltd* [1962] 2 Lloyd's Rep 238 (QB) (n 137).

[118] *Darbishire* (n 112) 1076 (Pearson LJ).

[119] ibid 1072.

[120] *Thai Airways International Public Co Ltd v KI Holdings Co Ltd* [2015] EWHC 1250 (Comm), [2016] 1 All ER (Comm) 675 [36]. See also *Dean v Ainley* [1987] 1 WLR 1729 (CA) 1736–37 (Kerr LJ).

[121] For example, if the cheapest option is a service provider with whom the claimant has had unsatisfactory dealings in the past, it may not be exceptional to avoid that option and opt instead for the second cheapest option. The New Zealand case of *Pipes NZ Limited v Steel Co Limited* [2014] NZHC 1216

The leading example of excessive cost is *The Borag*.[122] The claimant's ship was wrongfully arrested by the defendant. In order to secure release of the ship, the claimant was required to obtain a guarantee. However, the claimant funded the guarantee through its overdraft facility, such that it paid interest on the entire sum as though it was a loan.[123] Templeman LJ held that 'the owners could and should have adopted a form of mitigation which was reasonable either by refusing to pay the interest charges to their bankers or by seeking a guarantee elsewhere'.[124] In the course of argument, Templeman LJ described the charges as 'unheard of'.[125] In this context it is straightforward to conclude that the expense was outside the normal course of conduct, even taking into account the claimant's own position.

In assessing whether the costs incurred by the claimant were exceptional, it is necessary to take into account the claimant's characteristics, for better or worse. The claimant's conduct may be normal despite the fact that others in a similar position might have done better. For example, in *Thai Airways*, Leggatt J held that if the claimant had been a smaller company with less bargaining power, 'it could not seriously have been argued that its inability to negotiate a more favourable arrangement with [a third party] should be regarded as the effective cause of part of [the claimant's] loss'.[126] Similarly, in *The Hendrick*, Hewson J held that in determining whether the claimants had acted unreasonably, 'I must have in mind their lack of training in damage control and the absence of effective damage control gear on board their vessel'.[127]

Conversely, it appears that any special additional capacity of the claimant is similarly taken into account in determining whether its conduct was abnormal. This is illustrated by a series of car accident cases.[128] In *Beechwood Birmingham*, the claimant car dealer owned a large stock of cars, some of which were used by its employees.[129] When one of these cars was negligently damaged by the defendant,

[103] provides a helpful illustration, where taking the more expensive course of action was held not to be unreasonable in the claimant's circumstances.

[122] *Compania Financiera Soleada SA v Hamoor Tanker Corp Inc (The Borag)* [1981] 1 WLR 274 (CA). See also *The Pactolus* (1856) Sw 173, 166 ER 1079, 1081 (Dr Lushington); *Owners of the Georgidore v Owners of the Pacific Concord (The Pacific Concord)* [1961] 1 WLR 873 (PD) 881–82 (Lord Merriman); *Wandsworth LBC v Railtrack plc* [2001] EWCA Civ 1236, [2002] QB 756 [26] (Kennedy LJ); *Riyad Bank v Ahli United Bank (UK) plc* [2005] EWHC 279 (Comm), [2005] 2 Lloyd's Rep 409 [171] (Moore-Bick J).

[123] *The Borag* (n 122) 279 (Lord Denning MR).

[124] ibid 285.

[125] Reported by Lord Denning MR at ibid 282.

[126] *Thai Airways* (n 120) [176] (Leggatt J); cf *Shearson Lehman Hutton Inc v Maclaine Watson & Co Ltd (No 2)* [1990] 1 Lloyd's Rep 441 (QB) 443 (Webster J). See similarly in New Zealand: *Tucker v Sun* [2009] NZHC 1745, [42]–[45].

[127] *The Hendrik* [1964] 1 Lloyd's Rep 371 (PD) 379 (Hewson J).

[128] *Alexander v Rolls Royce Motor Cars Ltd* [1996] RTR 95 (CA) 101 (Beldam LJ); *Beechwood Birmingham Ltd v Hoyer Group UK Ltd* [2010] EWCA Civ 647, [2011] QB 357 [29]–[31] (Sir Mark Potter); *Singh v Yaqubi* [2013] EWCA Civ 23, [2013] RTR 15 [39] (Pill LJ).

[129] *Beechwood* (n 128).

the claimant hired a replacement car for its employee at the market rate. The Court of Appeal held that 'the claimant had ample capacity within its own stock of cars to absorb the loss of use of the particular car without any extra expenditure or loss of profit to its business *as was its usual practice*'.[130] Consequently, Sir Mark Potter concluded that 'the resort to outside hire was a failure to take a reasonable and less costly course open to *and customarily followed by* the claimant'.[131]

The judicial reasoning in *Beechwood Birmingham* is instructive. Sir Mark Potter focused on the course of conduct that was normal for the claimant itself, rather than (for example) a 'normal road user'. He emphasized the claimant's own 'usual' or 'customary' practice, taking into account its capacity to draw on a large fleet of vehicles. This approach established that the claimant did not normally incur the expense of hiring when paying out of its own pocket. The Court of Appeal's treatment of the claimant's special additional capacity is correct because it mirrors the proposition that the claimant's unfavourable characteristics (such as lack of bargaining power or inexperience) are also taken into account. In other words, the approach is the same, whether the claimant's special characteristics are positive or negative.[132]

2.2.4 The Ruxley debate

Where the claimant adopts the cheapest available mode of replication, its conduct will not usually be regarded as exceptional.[133] However, in rare cases it may be exceptional for the claimant to replicate the no-breach position at all. In *Ruxley v Forsyth*, the claimant was denied the cost of rebuilding a swimming pool that had been built to the wrong specification.[134] Lord Lloyd described the decision as an application of 'the principle that a plaintiff cannot always insist on being placed in the same physical position as if the contract had been performed, where to do so would be unreasonable'.[135] The cases applying this principle have all concerned the future (or hypothetical) conduct of the claimant after the trial;[136] perhaps for this reason, the decisions are not expressed as part of the law of mitigation and

130 ibid [29] (Sir Mark Potter) (emphasis added).

131 ibid [31] (Sir Mark Potter) (emphasis added).

132 However, a separate issue may be raised by analogy with the insurance rule: see Andrew Tettenborn, *The Law of Damages* (2nd edn, LexisNexis 2010) [5.71] and Chapter 9, Section 4.1. See in New Zealand: *Tucker v Sun* [2009] NZHC 1745 at [42] to [45].

133 See eg *Dominion Mosaics & Tile Co v Trafalgar Trucking Co* [1990] 2 All ER 246 (CA); *Stephenson Blake (Holdings) Ltd v Streets Heaver Ltd* [2001] Lloyd's Rep PN 44 (QB).

134 *Ruxley Electronics & Construction Ltd v Forsyth* [1996] AC 344 (HL).

135 ibid 371. See also 359 (Lord Jauncy), 361 (Lord Mustill); *Minscombe Properties v Sir Alfred McAlpine & Son* (1986) 279 EG 759, (1986) 2 Const LJ 303 (CA) 309 (O'Connor LJ): 'it may be unreasonable to insist on precise restoration where some other solution is equally effective and serviceable'.

136 See eg *Sealace Shipping Co Ltd v Oceanvoice Ltd (The Alecos M)* [1991] 1 Lloyd's Rep 120 (CA); *Southampton Container Terminals Ltd v Schiffahrisgesellsch 'Hansa Australia' MGH & Co (The Maersk Colombo)* [2001] EWCA Civ 717, [2001] 2 Lloyd's Rep 275; *Robot Arenas Ltd v Waterfield* [2010] EWHC 115 (QB).

thus strictly fall outside the scope of this book. On the other hand, the issue of the 'measure of damages' has sometimes been linked to mitigation.[137]

Although *Ruxley* was not expressed as a decision on the law of mitigation, two features of the case are relevant for present purposes. First, the only way that the claimant could have replicated the no-breach position was to rebuild the pool; no cheaper mode of replication was available. In particular, it would have been even more expensive (and obviously impractical)[138] for the claimant to have 'replaced' the pool by selling the property and buying another property with a pool of the correct specification.[139] Second, the House of Lords' decision was unaffected by the claimant's undertaking that he would in fact rebuild the pool if the cost of repair was awarded.[140] This aspect of the decision suggests that the result would have been the same even if the claimant had already rebuilt the pool,[141] thereby squarely raising the issue of mitigation.

This book does not attempt to resolve the *Ruxley* debate, but it offers an explanation for why the decision has proved so controversial.[142] The case is a rare example of a conflict between the replication and exceptionality rules, or, in other words, between legal and descriptive norms. Rebuilding the pool was descriptively exceptional, even taking into account the claimant's own preferences:[143] it is very unlikely that the claimant would have rebuilt the pool if paying out of his own pocket.[144] This consideration explains the irrelevance of the claimant's intention to

[137] See eg *Radford* (n 3) 1272 (Oliver J): 'No doubt the measure of damages and the plaintiff's duty and ability to mitigate are logically distinct concepts . . . But to some extent, at least, they are mirror images.' See also *Dodd Properties* (n 3) 453 (Megaw LJ); *Lagden v O'Connor (sub nom Burdis v Livsey)* [2003] UKHL 64, [2004] 1 AC 1067 [97] (Lord Walker).

[138] See discussion at *Ruxley Electronics & Construction Ltd v Forsyth* [1994] 1 WLR 650 (CA) 654 (Staughton LJ). The trial judge's finding that there was no 'difference in value' is thus something of a red herring, because it does not refer to any market transaction that was practically feasible.

[139] *Ruxley* (n 134) 371 (Lord Lloyd). In any event, having a pool of a particular depth in one house does not 'replicate' having a pool of the same depth in another house.

[140] ibid 362–63 (Lord Lloyd). Cf *Tito v Waddell (No 2)* [1977] Ch 106 (Ch) 183 (Megarry V-C). On the relevance of intention, see further David Winterton, *Money Awards in Contract Law* (Hart 2015) 191–99; Kramer (n 83) [4-196]–[4-201].

[141] cf Burrows, *Remedies* (4th edn) (n 64) 198: 'had Mr Forsyth already rebuilt the pool to the specified depth... he should have been entitled to the cost of cure.' It might be said that the claimant is not to be permitted to 'create' a new loss by giving an undertaking to cure, whereas the loss has ex hypothesi been suffered if the claimant has already cured the breach. However, in *both* situations the loss ultimately in contention is attributable to the claimant's choices.

[142] Another (different) explanation for the restriction in *Ruxley* is by analogy with the restrictions on specific performance or the agreed sum: see further Stephen Smith, 'Substitutionary Damages' in Charles Rickett (ed), *Justifying Private Law Remedies* (Hart 2008); Winterton (n 140) 201.

[143] *Ruxley* (n 134) 371 (Lord Lloyd): 'the judge, as is clear from his judgment, took Mr Forsyth's personal preferences and predilections into account. Nevertheless, he found as a fact that the cost of reinstatement was unreasonable.' See also 358–59 (Lord Jauncy).

[144] Although, if the claimant did so, and it could be shown that the decision to do so was not influenced by the prospects of obtaining damages, the position as regards mitigation might be otherwise.

rebuild *if awarded damages*.[145] It also explains why the House of Lords focused on whether the cost of repair was 'out of all proportion to the benefit to be obtained'.[146] Where the cost is disproportionate to the benefit, a reasonable claimant—and the court will usually take the claimant to be reasonable—would not normally chose to repair if paying out of its own pocket. On the other hand, rebuilding the pool would have replicated the no-breach position. The replication rule provides that where the claimant chooses not to replicate the no-breach position, damages are usually assessed as if it had done so.

In *Ruxley*, therefore, the legal norm of replication conflicted with the descriptive abnormality of replicating the no-breach position. In other words, there are two causally significant factors pulling in opposite directions. In these circumstances, our intuitions as to the reasonableness of the claimant's conduct are inevitably divided.[147] This book does not offer a solution to this conundrum, but it highlights the relevant issue. The focus of the House of Lords on ascertaining the 'true measure of the plaintiff's loss' rather than on arguments of legal policy,[148] fits with the explanation that the problem is rooted in conflicting causal intuitions.

3 The Effect on Damages

In Chapter 2, I showed that (despite earlier misunderstandings) it is now widely accepted that the application of mitigation results in a counterfactual assessment of the claimant's breach position, as if the claimant had acted reasonably.[149] In light of the replication and exceptionality rules, it is now possible to refine this proposition further. In particular, where the claimant made a choice not to replicate the no-breach position, damages are assessed as if it had replicated the no-breach position as nearly as possible. Where the claimant chose to replicate the no-breach position in an unusual way, damages are assessed as if it had adopted a usual method of replication. By contrast, where neither rule applies, the claimant will recover its factual loss based on its actual breach position evident at the date of trial.

[145] Note 140.

[146] *Ruxley* (n 134) 365 (Lord Lloyd); 360 (Lord Mustill). See also *The Maersk Colombo* (n 136) [30] (Clarke LJ).

[147] It has sometimes been argued that the claimant must always be entitled to the cost of cure unless a cheaper mode of replication is available: see eg *Radford* (n 3) 1284 (Oliver J).

[148] *Ruxley* (n 134) 368 (Lord Lloyd). See also 357 (Lord Jauncy): 'the reasonableness of an award of damages is to be linked directly to the loss sustained'; 360 (Lord Mustill), seeking 'the loss truly suffered by the promisee'.

[149] Section 3.3.

3.1 Where mitigation applies

3.1.1 Applying the counterfactual

Where the replication rule applies, the court must assess what would have happened if the claimant had attempted to replicate the no-breach position. For example, in *Commercial Fibres v Zabaida*, the sellers delivered yarn to the buyers in damaged packaging.[150] The buyers unreasonably attempted to transport the yarn without re-packaging it, such that most of the yarn was ruined. Donaldson J rejected the claim for the full value of the damaged yarn, but awarded £150 'as being the cost of re-cartoning', even though this re-packaging was never undertaken.[151] Similarly, in *Schering Agrochemicals v Resibel*,[152] Hobhouse J held that damages had to be assessed as if the claimants in that case had taken reasonable steps to repair a faulty alarm and safety system which they had purchased from the defendant.[153]

Where the exceptionality rule applies, the court must assess the cost that would have been incurred by the claimant if it had replicated the no-breach position in a normal way. So, in *The Borag*, although the Court of Appeal held that the claimant's method of financing a guarantee was abnormal, Templeman LJ clarified that 'The reasonable expenses of obtaining a guarantee must be recoverable'.[154] Similarly, in *Darbishire v Warran*, although the claimant's choice to repair rather than replace was held unreasonable, the Court of Appeal awarded damages based on the cost of buying a comparable car.[155] Where the claimant acted unusually by resorting to the market rather than accepting the defendant's offer, damages are assessed by reference to the cost that the claimant would have incurred if it had accepted the offer.[156]

To take an example from a well-known case,[157] in *Darbishire v Warran*, the claimant unreasonably spent £192 repairing his car when the value of the undamaged car was only £85.[158] The Court of Appeal held that 'the reasonable course for the plaintiff would have been to purchase a comparable car rather than repair

[150] *Commercial Fibres (Ireland) Ltd v Zabaida* [1975] 1 Lloyd's Rep 27.

[151] ibid 30. For a helpful application of the counterfactual, see in Canada *Caines v Bank of Nova Scotia* (1978) 90 DLR (3d) 271 at 276.

[152] *Schering* (n 4).

[153] ibid. cf *Beoco v Alfa Laval* (n 4), in which Stuart-Smith LJ criticized *Schering*, and—on very similar facts—declined to award damages in respect of the loss of production which would have resulted had the claimants taken steps to repair the system. The approach in *Beoco* is inconsistent with the other cases discussed thus far.

[154] *The Borag* (n 122) 284. See also 279–80 (Lord Denning).

[155] *Darbishire* (n 112).

[156] See further Section 1.2.2.1.

[157] See also *Payzu* (n 66) 587 (McCardie J): 'even if the plaintiffs had [acting reasonably] accepted the defendant's offer, they would nevertheless have lost the very useful period of credit which the contract gave them', citing *Cory v Thames Ironworks & Shipbuilding Co Ltd* (1867–68) LR 3 QB 181 (QB) as authority for this counterfactual assessment.

[158] *Darbishire* (n 112). This valuation was taken from Glass's Guide.

the damaged car',[159] and therefore rejected the claim for the cost of repairs. The court nevertheless awarded damages based on the cost of buying a comparable car, even though this cost was not in fact incurred because the original car had been repaired. The judges differed slightly as to the appropriate counterfactual: Harman LJ and Pennycuick J thought that the claimant could have obtained a comparable car for £85,[160] whereas Pearson LJ thought that it would have cost £105.[161] This difference of opinion nicely illustrates the application of the counterfactual assessment.

The Pacific Concord neatly illustrates the counterfactual assessment required by the exceptionality rule.[162] The claimant sought to repair its ship over the Christmas period, such that the ship was out of service for longer than if the repairs had been deferred until the New Year. Lord Merriman rejected the claim for the actual cost of repairs on the basis that the claimant's conduct had been unreasonable, but instead assessed damages as if the repairs had been deferred. In particular, he offered a detailed assessment of the costs that would have been (but were not in fact) incurred in these circumstances, holding that 'On the hypothesis that the work would have been done early in 1957 something must be allowed for the general rise in costs, said to amount to 8 per cent per annum, and I have taken this into account'.[163]

The process of counterfactual assessment inevitably raises certain evidential difficulties. However, it should not be thought that these difficulties are peculiar to mitigation. First, counterfactual reasoning is a basic and essential element of human thought,[164] reflected in the simple everyday question 'what if . . . ?'[165] Second, any assessment of damages already involves at least one counterfactual assessment, in order to assess the no-breach position.[166] The evidential difficulties faced in asking what would have happened if the claimant had acted normally (under the rules of mitigation) are no different in kind from those faced in asking what would have happened if the defendant had not breached its obligation (under the conventional application of the compensatory principle).[167] In this regard, as

[159] ibid 1079 (Pennycuick J, sitting in the Court of Appeal).
[160] ibid 1073 (Harman LJ), 1079 (Pennycuick J).
[161] ibid 1077 (Pearson LJ).
[162] *The Pacific Concord* (n 122).
[163] ibid 884.
[164] Christoph Hoerl, Tessa McCormack, and Sarah Beck (eds), *Understanding Counterfactuals, Understanding Causation: Issues in Philosophy and Psychology* (OUP 2011); Kevin Riggs and Donald Peterson, 'Counterfactual Thinking in Preschool Children: Mental State and Causal Inferences' in Peter Mitchell and Kevin Riggs (eds), *Children's Reasoning and the Mind* (Psychology Press 2000).
[165] See generally Neal Roese, 'Counterfactual Thinking' (1997) 121 Psychological Bulletin 133; Ruth Byrne, 'Mental Models and Counterfactual Thoughts about What Might Have Been' (2002) 6 Trends in Cognitive Sciences 426.
[166] See further Chapter 1, text to n 20. Counterfactual assessment may also be required in application of the remoteness rule: see eg *Cory* (n 157); *Victoria Laundry (Windsor) v Newman Industries* [1949] 2 KB 528 (CA); see further Chapter 11, Section 4.
[167] A key element of both assessments is that the court must 'adhere to reality subject only to giving full effect to the hypothesis': *Chilukuri v RP Explorer Master Fund* [2013] EWCA Civ 1307 [59] (Lewison LJ). See further HLA Hart and Tony Honoré, *Causation in the Law* (2nd edn, Clarendon 1985) 411–18.

Lord Bingham put it in *The Golden Victory*, 'the difficulty of accurate calculation is not a bar to recovery'.[168]

Where the claimant chose not to replicate the no-breach position, or replicated it in an unusual way, there may be a range of (counterfactual) normal responses that the claimant could have adopted instead. In this situation, as Kramer points out, 'the court must select one of the reasonable possibilities and will deem that to have been made'.[169] An analogous problem arises in applying the compensatory principle. It is very often necessary to ask what the defendant would have done but-for the breach.[170] In relation to negligent valuations where the defendant could have offered various reasonable valuations within a range, Lord Hoffmann proposed that the court should select the mean figure from the range because this was the 'most likely' figure that the defendant would have put forward but-for the breach.[171] Where the same loss would have been suffered even if the claimant had replicated no-breach position in the usual way, then the application of mitigation makes no difference to the assessment of damages.[172]

The counterfactual assessment of the claimant's conduct may occasionally raise 'loss of chance' problems, just as in relation to the compensatory principle. The damages award may need to reflect the likelihood (rather than the certainty) of a particular outcome on the hypothesis that the claimant acted normally. For example, in *Symrise*, Burton J held that the claimants unreasonably chose not to continue litigation with the Mexican Tax Authorities.[173] Burton J assessed the chance that the litigation would have been successful,[174] but was content on the facts to treat its success as proved on the balance of probability.[175] In *Steel v Robert George*, Viscount Simon held (obiter)[176] that in a case where a claimant unreasonably refused medical treatment, 'if the proposed operation can at best only work a partial

[168] *Golden Strait Corp v Nippon Yusen Kubishika Kaisha (The Golden Victory)* [2007] UKHL 12, [2007] 2 AC 353 [21]. In assessing the no-breach position, it has been said that 'this is not a question which can be considered on a mathematical basis. It has to be considered essentially, in the round, making... a "jury assessment"': *East v Maurer* [1991] 1 WLR 461 (CA) 468 (Beldam LJ), citing *Doyle v Olby (Ironmongers) Ltd* [1969] 2 QB 158 (CA) 169 (Winn LJ).

[169] Kramer (n 83) [15-78]. See similarly in Canada with respect to choosing a reasonable counterfactual scenario: *Agricultural Research Institute of Ontario v Campbell-High* 20 OR (2d) 401, 432.

[170] This raises the (much misunderstood) 'minimum obligations rule', recently clarified in *Durham Tees Valley Airport Ltd v bmibaby Ltd* [2010] EWCA Civ 485, [2011] 1 All ER (Comm) 731 [79] (Patten LJ). See further Michael Pratt, 'What Would the Defendant Have Done But For the Wrong?' (2019) 40 OJLS 28.

[171] *SAAMCO* (n 38) 221–22. See also *Lion Nathan Ltd v C-C Bottlers Ltd* [1996] 1 WLR 1438 (PC) 1445–47 (Lord Hoffmann).

[172] See eg *Standard Chartered Bank v Pakistan National Shipping Corp* [2001] EWCA Civ 55, [2001] 1 All ER (Comm) 822 [39], [41] (Potter LJ); *Energy Solutions EU Ltd v Nuclear Decommissioning Authority* [2015] EWHC 73 (TCC), [2015] PTSR 1106 [51] (Edwards-Stuart J); *Borealis AB v Geogas Trading SA* [2010] EWHC 2789 (Comm), [2011] 1 Lloyd's Rep 482 [105] (Gross LJ); *Stacey v Autosleeper Group Ltd* [2014] EWCA Civ 1551 [24] (Floyd LJ).

[173] *Symrise* (n 17) [86].

[174] ibid [65]–[66] (Burton J).

[175] ibid [87] (Burton J).

[176] On the facts, the claimant's refusal of treatment was not unreasonable.

cure, it does not appear to be an easy matter to fix what the reduced figure of compensation should be'.[177]

3.1.2 Cost to the claimant or defendant?

Where the claimant unreasonably refused the defendant's offer, the authorities are unsettled as to whether the counterfactual assessment should reflect the hypothetical cost to the claimant or (alternatively) to the defendant.[178] In *Copley v Lawn*, the claimant rejected the defendant's offer of a 'free' replacement car whilst her own car was being repaired.[179] Although the replacement would have been free to the claimant, it would obviously have cost the defendant something to provide. Longmore LJ held (obiter)[180] that 'if a claimant does unreasonably reject or ignore a defendant's offer of a replacement car, the claimant is entitled to recover at least the cost which [the claimant] can show [the defendant] would reasonably have incurred; he does not forfeit his damages claim altogether'.[181] In other words, Longmore LJ's approach focused on the hypothetical cost to the defendant.

In *Sayce v TNT*, the Court of Appeal subsequently cast doubt on Longmore LJ's approach.[182] Moore-Bick LJ accepted that the effect of mitigation was counterfactual, but focused instead on the counterfactual effect on the claimant, holding that 'If the claimant had accepted the defendant's offer he would not have needed to hire a replacement vehicle and would have suffered no loss arising out of the inability to use his own car'.[183] Moore-Bick LJ expressed concern that Longmore LJ's focus on the defendant was 'not an approach that is reflected in the earlier authorities' and was difficult 'to reconcile with the principle relating to avoidable loss'.[184] However, it was not necessary to conclude this issue on the facts of *Sayce* itself,[185] so the point remains unsettled.

The approach in *Sayce* is to be preferred: the counterfactual effect of mitigation should focus on the hypothetical cost to the claimant rather than to the defendant.[186] McGregor objects that 'this result leaves the defendant paying no damages at all in respect of the car hire claim although, had the claimant acted reasonably and accepted their offer, they would have had to bear the cost to them

[177] *Steele* (n 9) 500. See also *Houndsditch* (n 85) 581 (Stable J).

[178] See also W Courtney, 'Offers to Mitigate' (2020) 136 LQR 245.

[179] *Copley* (n 75). See also *Woodlands Oak* (n 128) [24]; however, this case may be better explained on the basis of an implied term: Kramer (n 83) [16-112]–[16-114].

[180] The issue did not arise on the facts because the Court of Appeal concluded that the claimant's refusal of the offer was not unreasonable: see further *Sayce* (n 113) [17] (Moore-Bick LJ).

[181] *Copley* (n 75) [32]. The brackets correct a typographical error: a similar amendment is made in *Sayce* (n 135) [29] (Moore-Bick LJ). See also *Evans v TNT Logistics Ltd* [2007] Lloyd's Rep IR 708 (CC).

[182] *Sayce* (n 113) [27]–[29] (Moore-Bick LJ).

[183] ibid [27].

[184] ibid [29].

[185] ibid [26].

[186] The only caveat is whether a separate principle should apply in relation to offers by the defendant in settlement of the dispute.

of the substitute car'.[187] This is true, but any windfall to the defendant is not a relevant consideration in assessing compensatory damages, which aim to redress the claimant's loss not the defendant's gain.[188] In *Copley*, Longmore LJ's error arose at an earlier stage when he held that the reasonableness test involved balancing the defendant's interests.[189] Properly understood, both the application and the effect of the avoidable loss rule are exclusively claimant-focused.

3.2 Where mitigation does not apply

3.2.1 Recovery of factual loss

Where mitigation does not apply, the claimant's breach position is assessed on the basis of what actually happened. In other words, the claimant will recover for its factual loss (no more and no less), subject to the application of other legal doctrines such as remoteness.[190] As Viscount Haldane put it in *British Westinghouse*, the court will 'look at what actually happened, and balance loss and gain'.[191] To put the same point the other way around, 'in order to displace the balance of actual loss and gain as the applicable measure of damages, it is necessary for the defendant to show that the action taken by the claimant was outside the reasonable range'.[192] In *Sainsbury's Supermarkets v Visa Europe*, the Supreme Court held unambiguously that 'The [claimants], having acted reasonably, are entitled to recover their factual loss.'[193]

For example, in a 'no transaction' case, the claimant can recover the actual costs of extrication including the transaction costs incurred in reselling.[194] Similarly, the claimant can recover the actual cost of repairing damaged property even where they turn out to cost more than expected.[195] Where the claimant has been defamed, they can recover the actual costs of employing a public relations consultant to restore their reputation.[196] This approach reflects the orthodox account

[187] Edelman (n 64) [9-076].

[188] See also Kramer (n 83) [16-124].

[189] For criticism of this approach, see Chapter 2, text to n 11. In *Sayce* (n 113) [29], Moore-Bick LJ acknowledged that Longmore LJ's view 'reflects the approach' that he took to application of the reasonableness test.

[190] See *Thai Airways* (n 120) [33] (Leggatt J); *Stephenson Blake* (n 133) [159] (Hicks QC). See similarly in Canada: *Winton v Robbins* [1959] SCR 775, 783.

[191] *British Westinghouse Electric & Manufacturing Co Ltd v Underground Electric Railways Co of London Ltd (No 2)* [1912] AC 673 (HL) 691.

[192] *Thai Airways* (n 120) [43] (Leggatt J). See also Kramer (n 83) [15-54] and [15-89]. Again, to the same effect in Canada, see *Winton v Robbins* [1959] SCR 775, 783.

[193] *Sainsbury's Supermarkets Ltd v Visa Europe Services LLC* [2020] UKSC 24, [2020] 4 All ER 807 [215].

[194] *East v Maurer* (n 168) 463–64 (Beldam LJ), 468 (Mustill LJ). See also *Waddell* (n 35) 681 (Bramwell LJ).

[195] *Humber Oil Terminal Trustee Ltd v Owners of the Sivand (The Sivand)* [1998] CLC 751 (CA) 761–62 (Evans LJ), 765 (Hobhouse LJ).

[196] *ReachLocal UK Ltd v Bennett* [2014] EWHC 3405 (QB), [2015] EMLR 7 [52] (Parkes QC). Similarly in Australia, the cost of employing a salesman to boost sales after the wrongful loss of an

of damages: the claimant recovers damages for its factual loss unless displaced by specific rules, including the rules of mitigation.

Of course, the non-application of the rules of mitigation does not prevent other legal rules from limiting or extending recovery of the claimant's factual loss. In particular, the rules of remoteness or contributory negligence may limit damages even where the claimant's conduct was not unreasonable.[197] Conversely, the claimant may recover more than its factual loss if either the insurance or benevolence 'exceptions' apply, again notwithstanding the non-application of the replication and exceptionality rules.[198] However, these other legal rules are finite in scope, and each rule requires its own justification distinct from mitigation.[199] Where no other legal rule applies, there is no reason to displace the assessment of factual loss prescribed by the compensatory principle.[200]

3.2.2 No special rule for expenses

Contrary to the account described above, the orthodox account of mitigation sometimes erects an artificial distinction between 'expenditure in mitigation' and other harm caused by the breach. McGregor confusingly suggests that 'The claimant, during their efforts to mitigate the damage, may incur further loss, which will often be a loss which is not in addition to, but in place of and less than, the loss which they are attempting to mitigate'.[201] Here, McGregor inadvertently uses the term 'loss' in more than one sense: first as 'factual loss', and then (roughly) as 'the harm that would have been suffered if the claimant had not acted', which by hypothesis was not in fact suffered. Where the claimant sought to replicate the no-breach position in the normal way, this second type of 'loss' is irrelevant; in assessing damages, the claimant simply recovers its factual loss, which includes the expenses incurred in replication.

In *The Borag*, Lord Denning firmly rejected the distinction between expenses and other types of harm, holding that this distinction 'fades into nothingness in most cases'.[202] Instead, 'when expenditure is incurred as a result of a wrongful act, the common law has always looked upon it as damages'.[203] By way of example, 'In

important contract was held to be recoverable: *Queensland Ice Supplies Pty Ltd v Anco Australasia Pty Ltd* [2000] QSC 072 [37].

[197] See further Chapter 11, Sections 4 and 5.

[198] See further Chapter 9, Section 4.1.

[199] For example, in *Dimond v Lovell* [2002] 1 AC 384 (HL) 400, Lord Hoffmann reasoned that 'The only way, therefore, in which Mrs Dimond could recover damages for the notional cost of hiring a car which she has actually had for free is if your Lordships were willing to create another exception to the rule against double recovery. I can see no basis for doing so'.

[200] This forms the proper understanding of the so-called '*Bwllfa* principle': see further Chapter 1, text to n 30.

[201] Edelman (n 64) [9-102]. See also *Compania Financiera Soleada SA v Hamoor Tanker Corp Inc (The Borag)* [1980] 1 Lloyd's Rep 111 (QB) 125–26 (Mustill J), overturned in *The Borag* (n 122).

[202] *The Borag* (n 122) 281.

[203] ibid 281.

a personal injury case the medical expenditure incurred is regarded as damages'; similarly, 'if you have a lorry or motor car which has been damaged and put out of action, the cost of providing a substitute is not regarded as sums expended in mitigation'.[204] Lord Denning's approach is straightforward and correct; there is no special rule for expenses. The only reason why it might look like there is a special rule is that the (hypothetical) cost of replication can be recovered even if the claimant chooses not to replicate the no-breach position, through the application of the replication rule.[205]

Why then do references to the so-called 'reasonable attempts rule' for recovery of expenses persist?[206] There are two likely reasons. First, the rule responds to the apparent peculiarity that the claimant's *actions* (in incurring expenditure) can result in an award of damages greater than if the claimant had done nothing at all.[207] But this is only peculiar if one becomes distracted by the distinction between acts and omissions,[208] whereas the relevant issue is whether the claimant's conduct (whether act or omission) departed from the normal course of events. Second, the rule responds to the apparent peculiarity that the claimant's conduct may be reasonable despite that it increased the eventual harm suffered.[209] But this is only peculiar if one becomes distracted by the *outcome* of the conduct,[210] whereas the relevant issue is the causal significance of the conduct itself.

Nolan has raised the problem of 'Preventive Damages',[211] asking whether 'expenses incurred to prevent threatened damage amount to recoverable damage in so far as reasonably incurred'.[212] Although this problem focuses on expenditure incurred *prior* to any other harm,[213] the question is again simply whether, in incurring the expense, the claimant either acted abnormally or made a choice

[204] ibid.

[205] In this context, it is sometimes suggested that 'it is not the cost of the repairs that constitutes the loss; the loss is the diminution in value of the chattel': *Coles v Hetherton* [2013] EWCA Civ 1704, [2015] 1 WLR 160 [29] (Aikens LJ). This misconception results from a failure to appreciate the counterfactual effect of the replication rule.

[206] See eg *Fulton Shipping Inc of Panama v Globalia Business Travel SAU (The New Flamenco)* [2014] EWHC 1547 (Comm), [2015] 1 All ER (Comm) 1205 [41] (Popplewell J).

[207] See eg Edwin Peel (ed), *Treitel on The Law of Contract* (15th edn, Sweet & Maxwell 2020) [20-109].

[208] See eg *Lagden* (n 137) [78] (Lord Scott): 'Mitigation is the process whereby the injured party attempts *by some course of action* to reduce the consequential loss he has suffered or will suffer *if nothing is done*.' (Emphasis added.)

[209] See eg Burrows, *Remedies* (4th edn) (n 64) 131: '[T]he fact that the incurring of expense has overall augmented the loss, rather than minimised it, i.e. it has not been a success, does not mean that it was unreasonably incurred.'

[210] In some circumstances, it may not even be known whether the harm would have been greater if the claimant had not acted: see eg *Skandia Property (UK) Ltd v Thames Water Utilities Ltd* [1999] BLR 338 (CA).

[211] Donal Nolan, 'Preventive Damages' (2016) 132 Law Quarterly Review 68.

[212] ibid 68, citing Principles of European Tort Law, Article 2.104.

[213] On this basis Nolan distinguishes the issue from mitigation, although he acknowledges that principles of mitigation 'may nevertheless provide helpful analogies': ibid 70–71.

not to replicate the no-breach position.[214] If not, the expenses were caused by the breach and are recoverable as part of the claimant's factual loss. For claims in the tort of negligence, the problem of pure economic loss can be overcome by what Nolan terms the 'pre-emptive right rationale'.[215] This rationale holds that where the claimant was forced to incur expense in order to avoid harm to its person or property, the defendant's conduct thereby directly infringes the claimant's right to bodily integrity or property.[216]

4 Procedural matters

The orthodox account of mitigation faces two procedural puzzles. First, the ambiguity of the 'question of fact' principle has already been highlighted.[217] The application of the reasonableness test is not itself a finding of primary fact and is often successfully appealed. This presents a puzzle for the orthodox account: which aspects of a trial judge's decision on mitigation can be overturned? Second, although in relation to avoidable loss it is well-settled that the defendant must prove that the claimant acted unreasonably, the burden of proof is less certain in other areas of mitigation. In relation to 'built-in mitigation' under the market rule and 'avoided loss', it may be in the interests of the claimant (rather than the defendant) to displace the assessment of factual loss. This presents another puzzle: who bears the burden of proof?

The causal explanation of mitigation resolves the question-of-fact puzzle. The choice and abnormality principles that explain the rules of mitigation are not specifically legal; they are questions of the kind that would (according to the old division) have appropriately been left to the jury. However, the application of the replication rule relies on a careful application of the compensatory principle to determine the claimant's no-breach position; this raises a question of law that, if wrongly applied, can be more readily interfered with on appeal. In relation to the market rule and avoided loss, the burden of proof puzzle is more difficult to resolve. The principle seems to be that the burden of proof is on the party who asserts that the assessment of the claimant's factual loss should be displaced on the grounds of an intervening cause.

[214] These two principles largely explain Nolan's list of 'limitations on recovery' in relation to preventive damages: see ibid 83–87.

[215] ibid 89–91.

[216] See further Peter Benson, 'The Basis for Excluding Liability for Economic Loss in Tort Law' in David Owen (ed), *Philosophical Foundations of Tort Law* (Clarendon 1995), 437–44.

[217] Chapter 2, Section 2.2.

4.1 Question of fact or law

The distinction between questions of law and fact originated in the division between the functions of judge and jury respectively.[218] Aside from the diminishing role of civil juries from the mid-nineteenth century onwards,[219] the boundary between questions of law and fact also shifted as new legal rules were developed, such that directions to the jury became more precise. In *British Westinghouse*, Viscount Haldane declared that 'The quantum of damage is a question of fact, and the only guidance the law can give is to lay down general principles which afford at times but scanty assistance in dealing with particular cases.'[220] Subsequently, in *The Chekiang*, Lord Sumner held that 'Damages may be a "jury question", that is a question of fact for the jury . . . but they must be measured under a proper direction, as to what the law requires.'[221]

Questions of fact were the issues that the jury was left to decide after having been directed (in accordance with the law) by the judge. The jury's decision on a question of fact could only be appealed in very narrow circumstances. In particular, the appellate courts historically had no power to reassess damages (unless both parties consented),[222] and the grounds for granting a new trial were limited to: misdirection by the judge;[223] misconduct by the jury;[224] or severe miscalculation such that 'the damages are so excessive that no twelve men could reasonably have given them.'[225] Provided that the jury was properly directed as to the question of fact to be decided, its decision on the issue was effectively final. The determination of an issue as one of fact or law therefore had significant procedural importance.

In the modern law of damages, the dichotomy between questions of fact and law is obsolete. On appeal, there is 'a spectrum of appropriate respect depending on the nature of the decision of the lower court which is challenged.'[226] At one end of the spectrum are decisions of primary fact;[227] at the other end are decisions of a 'purely legal nature', such as the interpretation of a statute.[228] In between, there are

[218] Edelman (n 64) [52-029].

[219] Discussed in *Ward v James* [1966] 1 QB 273 (CA) 290–91 (Denning LJ).

[220] *British Westinghouse* (n 191) 688.

[221] *Admiralty Commissioners v Owners of the SS Chekiang (The Chekiang)* [1926] AC 637 (HL) 643. For a modern equivalent (although misconceived, given the absence of juries), see *Ruxley* (n 134) 353 (Lord Bridge): 'the court, in assessing the measure of the claimant's loss has ultimately to determine a question of fact, although the law has of course developed detailed criteria which are to be applied.'

[222] Edelman (n 64) [53-007].

[223] See eg *Hadley v Baxendale* (1854) 9 Ex 341, 156 ER 145, 355 (Alderson B).

[224] *Wood v Gunston* (1655) Sty 462; *Ash v Ash* (1701) Comb 357.

[225] *Praed v Graham* (1889) 24 QBD 53 (CA) 55 (Lord Esher MR). See also *Smith v Schilling* [1928] 1 KB 429 (CA) 440 (Greer LJ). Note, however, that there was no power to order a new trial simply for the *smallness* of damages: *Hayward v Newton* (1732) 2 Str 940.

[226] *ST Dupont v EI du Pont de Nemours & Co* [2003] EWCA Civ 1368, [2006] 1 WLR 2793 [94] (May LJ). See further Adrian Zuckerman, *Zuckerman on Civil Procedure: Principles of Practice* (3rd edn, Sweet & Maxwell 2013) [24.198]–[24.220].

[227] *Dupont* (n 226) [94] (May LJ).

[228] Zuckerman, *Zuckerman on Civil Procedure: Principles of Practice* (3rd edn) (n 226) [24.205].

questions of 'mixed fact and law' that involve applying a legal standard to the facts of the case.[229] Where the question is of this middle kind, Hoffmann LJ has clarified that 'the vaguer the standard . . . the more reluctant an appellate court will be to interfere with the trial judge's decision.'[230] The important question, then, is which aspects of a trial judge's decision on mitigation are most amenable to interference by an appellate court?

This question raises a puzzle for the orthodox account of mitigation, because the reasonableness test suggests that there must be a single standard for interference in the application of the avoidable loss rule. The descriptive account of the replication and exceptionality rules instead reveals multiple issues, some of which are more amenable to appeal than others. The causal explanation of mitigation also resolves why and how the reasonableness test may have been regarded as a question of fact suitable for a jury.[231] Hart and Honoré conclude that 'All those issues which are on our analysis genuinely causal should be submitted to the jury',[232] essentially because they were not specifically legal questions. The popular idea that the reasonableness test raises a question of fact is thus explained by its reliance on ordinary causal principles.

In applying both the replication and exceptionality rules, the issue of choice is a question of fact in that it relies on ordinary causal principles to determine whether the claimant's conduct was sufficiently voluntary to be regarded as causally significant. The question whether (and when) the claimant had a 'choice' to replicate the position that it would have been in if the breach had not occurred, could appropriately have been put to a jury. The conclusion that the claimant had no choice is not restricted to absolute constraints on the claimant's conduct; the decision may involve balancing the claimant's conflicting interests.[233] However, this is no different to how people think about voluntariness in ordinary life for the purpose of attributing responsibility outside the law: the issue requires no specific legal knowledge.

In applying the exceptionality rule, the issue of descriptive exceptionality is also a question of fact in the sense that it applies ordinary causal principles. The issue whether the claimant departed from the normal course of conduct could appropriately have been put to the jury as a question of fact. The appropriate direction would be whether the claimant acted unusually having regard to their own circumstances, characteristics, and preferences, but ignoring the defendant's potential liability to pay damages.[234] In the modern law of damages, where mitigation

[229] *Re Grayan Building Services Ltd* [1995] Ch 241 (CA) 254 (Hoffmann LJ).

[230] ibid 254.

[231] At the time when the reasonableness test was firmly established by Viscount Haldane's classic statement of mitigation in *British Westinghouse* (n 191) 689, the role of civil juries was already significantly diminished. The point is that reasonableness came to be regarded as the type of issue that *would be* put to a jury.

[232] Hart and Honoré, *Causation in the Law* (2nd edn) (n 167) 428. See also *Hogan v Bentinck West Hartley Collieries* [1949] 1 All ER 588 (HL) 595–96 (Lord Normand).

[233] See further Chapter 6, Section 3.3.

[234] See further Chapter 6, Section 3.2.

is applied without a jury, the appellate court should not too readily interfere with the trial judge's decisions on the issues of choice and abnormality,[235] provided that these basic directions have been followed.[236] This approach probably best explains why the reasonableness test has often been characterized as a question of fact.

The remaining puzzle is why, if reasonableness is solely a question of fact, its application has so often successfully been appealed.[237] As Lord Hoffmann pointed out in relation to intervening causation, 'the existence of numerous appeals which raise questions of causation is a symptom of some deeper malaise . . . If the question is one of fact and common sense, why should this be so?'[238] His conclusion was that judges often misconstrue 'the rule which provides the context in which the question of causation is being asked. They have asked the wrong question rather than got the wrong answer'.[239] This perfectly captures the sense in which the application of the replication rule raises an important question of law. Before applying the replication rule, the judge must carefully assess the claimant's no-breach position. If the judge attempts to apply mitigation without engaging in this enquiry first, they risk asking themselves the wrong question.

The assessment of the no-breach position follows from the compensatory principle; it constitutes the legal concept of loss.[240] Although 'loss' (and thus 'mitigation of loss') may have many possible meanings outside the law,[241] within the law of damages this concept specifically entails a counterfactual comparison with the position as if the breach had not occurred. An enquiry into whether the claimant's conduct would have minimized its harm in some other sense involves asking the wrong question. The correct question is whether the claimant could have taken steps to replicate its no-breach position; only this is 'mitigation of loss' in the legally relevant sense. It follows, as Hobhouse LJ correctly emphasized in *Downs v Chappell*, that in applying the replication rule it is essential 'accurately to identify the wrong in respect of which the claimant is entitled to recover damages'.[242] This involves a question of law that may readily be appealed.

Once the judge has correctly identified the legal obligation that was breached and asked what would have happened but-for that breach, the remaining stages in the application of the replication rule (including the issue of choice) are less

[235] Edelman (n 64) [9-016]: 'once a court of first instance has decided that there has been, or has not been, a failure to mitigate, it is difficult to persuade an appellate court to come to a different view'.

[236] *County Ltd v Girozentrale Securities* [1996] 3 All ER 834 (CA) 858 (Hobhouse LJ): 'Causation involves taking account of recognised legal principles but, that having been done, it is a question of fact in each case'.

[237] See further Chapter 2, Section 2.2.

[238] Lord Hoffmann, 'Common Sense and Causing Loss' (Chancery Bar Association Lecture, 15 June 1999) 3.

[239] ibid 6.

[240] See further Chapter 1, Section 2.1.

[241] In particular, it may refer instead to an historical comparison with the position that the claimant *was* in before a particular event occurred.

[242] *Downs* (n 35) 438 (Hobhouse LJ).

amenable to appeal. The assessment of what steps would have replicated the no-breach position as nearly as possible is essentially a question of fact.[243] For example, in *Bulkhaul v Rhodia Organique*, the defendants repudiated their contract to hire chemical tanks.[244] To replicate the no-breach position would have involved hiring out the tanks to another customer; however, on the facts, there was no available market for hire. In these circumstances, the trial judge held that the nearest alternative involved selling the tanks;[245] the replication rule therefore applied because the claimants had chosen not to take these steps.[246] The Court of Appeal dismissed the appeal on reasonableness.[247]

4.2 The burden of proof

Although mitigation is an aspect of causation, its application involves causal *attribution*, rather than a dispute about primary facts. As Hart and Honoré put it, 'The determination, on causal principles, of the limits of responsibility in a case where the sequence of events is sufficiently established does not depend on adducing further evidence but on characterizing the upshot' of that evidence.[248] The issue of proof raised in mitigation is different from proof of so-called 'factual causation', which may raise issues of evidential uncertainty regarding what has happened, will happen in the future, or would have happened but-for the breach.[249] Instead, as regards the *application* of mitigation,[250] the issue of proof concerns who should bear the burden of proving that either the replication or exceptionality rule applies; in other words, it concerns proving the case rather than proving primary facts.

In relation to avoidable loss, the leading texts widely accept (and perhaps overemphasize) that the burden is on the defendant to prove that the claimant's conduct was 'unreasonable'.[251] Although a few rogue decisions have placed the burden on the claimant to prove that it acted reasonably,[252] judicial authority on this point

[243] Although the position is not entirely straightforward. The question is admittedly not a question of *primary* fact; the courts do employ some, unstated, legal criteria to determine what makes one alternative a 'better' replication than another; however, the application of these abstract criteria is likely to be intensely (primary) fact-sensitive

[244] *Bulkhaul* (n 20).

[245] ibid [21] (Smith LJ): 'It was reasonable to expect [the claimant] to make attempts to sell the tanks. That was because, if the contract had run its course, and the tanks ... would have been worth nothing at the end. Thus, Bulkhaul would be in no worse position if it sold the tanks than if it scrapped them at the end of the contract.'

[246] ibid [25] (Smith LJ).

[247] ibid [27], [37] (Smith LJ).

[248] Hart and Honoré (n 167) 407.

[249] See eg *Hotson v East Berkshire HA* [1987] AC 750 (HL); *Wilsher v Essex AHA* [1988] AC 1074 (HL); *Fairchild v Glenhaven Funeral Services Ltd* [2002] UKHL 22, [2003] 1 AC 32.

[250] For evidential issues concerning the effect of mitigation, see text to n 164.

[251] Edelman (n 64) [9-020]; Beale, *Chitty on Contracts* (34th edn) (n 112) [29-098]; Tettenborn, *Damages* (2nd edn) (n 132) [5.103]. See in Australia: *Watts v Rake* (1960) 108 CLR 158, 159.

[252] *Owners of the Temple Bar v Owners of the Guildford (The Guildford)* [1956] P 364 (PD) 370 (Lord Merriman); *Selvanayagam v University of the West Indies* [1983] 1 WLR 585 (PC) 589 (Lord Scarman),

is now well-settled.[253] In short, the defendant has the burden of proving that mitigation applies. More specifically, the defendant has the burden both of adducing sufficient evidence to raise the issue of mitigation (ie 'evidential burden'),[254] and also of persuading the judge that the replication or exceptionality rule applies on the facts (the 'legal burden').[255] Briggs LJ summarized that 'Where failure to mitigate is relied upon in answer to a claim for damages . . . it is for the defendant . . . both to plead and prove a case to that effect'.[256]

In relation to the market rule, which McGregor describes as 'built-in' mitigation,[257] the burden is on the party seeking to displace the prima facie measure of damages.[258] This is the obvious implication of the words 'prima facie' in the provisions of the Sale of Goods Act 1979,[259] but the same approach was adopted at common law prior to codification.[260] The prima facie measure reflects an application of the replication rule: damages are assessed as the cost of resorting to the market to obtain replacement performance, whether or not the claimant in fact did so.[261] Accordingly, where there is an available market, it appears that the burden is effectively on the party (whether claimant or defendant) who is seeking to show that the replication rule does *not* apply.[262] McGregor and Street correctly identify that this entails a reversal of the burden of proof compared with the position for avoidable loss.[263]

In relation to avoided loss, McGregor suggests that 'The legal onus to prove that a claimant has mitigated loss is on the defendant.'[264] There was previously

overruled on this point in *Geest plc v Lansiquot* [2002] UKPC 48, [2002] 1 WLR 3111 [14] (Lord Bingham); *Riyad Bank* (n 122) [171] (Moore-Bick J).

[253] *Hill v Showell* (1918) 87 LJKB 1106 (HL) 1114 (Lord Parmoor); *Richardson* (n 9) 73 (Viscount Simon), 75 (Lord Russell); *Standard Chartered (CA)* (n 172) [38]–[39] (Potter LJ); *Saunders v Williams* [2002] EWCA Civ 673, [2003] BLR 125 [22], [24] (Pill LJ); *Wilding* (n 34) [45] (Potter LJ), [55] (Sedley LJ). See in Australia *Watts v Rake* (1960) 108 CLR 158, 159. Similarly in Canada *Winton v Robbins* [1959] SCR 775, 783.

[254] For an example of the defendant's failure to discharge the evidential burden, see *Levy v Lewis* (CA, 26 November 1993) 2–3 (Steyn LJ).

[255] On the distinction between the evidential and persuasive burden, see generally, *Phipson on Evidence* (18th edn, Sweet & Maxwell 2013) [6-02]. In the context of assessing the claimant's factual loss, see also *Sony Computer Entertainment UK Ltd v Cinram Logistics UK Ltd* [2008] EWCA Civ 955, [2009] Bus LR 529 [37]–[51] (Rix LJ).

[256] *Anselm v Buckle* [2014] EWCA Civ 311 [24] (Briggs LJ).

[257] Edelman (n 64) [9-041].

[258] *Bence Graphics International Ltd v Fasson UK Ltd* [1998] QB 87 (CA) 97 (Otton LJ). See also *Garnac Grain Co Inc v HMF Faure & Fairclough Ltd* [1968] AC 1130 (HL) 1440 (Lord Pearson); *Louis Dreyfus Trading Ltd v Reliance Trading Ltd* [2004] EWHC 525 (Comm), [2004] 2 Lloyd's Rep 243 [25] (Andrew Smith J).

[259] Sale of Goods Act 1979, ss 50(3), 51(3), 53(3).

[260] *Roper v Johnson* (1873) LR 8 CP 167 (CP) 182 (Brett J), 183 (Grove J).

[261] See further Chapter 10.

[262] See also *Coles* (n 205) [27] (Aiken LJ), adopting the 'reasonable cost of repair' as the prima facie measure of damages in car accident cases.

[263] Edelman (n 64) [9-041], [32-067]; Harry Street, *Principles of the Law of Damages* (Sweet & Maxwell 1962) 37.

[264] Edelman (n 64) [9-115].

very little (if any) judicial authority to support this proposition.[265] However, it now finds support from *Sainsbury's Supermarkets v Visa Europe*, in which the Supreme Court noted (obiter) that 'In some cases of mitigation, the court is concerned with additional benefits which a claimant has gained from the mitigation action which it has taken. In such a case, it is for the defendant to show that the benefits should be set off against the prima facie claim of loss.'[266] Consistent with the causal explanation of the avoided loss rule, the court correctly identified that this issue raises 'delicate questions as to whether a benefit is sufficiently causally connected with the breach of contract or (in tort) the wrong or whether the benefit was the result of an independent commercial decision by the claimant.'[267]

At first glance, the burden of proof for avoided loss appears therefore to be the same as for avoidable loss: in both cases it is on the defendant. However, conceptually there is an important difference here. In relation to avoidable loss, the burden is on the defendant to displace evidence of the claimant's *factual loss* (ie based on the harms actually suffered) in favour of the counterfactual loss that would have been suffered if the claimant had acted 'reasonably' by replicating the no-breach position in the usual way. By contrast, in relation to avoided loss, the Supreme Court's position in *Sainsbury's Supermarkets* implies that the burden is on the defendant to displace the *counterfactual loss* that the claimant would have suffered if it had replicated the no-breach position in the usual way (the 'prima facie' loss), in favour of its factual loss (i.e. based on the benefits actually received). In other words, the position is precisely reversed.

Although relatively little attention has been paid to the burden of proof for the market rule and avoided loss, the current prevailing views appear to be inconsistent with the well-settled position in relation to avoidable loss. To align the law consistently with the established approach to avoidable loss, the burden would be on whichever party is asserting that a rule of mitigation applies to displace the claimant's factual loss.[268] This approach follows the general rule of evidence that 'the party who asserts must prove'.[269] However, it runs contrary to the current

[265] Although McGregor cites *Owners of the Andros Springs v Owners of the World Beauty (The World Beauty)* [1970] P 144 (CA), this case does not support his proposition because it concerned the burden of proving factual loss. However, the proposition may be supported by *Primavera* (n 52) [37], where Mance LJ asked 'whether any prima facie loss . . . was "mitigated" (or avoided) by the respondent's actual conduct'.

[266] *Sainsbury's Supermarkets* (n 193) [212].

[267] ibid.

[268] Kramer (n 83) [15-119]. In *Sony* (n 255) [37]–[51], Rix LJ held that the 'legal burden' rests on the claimant to prove its factual loss, although 'the evidential burden may shift depending on the circumstances'.

[269] *Robins v National Trust Co Ltd* [1927] AC 515 (PC) 520 (Viscount Dunedin); *Phipson on Evidence* (18th edn) (n 255) [6-04].

prima facie measure under the market rule, which presumptively applies the replication rule. One way of explaining this discrepancy is as a simple matter of convenience. Although it is wrong to assert that the prima facie measure must always be *recoverable* in order to avoid 'extensive and costly inquiries',[270] this consideration may be relevant in determining the burden of proof.

[270] *Joyner v Weeks* [1891] 2 QB 31 (CA) 43 (Lord Esher). See also *The Golden Victory* (n 168) [20] (Lord Bingham).

9
Avoided Loss

1 Introduction

This chapter restates the law of mitigation as it applies to the cases conventionally discussed under the rubric of 'avoided loss'. First, I argue that the *British Westinghouse* test for determining when benefits are taken into account in the assessment of damages reflects the application of the replication rule, which I introduced in Chapter 6. The vast majority of cases allowing recovery for so-called avoided loss are ones in which the claimant made a choice not to replicate the no-breach position as nearly as possible. Second, I show that in such cases, loss is assessed on a counterfactual basis as if the claimant had taken steps to replicate, ignoring any benefits actually received as a result of not replicating. By contrast, where the replication rule does not apply, the claimant will only recover for their factual loss. Finally, I discuss two other types of case which are also sometimes referred to as examples of recovery for 'avoided loss', but which are distinct from the replication rule.

2 Applying the *British Westinghouse* test

The orthodox account of mitigation provides that the claimant cannot recover for an avoided loss *except* where the benefit obtained by the claimant was 'collateral' to the breach.[1] The test, derived from *British Westinghouse*, is that 'the subsequent transaction, if to be taken into account, must be one arising out of the consequences of the breach and in the ordinary course of business'.[2] However, as I explained in Chapter 3, the leading texts on damages provide no guidance on how this test is applied. Instead, the conventional consensus is that 'the line between those avoided consequences which are collateral and those which are not is an exceedingly difficult one to draw'.[3] Several commentators have remarked, with

[1] See further Chapter 1, Section 3.2.

[2] *British Westinghouse Electric & Manufacturing Co Ltd v Underground Electric Railways Co of London Ltd (No 2)* [1912] AC 673 (HL) 690. See also 692, where Viscount Haldane distinguished between conduct that 'formed part of a continuous dealing with the situation in which they found themselves' and conduct that amounted to 'an independent or disconnected transaction'.

[3] James Edelman (ed), *McGregor on Damages* (21st edn, Sweet & Maxwell 2022) [9-111]. See also the judicial comments in *Hussain v New Taplow Paper Mills Ltd* [1988] AC 514 (HL) 528 (Bridge LJ); *Burdis v Livsey* [2001] 1 WLR 1751 (QB) 1757 (Gray J); *The New Flamenco (CA)* (n 46) [20] and [39] (Longmore LJ).

Mitigation in the Law of Damages. Andrew Summers, Oxford University Press. © Andy Summers 2025.
DOI: 10.1093/9780191864032.003.0009

despair, that the cases in this area are 'in a bit of a jumble',[4] 'a dreadful muddle',[5] and 'notoriously difficult to reconcile'.[6]

Instead, I argue that the replication rule neatly explains almost all of the cases in which the *British Westinghouse* test has successfully been applied. In other words, whenever the claimant has made a choice not to replicate the no-breach position as nearly as possible, the courts have consistently held that any benefits obtained as a result are treated as collateral under the *British Westinghouse* test. By contrast, where the claimant had no choice to replicate, or did in fact replicate, then the replication rule has no application. In these circumstances, the courts have consistently declined to treat the benefits as collateral and have assessed damages on basis of the claimant's factual loss. There are remarkably few cases that are inconsistent with this framework. Whilst judges have not always been clear in their reasoning, they have tended to reach the right results. It is the textbooks, rather than the cases, that are in a muddle.

2.1 The claimant chose not to replicate

Where the claimant made a choice not to replicate the no-breach position, damages are assessed as if it had done so, whether things turn out better than if they had attempted to replicate, or worse.[7] The application and effect of the replication rule was outlined in Chapter 6. The claimant's choice not to replicate the no-breach position may take several forms, such as a choice not to repair, seek replacement, or extricate from the breach. These sub-categories have no legal significance since they all reflect the same underlying rule; they are merely separated for ease of exposition. Finally, there are cases in which the claimant chose to take other steps that—although they would not have been taken but for the breach—were not part of any attempt to replicate the no-breach position. Such cases also fall within the effective ambit of the replication rule.

2.1.1 Repair

Damages have been awarded for the cost of repairing damaged or defective property even though in fact the claimant 'avoided' those losses by choosing not to undertake repairs. In *The London Corporation*, the claimants decided to sell their

[4] Harvey McGregor, 'The Role of Mitigation in the Assessment of Damages' in Djakhongir Saidov and Ralph Cunnington (eds), *Contract Damages: Domestic and International Perspectives* (Hart 2008) 366.

[5] David McLauchlan, 'Expectation Damages: Avoided Loss, Offsetting Gains and Subsequent Events' in Djakhongir Saidov and Ralph Cunnington (eds), *Contract Damages: Domestic and International Perspectives* (Hart 2008) 384.

[6] David Winterton, *Money Awards in Contract Law* (Hart 2015) 88. See also 249.

[7] Where things turn out for worse, the cases are conventionally considered under the rubric of avoidable loss: see further Chapter 8.

damaged ship to shipbreakers without repairing it.[8] In *Robinson v Maund*, the claimant's decided to sell their hotel without undertaking repairs required by the defendant's defective refurbishment.[9] In both cases, the Court of Appeal held that the claimants could recover the 'avoided' cost of repair even though as it turned out the subsequent sale prices were unaffected.[10] Similarly, in *Mueller Europe v Central Roofing*, the claimant manufacturers recovered damages for the cost of repairing machinery damaged in a fire started by the defendants, even though the claimants had in fact not undertaken the repairs, instead preferring to move their production to another factory.[11]

One explanation offered for these decisions is that the cost of repair is *always* recoverable regardless of the reason why it was in fact 'avoided', because this cost reflects the diminution in value of the property suffered at the time of breach. This explanation has been put forward by Robert Stevens in his rights-based account of substitutive damages,[12] and it also has some judicial support in two cases concerning the quantum of damages following a car accident.[13] In *Coles v Hetherton*, Aikens LJ held that 'the claimant is not obliged to repair the chattel to recover the direct loss suffered', because direct loss 'is suffered as soon as the chattel is damaged'.[14] This concept of direct loss is very different from factual loss because it is wholly unaffected by post-breach events.[15] The direct loss explanation holds that the claimant is entitled to substantial damages for breach regardless of the claimant's factual loss evident at the date of trial.

The replication rule provides an alternative and narrower explanation for the awards of damages in cases such as *The London Corporation*, *Robinson* and *Mueller*.[16] In each of these cases, the claimant made a choice not to repair the damaged property; that choice was an intervening cause for which the claimant was responsible for better or worse. On the facts, the claimants' choice redounded to their own benefit, but if they had instead made a significant loss as a result of their

[8] *The London Corporation* [1935] P 70 (CA).

[9] *Robinson v Maund* (CA, 20 January 1993).

[10] *The London Corporation* (n 8) 77 (Greer LJ); *Robinson* (n 9) (Steyn LJ). See also, in relation to defective services: *White Arrow Express Ltd v Lamey's Distribution Ltd* [1995] CLC 1251 (CA) 1255–56 (Sir Thomas Bingham MR).

[11] *Mueller Europe Ltd v Central Roofing (South Wales) Ltd* [2013] EWHC 237 (TCC), 147 Con LR 32 [148] (Stuart-Smith LJ): '[T]he fact that the group has taken a decision that the facility will be partially replaced by building in the USA is immaterial.'

[12] Robert Stevens, *Torts and Rights* (OUP 2007) 69–70; Robert Stevens, 'Damages and the Right to Performance: A Golden Victory or Not?' in Jason Neyers, Richard Bronaugh, and Stephen Pitel (eds), *Exploring Contract Law* (Hart 2009) 182.

[13] *Burdis v Livsey (sub nom Lagden v O'Connor)* [2002] EWCA Civ 510, [2003] QB 36 [84] (Aldous LJ); *Coles v Hetherton* [2013] EWCA Civ 1704, [2015] 1 WLR 160 [27]–[33] (Aikens LJ).

[14] *Coles* (n 13) [27].

[15] ibid [27] (Aikens LJ): 'Events occurring after the infliction of the damage are irrelevant to calculating the diminution in value measure of damages', citing *Burdis* (n 13) [95] (Aldous LJ). However, in *Burdis*, Aldous LJ held that damages for direct loss *could* be reduced by post-breach events 'in so far as such events are referable to the claimant's duty to mitigate his loss': [88].

[16] Note 8, n 9, and n 11, respectively.

decision not to repair, damages would still have been limited to the cost of repair.[17] In other words, the risk arising from not repairing was down to the claimant either way. Unlike the 'direct loss' explanation, the replication rule only applies where the claimant exercised a *choice* not to repair. Where the cost of repairs is 'avoided' for a different reason, the replication rule has no application and the claimant will be limited to its factual loss, unless another relevant rule applies.[18]

Where repairs have not yet been undertaken by the date of trial and may or may not be undertaken in the future, it is well-established that the absence of an intention to undertake repair does not count conclusively against an award of 'cost of cure' damages.[19] This approach can now be explained in light of the replication rule. The relevant issue is whether the repair would (if undertaken) replicate the no-breach position as nearly as possible, rather than whether the cost of repair will actually be incurred. Put another way: if the hypothetical cost of repair can be awarded even where it is known that the claimant has already chosen not to repair and can no longer do so (for example, because they have already resold the relevant property), it follows that evidence of an intention not to repair in future cannot be decisive.

2.1.2 Replacement

Damages have also been awarded for the cost of replacing the defendant's non-performance or defective performance even though in fact the claimant chose not to seek a replacement, either immediately or at all. Many such 'avoided loss' cases have arisen in the context of sales of goods or other property where the claimant had an opportunity to resort to an available market for a replacement. Where the claimant made a choice not to resort to the market as soon as possible after the breach, damages are assessed as if it had done so, even if (as it turns out) the choice reduces the harm in fact suffered by the claimant. Just as in relation to avoidable loss,[20] such cases are often expressed as an application of the so-called 'market rule'.[21] As I explain in detail in Chapter 10, the market rule is simply an application of the replication rule, and crucially depends on the claimant having made a *choice* not to resort to the market.[22]

Jamal v Moolla Dawood illustrates the application of the replication rule in the context of non-acceptance of shares.[23] Rather than re-selling the shares as soon as

[17] See further Chapter 8, Section 2.1.1.

[18] See further Section 4.

[19] *Darlington BC v Wiltshier Northern Ltd* [1995] 1 WLR 68 (CA) 80 (Steyn LJ); *Ruxley Electronics & Construction Ltd v Forsyth* [1996] AC 344 (HL) 357, 359 (Lord Jauncey), 372 (Lord Lloyd); *Giedo Van Der Garde BV v Force India Formula One Team Ltd* [2010] EWHC 2373 (QB) [484] (Stadlen J); *De Beers Ltd v Atos Origin IT Services UK Ltd* [2010] EWHC 3276 (TCC) [345] (Edwards-Stuart J). See further David Winterton (n 6) 191–99.

[20] See Chapter 8, Section 2.1.2.

[21] As McGregor put it: 'mitigation has become incorporated into the normal measure of damages': McGregor (n 4) 332.

[22] See Chapter 10, Section 1.2.

[23] *AKAS Jamal v Moolla Dawood Sons & Co* [1916] 1 AC 175 (PC).

possible after accepting the defendant's repudiation, the claimant chose to wait for two months before selling the shares gradually in several batches. In the meantime, the market value of the shares rose, such that the claimant obtained a higher price for the shares than it would have done if it had sold at the date of breach, when it first had the opportunity to do so. The defendant argued that damages should be assessed as the difference between the contract price and the actual sale prices, ie the claimant's factual loss. The Privy Council (whose panel included Viscount Haldane)[24] disagreed, instead awarding damages as if the claimant had sold the shares at the date of breach on the basis that:

> If the seller retains the shares after the breach, the speculation as to the way the market will subsequently go is the speculation of the seller, not of the buyer; the seller cannot recover from the buyer the loss below the market price at the date of the breach if the market falls, nor is he liable to the purchaser for the profit if the market rises.[25]

Although Burrows criticizes this reasoning,[26] McGregor and *Chitty* accept that the decision can be explained as an application of Viscount Haldane's second limb in *British Westinghouse v London Underground*, concluding that the subsequent sale of the shares was 'to be regarded as an independent transaction'[27] and 'does not arise from any act of mitigation'.[28] However, this explanation merely restates the *British Westinghouse* test and does not explain *why* the transaction in *Jamal* was independent, especially given that McGregor reaches the opposite conclusion for several other 'speculation' cases to which the so-called avoided loss rule has been applied.[29] The better explanation is that the Privy Council's reasoning reflects the application of the replication rule and its reliance on 'speculation' further reflects the importance of the claimant's *choice* not to resort to the market.

The reasoning in *Jamal* was subsequently applied by the Court of Appeal in *Campbell Mostyn v Barnett Trading*, a case involving the non-acceptance of goods.[30] The claimants decided not to resell immediately, and the market price subsequently rose. The Court of Appeal unanimously awarded damages as if the

24 Viscount Haldane also gave the judgment in *British Westinghouse* (n 2) that established the so-called 'avoided loss rule'.

25 *Jamal* (n 23) 179.

26 Andrew Burrows, *Remedies for Torts and Breach of Contract* (4th edn, OUP 2019) 196: 'This approach leaves a claimant in a better position than if the contract had been performed and therefore runs contrary to the avowed compensatory goal'.

27 Edelman, *McGregor on Damages* (21st edn) (n 3) [9-135]. See also McGregor (n 4) 340.

28 Hugh Beale (ed), *Chitty on Contracts* (34th edn, Sweet & Maxwell 2022) [29-115].

29 Edelman, *McGregor on Damages* (21st edn) (n 3) [9-174]–[9-184], criticizing the application of the rule in *Rodocanachi, Sons & Co v Milburn Bros* (1887) LR 18 QBD 67 (CA); *Williams Bros v Ed T Agius Ltd* [1914] AC 510 (HL); *Slater v Hoyle & Smith Ltd* [1920] 2 KB 11 (CA).

30 *Campbell Mostyn (Provisions) Ltd v Barnett Trading Co* [1954] 1 Lloyd's Rep 65 (CA). See also *Gardner v Marsh & Parsons* [1997] 1 WLR 489 (CA) 507 (Peter Gibson LJ).

claimant had sold the goods at the date of breach, even though, as Birkett LJ acknowledged, 'on the facts as we now know them, the plaintiffs . . . suffered no loss at all'.[31] Again, the court's reasoning reflected the symmetry in the application of the replication rule. Somervell LJ emphasized that 'if the market had gone even worse than it was on [the date of breach] [the defendants] would not have been liable to pay more than whatever sum was fixed . . . on that day'.[32] In other words, the claimant was responsible for its choice not to resort to the market, for better or worse.

The same approach is evident in several cases on non-delivery.[33] In *Williams Bros v Agius*, the defendants failed to deliver coal to the claimant at a price of 16s 3d per ton.[34] The market price at the date of breach was 23s 6d per ton. The claimant had already concluded a sub-sale to a third party at 19s per ton. The House of Lords unanimously assessed damages as the difference between the contract price and the market price at the date of breach, even though in fact the claimant chose not to resort to the market and simply cancelled the sub-sale without liability. Proponents of the orthodox account of mitigation have criticized the award on the basis that it 'overcompensated the claimant' because it exceeded the claimant's factual loss, arguing that the award should instead have been assessed by reference to the sub-sale.[35]

The reasoning in *Williams Bros* reflects the replication rule. Lord Moulton held that the difference between the contract price and market price was 'the true measure of [the claimant's] loss from the breach, for it is that which it will cost him to put himself in the same position as if the contract had been fulfilled'.[36] In other words, the claimant was awarded the cost of replicating the no-breach position. Viscount Haldane expressly noted that even though this cost was not in fact incurred, the award was 'quite in harmony with what was recently said in this House in *British Westinghouse*'.[37] Viscount Haldane and Lord Dunedin also reasoned that 'if the plaintiff had sold the goods before the breach for more than the market price at that date he could not recover on that footing . . . it would therefore be unjust if the market price did not govern when he had sold for less'.[38]

[31] *Campbell Mostyn* (n 30) 69.
[32] ibid 68.
[33] *Rodocanachi* (n 29); *Williams Bros* (n 29); *Bear Stearns Bank plc v Forum Global Equity Ltd* [2007] EWHC 1576 (Comm); *Oxus Gold plc v Templeton Insurance Ltd* [2007] EWHC 770 (Comm). cf *Euro-Asian Oil SA v Credit Suisse AG* [2018] EWCA Civ 1720.
[34] *Williams Bros* (n 29).
[35] Burrows (n 26) 192. See also McLauchlan, 'Expectation Damages: Avoided Loss, Offsetting Gains and Subsequent Events' (n 5) 366.
[36] *Williams Bros* (n 29) 531. See also 523 (Lord Dunedin).
[37] ibid 520. See also 523 (Lord Dunedin): 'it is absurd to suppose that a contract with a third party as to something else, just because it is the same kind of thing, can reduce the damages which the unsatisfied buyer is entitled to recover under the original contract'.
[38] ibid 520. See also 522–23 (Lord Dunedin).

The replication rule also applies where the claimant chooses not to seek a replacement after receiving patently defective goods.[39] The best-known example is *Slater v Hoyle*,[40] which as McGregor puts it, 'has received much attention over the years'.[41] The claimant purchased unbleached cotton from the defendant for the purpose of bleaching and selling on to a third party for use in manufacturing shirts. Although the claimant knew that the deliveries were 'persistently of a quality not in accordance with the contract',[42] it proceeded to sell the cloth to the third party, apparently without incurring any liability under the sub-contract.[43] The Court of Appeal awarded damages based on the difference in market value between the cotton promised and the cotton actually delivered, even though (as it turned out) the claimant was able to use the cotton without suffering any factual loss.

The award in *Slater* has been criticised by proponents of the orthodox account of mitigation on the basis that 'there are difficulties in justifying it on compensatory reasoning because it appears to leave the claimant in a better position than if the contract had been properly performed'.[44] However, the Court of Appeal clearly thought that the award was compensation for loss, albeit not a factual loss. Warrington LJ and Scrutton LJ both described the difference in market value as a 'loss',[45] and Bankes LJ expressly rejected the argument that the claimants had 'suffered no loss'.[46] Scrutton LJ acknowledged that the award gave the claimants 'more if the goods were inferior than they would have got if they were sound',[47] but nevertheless concluded that '[t]he rules of English law do not always give exact indemnity, and in this case I think they do not'.[48]

The reasoning and result in *Slater* neatly exemplify the application of the replication rule. The claimants made a choice not to replicate the no-breach position by selling the defective cotton and buying replacement cotton. As Scrutton LJ noted, 'the buyers were under no obligation to deliver the goods of the original contract to the sub-buyer';[49] instead they 'could supply the sub-contract by buying

[39] cf *latently* defective goods, as in *Bence Graphics International Ltd v Fasson UK Ltd* [1998] QB 87 (CA), discussed at text to n 129.

[40] *Slater* (n 29). See also *Jones v Just* (1867–68) LR 3 QB 197 (QB); *Derby Resources AG v Blue Corinth Marine Co Ltd (The Athenian Harmony) (No 1)* [1998] 2 Lloyd's Rep 410 (QB) 415–16 (Colman J).

[41] Edelman, *McGregor on Damages* (21st edn) (n 3) [9-177].

[42] The headnote records that the contract specified the length, width, yarn, warp, and weft of the cloth: *Slater* (n 29) 12. See also 16 (Warrington LJ), noting that some of the cotton was 'persistently of a quality not in accordance with the contract'.

[43] Scrutton LJ recorded that 'The sub-buyer made oral complaints but did not reject the goods, and though at the time of the trial he was claiming on the buyers, he had not taken any actual legal proceedings': ibid 19.

[44] Burrows (n 26) 193. See also Edelman, *McGregor on Damages* (21st edn) (n 3) [9-180]; McLauchlan, 'Expectation Damages: Avoided Loss, Offsetting Gains and Subsequent Events' (n 5) 370–72.

[45] *Slater* (n 29) 18 (Warrington LJ), 22 (Scrutton LJ).

[46] ibid 14. See also 16 (Warrington LJ), rejecting the argument that 'the defendants in fact suffered no damage'.

[47] ibid 20.

[48] ibid 24.

[49] ibid 20. See also 22.

in the market'.[50] It followed that 'If the buyer delivers under the sub-contract the damaged goods and has to pay damages, these damages ... will clearly not be recoverable';[51] this proposition is well-established in the context of avoidable loss. Scrutton LJ emphasized that this reasoning cut both ways: the claimants could not recover damages for the losses on the sub-sale if they turned out to be greater than the cost of resorting to the market, but 'The result seems the same if they are less ... [the sub-sale] cannot affect his claim one way or the other'.[52]

The decision in *Bence Graphics v Fasson* has conventionally been regarded as inconsistent with *Slater*,[53] but as I explain in detail below, in fact the two cases can be reconciled.[54] By contrast, the decision in *Pagnan & Fratelli v Corbisa* is a real outlier.[55] The defendant sellers supplied the claimant with damaged goods. The claimant initially rejected the delivery, but later repurchased the same goods (which were already in its possession) from the defendant at a reduced price. The Court of Appeal rejected a claim for damages based on the difference between the market value of the damaged goods and their value in the promised condition. Salmon LJ concluded that 'the buyers suffered no loss' because they had profited from repurchasing the damaged goods at below their market value.[56] In particular, he held that the repurchase 'formed part of a continuous dealing with the situation in which they found themselves and was not an independent or disconnected transaction'.[57]

Pagnan is wrongly decided because it overlooks that the claimant *chose* not to replicate their no-breach position. As Salmon LJ acknowledged, the claimant was not bound to repurchase the damaged goods;[58] it could have resorted to the market to purchase goods of the contractual specification. Just as in *Slater*, the claimant should have been held responsible for its choice not to replicate, for better or worse. The failure to see the connection with *Slater*, which was not cited in *Pagnan*, illustrates the pitfalls of the 'continuous dealing' test. The subsequent dealings in *Pagnan* appeared 'continuous' with the original transaction in that they involved the same parties and the same goods; however, the repurchase nevertheless involved a fresh choice by the claimants to make do with sub-standard goods rather than seeking conforming goods.

[50] ibid 21 (Scrutton LJ).
[51] ibid 22 (Scrutton LJ).
[52] *Slater* (n 29) 22. See also 23–24.
[53] *Bence* (n 39).
[54] Text to n 129.
[55] *R Pagnan & Fratelli v Corbisa Industrial Agropacuaria Ltd* [1970] 1 WLR 1306 (CA).
[56] ibid 1316.
[57] ibid 1315–16.
[58] ibid 1315.

2.1.3 Extrication

Further applications of the so-called avoided loss rule arise from the claimant's choice not to extricate itself from the breach. The Court of Appeal has noted that 'Reported cases in this field are legion',[59] and indeed a careful search of the unreported cases indicates that they are even more numerous than is conventionally acknowledged.[60] The relatively few cases mentioned by the leading texts are written off as 'wrongly decided' on the basis that the award exceeded the orthodox 'factual loss cap' on damages; these cases have led many scholars to conclude that the application of the avoided loss rule is in a 'dreadful muddle'.[61] However, the awards are consistent with the application of the replication rule, and the judicial focus on the claimant's choice not to extricate strongly supports this explanation.

The claimant's choice not to extricate from the breach may take one of two main forms depending on the assessment of the no-breach position. The first category of cases involve a choice by the claimant (after discovering the breach) to retain property that it would otherwise have sold but-for the breach.[62] The second category of cases involve a choice not to undo a transaction (by reselling property) that the claimant would never have entered into in the first place but-for the breach.[63] In both sets of cases, the courts have reasoned that the claimant is responsible for the consequences of its choice to retain the property, for better or worse. The claimant is awarded damages as if it had sold the property when it could have done so, even though in fact it did not. An important consequence of this reasoning is that the claimant may end up recovering damages greater than its factual loss.

In relation to the first category of extrication cases, the Court of Appeal's decision in *Blue Circle Industries v MOD* perfectly illustrates the application of the replication rule.[64] The defendants leaked radioactive material on to the claimant's land. If the leak had not occurred, the claimant would have sold the land to a prospective purchaser for around £10mil in 1993.[65] By the time the land became available to sell in 1994 after having been decontaminated,[66] an intervening slump in

[59] *Bacciottini v Gotelee & Goldsmith* [2016] EWCA Civ 170, [2016] 4 WLR 98 [34] (Davis LJ).

[60] See eg *Bondwheat Ltd v Riddington & Co* (CA, 10 July 1991); *Constantine (Tavistock Antiques) v TotalFinaElf UK Ltd* [2003] EWHC 428 (Ch). See also, in specialist reports: *Daisley v BS Hall & Co* (1972) 225 EG 1553 (QB); *Marder v Sautelle & Hicks* [1988] 2 EGLR 187 (CA); *Pankhania v Hackney LBC* [2004] EWHC 323 (Ch), [2004] 1 EGLR 135.

[61] McLauchlan, 'Expectation Damages: Avoided Loss, Offsetting Gains and Subsequent Events' (n 5) 384. See further Chapter 3, text to n 58.

[62] See eg *Blue Circle Industries plc v Ministry of Defence* [1999] Ch 289 (CA); *Primavera v Allied Dunbar Assurance plc* [2002] EWCA Civ 1327, [2003] Lloyd's Rep PN 14; *Constantine* (n 60).

[63] See eg *Daisley* (n 60); *Perry v Sidney Phillips & Son* [1982] 1 WLR 1297 (CA); *Marder* (n 60); *Hussey v Eels* [1990] 2 QB 227 (CA); *Bondwheat* (n 60); *Devine v Jefferys* [2001] Lloyd's Rep PN 301 (QB); *Pankhania* (n 60). See also *Glencore Energy UK Ltd v Cirrus Oil Services Ltd* [2014] EWHC 87 (Comm), in which the claimant prevented the acquisition of property that was to be used in a sub-sale, rather than re-selling the property after acquisition.

[64] *Blue Circle* (n 62).

[65] ibid 314 (Chadwick LJ).

[66] ibid 308 (Aldous LJ), 315 (Chadwick LJ): 'The estate was unsaleable, whether as a whole or in parts, until the completion of the clean-up operation.'

the property market had reduced its value to only £4mil. The claimant chose not to sell the land in 1994, and by the date of trial in 1996 the value of the land had risen to £5mil. The Court of Appeal awarded damages as if the claimant had sold the land in 1994, even though in fact the claimant did not sell the land then, or at any time prior to trial.

In reaching this conclusion, the Court of Appeal expressed the issue as one of causation.[67] Aldous LJ held that after 1994, the question 'whether or not the [defendants] would be liable for a further decrease in value or would have the benefit of an increase must depend on whether that further increase or decrease was caused by the contamination'.[68] He reasoned that '[t]he chain of causation will end at a particular date whether or not the value increased or decreased thereafter'.[69] The chain of causation was broken in 1994 because thereafter the claimants were no longer '"locked into" the situation produced by the contamination'[70] and were 'free once again to exercise their own choice as to the use or marketing of the estate'.[71] It did not matter that the claimants did not in fact sell in 1994, nor that the claimant's factual loss had subsequently been reduced by the rising market.

The Court of Appeal emphasized that the decision to retain the property after 1994 was one that the claimant 'was free to take in its own interests'.[72] In particular, the issue was whether the claimants made a 'choice' rather than whether it acted 'reasonably in retaining the land'.[73] Chadwick LJ expressly acknowledged a 'logical symmetry' in the application of the rule and noted that 'The symmetry has attracted the other members of this court'.[74] The questions of whether the claimants could recover for the further harm if the market fell or must give credit if the market rose, 'must be answered the same way, whichever way it is'.[75] Simon Brown LJ's concluding comments encapsulate the key elements of the replication rule, including its symmetrical application, its link to causation and the importance of choice:

> [The claimants'] decision here to retain their estate after December 1994 should not properly be regarded 'as part of a continuous transaction' . . . The loss caused by that breach of statutory duty ended once the land was reinstated and again became available to be retained or sold as [the claimants] chose. Any further loss would have been caused by [the claimants'] decision to retain the land; likewise any gain. The speculation from that point was on their own account.[76]

[67] ibid 305 (Aldous LJ), 316 (Chadwick LJ), 321–22 (Simon Brown LJ).
[68] ibid 305.
[69] ibid 308.
[70] ibid 308 (Aldous LJ).
[71] ibid 315 (Chadwick LJ). See also 321 (Simon Brown LJ).
[72] ibid 316 (Chadwick LJ).
[73] ibid 321 (Simon Brown LJ). See also 316 (Chadwick LJ).
[74] ibid 317.
[75] ibid 321.
[76] ibid 321.

The same reasoning is evident in *Primavera v Allied Dunbar Insurance*.[77] The defendant failed to advise the claimant of the need to make salary contributions to a pension scheme; if the claimant had been properly advised, he would have made the relevant contributions and would have closed the fund in 1995.[78] Instead, when the claimant discovered the breach in 1995, he chose to retain the fund, which subsequently increased in value. Mance LJ identified the issue as being 'whether any prima facie loss suffered as at March 1995 was "mitigated" (or avoided) by the respondent's actual conduct' in retaining the fund.[79] The Court of Appeal assessed damages as if the claimant had closed the fund in 1995, even though in fact the fund remained open until at least 2002 and (as things turned out) the claimant was left in a better financial position than if he had been properly advised.

The Court of Appeal's reasoning was again based on causation, concluding that although 'there was a causal link between the appellants' negligence and the eventual profit . . . the negligence merely set the scene for that profit rather than directly causing it'.[80] The judges emphasised the importance of the claimant's choice to retain the fund. Mance LJ reasoned that 'Rather than crystallise his loss . . . the respondent chose to keep the pension policy and the loan in existence to their full extent. That may or may not have proved beneficial overall, but it was, in legal terms, his "speculation"'.[81] All of the judges recognised the symmetry of this proposition. As Latham LJ put it, 'Had that investment decision proved disadvantageous, [the claimant] would not have had any claim for such loss against the [defendants] . . . The corollary is that the [defendants] are not entitled to take advantage of any benefits'.[82]

In *Primavera*, the judges also sought to relate their reasoning to the orthodox avoided loss rule. Latham LJ acknowledged that 'I was at first attracted by the [defendant's] argument, essentially based on *British Westinghouse* . . . that the [claimant] simply did that which a reasonable and prudent man would have done in the circumstances'.[83] However, on reflection he agreed with Simon Brown LJ's conclusion that 'the benefits accruing to the fund through its being left in place during the five and a half years in question were . . . not part of a continuous transaction of which that negligence was the inception; rather they were the result of a number of decisions by the [claimant]'.[84] In substance, the reason why the *British Westinghouse* test was satisfied was because the claimant made a free choice not to

[77] *Primavera* (n 62).

[78] ibid [7] (Simon Brown LJ), [36] (Lord Mance). See especially [52] (Latham LJ), noting that 'the purpose of the original transaction . . . was to enable the respondent to raise a loan of £500,000 which he could redeem in 1995. The respondent had not intended the transaction to continue beyond that'.

[79] ibid [37].

[80] ibid [21] (Simon Brown LJ). See also [50] (Latham LJ).

[81] ibid [40]. See also [29] (Simon Brown LJ), [52] (Latham LJ).

[82] ibid [52] (Latham LJ). See also [29] (Simon Brown LJ), [40] (Mance LJ).

[83] ibid [51] (Latham LJ).

[84] ibid [21] (Simon Brown LJ). See also [38] (Mance LJ).

extricate from the breach, regardless of whether that decision was in some sense 'reasonable'.

The second category of extrication cases is illustrated by *Hussey v Eels*,[85] one of the best-known and perhaps most controversial instances of recovery for avoided loss. The claimants were induced to buy a house by the defendant's negligent misrepresentation that the property was free from subsidence. Upon discovering the subsidence, the claimants chose not to resell the house immediately, but instead sought planning permission to develop a second house on the same site. Two years later, after receiving planning permission, the claimants sold the property for substantially more than they had paid for it. The Court of Appeal awarded damages based on 'the difference between the price paid . . . and the actual market value of the property at the date of completion' even though the claimants had in fact resold the property at a profit.

Mustill LJ acknowledged that 'in one sense there was a causal link between the inducement of the purchase by misrepresentation and the sale two-and-a-half years later'.[86] However, applying the *British Westinghouse* test, he concluded that 'when the plaintiffs unlocked the development value of their land they did so for their own benefit, and not as part of a continuous transaction of which the purchase of land and bungalow was the inception'.[87] This conclusion has been criticized in the leading texts on damages. McGregor and Burrows describe *Hussey* as a 'particularly suspect'[88] and 'controversial'[89] decision, because 'the acts of applying for planning permission and then selling upon obtaining it were designed to deal with the difficulties raised by the subsidence affecting the property' such that 'those acts arose from the consequences of the wrong and the benefit from acts taken in mitigation'.[90] In *Gardner*, Peter Gibson LJ stated that *Hussey* was 'an exceptional case turning on its own facts'.[91]

These criticisms of *Hussey* overlook how the replication rule works. After discovering the misrepresentation, the claimants could have extricated themselves from the transaction by reselling the property immediately.[92] As Mustill LJ put it, the claimant's decision to retain the property whilst they sought planning permission 'represented a choice of one of the options with which the plaintiffs had been presented by the defendants' wrongful act'.[93] If this choice had proved unwise, for example if their planning application had been unsuccessful or if the property had

[85] *Hussey* (n 63).
[86] ibid 241.
[87] ibid 241.
[88] McGregor (n 4) 399.
[89] Burrows (n 26) 150.
[90] Edelman, *McGregor on Damages* (21st edn) (n 3) [9-144]. See also Burrows (n 26) 150–51.
[91] *Gardner* (n 30) 510. Cf *Quilter v Hodson Developments Ltd* [2016] EWCA Civ 1125 [36] (Floyd LJ), noting that *Hussey* 'does not seem to us to be. . . exceptional'.
[92] Although there is no report of an express finding that the claimants would not have entered into the transaction but-for the misrepresentation, this finding can reliably be inferred from the context.
[93] *Hussey* (n 63) 241. See also 233.

otherwise decreased in value during the intervening period, the defendant would not have been responsible for the additional harm suffered. It follows, as Kramer correctly identifies, that the consequences of retaining and later developing the site are also irrelevant where they turned out to be beneficial to the claimant.[94]

Although commonly omitted from the leading texts, numerous other cases support the approach in *Hussey*. In reality, the cases acknowledged and criticised by the orthodox account are just the tip of the iceberg. Three decisions predating *Hussey* all awarded damages for avoided loss based on the claimant's choice not to extricate after being induced to purchase property by the defendant's negligent survey.[95] In each case, the court awarded damages as if the claimants had extricated by reselling the property immediately, even though in fact the claimants had not resold the property, either immediately or at all, and had not suffered any factual loss. In one of these decisions, Bristow J reasoned that 'What is sauce for the goose is sauce for the gander, and if [the claimant] would never be entitled to recover more than [the cost of extrication], it must follow that he will never be entitled to recover less'.[96]

Since the decision in *Hussey*, at least three further decisions have allowed recovery for avoided loss in circumstances where the claimant made a choice not to extricate.[97] These cases have either been overlooked altogether or dismissed as wrongly decided by the leading texts.[98] In the most recent case, *Pankhania v Hackney LBC*, the claimant property developer was induced to buy a car park on the basis of the defendant's misrepresentation that the car park was occupied under a contractual licence, when in fact the occupier held a protected tenancy.[99] Vos J awarded damages as if the claimant had resold the car park upon discovering the misrepresentation, even though in fact he chose to retain the car park and succeeded in obtaining possession from the protected tenant, thereby reducing his factual loss. Vos J reasoned that:

> the decision to retain the Properties was indeed collateral to the tort, because [the claimant] would not have bought the Properties, but for the tort. He could have been expected to sell the Properties when he found out about the Tenancies, but he chose not to in the circumstances then prevailing. That was not part of a continuous transaction of which the misrepresentation was the inception.[100]

[94] Adam Kramer, *The Law of Contract Damages* (3rd edn, Hart 2022) [3-36].
[95] *Daisley* (n 60); *Perry* (n 63); *Marder* (n 60).
[96] *Daisley* (n 60) 1557.
[97] *Bondwheat* (n 60); *Devine* (n 63); *Pankhania* (n 60).
[98] See eg Edelman, *McGregor on Damages* (21st edn) (n 3) [9-164], criticizing *Devine* (n 63) and omitting the other two cases. Other proponents of the orthodox account of mitigation have omitted all three cases from their analysis.
[99] *Pankhania* (n 60).
[100] ibid [45].

As an application of the replication rule, this reasoning is impeccable: Vos J started by assessing the no-breach position, clarifying that the claimant would not have entered into the transaction but-for the breach; he then reasoned that the claimant could have resold the car park (thus replicating the no-breach position) but instead made a choice not to do so. It was on this basis that the claimant's conduct was not part of a 'continuous transaction' under the *British Westinghouse* test. Vos J also noted counsel's argument that 'Things could have gone disastrously wrong for [the claimant] and he would not have been able to claim more. But if things went well for [the claimant], that is his good fortune.'[101] Although Vos J expressed the award as the 'normal measure of damages', he noted that this measure was 'intimately bound up with' questions of mitigation and causation.[102]

Two Court of Appeal cases—with essentially similar facts—illustrate the importance of explicitly considering the no-breach position when deciding issues of mitigation and avoided loss.[103] In *Bacciottini v Gotelee & Goldsmith*, the defendants negligently failed to advise the claimants of a planning restriction on a property that the claimants were thinking of buying.[104] After going ahead with the purchase and discovering the error, the claimants succeeded in having the restriction lifted but nevertheless claimed damages for the diminution in value of the property at the date of completion. In *LSREF III Wight v Gately*, the defendants negligently failed to advise the claimant lenders about an insolvency clause in a lease that resulted in the claimant's loan being under-secured.[105] The claimant subsequently succeeded in negotiating the removal of the clause, thereby restoring adequate security, but nevertheless claimed damages representing the diminution in value of the security at the date of the transaction.

In both *Bacciottini* and *LSREF*, the Court of Appeal rejected the application of the avoided loss rule and held that the claimants could only recover for the costs actually incurred in removing the planning restriction and insolvency clause respectively.[106] It is difficult to say whether or not these decisions are correct, because in both cases the trial judge failed to make any findings as to what would have happened if the claimants had been properly advised.[107] The Court of Appeal was untroubled by these omissions and indeed sought to discourage such 'speculation'.[108] In *LSREF*, Briggs LJ noted that the question of what would have happened but-for the breach made 'no difference for present purposes'.[109] This approach

[101] ibid [14].
[102] ibid [22].
[103] See also *Quilter v Hodson* [2016] EWCA Civ 1125, which implicitly relies on an assumption that, but for the defendant's breach, the claimant would have bargained successfully for a lower price rather than pulling out of the transaction altogether.
[104] *Bacciottini* (n 59).
[105] *LSREF III Wight Ltd v Gateley LLP* [2016] EWCA Civ 359, [2016] PNLR 21.
[106] *Bacciottini* (n 59) [63] (Davis LJ); *LSREF* (n 105) [40]–[43] (Briggs LJ).
[107] *Bacciottini* (n 59) [29] (Davis LJ); *LSREF* (n 105) [14] (Briggs LJ).
[108] *Bacciottini* (n 59) [69] (Davis LJ); *LSREF* (n 105) [14] (Briggs LJ).
[109] *LSREF* (n 105) [14].

misunderstands the legal concept of loss, because without assessing the claimant's no-breach position, it is impossible to apply correctly either the replication rule or the wider compensatory principle.

The Court of Appeal's reasoning in *Bacciottini* and *LSREF* highlights a common error in the analysis of the avoided loss cases. In both cases, the court focused on rebutting counsel's argument that damages for the diminution in value as at the date of breach were *always* recoverable.[110] This argument was rightly rejected, but it is a straw man. The so-called 'diminution in value' measure, often invoked in the context of avoided loss, is predicated on the counterfactual effect of the replication rule. In the context of extrication, the replication rule only applies where the claimant made a choice not to resort to the market to undo a transaction that it would not have entered into but-for the breach. It is therefore true that the claimant cannot *always* recover damages for diminution in value (as where the claimant had no choice), but it does not follow that the claimant can *never* recover on this basis.

Although there was no finding on the no-breach position in either *Bacciottini* or *LSREF*, if the trial judge had found that the claimants would not have entered into the transaction but-for the breach, there would have been a good argument that the replication rule should have applied. This is because in both cases the claimants chose not to undo the transaction after discovering the breach. On this basis, the cases appear indistinguishable from *Hussey* and related decisions.[111] One might object that the claimants would then have recovered damages greater than their factual loss. However, this point cannot be conclusive because it is also true of the numerous other cases described in this chapter. It must also be remembered that the replication rule cuts both ways; if the claimants' choice not to extricate had proved disadvantageous, they could not have recovered for the additional harm suffered.

On the other hand, in *Bacciottini*, the steps that the claimants in fact took were exceptionally straightforward compared with the process of undoing the transaction by reselling the house. The trial judge and Court of Appeal emphasized that the removal of the planning restriction was 'simple, obvious and cheap'.[112] In these circumstances, it may have been descriptively unusual for the claimants to have replicated the no-breach position by reselling the house. If so, this case would raise the same tension between legal and descriptive norms as in *Ruxley v Forsyth*, whereby the application of the replication and exceptionality rules conflict.[113] The same cannot be said on the facts of *LSREF*, because there the choice to negotiate the removal of the insolvency clause does not appear to have been obviously

[110] *Bacciottini* (n 59) [58] (Davis LJ); *LSREF* (n 105) [35] (Briggs LJ).
[111] Text to n 64 and following.
[112] *Bacciottini* (n 59) [59] (Davis LJ).
[113] *Ruxley* (n 19). See further Chapter 8, Section 2.2.4.

cheaper or more straightforward than extricating from the transaction by selling the under-secured loan.[114]

2.1.4 Other choices

The claimant may choose to take other steps that, although prompted by the breach,[115] were not part of any attempt to replicate the no-breach position.[116] For example, suppose that the claimant is injured by the defendant and whilst recovering in hospital, he uses his spare time to set up a business or buy a lottery ticket. The business profits or lottery winnings are not taken into account in the assessment of damages.[117] This proposition is readily accepted by proponents of the orthodox account of damages, even though the benefit would not have arisen but-for the breach.[118] In relation to the lottery ticket example, Burrows concludes that the 'benefit should not be deducted because it was too indirectly related to the tort or breach of contract'.[119] This reasoning is correct, but very hard to square with Burrows' staunch opposition to putting the claimant in a better position than if the breach had not occurred.[120]

The best-known example from the cases is *Lavarack v Woods of Colchester*.[121] The claimant was wrongfully dismissed. He subsequently took employment with a rival company and also purchased shares in another rival company called Ventilation. Neither of these steps could have occurred but-for the breach because both were prohibited during the course of his original employment. The Court of Appeal held that although the remuneration from the substitute employment was to be taken into account in assessing the claimant's loss, the benefit of the investment in Ventilation was not. Lord Denning MR reasoned that although 'the plaintiff was only at liberty to invest in Ventilation because his employment was terminated ... nevertheless the benefit from that investment was not a direct result of his dismissal. It was an entirely collateral benefit'.[122]

[114] *LSREF* (n 105). Although the Court of Appeal rejected the trial judge's conclusion that the renegotiation was 'complicated and potentially open-ended' (at [52]), it did not attempt any comparison with the difficulty of extrication.

[115] In other words, the claimant would not have taken such steps but for the breach.

[116] Contrast cases where the claimant would still have obtained the benefit even if the breach had not occurred: see eg *Assetco Plc v Grant Thornton UK LLP* [2019] EWHC 150 (Comm) [897]–[898] (Bryan J).

[117] Law Commission, *Damages for Personal Injury: Medical, Nursing and Other Expenses; Collateral Benefits* (Law Com No 262, 1999) [10.4].

[118] Burrows (n 26) 148.

[119] ibid 148.

[120] See further Chapter 1, Section 2.3.

[121] *Lavarack v Woods of Colchester* [1967] 1 QB 278 (CA). See also *Hill v Showell* (1918) 87 LJKB 1106 (HL) 1115 (Lord Parmoor); *Jewelowski v Propp* [1944] KB 510 (KB); *Famosa Shipping Co Ltd v Armada Bulk Carriers Ltd (The Fanis)* [1994] 1 Lloyd's Rep 633 (QB); *Goknur v Organic Village Ltd* [2019] EWHC 2201 (QB) [61].

[122] *Lavarack* (n 121) 290. See also 300 (Russell LJ).

The decision in *Lavarack* has been supported by the leading texts on the basis that 'while the profit on the Ventilation shares was a compensating advantage, it should not be deducted because it was too indirectly related to the breach, as it did not follow from action taken to avoid its consequences'.[123] Although this 'directness' reasoning hints that the decision is concerned with the application of causal principles, the test itself is too vague. In *The Fanis*, Mance J articulated a more specific test based on whether 'the profit was an element or consequence of the *substitute*' for performance.[124] For example, in *Lavarack*, the claimant's choice to purchase the Ventilation shares was not part of his attempt to secure substitute employment; similarly, the decision to purchase a lottery ticket whilst in hospital is not part of a claimant's attempt to treat his injury.

The substitute performance test articulated by Mance J reflects a further application of the replication rule. So far it has been argued that the replication rule only applies where the claimant made a choice *not* to replicate the no-breach position. However, even where the claimant did replicate the no-breach position, it may *also* choose to take steps that are not part of the attempt at replication (or 'substitute' performance). The reason why these steps are regarded as 'indirect' or 'independent' even though they would not have arisen but-for the breach is that they are voluntary and not part of an attempt at replication. Again, this rule cuts both ways and applies to costs as well as to benefits;[125] for example, the claimant cannot recover for the cost of buying the lottery ticket if he does not win, any more than his winnings are taken into account if he does.

Of course, it may not always be entirely straightforward to determine whether any of the steps actually taken by the claimant were distinct from the attempt at replication. *Chitty* gives an indication of this issue in acknowledging that 'the courts have seldom taken [the claimant's] benefit into account where the alternative use chosen by the claimant was substantially different from his promised performance under the original contract'.[126] But by contrast, 'Where the alternative use has a similar goal (e.g. the earning of profits or wages), the courts have been more likely to take it into account in assessing damages'.[127] In other words, although the line may be difficult to draw precisely, the aim is to distinguish steps taken in replication from steps that serve some different purpose altogether.

[123] Burrows (n 26) 149. See also Edelman, *McGregor on Damages* (21st edn) (n 3) [9-129].

[124] *The Fanis* (n 121) 637.

[125] See eg HLA Hart and Tony Honoré, *Causation in the Law* (2nd edn, Clarendon 1985) 158: 'For a man who has suffered a serious injury owing to defendant's negligence it may be natural to decide to take a holiday, and it may be probable that he will do so, but it does not follow that he can charge the tortfeasor with the cost of it.'

[126] Beale, *Chitty on Contracts* (34th edn) (n 28) [29-120].

[127] ibid [29-101].

2.2 The claimant had no choice to replicate

Where the claimant was unable to replicate the no-breach position, it cannot have made a choice not to replicate. Hence the replication rule has no application and recovery for an 'avoided loss' will be denied.[128] This explains the decision in *Bence Graphics v Fasson*.[129] The claimant purchased vinyl film from the defendant to be used in manufacturing decals for sub-sale to third parties. The vinyl contained insufficient stabilizer to protect against ultra-violet light and therefore degraded faster than promised. This defect only became apparent after the claimant had already supplied the decals to its sub-buyers.[130] The claimant sought damages based on the difference in market value between the vinyl promised and supplied, even though in fact the claimant had obtained full price for the decals and received only one complaint from amongst its sub-buyers.

The Court of Appeal rejected the claim for difference in market value, holding that the claimant could only recover the much smaller sum representing the 'actual losses (if any) suffered by the plaintiffs under or arising from [the sub-sales]'.[131] The leading texts regard this decision as impossible to reconcile with the earlier Court of Appeal authority in *Slater*.[132] Bridge concludes that 'The *Slater* and *Bence* cases display radically different philosophies of damages assessment'.[133] The decision in *Bence* is preferred over *Slater* by proponents of the orthodox loss-based account of damages,[134] whereas proponents of the rival rights-based account have criticized *Bence*.[135] These analyses of *Bence* and *Slater* reflect the conventional split between those who think that damages greater than factual loss are *never* available, and those who think that they are *always* available.

On my account of mitigation, both *Slater* and *Bence* are correctly decided.[136] The key distinction between the cases is that in *Bence* (unlike in *Slater*), the defect was latent. The claimant only discovered that the vinyl was faulty after it had already been supplied to the sub-buyers;[137] it therefore had no choice to replicate the no-breach position by resorting to the market to purchase replacement vinyl of the contractual specification. In these circumstances, the so-called 'difference in

[128] Unless a different legal rule applies: see further Section 1.4.

[129] *Bence Graphics* (n 39).

[130] ibid 108 (Thorpe LJ), 106 (Auld LJ).

[131] ibid 91 (Otton LJ). The sub-sale losses amounted to £22,000 in respect of returned stock, whereas the difference in value was £564,328.

[132] *Slater* (n 29). See further the discussion at text to n 40.

[133] Michael Bridge, 'Markets and Damages in Sale of Goods Cases' (2016) 132 Law Quarterly Review 404, 417.

[134] Burrows (n 26) 194; Edelman, *McGregor on Damages* (21st edn) (n 3) [9-180]; McLauchlan, 'Expectation Damages: Avoided Loss, Offsetting Gains and Subsequent Events' (n 5) 370–72.

[135] Stevens, 'Damages and the Right to Performance' (n 12) 179–80.

[136] See further, for the first articulation of this argument, Andrew Dyson and Adam Kramer, 'There is No "Breach Date Rule": Mitigation, Difference in Value and Date of Assessment' (2014) 130 LQR 259.

[137] *Bence* (n 39) 108 (Thorpe LJ). Cf *OMV Petrom SA v Glencore International AG* [2017] 3 All ER 157, which also concerned a latent breach: see further Chapter 7, text to n 84.

value' measure of damages is irrelevant. In the absence of any intervening cause, the defendant is responsible for the actual consequences of the breach, for better or worse. This symmetry was expressly recognised by Otton LJ, who noted that he would have reached the same decision if the claimant's factual loss on the sub-sales had instead turned out to be greater than the difference in value rather than less.[138]

This explanation of the decision in *Bence* is consistent with Treitel's analysis.[139] Treitel argued that where the claimant 'had (legally) no choice as to the disposal of the goods', then damages should be measured by reference to the actual losses under the sub-sale rather than the difference in value.[140] This reasoning, often evident in 'string contracts', aptly reflects the scope of the replication rule. However, Treitel went on to conclude that *Bence* was wrongly decided because there the claimants were not contractually obliged to use the vinyl supplied by the defendants for their sub-sale.[141] Although Treitel's reasoning is correct as a matter of *legal* choice, it overlooks the fact that the claimants did not have any *practical* choice because they were unaware of the breach. In other words, whilst having no legal choice to replicate is one reason why the replication rule may be inapplicable, having no practical choice (for example when the defect is latent) is another. The award of damages for 'avoided loss' has similarly been rejected in other cases involving a latent breach.[142]

One might think that on the facts of *Bence*, the law as I have stated it leads to a harsh result. The claimant received less in damages because the defendant's breach was harder to detect, compared with *Slater* where the breach was patent. This is true, as things turned out. But it overlooks that the replication rule cuts both ways. If the sub-sales had turned out to be disastrous in *Slater*—for example, leading to mass returns and reputational damage—then the defendant would not have been liable for these consequences, whereas in *Bence* they would.[143] Accordingly, the law does not offer the defendant any incentive to conceal the breach, and nor does it penalize claimants who manage to discover wrongdoing. Discovery of the breach shifts responsibility on to the claimant, but whether or not this is to the claimant's advantage depends on the outcome of whatever choices they subsequently make.

Like *Slater*, the decision in *Wertheim v Chicoutimi Pulp* is also commonly cited in support of the orthodox 'factual loss cap' on damages.[144] It is true that the Privy

[138] *Bence* (n 39) 101. The Court of Appeal made clear that the defendants would also be liable to compensate the claimant should future claims against the claimants arise: 101 (Otton LJ); 107 (Auld LJ).

[139] Guenter Treitel, 'Damages for Breach of Warranty of Quality' (1997) 113 Law Quarterly Review 188.

[140] ibid 192.

[141] ibid 193.

[142] *McKinnon v E Surv Ltd* [2003] EWHC 475 (Ch), [2003] Lloyd's Rep PN 174; *Rubenstein v HSBC Bank plc* [2012] EWCA Civ 1184, [2012] 2 CLC 747 [133]–[136] (Rix LJ). See also the reasoning in *Gardner* (n 30) 507 (Peter Gibson LJ).

[143] In *Bence* (n 39), Otton LJ (at 101) and Auld LJ (at 107) both expressly stated that the defendants would be liable to compensate the claimant if they faced further claims by sub-buyers.

[144] See further Chapter 1, text to n 53.

Council's reasoning appears to adopt this understanding; Lord Atkinson held that it would be 'against all justice' if the claimant was 'permitted to make a profit by the breach of . . . and be put, as far as money can do it, not in the same position in which he would have been if the contract had been performed, but in a much better position'.[145] However, the outcome of *Wertheim* is consistent with the scope of the replication rule.[146] On the facts, replication of the no-breach position was impossible because the breach consisted of *delayed* delivery, which cannot be undone or corrected. This distinguishes *Wertheim* from the non-delivery cases such as *Williams Bros*,[147] in which the claimant made a choice not to obtain replacement goods at all.

Finally, just as the claimant can recover damages for any additional harm suffered whilst it remained 'locked in' to a transaction that it would not have entered into but-for the breach,[148] any benefits must also be taken into account.[149] The decision in *Wapshott v Davis Donovan* may be doubted on this basis.[150] The defendant solicitors failed to identify a defect in title to property purchased by the claimants. The claimants were unable to resell the property until the defect was cured. The Court of Appeal awarded damages based on the difference in value of the property at the date of breach, even though in fact the claimants had profited from the rise in property prices whilst the property remained unsaleable. This benefit should have been taken into account in the assessment of damages because the claimants had no choice to sell earlier.

2.3 The claimant did replicate

The vast majority of cases given as authority for the proposition that 'the claimant cannot recover for an avoided loss',[151] are explicable on the narrower basis that the relevant benefit was obtained through the claimant's own steps to replicate the no-breach position. *British Westinghouse* itself exemplifies this proposition.[152]

[145] *Wertheim v Chicoutimi Pulp Co* [1911] AC 301 (PC) 308.

[146] The explanation for the precise award in *Wertheim* is unclear and does not appear to have any supporters in the leading texts: see eg Burrows (n 26) 195; Edelman, *McGregor on Damages* (21st edn) (n 3) [9-181]. See also Stevens, 'Damages and the Right to Performance' (n 12) 183, concluding that the award 'neither reflects the value of the right nor the loss suffered'.

[147] Lord Atkinson also gave judgment in *Williams Bros* (n 29), and expressly distinguished *Wertheim* as a case about delay rather than non-delivery: 529. See also ibid 522 (Lord Dunedin).

[148] See eg *Smith New Court Securities Ltd v Citibank NA* [1997] AC 254 (HL). See further Chapter 7, Section 4.1.

[149] For example, where the claimant benefits whilst being locked in to a 'string contract' for the subsale of identical goods: *Slater* (n 29) 15 (Bankes LJ, obiter); Treitel, 'Damages for Breach of Warranty' 192–93. See too in Australia: *Cardno BSD Pty Ltd v Water Corporation* [2001] WASCA 161 [154]–[157].

[150] *Wapshott v Davis Donovan & Co* [1996] PNLR 361 (CA).

[151] See further Chapter 1, text to n 171.

[152] *British Westinghouse* (n 2). This explanation of *British Westinghouse* is reflected in *The Fanis* (n 121) 636 (Mance J) and Edelman, *McGregor on Damages* (21st edn) (n 3) [9-121]. For a more

In purchasing the replacement turbines, the claimant was merely replicating the position (as nearly as possible) as if the defendant had supplied turbines of the correct specification.[153] Accordingly, in *Dimond v Lovell*, Lord Hoffmann correctly held that *British Westinghouse* exemplified 'the rule that requires additional benefits obtained as a result of taking reasonable steps to mitigate loss to be brought into account in the calculation of damages'.[154] Reflecting the same understanding, Leggatt J has further emphasized that 'There is thus no need to invoke McGregor's "avoided loss" rule in order to explain the decision'.[155]

Several other cases are explicable on the same basis.[156] In *Erie County National Gas v Carroll*, the benefit resulted from the claimant's use of its own gas supply in substitution for the gas promised by the defendant, hence amounted to steps taken in an attempt at replication.[157] Likewise, in *Bellingham v Dhillon*, the claimant driving instructor was negligently injured by the defendant.[158] The claimant adduced evidence that if he had not been injured, he would have purchased a driving simulator and made profits from operating it. In assessing this head of damages, Forbes J took into account the fact that the claimant had subsequently purchased the simulator at a significant discount. Forbes J reasoned that 'The action of the plaintiff was that of a reasonable and prudent man of business. It was his duty to mitigate his damage by buying this equipment'.[159] The language of reasonableness is a distraction here: what matters is that the purchase entailed actual replication of the claimant's no-breach position, so the consequences were correctly included in the assessment of damages, even though they took place long after the breach.[160]

There is one outlying decision in which the claimant was awarded damages for avoided loss even though the benefit resulted from the claimant's own steps taken to replication the no-breach position. In *Mobil North Sea v PJ Pipe & Valve*, the

detailed analysis of *British Westinghouse*, see further Andrew Dyson, 'British Westinghouse Revisited' [2012] Lloyd's Maritime and Commercial Law Quarterly 412.

[153] Another way of putting this, with the same effect, is that the claimant had no choice but to supersede its no-breach position: see further Chapter 11, text to 83.

[154] *Dimond v Lovell* [2002] 1 AC 384 (HL) 401–02. See also, in support of this view: *Hussey* (n 201) 236 (Mustill LJ); *Famosa Shipping Co Ltd v Armada Bulk Carriers Ltd (The Fanis)* [1994] 1 Lloyd's Rep 633 (QB) 635–36 (Mance J); *Gardner* (n 30) 498 (Hirst LJ) and 514 (Pill LJ); *Thai Airways International Public Co Ltd v KI Holdings Co Ltd* [2015] EWHC 1250 (Comm), [2016] 1 All ER (Comm) 675 [41] (Leggatt J).

[155] *Thai Airways* (n 154) [45].

[156] See eg *Staniforth v Lyall* (1830) 7 Bing 169, 131 ER 65; *Hill* (n 121); *Nadreph Ltd v Willmett & Co* [1978] 1 WLR 1537 (Ch); *Gregory v Shepherds* [2000] Lloyd's Rep PN 724 (CA); *The Kildare* (n 191) [67] (Steel J).

[157] *Erie County Natural Gas & Fuel Co Ltd v Carroll* [1911] AC 105 (PC). See especially Lord Atkinson's reasoning at 117. Lord Atkinson also noted by way of symmetry that 'It may well be that if several reasonable but abortive attempts had been made to procure this gas the cost of these would have been properly treated as part of the cost of ultimately obtaining it': 119.

[158] *Bellingham v Dhillon* [1973] QB 304 (QB).

[159] ibid 309.

[160] *Hussey* (n 63) 236–38 (Mustill LJ)

defendants supplied latently defective valves that were subsequently used by the claimant in its building project.[161] Upon discovering the defect, the claimant took steps to settle claims made against it by the main contractor on the project. The Court of Appeal held that any benefit to the claimants from this settlement was to be ignored. Although Rix LJ concluded that the settlements were 'an entirely independent and collateral matter arising not in the context of mitigation at all',[162] this conclusion may be doubted because the steps taken to minimize liability to third parties were part of an attempt to replicate the no-breach position. Perhaps the best rationalization of the case is that there exists a qualitative difference between a settled claim and a claim which never arose, such that the settlements *did not* in fact replicate the no-breach position.

Where the claimant did in fact take steps to replicate its no-breach position, the replication rule has no application. But what about the exceptionality rule? In principle, I think this rule could apply to cases of 'avoided loss'—mirroring its application to avoidable loss—where the claimant obtained benefits as a result of replicating in an exceptional way, which would not have arisen if it had replicated in the usual way.[163] As emphasized in Chapter 6, the test for exceptionality is essentially subjective and takes into account the claimant's own circumstances, characteristics, and preferences. It will therefore rarely be triggered. This may explain why in *Hill v Showell*, Viscount Haldane held that a benefit obtained by the claimant (through steps in replication) will be taken into account even though the claimant 'may have gone somewhat out of his way to make fresh efforts'.[164] I am not aware of any cases in which a claimant has recovered for an avoided loss pursuant to the exceptionality rule, but it may just be that no suitable case has yet arisen.

2.4 Replication 'as nearly as possible'

The replication rule only applies where the claimant made a choice not to replicate the no-breach position *as nearly as possible*. As I highlighted in Chapter 1, it is very often not possible for the claimant (or anyone else) to replicate the no-breach position exactly.[165] The most common reason for this is simply the passage of time: if the due date for performance has already passed,[166] then it is strictly too late to replicate exactly the position that the claimant was entitled to in the first place. Of course, in these circumstances, we do not say that mitigation no longer has any

[161] *Mobil North Sea Ltd v PJ Pipe & Valve Co Ltd* [2001] EWCA Civ 741, [2001] 2 All ER (Comm) 289.
[162] ibid [30].
[163] For the application to avoidable loss, see Chapter 8, Section 2.2.
[164] *Hill* (n 121) 1108.
[165] See further Chapter 1, text to n 18.
[166] For example, cases where the breach consists of late performance, or cases of defective or non-performance where the due date for compliant performance has since passed.

application. Instead, the claimant remains responsible for its choice not to replicate as nearly as possible. Where the only issue is delay, it is typically taken for granted that replication as nearly as possible means seeking the same performance as *soon* as possible. However, in other circumstances, difficult questions can arise about whether the steps that the claimant in fact took amounted to replication as nearly as possible, or a choice to depart from this benchmark.[167]

The controversial decision of the Supreme Court in *The New Flamenco* exemplifies this point.[168] I have written about this case elsewhere at greater length.[169] Here, I focus on two main points. First, the reasoning of the Supreme Court, albeit brief, nicely illustrates the importance of choice that characterizes my account of mitigation, as well as the fact that the rules of mitigation have symmetrical effect. Second, the correctness of the result given by the Supreme Court turns on the range of options that were available to the claimant following the breach, which was ambiguous on the facts of the case. More generally, there remains some conceptual uncertainty about how to define which position—out of a range of options available to the claimant—should be treated as closest to the no-breach position for the purpose of applying the replication rule.

The basic facts of *The New Flamenco* were as follows. The respondent charterers repudiated a two-year time charter of a small cruise ship, the New Flamenco. At the time there was no substitute two-year time charter available in the market. The owners immediately sold the ship for a price of $US23,765,000. The arbitrator appears to have accepted that the owners would not have taken this step but for the breach.[170] The owners subsequently sought to recover the net loss of profits they would have earned (some €7.5m) if the charter had not been repudiated. However, the value of the ship when the charter was due to end would have been a mere $7,000,000, primarily because of the fall in the charter market brought about by the Lehman Brothers collapse in 2008. The charterers argued that the difference of $16,765,000 between this sum and the actual sale price must be brought into account, resulting in an award of nominal damages because this benefit exceeded the lost profits claimed.

[167] There are echoes here of the 'continuity thesis', which claims to justify (and define) the secondary obligations that arise from wrongdoing. See eg John Gardner, 'Wrongs and Faults' (2005) 59 The Review of Metaphysics 95, 103: 'If one does not fully conform to a reason ... the reason does not evaporate ... Instead, it now counts as a reason for doing the next best thing, and failing that, the next best thing again, and so on.' See also Neil MacCormick, 'The Obligation of Reparation' in MacCormick (ed), *Legal Right and Social Democracy: Essays in Legal and Political Philosophy* (OUP 1992) 212–13.

[168] *Fulton Shipping Inc of Panama v Globalia Business Travel SAU (formerly Travelplan SAU) of Spain (The New Flamenco)* [2017] UKSC 43, [2017] 1 WLR 2581.

[169] See further Andrew Summers, 'Choice, Benefits and the Basis of the Market Rule' [2016] LMCLQ 202, reviewing the Court of Appeal decision; and David McLauchlan and Andrew Summers, 'Mitigation and Causation of Benefits' [2018] LMCLQ 171, reviewing the Supreme Court decision.

[170] See also *The New Flamenco* [2014] EWHC 1547 (Comm), [2014] 2 Lloyd's Rep 230 [12] (Popplewell J): 'The arbitrator made findings that the sale of the Vessel by the Owners in October 2007 was caused by the Charterers' breach ... ' Regardless of whether this refers to factual or legal causation, it appears to entail that the arbitrator regarded the but for test as satisfied.

The New Flamenco contains a factual ambiguity regarding the range of options available to the claimants at the time of the repudiation. In particular, the arbitrator's findings left open whether there was no alternative employment available for the vessel at all (either on the spot market or pursuant to shorter-term time charters), or whether there was merely no substitute *two-year* time charter available as a direct substitute for the outstanding term of the original charter.[171] It appears that Lord Clarke, giving the judgment of the Supreme Court, assumed that at the time of breach there *was* still an available spot market for hire.[172] As I explain further below, this factual assumption is potentially important for the correctness of the Supreme Court's decision.

In the Supreme Court, giving the sole judgment, Lord Clarke held that the sale of the ship was not to be brought into account in the assessment of damages. Instead, 'the measure of the loss is the difference between the contract rate and what was or ought reasonably to have been earned from employment of the vessel under shorter charterparties, as for example on the spot market'.[173] In effect, this entailed the difference between the claimants' no-breach position and a counterfactual assessment of their breach position as if they had employed the vessel on the spot market. This is the correct application of the replication rule, if it is assumed that hiring on the spot market would have replicated the no-breach position as nearly as possible (given that no two-year charter was available), and that the claimants chose to depart from this position by selling the vessel.

The Supreme Court's reasoning also strongly supports the main features of my account of mitigation. First, Lord Clarke expressly articulated his decision in terms of causation: the sale of the vessel 'was . . . not on the face of it caused by the repudiation of the charterparty'.[174] Second, he emphasized that the claimant's made a choice: 'there was nothing about the premature termination of the charterparty which made it necessary to sell the vessel'.[175] Allied to this, Lord Clarke held that the claimants were responsible for the consequences of their choice: 'If the owners decide to sell the vessel, whether before or after termination of the charterparty, they are making a commercial decision at their own risk'.[176] Finally, in common with both Popplewell J at first instance and the Court of Appeal, Lord Clarke recognized that his conclusion on causation cut both ways, and he would have reached the same conclusion that the sale of the vessel should be ignored even if the market had subsequently risen rather than fallen.[177]

[171] *The New Flamenco* [2014] EWHC 1547 (Comm), [2014] 2 Lloyd's Rep 230 [12].
[172] *The New Flamenco* (n 168) [34].
[173] ibid.
[174] ibid [32].
[175] ibid.
[176] ibid.
[177] ibid [33].

The assumption by Lord Clarke that the claimants could have hired out the vessel on the spot market instead of selling it was significant.[178] As mentioned above, the arbitrator's findings of fact on this point were ambiguous, and it might have been that there was no alternative employment for the vessel at all.[179] In this case, it appears that Lord Clarke would still have treated the sale caused by the claimant owners and not the defendant charterers,[180] on the basis that a sale 'was incapable of mitigating the loss of the income stream'.[181] This is too categorical. If there were no hire options available, then it is conceptually (as well as factually) unclear what steps would amount to replicating the no-breach position as nearly as possible. Plausibly, selling the vessel might have been the only and closest steps that the claimant could have taken. In that case, the consequences of the sale—for better or worse—should have been taken into account in the assessment of the claimants' breach position.[182]

3 The Effect on Damages

The leading texts on damages promote the view that claimants cannot, other than in exceptional circumstances, recover for an 'avoided loss'.[183] Indeed, the orthodox account of damages has no framework capable of explaining how a claimant can *ever* recover for an avoided loss. This is because it envisions a two-stage process whereby the court must first assess the claimant's factual loss taking into account everything that has occurred up to the date of trial,[184] and then apply 'limitations' on damages to cut back the amount that the claimant can recover.[185] There is accordingly no space within the orthodox account for doctrines whose effect is to *increase* the award of (compensatory) damages compared with the claimant's factual loss. This explains why so many commentators on damages have taken the extreme view that all or nearly all of the so-called avoided loss cases must be wrongly decided.[186]

[178] Note 172. See also Adrian Lee, '*The New Flamenco* Appraised: A New Framework for Avoided Loss and Mitigation' [2021] LMCLQ 98, adopting a similar argument.

[179] Note 171. See further McLauchlan and Summers, 'Mitigation and Causation of Benefits' (n 169), text to fn 7.

[180] *The New Flamenco* (n 168) [33].

[181] ibid [34].

[182] Indeed, this is close to the Court of Appeal's reasoning: see further Summers, 'Choice, Benefits and the Basis of the Market Rule' (n 169).

[183] See further Chapter 1, Section 2.3 and Chapter 3, Section 3.1.

[184] For a definition, see Chapter 1, text to n 27.

[185] See further Chapter 1, Sections 2.1 and 2.2.

[186] See eg McLauchlan, 'Expectation Damages: Avoided Loss, Offsetting Gains and Subsequent Events' (n 5) 360–88; Burrows (n 26) 150–52, 191–96; Edelman, *McGregor on Damages* (21st edn) (n 3) [9-133]–[9-184].

By contrast, I argue that the replication rule is capable of explaining not only when so-called 'avoided loss' is recoverable, but also precisely how damages are assessed in such cases. Where the claimant made a choice not to replicate the no-breach position as nearly as possible, damages are assessed on a counterfactual basis, as if they had replicated (incurring expenses in so doing), even though they did not. But where the replication rule does not apply, there are typically no grounds for displacing the assessment the claimant's factual loss.[187] Below, I address how each of these modes of assessment work in the context of the so-called avoided loss cases. However, the underlying effect (or non-effect) of the replication rule here is exactly the same as in the avoidable loss context, so readers may also refer to the corresponding discussion in Chapter 8.[188]

3.1 Where the replication rule applies

Where the replication rule applies, damages are assessed on a counterfactual basis, as if the claimant had replicated. This proposition more accurately captures how the assessment of avoided loss works, than the so-called 'ignoring heuristic', which I critiqued in Chapter 3.[189] Honoré gives a useful (non-legal) example to illustrate the distinction.[190] Consider the statement: 'Churchill kept Britain in the war in 1940'. To test this assertion, we would not merely eliminate or 'ignore' Churchill's actual role as Prime Minister. Instead, we would need to substitute another Prime Minister whose hypothetical conduct would have affected whether Britain remained in the war. In other words, we would need to engage in a counterfactual assessment of what would have happened if (for example) Halifax had been Prime Minister, and then ask whether Halifax would have been able to convince Parliament and the public to continue the war. 'Ignoring' Churchill's actual conduct is only half of the process.

In Chapter 3, I cited *Primavera* and *The New Flamenco* as two cases illustrating how the 'ignoring heuristic' falls short of fully explaining how damages for avoided loss are assessed. The correct counterfactual nature of the assessment has occasionally been acknowledged directly by the courts. The best example is *Hussey v Eels*, where Mustill LJ described the loss for which damages were awarded as resulting from a 'deemed mitigation' by the claimant.[191] This nicely captures the

[187] The qualifier 'typically' applies because there are other distinct doctrines than can result in a counterfactual assessment of the claimant's breach position: see further Section 4.1.

[188] See further Chapter 8, Section 3.

[189] Chapter 3, Section 3.2.

[190] Tony Honoré, 'Necessary and Sufficient Conditions in Tort Law' in David G Owen (ed), *The Philosophical Foundations of Tort Law* (OUP 1997) 371.

[191] *Hussey* (n 63) 233. See also *Radford v De Froberville* [1977] 1 WLR 1262 (Ch) 1285–86 (Oliver J); *Coastal (Bermuda) Petroleum Ltd v Vtt Vulcan Petroleum SA (The Marine Star)* [1994] CLC 1019 (QB) 1025 (Mance J); *Golden Strait Corp v Nippon Yusen Kubishika Kaisha (The Golden Victory)* [2007] UKHL 12, [2007] 2 AC 353 [57] (Lord Carswell); *Zodiac Maritime Agencies Ltd v Fortescue Metals*

true effect of the replication rule. Specifically, where the claimant made a choice not to replicate the no-breach position as nearly as possible, damages are assessed counterfactually as if they had done so.[192] Not only is the claimant's actual conduct (and the resulting benefits) 'ignored', but the expenses of the hypothetical steps taken in replication are awarded instead. It is these expenses that constitute the claimant's so-called 'avoided loss'. They are, in effect, the losses that the claimant would have incurred if they had undertaken the normal response to the breach, even though in fact they did not.

Even though there is a vast and diverse range of cases allowing recovery of avoided loss where the replication rule applies (as I showed in Section 2.1 above), at the highest level this recognition currently appears to be somewhat precarious, as revealed in the recent Privy Council case of *Sagicor Bank v Seaton*.[193] There, the claimant's bank account was wrongfully frozen and debited by the defendant bank. The claimant chose not to go into the market to borrow the sums elsewhere, but nevertheless claimed compound interest. The Privy Council refused, holding that 'A plaintiff seeking interest as damages where the defendant has withheld money in breach of contract must plead and prove its loss',[194] where loss meant 'actual loss of interest' rather than 'theoretical and non-existent loss'.[195] Lord Hodge (with whom the rest of the Board agreed) specifically held that there was no automatic right to recover interest, on the basis that 'while such a norm might promote legal certainty in relation to such claims, there is no principle on which it is based'.[196]

It may be significant that in *Sagicor*, the Board included Lord Burrows,[197] whose previous writings reflect a strong preference for what I have termed a 'factual loss cap'.[198] However, such a rule is untenable as a matter of authority: in addition to the avoided loss cases outlined in this chapter, the plethora of cases applying the so-called 'market rule' (addressed in Chapter 10) also clearly exemplify counterfactual assessment. The principle on which interest should have been recoverable in

Group Ltd (The Kildare) [2010] EWHC 903 (Comm), [2011] 2 Lloyd's Rep 360 [65] (Steel J); *Deutsche Bank AG v Total Global Steel Ltd* [2012] EWHC 1201 (Comm) [166] (Andrew Smith J).

[192] Note that the application of the replication rule does not result in 'stopping the clock' in respect of all post-breach events. Any other post-breach events that would still have occurred even if the claimant had replicated in the usual way, will still be relevant.

[193] *Sagicor Bank Jamaica Ltd v YP Seaton* [2022] UKPC 48, [2023] 2 All ER 81. See also, on very similar facts but reaching the opposite conclusion: *Equitas Ltd v Walsham Bros & Co Ltd* [2013] EWHC 3264 (Comm), [2014] PNLR 8.

[194] ibid [37].

[195] ibid [33].

[196] ibid [34].

[197] The other judges were Lord Hodge, Lord Kitchin, Lord Stephens, and Lady Rose.

[198] See further Chapter 1, Section 2.3. The Privy Council's reasoning is also redolent of earlier cases that were sceptical of counterfactual assessment on grounds that 'the court must not speculate when it knows the facts': *Curwen v James* [1963] 1 WLR 748 (CA) 753 (Harman LJ); *Jobling v Associated Dairies* [1982] AC 794 (HL) 802 (Lord Wilberforce), 807 (Lord Edmund-Davies), 813 (Lord Keith). See also *Bwllfa and Merthyr Dare Steam Collieries (1891) Ltd v Pontypridd Waterworks Co* [1903] AC 426 (HL) 431 (Lord Macnaghten).

Sagicor is mitigation, specifically the replication rule. The right to recover interest even though no factual loss was incurred, is just the flipside of the proposition (which the Privy Council endorsed),[199] that if the choice not to borrow had resulted in missing a profitable opportunity, the claimant would still have recovered the interest only. The effect of the rule cuts both ways. It is a mistake to object to the counterfactual assessment entailed by the replication rule only when it results in an award of damages greater than the claimant's factual loss.

3.2 Where the replication rule does not apply

Where the claimant did in fact replicate the no-breach position as nearly as possible, no intervening cause arises to displace the assessment of the claimant's factual loss. Accordingly, the claimant will recover for any harm or expenses actually incurred, but any benefits arising from their conduct will also be taken into account in assessing damages. As Viscount Haldane clarified in *British Westinghouse*, in these circumstances the court must simply 'look at what actually happened, and balance loss and gain'.[200] On the facts of British Westinghouse itself, the claimant's conduct did amount to replication. Accordingly, as Mustill LJ has subsequently emphasized, 'To compensate the appellants for the cost of replacement whilst ignoring the additional benefits which this replacement had brought would have been palpable injustice'.[201]

Similarly, where the claimant had no choice to replicate, they will recover for their factual loss for better or worse, because the replication rule will not apply. *Bence Graphics* is the classic example, turning on the fact the claimant was unaware of the breach at the time when they resold the defective goods.[202] The decision in *JSC BTA Bank v Ablyazov* is also explicable on this basis,[203] and is worth highlighting because it provides a useful contrast with the facts of *Sagicor*.[204] The claimant had been defrauded out of his money by the defendant. As in *Sagicor*, the court refused to award interests as damages, holding that 'the Bank . . . has not alleged "its actual interest losses"'.[205] However, in *JSC BTA Bank*—unlike in *Sagicor*—the claimant was unaware of the breach. It was therefore correct to hold the defendants causally responsible for the actual consequences of their wrong, for better or worse, until the claimants had discovered the fraud.[206]

[199] *Sagicor* (n 193) [37] (Lord Hodge).
[200] *British Westinghouse* (n 2) 691.
[201] *Hussey v Eels* [1990] 2 QB 227 (CA) 236.
[202] See further text to n 129. See also *Wertheim* (n 145) and the other cases cited in Section 2.2.
[203] *JSC BTA Bank v Ablyazov* [2013] EWHC 867 (Comm).
[204] Note 193.
[205] *JSC BTA Bank* (n 203) [12].
[206] For this reason, *JSC BTA Bank* (n 203) is not incompatible with *Sagicor* (n 193), or with the earlier decision of *Equitas* (n 193). Contra Burrows (n 26) 299–301.

Finally, *Kennedy v Van Emden* also exemplifies the non-application of the replication rule.[207] The defendant solicitors negligently advised the claimant in relation to a lease. But-for the breach, the claimant would not have entered into the lease.[208] However, by the time the error was discovered, the problem had already been fully corrected by legislation. Nourse LJ held that 'Compensation is a reward for real, not hypothetical, loss. It is not to be made an occasion for recovery in respect of a loss which might have been, but has not been, suffered'.[209] This reasoning is plainly too broad because it ignores the many other cases where damages have been awarded for an avoided loss. Instead, the decision is better explained on the narrower basis that the breach was latent. The difference in value of the lease at the date of breach was irrelevant because the claimant had no choice to replicate the no-breach position by extricating from the transaction at that date.

4 Distinct 'avoided loss' cases

In this chapter I have so far proceeded as though the replication rule is the *only* ground where the claimant can recover for an avoided loss. However, as I outlined in Chapter 1, there are two other well-established grounds on which the claimant may recover damages greater than their factual loss: the 'insurance' and 'benevolence' rules.[210] The benevolence rule is clearly distinct from the law of mitigation, since it revolves around the conduct of third parties rather than the claimant's own conduct. The insurance rule has a more plausible connection to mitigation because it concerns a payment (the insurance premium) made by the claimant. However, for reasons I explain below,[211] I think there are key differences between the insurance rule and either the replication or exceptionality rules, such that this rule should be treated as distinct.

Besides the cases that expressly apply either the insurance or benevolence rules, there appear to be two types of case that have awarded damages for an avoided loss but which do not appear to fit the replication rule. I address each of these below. First, are cases where the claimant had 'earned' an opportunity to replicate the no-breach position at a lower cost than expected. In my view, these cases are distinct from the law of mitigation and are instead best understood as an extension of the insurance rule. Second, are cases in which the claimant's no-breach position was replicated by a third party, but in circumstances where the benevolence rule

[207] *Kennedy v Van Emden & Co* [1996] PNLR 409 (CA).
[208] ibid 414 (Nourse LJ).
[209] ibid 414.
[210] *British Transport Commission v Gourley* [1956] AC 185 (HL) 197–98 (Earl Jowitt); *Hussain v New Taplow Paper Mills Ltd* [1988] AC 514 (HL) 527 (Lord Bridge); *Swynson Ltd v Lowick Rose LLP (In Liquidation) (formerly Hurst Morrison Thomson LLP)* [2017] UKSC 32, [2018] AC 313 [11] (Lord Sumption), [47] (Lord Mance), [98] (Lord Neuberger). See further Chapter 1, Section 2.3.
[211] Text to n 228.

as conventionally understood does not apply because there was no intention to benefit the claimant. I argue that these cases are also distinct from mitigation and are sufficiently anomalous—and few in number—that they ought to be treated as wrongly decided.

4.1 Earned benefits

There are several cases awarding damages for 'avoided loss' where the claimant took advantage of an opportunity to replicate the no-breach position at a lower cost than expected. The best-known example is *The Mediana*, in which the claimant's lightship 'Comet' was negligently damaged by the defendant.[212] The claimant sought to replicate its no-breach position by providing a temporary replacement for the lightship during the period of repair. However, rather than hiring a replacement lightship, the claimant was able to make use of its spare lightship 'Orion', which it had maintained ready for emergencies. The claimant recovered damages (in an amount agreed by the parties) for 'loss of the use of the Lightship "Comet" or hire of the services of the Lightship "Orion"',[213] even though the claimant was in fact able to deploy the Orion without incurring any out-of-pocket expense.[214]

Other cases appear to raise similar issues. In *Jebsen v East & West India Dock Company*, the claimants transported passengers by steam-liner from Norway to America.[215] In breach of contract the defendants detained one of the claimants' ships in their port, such that its voyage was delayed. The claimant recovered damages (in an amount assessed by the jury) that included the loss of fares that would have been earned from passengers due to travel on the ship,[216] even though the claimants in fact managed to reallocate most of the passengers to other ships within its fleet.[217] More recently, in *Coles v Hetherton*, the claimant recovered damages for the 'reasonable cost' of repairing its car 'assessed by reference to the position of the

[212] *Owners of the Steamship Mediana v Owners of the Lightship Comet (The Mediana)* [1900] AC 113 (HL). See also *Koch Marine Inc v d'Amica Societa di Navigazione arl (The Elena d'Amico)* [1980] 1 Lloyd's Rep 75 (QB) 90 (Goff J).

[213] *The Mediana* (n 212) 114, where the headnote refers to the pleadings. cf James Edelman, 'The Meaning of Loss and Enrichment' in Robert Chambers, Charles Mitchell, and James Penner (eds), *Philosophical Foundations of the Law of Unjust Enrichment* (OUP 2009) 216, suggesting that the amount equated to the cost of maintaining the spare. Edelman's analysis cannot be correct because Lord Shand noted (at 121–22) that the cost of maintaining the spare was £1,000 per annum, equating to £203 pro rata for the seventy-four days of deprivation, whereas the agreed sum was £311.

[214] See also *Erie County* (n 157), where the claimant was able to use its own gas reserves rather than resorting to the market, following the defendant's failure to supply the gas.

[215] *Jebsen v East & West India Dock Co* (1874–75) LR 10 CP 300 (CP). cf *Platt v London Underground Ltd* [2001] 2 EGLR 121 (Ch), where on similar facts Neuberger J rejected a claim for loss of profits.

[216] *Jebsen* (n 215) 300, where the headnote refers to the loss of 'passage-money payable by certain emigrants'.

[217] This award was approved by Viscount Haldane in *British Westinghouse* (n 2) on the basis that 'what was relied on as mitigation did not arise out of the transactions the subject-matter of the contract': 690.

individual claimant',[218] even though in fact the claimant had arranged the repairs through its insurer at a cheaper rate.

The rules of mitigation do not appear to explain these decisions. In principle, the exceptionality rule could apply to saved expenses ('avoided loss') just as to excessive costs ('avoidable loss'), in circumstances where the claimant made a choice to replicate the no-breach position in an unusual way.[219] However, the cases on avoidable loss clarify that descriptive exceptionality relies on an agent-level rather than population-level norm.[220] In other words, the claimant's conduct must have been abnormal for that particular claimant, not merely unusual for most claimants in that position. On the facts of the cases highlighted, the steps taken by claimant (for example, making use of a spare ship within the claimant's own fleet) do not appear to have been unusual in light of the claimants' own circumstances.

An alternative explanation involves applying the principles underlying the insurance rule. In *Parry v Cleaver*, Lord Reid held 'that the real and substantial reason for disregarding [insurance pay-outs] is that the plaintiff has bought them and that it would be unjust and unreasonable to hold that the money which he prudently spent on premiums and the benefit from it should enure to the benefit of the [defendant]'.[221] This reasoning explains why the insurance rule only applies where the claimant (rather than the defendant or a third party) paid the premiums on the insurance policy.[222] The House of Lords has established that the same rule extends to pension payments, provided that the claimant made the contributions.[223] The rule thus applies generally to earned benefits rather than merely to insurance payouts specifically. As Lord Sumption noted in *Swynson*, cases of this kind are those where 'the benefit[s] ... are attributable to his [the claimant's] premiums, his contributions, *or his work*'.[224]

The decisions in *The Mediana*, *Jebsen*, and *Coles* can all be explained by applying the insurance rule to saved expenses, by analogy with the receipt of benefits. In *The Mediana*, Smith LJ (giving judgment in the Court of Appeal) expressly drew an analogy between the claimant's decision to maintain a spare for emergencies and contributions to an insurance policy, holding that by maintaining a spare,

[218] *Coles* (n 13) [16] (Aikens LJ). See also *Bee v Jenson* [2007] EWCA Civ 923, [2007] 4 All ER 791, raising the same issue in relation to hire charges.

[219] *Thai Airways* (n 154) [176] (Leggatt J). See further text to n 163.

[220] See eg *Beechwood Birmingham Ltd v Hoyer Group UK Ltd* [2010] EWCA Civ 647, [2011] QB 357, where a car dealership was held to have acted unreasonably by hiring a spare vehicle when it could have deployed a spare. See further Chapter 6, Section 3.2.

[221] *Parry v Cleaver* [1970] AC 1 (HL) 14. See also 31 (Lord Morris), 35 (Lord Pearce), 39 (Lord Wilberforce), 49 (Lord Pearson); *Forgie v Henderson* (1818) 1 Murray 410, 418 (Lord Chief Commissioner Adam); *Hussain v New Taplow Paper Mills Ltd* [1988] AC 514 (HL) 528 (Lord Bridge); *Shearman v Folland* [1950] 2 KB 43 (CA) 46 (Asquith LJ).

[222] *Hussain* (n 221) 527 (Lord Bridge); *Hodgson v Trapp* [1989] AC 807 (HL) 819 (Lord Bridge); *McCamley v Cammell Laird Shipbuilders Ltd* [1990] 1 WLR 963 (CA) 970 (O'Connor LJ).

[223] *Parry* (n 221); *Smoker v London Fire and Civil Defence Authority* [1991] 2 AC 502 (HL) 543 (Lord Templeman); *Hopkins v Norcros plc* [1994] ICR 11 (CA).

[224] *Swynson* (n 210) [11] (emphasis added).

the claimants 'stand for the purpose their own insurers'.[225] In *Jebsen*, Denman J relied on the decision in *Bradburn v Great Western Railway*, the leading authority on the insurance rule.[226] In *Coles*, Aikens LJ reasoned that 'what the insurer can obtain on the open market . . . is irrelevant, because the position of the insurer is, as a matter of law, irrelevant'.[227] In this way, all of the decisions reflect the application of the insurance rule.

In my view, the insurance rule is distinct from the law of mitigation. First, it does not rely on the choice principle; the claimant may 'earn' the benefit even though its contributions (for example, to an insurance policy or pension) were compulsory. Second, the claimant's contributions need not be descriptively unusual: it does not matter that everyone takes out insurance. Third, the insurance rule applies to action taken by the claimant prior to breach. Although Hart and Honoré give some indication that they regard the insurance rule as causal, they also rely on the more general proposition that it would be 'unjust' to deprive the claimant of the benefit.[228] In *Parry v Cleaver*, Lord Pearce expressly rejected causal reasoning and instead concluded that the insurance rule was based on considerations of 'fairness and justice and public policy'.[229]

4.2 Replication by third parties

Where the claimant's no-breach position is replicated by a third party without cost to the claimant, the replication rule has no application. Unless the benevolence rule applies, then the claimant will normally be restricted to their factual loss as reduced by the third party. The leading authority is *Dimond v Lovell*, where following a car accident, the claimant obtained a hire car without paying for it due to an unenforceable credit agreement with a third party.[230] The House of Lords rejected a claim for the reasonable cost of hire on the basis that it was not actually incurred. Lord Hoffmann held that 'the only way . . . in which Mrs Dimond could recover damages . . . is if your Lordships were willing to create another exception to the rule against double recovery. I can see no basis for doing so'.[231]

There are nevertheless a handful of cases in which damages for an avoided loss were awarded even though none of the established rules (for insurance,

[225] *Owners of the Steamship Mediana v Owners of the Lightship Comet (The Mediana)* [1899] P 127 (CA) 137.
[226] *Jebsen* (n 215) 305, citing *Bradburn v The Great Western Railway Co* (1874–75) LR 10 Ex 1 (Ex Ch).
[227] *Coles* (n 13) [37]. See further [34]–[42].
[228] Hart and Honoré (n 125) 160.
[229] *Parry* (n 221) 33, 37.
[230] *Dimond* (n 154).
[231] ibid 400 (Lord Hoffmann).

benevolence, or mitigation) appeared to apply.[232] The most famous and controversial example is *Burdis v Livsey*.[233] In that case, the claimant's car was repaired without cost pursuant to an unenforceable credit agreement, yet the Court of Appeal held that damages equal to the normal cost of repair were still recoverable. Aldous LJ reasoned that the cost of repairs reflected a 'direct loss' whereas hire costs were distinguished as a 'potential future loss'.[234] The better view is that *Burdis* is inconsistent with *Dimond* and should be treated as wrongly decided. Both are cases where the replication rule had no application because the no-breach position was in fact replicated as nearly as possible, and there appear to be no grounds for applying the benevolence rule given that the third party creditor did not intend to benefit the claimant.

Another example is *Gardner v Marsh & Parsons*.[235] The claimant purchased a long lease in a property following the defendant's negligent failure to warn of serious structural defects requiring repair. The Court of Appeal awarded damages based on the difference in value of the lease at the date of breach, even though in fact the landlords had subsequently undertaken the repair at no cost to the claimant. For the majority (Peter Gibson LJ dissenting), Hirst LJ relied on *Phillips v Ward* in support of the proposition that the difference in value measure was always recoverable.[236] However, this measure is predicated on the counterfactual effect of the replication rule where the claimant made a choice not to extricate from the breach; it had no application in *Gardner*, where the claimant was initially unaware of the breach,[237] and replication was undertaken by a third party.[238] Again, given that the benevolence rule also did not apply, *Gardner* appears to be wrongly decided.

Finally, in *Needler v Taber Financial Services*, the claimant was the victim of a pensions mis-selling.[239] Prior to the claimant's discovery that they had been negligently advised, the fund in which they had been induced to invest benefited substantially from a demutualization. Sir Andrew Morritt VC held that 'the benefit was not caused by and did not flow, as part of a continuous transaction, from the negligence'.[240] The replication rule does not apply, because the claimant did not

[232] In addition to the cases discussed below, see also *Smiley v Townshend* [1950] 2 KB 311 (CA) and *Donelly v Joyce* [1974] QB 454.
[233] *Burdis* (n 13). See also *Jones v Stroud* (n 232).
[234] ibid [87] (Aldous LJ). This distinction was originally advanced by Harvey McGregor QC as counsel for the claimant: [78] (Aldous LJ).
[235] *Gardner* (n 30).
[236] ibid 496 (Hirst LJ).
[237] ibid 491 (Hirst LJ).
[238] Although the trial judge failed to reach a firm conclusion as to what would have happened but-for the breach, it can be inferred that the claimant would probably have gone ahead with the transaction but would have negotiated for the repairs to be undertaken prior to completion: ibid 492, 497 (Hirst LJ).
[239] *Needler Financial Services Ltd v Taber* [2002] 3 All ER 501 (Ch). See also *Titan Europe 2006-3 Plc v Colliers International UK Plc* [2015] EWCA Civ 1083, [2016] 1 All ER (Comm) 999 [36]–[38] (Longmore LJ), but this decision is explicable on the distinct ground of 'reflective loss'.
[240] ibid [26].

have a choice to extricate themselves from the fund, since (at the relevant time) they were unaware of the breach.[241] As in *Burdis* and *Gardner*, there were also no grounds for applying the benevolence rule. It therefore follows from Dimond that the benefit should have been taken into account, just as any additional loss from remaining invested in the fund would have been recoverable so long as the breach remained latent.

[241] Contrast *Primavera* (n 62), in which the claimant was aware of the breach: see further text to n 77. cf Burrows (n 26) 149–50, who treats these two cases as indistinguishable.

10
The Market Rule

1 Introduction

The 'market rule' of damages is conventionally expressed as the rule that where there is an available market for substitute performance, the claimant's damages will be assessed by reference to that market value, rather than what actually happened. The rule has been codified in the Sale of Goods Act 1979 in the case of damage for non-acceptance, non-delivery, and defective goods,[1] but also applies at common law in other goods cases, as well as to services, property damage, and many other contexts.[2] Broadly two types of explanation have been given for the rule. The first is one of practical expedience—assessment by reference to market value (usually) provides predictability and certainty for the parties so is conducive to commercial transactions.[3] The second, frequently disputed by proponents of the first,[4] is that the market rule is an aspect of mitigation.

I argue that the market rule is indeed best explained as an aspect of mitigation.[5] More specifically, it entails an application of the replication rule. If the claimant could have replicated its no-breach position by having recourse to a market for substitute performance, but chose not to, then damages will nevertheless be assessed as if it had done so. The so-called market rule thus blends seamlessly with the multitude of other cases that apply the replication rule, particularly in the context of choices not to seek a replacement, which I discussed in Chapters 8 and 9.[6] The advantage of conceiving of the market rule in these terms is that it fully explains

[1] Sale of Goods Act 1979, ss 50(3), 51(3), and 53(3) respectively. See further Section 2.3.

[2] See eg *Smith New Court Securities Ltd v Citibank NA* [1997] AC 254 (HL) 279 (Lord Steyn): 'the same legal principle must govern sales of shares, goods, a business or land'. See also *Golden Strait Corp v Nippon Yusen Kubishika Kaisha (The Golden Victory)* [2007] UKHL 12, [2007] 2 AC 353 [80] (Lord Brown), noting its application to 'building or repairing contracts' and 'breached charterparties'.

[3] See eg Michael Bridge, 'Markets and Damages in Sale of Goods Cases' (2016) 132 LQR 404; and David McLauchlan, 'Expectation Damages: Avoided Loss, Offsetting Gains and Subsequent Events' in D Saidov and R Cunnington (eds), *Contract Damages: Domestic and International Perspectives* (Hart 2008) 376.

[4] Bridge, 'Markets and Damages' (n 3) 410. See further text to n 15.

[5] See further Andrew Dyson and Adam Kramer, 'There is No "Breach Date Rule": Mitigation, Difference in Value and Date of Assessment' (2014) 130 LQR 259, in which I first advanced this argument. I stand by almost all of what I wrote (with Adam Kramer) then, except that my references to a 'choice to depart from the normal response to breach' can now be more precisely understood as a 'choice not to replicate the no-breach position as nearly as possible', per my formulation of the replication rule.

[6] See further Chapter 8, Section 2.1.2 and Chapter 9, Section 2.1.2.

Mitigation in the Law of Damages. Andrew Summers, Oxford University Press. © Andy Summers 2025.
DOI: 10.1093/9780191864032.003.0010

when and why the rule is sometimes held not to apply: in particular, whenever the claimant had no choice to obtain substitute performance at the relevant time.

In this chapter, I begin by setting out the case for treating the market rule as an aspect of mitigation. This explanation already has extensive judicial support, but my contribution is to show more precisely how the market rule aligns with the revised account of mitigation that I have developed in this book. In particular, to understand the scope of the market rule, it is essential to appreciate the importance of the claimant's *choice* not to resort to the market. I classify cases in which the market rule has been displaced according to the various circumstances in which the claimant lacks such a choice. Finally, I show that the effect of the market rule mirrors precisely the effect of the replication rule as outlined in Chapters 8 and 9.

2 The Market Rule as Mitigation

There is voluminous judicial support for the proposition that the market rule is an aspect of mitigation. Indeed, given recent expositions of the rule in the Supreme Court, this proposition can now hardly be doubted as a matter of judicial authority. Nevertheless, there remains some apparent uncertainty about how exactly the market rule fits with certain key features of mitigation *as conventionally understood*, which has allowed some doubts to persist. In this section, I explain how these residual doubts are based on a misunderstanding of how mitigation works. Once mitigation is restated along the lines that I proposed in Chapter 6 (and illustrated in Chapters 8 and 9), it becomes clear that the market rule is a straightforward application of the replication rule—indeed, one might say the archetypal case. In particular, the emphasis on choice that characterizes my account of mitigation is front-and-centre in the cases on the market rule, revealing their common basis.

2.1 What explains the market rule?

It is already conventional to explain the market rule as an aspect of mitigation.[7] McGregor has described the rule as 'built-in mitigation'.[8] In *The Marine Star*,

[7] See eg *The Golden Victory* (n 2) [79]; *Hussey v Eels* [1990] 2 QB 227 (CA), 233 (Mustill LJ); *Bunge SA v Nidera BV* [2015] UKSC 43, [2015] 3 All ER 1082 [17] (Lord Sumption) and further authorities cited in Dyson and Kramer (n 5) 270 fn 83.

[8] Harvey McGregor, 'The Role of Mitigation in the Assessment of Damages' in D Saidov and R Cunnington (eds), *Contract Damages: Domestic and International Perspectives* (Hart 2008) 332. Judges have occasionally reasoned directly in terms of mitigation instead of the market rule, even in cases involving supply of goods: see eg *Bulkhaul Ltd v Rhodia Organique Fine Ltd* [2008] EWCA Civ 1452, [2009] 1 Lloyd's Rep 353 [4], [26] (Smith LJ), which involved non-acceptance of goods via early termination of a lease agreement.

Mance J stated that: 'An available market is a means of mitigating any loss otherwise contemplated which has become incorporated into the general measure of recovery'.[9] This point has subsequently been emphasized on several occasions by Lord Leggatt.[10] For example, in *Nagel v Pluczenik Diamond Company*, Leggatt LJ (as he then was) clarified that the market rule is 'merely a rule of thumb which reflects the usual result in practice of applying the mitigation principle where there is an available market'.[11] He also emphasized that the rule 'is not an exercise in valuing the contract considered as an asset but an inquiry into the loss actually sustained by the claimant as a result of non-performance'.[12] In *Stanford International Bank v HSBC*, Lord Leggatt reframed the rule expressly as the 'market *mitigation* rule':

> The reason why in some types of case—for example, cases involving loss of or damage to goods—it is often appropriate to take a valuation date at or near to the date of breach is the effect of a rule which I will call the market mitigation rule. This rule is that, where there is an available market in which an adequate substitute can be obtained for goods or services of which the defendant's breach of duty deprived the claimant, damages are to be assessed as if the claimant entered the market and obtained such a substitute at the earliest reasonable opportunity whether or not the claimant in fact did so.[13]

However, some legal scholars have rejected the mitigation explanation and offered alternative accounts. Most notably, Bridge has described the market rule as 'an abstract method of damages assessment' and a 'hard rule displaced in relatively infrequent circumstances'.[14] He argues that 'the market rule is more than the application of the rule of mitigation of damages',[15] and instead explains that the rule stems from commercial considerations. Foremost amongst these is that 'The demands of certainty . . . outweigh any principle that claimants should receive individualised compensation'.[16] For the same reason, Bridge is generally sceptical of

[9] *Coastal (Bermuda) Petroleum Ltd v Vtt Vulcan Petroleum SA (The Marine Star)* [1994] CLC 1019 (QB) 1025.

[10] In addition to the cases cited below, see *Hirtenstein v Hill Dickinson LLP* [2014] EWHC 2711 (Comm) [117] (Leggatt J); *Novus Aviation Ltd v Alubaf Arab International Bank* [2016] EWHC 1575 (Comm) [129] (Leggatt J); *Marathon Asset Management v Seddon* [2017] EWHC 300 (Comm) [250] (Leggatt J).

[11] *Nagel v Pluczenik Diamond Company NV* [2018] EWCA Civ 2640 [41].

[12] ibid.

[13] *Stanford International Bank Ltd v HSBC Bank PLC* [2022] UKSC 34, [2023] 2 WLR 79 [43].

[14] Bridge, 'Markets and Damages' (n 3) 407.

[15] ibid 410.

[16] ibid 412. See also 413, noting that the market rule 'allows a dispute to be determined bilaterally and facilitates arbitral settlement where the sub-buyer is not a party to any relevant arbitration agreement'. See also *Equitas Ltd v Walsham Bros & Co Ltd* [2013] EWHC 3264 (Comm), [2014] PNLR 8 [123] (Males J), for judicial reference to the market rule as a tool for enhancing commercial certainty.

decisions that have disapplied the market rule in cases where an available market existed.[17]

The certainty afforded by the market rule is largely illusory because (as I will show in the following section), there are a multitude of cases where reference to market value has been displaced on account of the claimant's specific circumstances, even though there was in some sense an available market.[18] But if not commercial considerations, what explains the rule? I argue that the market rule is indeed an aspect of mitigation, specifically the replication rule. Before developing this case below, it may first be helpful to address the reasons why Bridge sees the market rule as distinct from and incompatible with mitigation. In short, all of these objections follow from misapprehensions about how mitigation works, which are understandable on the orthodox understanding of mitigation but are corrected under my new account.

First, Bridge argues that 'mitigation supposes deterioration not market volatility.'[19] This apparent mismatch is based on the conventional understanding of mitigation as a limitation on damages, applicable only when the claimant's factual loss turns out to be greater than the loss they would have suffered if they had taken mitigating steps. By contrast, as I have argued, the replication rule—which underpins the so-called market rule—is entirely symmetrical in its application. In other words, it applies in the same way whether the claimant's choice not to replicate its no-breach position turned out for better or worse.[20] Accordingly, mitigation is exactly suited to explaining the indifference of the market rule to market volatility. The problem is just that the orthodox account of mitigation has hitherto obscured this.

Second, Bridge also notes that the market rule cannot be explained by mitigation because of 'the absence of any *requirement* that the claimant enter the market to conclude a substitute transaction.'[21] McLauchlin has similarly argued that in available market cases, 'the references to mitigation ... are confusing. We may wish to restrict the seller to recovery of the contract/market price differential at the date of the breach, but there ought to be no question of an "obligation" to resell.'[22] These objections stem from the misapprehension that mitigation really is prescriptive, whereas the market rule obviously is not. In *The Elena D'Amico*, Robert Goff J correctly stressed that the claimant is 'fully entitled' not to resort to the market.[23]

[17] See eg ibid 417–20, Bridge's discussion of *Bence Graphics International Ltd v Fasson UK Ltd* [1998] QB 87 (CA).

[18] See further Sections 3.2 to 3.4.

[19] Bridge, 'Markets and Damages' (n 3) 410.

[20] See Chapters 8 and 9 respectively.

[21] Bridge, 'Markets and Damages' (n 3) 409 fn 41 (emphasis added).

[22] McLauchlan (n 3) 376.

[23] *Koch Marine Inc v d'Amica Societa di Navigazione arl (The Elena d'Amico)* [1980] 1 Lloyd's Rep 75 (QB) 87. See also *Ruxley v Forsyth* [1994] 1 WLR 650, 655 (Staughton LJ): '[T]he transaction is notional because the loser is not obliged to sell his building or chattel and purchase another; I have never heard it suggested that he is. He merely recovers damages measured on the loss that he would have suffered if

However, it is similarly true that claimants are under no 'duty' to mitigate.[24] As I explained in Chapter 7, mitigation serves to attribute responsibility for the claimant's conduct, but does not prescribe how claimants should behave.[25] Again, on my account of mitigation, there is no tension with the market rule.

Finally, one might think that the market rule is incompatible with mitigation because under the market rule, the reasonableness of the claimant's conduct is irrelevant. This point is very well-established in the cases that apply the market rule.[26] It does not matter whether the claimant's choice not to resort to the market was a 'sensible business decision' and hence supported by good reasons.[27] As Devlin J put it in *Biggin v Permanite*, 'The man who buys shares on the stock exchange in the belief that they will go up is acting quite as reasonably as the man who sells the same shares in the belief that they will go down.'[28] Consequently, as Romer LJ argued in *Campbell Mostyn v Barnett*, 'a seller who decided not to take advantage of [the market] could scarcely charge the buyer with a further deterioration in price, on the ground that he had behaved reasonably, if he acted upon his own initiative.'[29]

Instead, the cases applying the market rule routinely emphasize that—however 'reasonable' the claimant's decision was—by choosing not to resort to the market the claimant was 'speculating' and 'does so at his own risk.'[30] This rejection of the reasonableness test in favour of an emphasis on speculation is indeed incompatible with the orthodox understanding of mitigation. However, it is entirely consistent with my new account, which focuses on the significance of the claimant's *choice* not to replicate its no-breach position, for better or worse. As I highlighted in Chapter 2, when applying the so-called avoidable loss rule, judges have similarly noted that reasonableness does not follow its ordinary meaning.[31] Accordingly, for

he had done so.' In Australia, see: *Hardi Finance Corporation Pty Ltd v Ahern (No 3)* [2010] WASC 403, [764]; *Karacominakis v Big Country Developments Pty Ltd & Ors* [2000] NSWCA 313 [187].

[24] See eg *Bunge* (n 7) [81] (Lord Toulson): 'It is well recognised that the so-called duty to mitigate is not a duty in the sense that the innocent party owes an obligation to the guilty party to do so.'

[25] See Chapter 7, Section 2.

[26] *Standard Chartered Bank v Pakistan National Shipping Corp* [1999] 1 Lloyd's Rep 747, [1999] CLC 761 (QB) 778 (Toulson J). See also: *Habton Farms v Nimmo* [2003] EWCA Civ 68, [2004] QB 1 [66], [100] (Clarke LJ); *Campbell Mostyn (Provisions) Ltd v Barnett Trading Co* [1954] 1 Lloyd's Rep 65 (CA) 71 (Romer LJ); *Downs v Chappell* [1997] 1 WLR 426 (CA) 437 (Hobhouse LJ); *Blue Circle Industries plc v Ministry of Defence* [1999] Ch 289 (CA) 306 (Aldous LJ); 321 (Simon Brown LJ).

[27] *The Elena d'Amico* (n 23) 89 (Goff J). This part of Goff J's judgment was repeated in *Glory Wealth Shipping Pte Ltd v Korea Line Corp (The Wren)* [2011] EWHC 1819 (Comm) [16] (Blair J) and *Fulton Shipping Inc of Panama v Globalia Business Travel SAU (The New Flamenco)* [2014] EWHC 1547 (Comm), [2015] 1 All ER (Comm) 1205 [64] (Popplewell J).

[28] *Biggin & Co Ltd v Permanite Ltd* [1951] 1 KB 422 (KB) 429.

[29] *Campbell Mostyn* (n 26) 70–71 (Romer LJ).

[30] *The Golden Victory* (n 2) [79] (Lord Brown). See also *AKAS Jamal v Moolla Dawood Sons & Co* [1916] 1 AC 175 (PC) 179 (Lord Wrenbury); *Kaines (UK) v Oesterreichische Warenhandelsgesellschaft Austrowaren GmbH* [1993] 2 Lloyd's Rep 1 (CA) 11 (Bingham LJ), 13 (Dillon LJ); *Transfield Shipping Inc v Mercator Shipping Inc (The Achilleas)* [2007] EWCA Civ 901, [2008] 1 All ER (Comm) 685 [102] (Rix LJ); *Bunge* (n 7) [80] (Lord Toulson).

[31] See further Chapter 2, Section 2.1.

both mitigation and the market rule, one could clarify that 'a special sense of "reasonable" is meant',[32] although in both cases it would more helpful simply to recognize directly that choice rather than reasonableness is the relevant touchstone.[33]

2.2 Applying the replication rule

The market rule is simply an application of the replication rule in contexts where the claimant can replicate the no-breach position by resorting to the market. Accordingly, the market rule is entirely 'as one' with mitigation, properly understood. Just as in the avoidable and avoided loss cases, there is a strong emphasis on the voluntariness of the claimant's conduct. For example, in *Kwei Tek Chao v British Traders*, Devlin J held that 'if [the claimant] chooses not to sell the goods he is not to be put in any better or worse position by delaying for his own purposes'.[34] In *The Elena D'Amico*, Goff J reasoned that 'the decision not to take advantage of the available market is the independent decision of the innocent party, independent of the wrongdoing which has taken place'.[35] In *The New Flamenco*, Longmore LJ stated that the market rule 'depends on there being an available market which the innocent party *decides for reasons of his own* to ignore'.[36] The same emphasis on choice is clear in the cases on shares,[37] financial products,[38] charterparties,[39] businesses,[40] and land.[41]

It follows from this reasoning that the market rule will be irrelevant where the claimant had no choice to resort to the market.[42] In *The New Flamenco*, the Court of Appeal emphasized that the market rule 'depends on there being an available market which the innocent party *decides for reasons of his own* to ignore'.[43] Where the claimant chooses not to seek a replacement, this choice is regarded as an intervening cause for which the defendant is not responsible, even though of

[32] Adam Kramer, *The Law of Contract Damages* (3rd edn, Hart 2022) [16-52]. See also Dyson and Kramer (n 5) 265.

[33] See further Chapter 8, Section 2 and Chapter 9, Section 2.1.

[34] *Kwei Tek Chao v British Traders & Shippers Ltd* [1954] 2 QB 459 (QB) 494.

[35] *The Elena d'Amico* (n 23).

[36] *Fulton Shipping Inc of Panama v Globalia Business Travel SAU (The New Flamenco)* [2015] EWCA Civ 1299, [2016] 1 Lloyd's Rep 383 [25] (Longmore LJ) (emphasis added).

[37] *Jamal v Moolla Dawood* (n 30) (Lord Wrenbury); *Gestmin SGPS SA v Credit Suisse (UK) Ltd* [2013] EWHC 3560 (Comm) [186] (Leggatt J).

[38] *Primavera v Allied Dunbar Assurance plc* [2002] EWCA Civ 1327, [2003] Lloyd's Rep PN 14 [40] (Mance LJ), [52] (Latham LJ) (pension fund); *Dampskibsselskabet Norden A/S v Andre & Cie SA* [2003] EWHC 84 (Comm), [2003] 1 Lloyd's Rep 287 [42] (Toulson J) (freight swap agreement).

[39] *The Elena d'Amico* (n 23) 87 (Goff J); *The Achilleas (CA)* (n 30) [102] (Rix LJ); *The Wren* (n 27) 402 [16] (Blair J); *The New Flamenco (CA)* (n 36) [49] (Christopher Clarke LJ).

[40] *Downs v Chappell* [1997] 1 WLR 426 (CA) 437 (Hobhouse LJ).

[41] *Blue Circle Industries plc v Ministry of Defence* [1999] Ch 289 (CA) 317 (Chadwick LJ), 321 (Simon Brown LJ).

[42] See further Section 3. See also Dyson and Kramer (n 5) 273–80.

[43] *The New Flamenco (CA)* (n 39) [25] (Longmore LJ) (emphasis added).

course 'It is perfectly true that [the claimant's] decision is made in the context of a pre-existing breach'.[44] The root explanation of the market rule lies in the same commonsense principles of causation that explain the law of mitigation. In *Bunge v Nidera*, Lord Toulson expressed this causal explanation perfectly, linking the claimant's choice to the attribution of responsibility:

> The *option* to re-enter or stay out of the market arises from the breach, but it does not follow that there is a causal connection between the breach and his *decision* whether to re-enter or to stay out of the market, so as to make the guilty party responsible for that decision and its consequences.[45]

In *SAAMCo*, Lord Hoffmann similarly held that 'where there is an available market, any additional loss which the buyer suffers through not having immediately bought equivalent goods at the market price is prima facie caused by his own change of mind'.[46] Again, the emphasis here is on choice rather than reasonableness. As Leggatt J summarized in *Hirtenstein v Hill Dickinson*, 'As with any "failure to mitigate", the essential point is that the decision whether or not to resort to the market is a voluntary choice made by the claimant which breaks the chain of causation from the defendant's breach'.[47] Similarly in *Glencore v Cirrus*, Cooke J reasoned that '[m]ovement in the market thereafter is... excluded... on the basis that any change in the figures affected thereby is the result of the seller's own decision to play the market'.[48]

The symmetrical application of the replication rule in the context of an available market was clearly explained in *The Elena D'Amico*, where Goff J reasoned that the claimant's choice not to resort to the market amounts to a 'decision independent of the wrong; and the consequences of that decision are his. If he judges the market correctly he reaps the benefit; if he judges it incorrectly, then the extra cost falls upon him'.[49] In *Bunge v Nidera*, Lord Toulson similarly emphasized that where the claimant had a 'free choice whether to re-enter the market', the defendant 'is not liable to the innocent party for the adverse effect of market changes . . . nor is the innocent party required to give credit to the guilty party for any subsequent market movement in favour of the innocent party'.[50] In other words, 'The speculation which way the market will go is the speculation of the claimant'.[51]

[44] *The Elena d'Amico* (n 23) 89 (Goff J).

[45] *Bunge* (n 7) [80] (emphasis in original). See also *Norden* (n 38) [42] (Toulson J).

[46] *South Australia Asset Management Corp v York Montague Ltd ('SAAMCo')* [1997] AC 191 (HL) 221.

[47] *Hirtenstein* (n 10) [117]. See also *Bunge* (n 7) [17] (Lord Sumption), [80] (Lord Toulson); *Thai Airways International Public Co Ltd v KI Holdings Co Ltd* [2015] EWHC 1250 (Comm), [2016] 1 All ER (Comm) 675 [35] (Leggatt J).

[48] *Contigroup Companies Inc v Glencore AG* [2004] EWHC 2750 (Comm), [2005] 1 Lloyd's Rep 241 [99]. See also *Gardner v Marsh & Parsons* [1997] 1 WLR 489 (CA) 507 (Peter Gibson LJ): 'The decisions to retain and subsequently sell the goods are independent of the breach.'

[49] *The Elena d'Amico* (n 23) 89.

[50] *Bunge* (n 7) [80] (Lord Toulson).

[51] ibid [80].

2.3 The Sale of Goods Act 1979

For sale of goods cases involving non-acceptance, non-delivery, or defective goods, the market rule is codified in the Sale of Goods Act 1979.[52] The Act provides for a 'prima facie' measure based on the market value at the date of breach under sub-section 3, which may be displaced in appropriate cases by the 'primary' rule under sub-section 2.[53] The latter awards 'the estimated loss directly and naturally resulting, in the ordinary course of events' from the defendant's breach of contract. The prima facie rule under sub-section 3 is expressly predicated on there being an 'available market' for the goods. These provisions were carried over from the original Sale of Goods Act 1893, which in turn was expressly intended 'to reproduce as exactly as possible the statutory and common law rules relating to the sale of goods'.[54]

The cases pre-dating codification clearly recognized that the market measure (which later became sub-section 3) assumed that the claimant could resort to the market at the date of breach to obtain substitute performance. For example, in *Borries v Hutchinson*, Erle CJ held:

> As a general rule, a vendor who fails to deliver goods according to his contract, must pay as damages to the vendee the difference between the value of the goods at the time of breach of contract as compared with the contract-price: or, in other words, if the vendee can go into the market and get the article contracted for, the vendor must reimburse him the difference between that which he has been compelled to pay for it and the price at which the vendor had contracted to deliver for it.[55]

In the 1891 case of *Duff v Iron and Steel Fencing*, Lord M'Laren explained that even if the injured party does not in fact resort to the market to obtain substitute performance, damages will be assessed as if he had done.[56] Accordingly, Mustill J has subsequently described sub-section 3 as 'founded on a presumed mitigation'.[57]

[52] Sale of Goods Act 1979, ss 50(3), 51(3), and 53(3) respectively.

[53] In *The Elena d'Amico* (n 23) 87, Robert Goff J emphasized that s 51(2) 'is the governing principle'. See also *Bence Graphics* (n 17) 102 (Auld LJ); *R Pagnan & Fratelli v Lorico (Lebanese Organisation for International Commerce) (The Caloric)* [1981] 2 Lloyd's Rep 675, 678 (Lloyd J).

[54] M Chalmers, *The Sale of Goods, Including the Factors Act, 1889* (London: Clowes, 1890), iv. The introductory text to the 1893 Act describes it as 'an Act for codifying the Law relating to the Sale of Goods'. See also *Bunge* (n 7) [16] (Lord Sumption).

[55] *Borries v Hutchinson* (1865) 144 ER 518, 524. See also *Gainsford v Carroll* (1824) 2 B & C 624, 107 ER 516, 624–25; *Shaw v Holland* (1846) 15 M & W 136, 153 ER 794, 798 (Parke B).

[56] *Duff & Company v the Iron and Steel Fencing and Buildings Company* (1891) 19 R 199, 204.

[57] *Empresa Exportadora De Azucar v Industria Azucarera Nacional Sa (The Playa Larga and Marble Islands)* (Unreported 29 February 1980). See also *The Marine Star* (n 9) (Mance J); *Tharros Shipping Co Ltd v Bias Shipping Ltd (The Griparion) (No 2)* [1994] 1 Lloyd's Rep 533, 547 (Rix J); *Bem Dis a Turk Ticaret S/A Tr v International Agri Trade Co Ltd (The Selda)* [1999] 1 Lloyd's Rep 729, 732 (Hirst LJ).

Similarly Lord Brown stated that the explanation for section 51(3) 'is that the injured party should ordinarily go out into that market to make a substitute contract to mitigate (and generally thereby crystallise) his loss', adding that the same principle applied at common law outside the sale of goods context.[58] This accurately explains how the market measure in the Sale of Goods Act 1979 also derives from the replication rule, although the word 'should' (which incorrectly implies a prescriptive purpose), is best avoided.[59]

The replication rule assists in explaining when and why the prima facie market measure under sub-section 3 of the Sale of Goods Act 1979 provisions may be displaced. This measure only applies where the claimant had a choice to resort to the market to obtain substitute performance at the date of breach.[60] Where they did not have such a choice—either because there was no available market, or for another reason—sub-section 3 will not apply.[61] For this reason it is a mistake to conclude, as Webster J did in *Shearson Lehman Hutton v Maclaine Watson*, that 'the requirements of reasonable mitigation, which would ordinarily apply to a claim for damages, do not apply when the measure of damages is governed by [sub-section 3]'.[62] Such a statement fails to see the wood for the trees, since sub-section 3 is itself founded on an application of mitigation, which is the key to understanding its scope.

3 (Dis)applying the Market Rule

The market rule will not apply where the claimant had no choice to resort to the market to obtain substitute performance. This follows from the replication rule, because resort to the market is the just means by which the claimant is usually able to replicate its no-breach position as nearly as possible. Obviously, where there is no available market for substitute performance then the market rule will not apply. Here, the replication rule helps to explain what an 'available market' means in

[58] *The Golden Victory* (n 2) [79]. For further dicta also explaining the 1979 Act market measure as an application of mitigation, see *Melachrino v Nickoll* [1920] 1 KB 693, 697 (Bailhache J); *Lesters Leather & Skin Co Ltd v Home and Overseas Brokers Ltd* (1948–49) 82 Lloyd's Rep 202, 205 (Lord Goddard CJ); *Radford v De Froberville* [1977] 1 WLR 1262, 1285 (Oliver J); *Gardner v Marsh & Parsons* [1997] 1 WLR 489, 507 (Gibson LJ); *Bp Plc v Aon Ltd (No 2)* [2006] EWHC 424 (Comm); [2006] 1 All ER (Comm) 789 [312] (Colman J); *The Achilleas (CA)* (n 30) [102] (Rix LJ); *Deutsche Bank AG v Total Global Steel Ltd* [2012] EWHC 1201 (Comm) [155] (Andrew Smith J). See also Michael Bridge (ed), *Benjamin's Sale of Goods, 8th edn* (2010) [16-052]; Andrew Tettenborn, *Contractual Duties: Performance, Breach, Termination and Remedies* (Sweet & Maxwell, 2011) [21-088].

[59] See further text to n 23.

[60] *Bunge* (n 7) [17] (Lord Sumption); *Flame SA v Glory Wealth Shipping Pte Ltd* [2013] EWHC 3153 (Comm), [2013] 2 Lloyd's Rep 653 [18] (Teare J); *Lakatamia Shipping Co Ltd v Su* [2014] EWHC 3611 (Comm), [2015] 1 Lloyd's Rep 216 [111] (Cooke J); *Tharros Shipping Co Ltd v Bias Shipping Ltd (The Griparion) (No 2)* [1994] 1 Lloyd's Rep 533 (QB) 537 (Rix J).

[61] *The Marine Star* (n 9) 1025 (Mance J).

[62] *Shearson Lehman Hutton Inc v Maclaine Watson & Co Ltd (No 2)* [1990] 1 Lloyd's Rep 441, 443.

this context. However, even where there is (in some sense) an available market, the market rule will have no application where the claimant was unaware of the breach, or where the claimant was unable to access the market owing to its specific circumstances. For ease of exposition, these cases are sub-divided into common types below; however, in practice these categories can overlap, and all are governed by the same underlying principles.

3.1 No available market

The application of the market rule 'presupposes the existence of an available market'.[63] The statutory provisions for non-delivery and non-acceptance of goods make clear that the prima facie measure only applies '[w]here there is an available market for the goods in question'.[64] Exactly the same condition operates at common law. As Steel J put it in *The Kildare* (a case in which there was held to be no available market), the claimant's conduct 'could not be the outcome of an independent decision since no alternative form of mitigation was available'.[65] More recently, Lord Leggatt made the same point, noting that the market rule does not apply 'where there is no available market in which an adequate substitute for the lost performance can be obtained'.[66]

The courts have often struggled to precisely define what is meant by an 'available market'.[67] Judicial attempts at definition have included whether there is a 'particular level of trade';[68] whether the price can fluctuate in response to supply and demand;[69] or whether there are 'sufficient traders who are in touch with each other'.[70] The courts have also faced further questions regarding the geographical scope of the market,[71] whether the availability of the market depends on the ability to sell in a particular volume,[72] and whether market transactions must be immediately available.[73] If the market rule is understood as an abstract measure of

[63] *Bunge* (n 7) [82] (Lord Toulson).

[64] Sections 50(3) and 51(3), Sale of Goods Act 1979.

[65] *Zodiac Maritime Agencies Ltd v Fortescue Metals Group Ltd (The Kildare)* [2010] EWHC 903 (Comm), [2011] 2 Lloyd's Rep 360 [63].

[66] *Stanford International Bank* (n 13) [43]. See similar comments in Australian case law: *Cardno BSD Pty Ltd v Water Corporation* [2001] WASCA 161 [156].

[67] See further Bridge (ed) *Benjamin's Sale of Goods* (11th edn, Sweet & Maxwell 2022) [16-068].

[68] *Heskell v Continental Express Ltd* [1950] 1 All ER 1033 (KB) 1056 (Devlin J).

[69] *Charter v Sullivan* [1957] 2 QB 117 (CA) 128 (Jenkins LJ).

[70] *ABD (Metals and Waste) Ltd v Anglo Chemical & Ore Co Ltd* [1955] 2 Lloyd's Rep 456 (QB) 466 (Sellers J).

[71] See eg *Lesters Leather & Skin Co Ltd v Home and Overseas Brokers Ltd* (1948) 82 Ll L Rep 202 (CA) 205 (Lord Goddard CJ); *WL Thompson Ltd v R Robinson (Gunmakers) Ltd* [1955] Ch 177 (Ch) 188 (Upjohn J).

[72] See eg *Garnac Grain Co Inc v HMF Faure & Fairclough Ltd* [1968] AC 1130 (HL) 1138 (Lord Pearson).

[73] See eg *Hooper v Oates* [2013] EWCA Civ 91, [2014] Ch 287 [38] (Lloyd LJ).

damages (for example as a tool for enhancing commercial certainty),[74] there seems no clear way to resolve these problems.

By contrast, applying the replication rule, an available market simply means that the claimant had an opportunity to transact with a third party to replicate the no-breach position as nearly as possible, for example via repair or replacement. In *Shearson Lehman Hutton*, Webster J concluded that there was an available market if 'there is one actual buyer on that day at a fair price'.[75] In other words, a single opportunity to buy and sell is enough to constitute an available market. This is the correct approach because (despite the objective-sounding label), the concept of an available market is essentially subjective: 'the essence of an "available market" is that it should in fact be available to the innocent party'.[76] The question of whether there is an *available market* thus directly shades into the issue of whether the claimant can *access* the market, which is discussed further below.[77]

Connected to the question of 'availability' is the question of what is the relevant 'market' which must be available. In the context of a claim brought by the buyer for non-delivery, Males J said that '"the goods in question" for the purpose of section 51(3) [Sale of Goods Act 1979] need not necessarily be identical in every respect to the goods which were the subject of the sale'.[78] Recently, in *Stanford International Bank*, Lord Leggatt conditioned the operation of the market rule on the presence of an available market 'in which an adequate substitute for the lost performance can be obtained'.[79] This reflects the proposition that the replication rule applies where the claimant made a choice not to replicate its no-breach position *as nearly as possible*. As discussed in Chapter 9, determining what amounts to replication 'as nearly as possible' can be tricky where the claimant is faced with a range of options, none of which replicate their no-breach position exactly.[80] Nevertheless, in principle this is the correct approach.

3.2 Claimant was unaware of the breach

The market rule will not apply if (and for so long as) the claimant was unaware of the breach. The follows from the fact that the claimant cannot exercise a 'choice' not to replicate their no-breach position until they are aware that a breach has

[74] See further text to n 16.

[75] *Shearson* (n 62) 447. This definition was also later adopted in *The Kildare* (n 65) [56] (Steel J).

[76] *Air Studios Ltd v Lombard North Central plc* [2012] EWHC 3162 (QB), [2013] 1 Lloyd's Rep 63 [95] (Males J). Furthermore, the relevant 'market' must provide an equivalent to the claimant's no-breach position: *The Kildare* (n 65) [57] (Steel J).

[77] See further Section 3.4.

[78] *Air Studios* (n 76) [94]. Note that this remark was prefaced with 'particularly in the case of second-hand goods'. See also *Goknur v Organic Village Ltd* [2019] EWHC 2201 (QB) [47] (Martin Chamberlain QC).

[79] *Stanford International Bank* (n 13) [43].

[80] See further Chapter 9, Section 2.4.

occurred.[81] The requirement of knowledge of the breach has been recognised in a number of cases. For example, in *Kwei Tak Chao,* Devlin J stated that:

> As to the consequences of a wrong which deceives the aggrieved party, whether it be in tort or in breach of contract, the aggrieved party cannot be expected to act in such a manner as to compensate himself until he has ascertained the fact. It seems to me quite fictitious to talk of the buyers having to be treated as if they had gone out into the market . . . [when] they had no notion, and could have had no notion, that they had any rights with regard to the contract.[82]

The same point was made by Leggatt J in *Marathon Asset Management v Seddon,* where he noted that 'the assumption that there is an available market in which the injured party can immediately obtain a substitute for the defendant's performance in order to mitigate its loss' does not hold when 'the claimant did not discover the breach until a later date'.[83] More recently, in *Stanford International Bank*, Lord Leggatt stated that 'where the claimant is not aware of the defendant's breach until some time later [. . .] the relevant loss will occur, and the damages will therefore be measured, at a different date'.[84] As I discuss in Chapter 7, and notwithstanding Devlin J's passing reference to constructive knowledge, the better view appears to be that the market rule (following the replication rule) is not engaged until the claimant has actual knowledge of the breach.[85]

It is for this reason that, where the claimant acquires latently defective goods for use in commercial production, the 'market rule' will not prevent recovery of lost profits arising from the defect.[86] Where the defective goods are sold on by the claimant without knowledge of the defect, the cost of any claims by sub-buyers,[87] or the expense of a product recall,[88] will also be recoverable, subject to the application of other doctrines such as remoteness. However, where, as in *Bence Graphics*, the losses under sub-sales turn out to be less than the difference

[81] See further Chapter 7, Section 4.1.

[82] *Kwei Tek Chao* (n 34) 496. See also in Canada: *Armstrong v Roslyn Park Land Co Ltd* (1951) 4 WWR (NS) 270 approved in *329383 Alberta Corporation v Wass* 1999 ABPC 90 at [21].

[83] *Marathon Asset Management* (n 10) [250]. See to the same effect in Canadian case law: *410784 Ontario Ltd v Little Zinger Inc (Corktown Esso)* 2016 ONCA 90 [210]–[211]; *Armstrong v Roslyn Park Land Co Ltd* (1951) 4 WWR (NS) 270.

[84] *Stanford International Bank* (n 13) [43].

[85] See further Chapter 7, Section 4.1.

[86] See eg *Wagstaff v Shorthorn Dairy Co* (1884) C & E 324 (QB); *George Mitchell (Chesterhall) Ltd v Finney Lock Seeds Ltd* [1983] 2 AC 803 (HL); *GKN Centrax Gears Ltd v Matbro Ltd* [1976] 2 Lloyd's Rep 555 (CA).

[87] See eg *Randall v Raper* (1858) 120 ER 438; *Hammond & Co v Bussey* (1887) 20 QBD 79 (CA); *Kasler v Slavouski* [1928] 1 KB 78 (KB); *Biggin* (n 28); *Henry Kendall & Sons v William Lillico & Sons Ltd* [1969] 2 AC 31 (HL); *Ashington Piggeries Ltd v Christopher Hill Ltd* [1972] AC 441 (HL); *Centrax Gears* (n 86); *Bence Graphics* (n 17) 101.

[88] See eg *Bacardi-Martini Beverages Ltd v Thomas Hardy Packaging Ltd* [2002] EWCA Civ 549, [2002] 2 Lloyd's Rep 379; *Britvic Soft Drinks Ltd v Messer UK Ltd* [2002] 1 Lloyd's Rep 20 (QB).

in market value, the inapplicability of the market rule will be to the defendant's advantage. When applying the market rule, the courts have generally valued the repair or replacement at the date when the defect was discovered, and not at the date of breach.[89]

The same principles apply where replication of the no-breach position entails extrication from the original transaction rather than repair or replacement. For example, in *SAAMCO*, Lord Hoffmann rejected the proposition that a lender had acted 'unreasonably' where it had not extricated itself immediately from an under-secured loan. He reasoned that 'it seems to me impossible to say that the loss was caused by any decision of the lenders not to go into the market . . . They did not know until some time afterwards that the valuations were wrong'.[90] This equally explains why, when applying the market rule to property that has been the subject of a misrepresentation, the property is valued at the date when the claimant discovered that the representation was false, and not when the representation was made.[91] It is only after discovery of the misrepresentation that the claimant is able to exercise a choice whether or not to extricate itself from the transaction.[92]

The importance of awareness of the breach also explains the divergent results in *Equitas Ltd v Walsham Bros* and *JSC BTA Bank v Ablyazov*.[93] In both cases the claim was for interest as damages, and for the interest rate to be measured as at the date of breach. In *JSC*, the claimant had parted with their money as a result of the defendant's fraudulent misrepresentation. Since the claimant was initially unaware of the breach, this explained why the cost of borrowing at the date of breach was irrelevant. By contrast, *Equitas* was a breach of contract case where sums were owed to the claimant but wrongfully withheld by the defendant, and the claimant had immediate knowledge of the breach. Accordingly, the market rule correctly operated by deeming the claimant to have had resort to lenders at the date of breach, and why market compound interest rates from this date were appropriate.

89 In relation to replacement, see eg: *Van Den Hurk v R Martens & Co Ltd* [1920] 1 KB 850 (KB); *Applegate v Moss* [1971] 1 QB 406 (CA); *Naughton v O'Callaghan* [1990] 3 All ER 191 (QB); *Bominflot Bunkergesellschaft fur Mineralole mbH & Co v Petroplus Marketing AG* [2012] EWHC 3009 (Comm), [2013] 1 All ER (Comm) 610. In relation to repair, see eg *East Ham Corp v Bernard Sunley & Sons* [1966] AC 406 (HL).

90 *SAAMCO* (n 46) 221. See also *Standard Chartered Bank* (n 26) (Toulson J).

91 See eg *Naughton* (n 89) 198 (Waller J); *Reeves v Thrings & Long (No 1)* [1996] PNLR 265 (CA) 278 (Bingham MR); *Joyce v Bowman Law Ltd* [2010] EWHC 251 (Ch), [2010] PNLR 22 [98] (Vos J). See further Dyson and Kramer (n 5) 275 fn 112. For an incorrect application of the 'breach date rule', see *Wapshott v Davis Donovan & Co* [1996] PNLR 361 (CA) 375 (Bedlam LJ).

92 *Salford City Council v Torkington* [2004] EWCA Civ 1646 [48] (Potter LJ); [64] (Mance LJ)

93 *Equitas* (n 16); *JSC BTA Bank v Ablyazov* [2013] EWHC 867 (Comm). See further Chapter 9, text to n 200.

3.3 Claimant was legally 'locked in'

The claimant may be legally 'locked in' to the original transaction with the defendant, and thus unable to resort to the market at the date of breach, or at all.[94] This can occur under 'string contracts' where the claimant buys goods from the defendant and is contractually obliged to deliver those *exact same goods* to a sub-buyer.[95] In these circumstances 'the measure of loss of profit on re-sale is the right measure'.[96] Treitel correctly identified that this is because the claimant has '(legally) no choice as to the disposal of the goods'.[97] Consequently, the replication rule does not apply.[98] In *Contigroup Companies v Glencore*, Glick QC held that it would be 'entirely artificial' to measure damages by reference to the market where the sub-sale was on terms back-to-back with the original transaction.[99] However, where the sub-sale is merely for goods of an *equivalent specification*, the claimant remains able to resort to the market (unless some other constraint applies) such that if it chooses not to, the replication rule will apply.

The case of *Euro-Asian Oil v Credit Suisse* appears wrongly decided on this basis.[100] The claimant buyer struck a contract with the defendant for the purchase of oil. The claimant also struck a collateral contract with a third-party, under which they contracted to sell oil matching the same description and amount of that purchased under the first contract with the defendant. At the time of breach for non-delivery by defendant, the market price of the oil was £18 million. The collateral contract with the third party was for £16 million. Affirming the decision of the judge at first instance, the Court of Appeal concluded that the proper measure for the assessment of damages was the loss under the collateral contract (ie £16 million), and not the amount that it would have cost to purchase substitute oil on the market (ie £18 million).

In deciding that the market value of the goods at the date of breach had been displaced in favour of the contract price with the third party, Simon LJ (with whom the other judges agreed) drew heavily on *Kwei Tek Chao*.[101] He quoted with approval a passage where Devlin J gives an example of circumstances where the market measure may be displaced, namely where the very goods to be acquired

[94] See further Dyson and Kramer (n 5) 276–77.

[95] See eg *Louis Dreyfus Trading Ltd v Reliance Trading Ltd* [2004] EWHC 525 (Comm), [2004] 2 Lloyd's Rep 243 [21] (Andrew Smith J). Apart from contractual obligations, it is possible that the claimant's choice may be constrained by other legal obligations in tort or criminal law.

[96] *Kwei Tek Chao* (n 34) 490 (Devlin J). For an application, see eg *R&H Hall Ltd v WH Pim Junr & Co Ltd* (1928) 30 Ll L Rep 159 (HL).

[97] Treitel, 'Damages for Breach of Warranty of Quality' (1997) 113 LQR 188, 192. This statement was in the context of the avoided loss rule: see further Chapter 9, text to n 138.

[98] However, there will be a separate issue whether the losses under the sub-sale were unforeseeable and therefore too remote: see further Kramer, *Contract Damages* (n 32) [4-51]–[4-53].

[99] *Glencore* (n 48) [80].

[100] *Euro-Asian Oil SA v Credit Suisse AG* [2018] EWCA Civ 1720, [2019] 1 All ER (Comm) 706.

[101] *Kwei Tek Chao* (n 34).

under the initial contract had been re-sold to a third party. Since it assumed such importance in the court's reasoning in *Euro-Asian*, this passage from *Kwei Tek Chao* is worth quoting at length:

> Similarly, it may very well be that in the case of string contracts, if the seller knows that the merchant is not buying merely for re-sale generally, but upon a string contract where he will re- sell those specific goods and where he could only honour his contract by delivering those goods and no others, the measure of loss of profit on re-sale is the right measure.[102]

Simon LJ went on to reason that although this was not strictly a case involving a string contract (in the sense that the claimant was legally obliged to deliver the exact same goods to the sub-buyer), there had nevertheless been a 'proper factual foundation' for the trial judge to conclude that the resale of the same oil to the third party had always had been contemplated by the defendant, so that the price on the re-sale ought to be the correct measure for the purpose of calculating loss. While Simon LJ thought he was giving effect to the principle underlying Devlin J's remarks in *Kwei Tek Chao*, he was not. Whereas Devlin J's approach, when properly understood, gives effect to the replication rule as I have stated it, Simon LJ's does not.

It is essential to see that, according to Devlin J in *Kwei*, for the price under the subsequent contract to displace the market measure in the assessment of damages, there are two cumulative requirements.[103] First, that there is a real string contract, such that the buyer is legally locked into the transaction with the seller. Second, that the string contract is contemplated by the seller. The first requirement is made clear by Devlin J's reference to a contract where the buyer 'could only honour his contract [with C] by delivering those goods *and no others*'[104] (emphasis provided). The second requirement is made clear by Devlin J stating that the sub-sale will only displace the market measure 'if the seller knows that the buyer is not buying merely for re-sale generally, but upon a string contract'.[105] The first requirement concerns mitigation, whilst the second concerns remoteness.

Since in *Euro-Asian* there was no real string contract, the claimant was not legally 'locked in' to the transaction with the defendant and could still have replicated their no-breach position by resorting to the market to buy replacement oil. It is not enough that there was contemplation by the defendant of the subsequent sale to the third party, since there was nothing to stop the claimant using replacement goods from the market to supply that sub-sale. Applying the replication

[102] ibid 489–90 (Devlin J).
[103] See too Kramer, *Contract Damages* (n 32) [4-52].
[104] ibid 490.
[105] ibid 489.

rule, the claimant was entitled to recover the market value of the oil at the date of breach, being the cost of replicating its no-breach position, even though it did not in fact do so. This would have left the claimant with its profits under the sub-sale. Accordingly, *Euro-Asian* is wrongly decided since the 'market rule' should have applied in this case.[106]

3.4 Claimant was unable to access the market

There may be circumstances in which, although there exists in some general sense a 'market' for repair, replacement, or extrication, the claimant is unable to access it. Such circumstances include: first, where the claimant needs time to access the market; second, where the claimant is impecunious and therefore cannot afford to pay to replicate his no-breach position in advance of receiving damages; and finally, miscellaneous other cases in which the claimant effectively has no choice to access the market. In each of these cases, the replication rule (and hence the so-called market rule) will not apply. The unifying principle underlying this conclusion is again that the claimant did not have a choice to replicate its no-breach position at the date of breach and, therefore, 'the relevant loss will occur [. . .] at a different date'.[107]

First, the claimant may need time to access the market. The so-called 'breach-date rule' for the assessment of damages rests on the premise that the claimant can resort immediately to the market to replicate its no-breach position.[108] This assumption is usually apt for straightforward transactions in highly liquid markets.[109] Here, the breach-date rule provides a satisfactory (albeit imperfect)[110] proxy for the replication principle, given the claimant will mitigate its loss by seeking a substitute performance from the market upon breach.[111] However, replication sometimes involves buying or selling illiquid assets in complicated or protracted

[106] Arguing that *Euro-Asian* is wrongly decided: Hugh Beale (ed), *Chitty on Contracts* (34th edn, Sweet & Maxwell 2022) [46-401]. Arguing that *Euro-Asian* is rightly decided: Kramer, *Contract Damages* (n 32) [4-128]; James Edelman (ed), *McGregor on Damages* (21st edn, Sweet & Maxwell 2022) [9-184].

[107] *Stanford International Bank* (n 13) [43].

[108] See further Dyson and Kramer (n 5) 271–72. See also *Marathon Asset Management* (n 10) [250] (Leggatt J).

[109] In *Hooper* (n 73) [34], Lloyd LJ gave commodities, listed shares, freight forward agreements, and charterparties as commercial examples. The majority of consumer retail purchases (but not consumer sales) also fall into this category.

[110] In *The Golden Victory* (n 2) [34], Lord Scott highlighted that even in relation to liquid markets 'some period must usually be allowed to enable the necessary arrangements for the substitute sale or purchase to be made', citing *Kaines* (n 30). See also *Waddell v Blockey* (1879) 4 QBD 678 (CA) 681 (Bramwell LJ). For an example where the date of assessment was postponed on this basis, see *C Sharpe & Co Ltd v Nosawa & Co* [1917] 2 KB 814, 821 (Atkin J).

[111] *Novus Aviation* (n 10) [129] (Leggatt J).

transactions.[112] Here, 'time may well be needed before the injured party can reasonably be required to re-enter the market'.[113] As a result, the so-called breach date rule is inappropriate in these circumstances because the claimant (in all practical senses) has no choice to replicate the no-breach position at the date of breach.

Second, if the claimant is impecunious and cannot afford to buy substitute performance in advance of receiving damages, then they may have no practical choice to resort to the market despite there existing an 'available market' from an objective standpoint.[114] Clearly, if at the date of breach going to market to replicate the position is a financial impossibility (ie the claimant does not have enough funds of its own and is unable to borrow them), then on any understanding the claimant does not have a 'choice' to replicate and the market rule does not apply. However, 'impecuniosity' has also been given a broader meaning such that the claimant will not be faced with a 'choice' where replicating at the date of breach would involve 'making sacrifices [she] could not reasonably be expected to make'.[115] I discuss in more detail these 'edge cases' regarding the meaning of choice, in Chapter 6.[116]

Finally, and relatedly, there are various other miscellaneous reasons why the claimant may effectively lack a choice to resort to the market, such that the market rule will be held inapplicable. For example, in *Smith New Court Securities*, the defendant fraudulently induced the claimant to buy shares.[117] The House of Lords held that the claimant was 'in a special sense locked into the shares' because it had purchased them as a 'market-making risk' such that immediate sale was uneconomical.[118] A similar issue arose where the required volume of sales was so large in proportion to the market that the claimant could not resell immediately without triggering a collapse in the market price.[119] In both cases, the court held that it would be inappropriate to take the abstract 'market price' in these circumstances.

Of course, the claimant can almost always access some market at some price. For example, in *Gestmin v Credit Suisse*, Leggatt J held that the claimant 'could probably have sold all [the shares] over time if it had been willing to accept lower prices'.[120] Nevertheless, he concluded that 'the relevant question in my view is whether there was a time at which [the claimant] could have sold the shares at a

[112] See eg *Hooper* (n 73) [34] (Lloyd LJ) (sale of land); *Habton Farms v Nimmo* [2003] EWCA Civ 68, [2004] QB 1 [129] (Auld LJ) (sale of a racehorse); *East v Maurer* [1991] 1 WLR 461 (CA) 463 (Bedlam LJ) (sale of a business). See in Canada: *100 Main Street Ltd v WB Sullivan Construction Ltd* (1978) 88 DLR (3d) 1 (Ont CA) at 428–32.

[113] *The Golden Victory* (n 2) [80] (Lord Brown).

[114] *Lagden v O'Connor* [2003] UKHL 64, [2004] 1 AC 1067. See in the Australian context: *Hardi Finance Corporation Pty Ltd v Ahern (No 3)* [2010] WASC 403 [770]; *Burns v MAN Automotive (Australia) Pty Ltd* [1986] HCA 81, [8]–[10] (Brennan J).

[115] *Lagden* (n 114) [9] (Lord Nicholls). See similarly in Australia: *Newmarket Corporation Pty Ltd v Kee-Vee Properties Pty Ltd* [2003] WASC 157 [186].

[116] See further Chapter 6, Section 3.3.

[117] *Smith New Court Securities* (n 2).

[118] ibid 268 (Lord Browne-Wilkinson).

[119] *Shearson* (n 62).

[120] *Gestmin SGPS SA v Credit Suisse (UK) Ltd* [2013] EWHC 3560 (Comm) [190].

price which fairly reflected their value'.[121] It was inappropriate to adopt the market value at the date of breach (or any other date prior to trial) because the claimant 'could not at any time have sold its (very large) shareholding . . . other than with difficulty and a significant loss of value'.[122] One might object that this kind of consideration brings reasonableness back into the 'choice' requirement by the back door. However, there is an important distinction because the focus is still on the quality of options available to the claimant rather than any exercise in balancing the defendant's interests.

4 The Effect on Damages

The effect of the market rule is identical to that of the so-called avoidable and avoided loss rules because all these rules are just instantiations of the same underlying replication rule. Consequently, where the market rule applies the claimant's breach position is assessed as if they had resorted to the market at the relevant time, because these are the steps that would have replicated their no-breach position as nearly as possible. In *The Golden Victory*, Lord Bingham held that damages are assessed 'on the assumption' that the claimant resorted to the market 'whether in fact the injured party acts in that way or, for whatever reason, does not'.[123] Similarly, in *Stanford International Bank*, Lord Leggatt held that 'where there is an available market [. . .] damages are to be assessed as if the claimant entered the market [. . .] whether or not the claimant in fact did so'.[124] In *Hussey v Eels*, Mustill LJ aptly described this as a 'deemed mitigation'.[125] Just as under the so-called avoidable and avoided loss rules, this entails a counterfactual assessment: 'The actual facts are ordinarily irrelevant'.[126]

Where the market rule applies, there is no liability for any additional harms actually incurred by the claimant as a result of not resorting to the market. This has sometimes been explained on grounds of commercial expedience.[127] However, it is better understood in terms of causation, and the proposition that the claimant is

[121] ibid. See also See *Tattersalls v McMahon* [2021] EWHC 1629 (QB) [15]–[16] (Carver J), discussing different modes of resale following the original buyer's failure to pay the price.

[122] *Gestmin* (n 120) [190] (Leggatt J).

[123] *The Golden Victory* (n 2) [10]. See also *The Achilleas* (CA) (n 30) [102] (Rix LJ); *Hirtenstein* (n 10) [117] (Leggatt J); and *Sainsbury's Supermarkets Ltd v Visa Europe Services LLC* [2020] UKSC 24, [2020] 4 All ER 807 [214], quoting Dyson and Kramer (n 5).

[124] *Stanford International Bank* (n 13) [43].

[125] *Hussey* (n 7) 232–33. See also *Radford v De Froberville* [1977] 1 WLR 1262 (Ch) 1285–86 (Oliver J); *The Marine Star* (n 9) 1025 (Mance J); *The Golden Victory* (n 2) [57] (Lord Carswell); *The Kildare* (n 65) [65] (Steel J); *Deutsche Bank v Total Global Steel* (n 58) [166] (Andrew Smith J).

[126] *The Golden Victory* (n 2) [10]. See also *The Achilleas* (CA) (n 30) [102] (Rix LJ); *Derby Resources AG v Blue Corinth Marine Co Ltd (The Athenian Harmony) (No 1)* [1998] 2 Lloyd's Rep 410 (QB) 415–16 (Colman J).

[127] See eg *Smith New Court Securities* (n 2) 266 (Lord Browne-Wilkinson). See also *Equitas* (n 16) [123] (Males J).

responsible for the consequences of its own choice not to resort to the market, for better or worse. In *SAAMCO*, Lord Hoffmann held that 'where there is an available market, any additional loss which the buyer suffers through not having immediately bought equivalent goods at the market price is prima facie caused by his own change of mind'.[128] Accordingly, the claimant will not be able to recover for any 'consequential losses' in fact suffered as a result of not resorting to the market for substitute performance, such as claims by sub-buyers or loss of business profits.[129]

It is important to note that the effect of the market rule is not simply to 'freeze' the damages assessment at the time when the claimant could have resorted to the market. Other subsequent events in the real world may remain relevant: both for assessment of the claimant's no-breach position, and for their breach position to the extent that these events would also have affected the counterfactual world in which the claimant had resorted to the market. For this reason, Lord Sumption was correct in *Bunge v Nidera* to argue that, even where the market rule applies, 'There is no principled reason why, in order to determine the value of the contractual performance which has been lost by the repudiation, one should not consider what would have happened if the repudiation had not occurred'.[130] This follows from the fact the application of the market rule entails a counterfactual assessment that modifies only the fact that the claimant did not resort to the market; it does not impose a crude 'stop the clock' approach for all purposes.

Where the claimant had no choice to replicate its no-breach position by resorting to the market, such that the market rule does not apply, it will recover damages for its factual loss for better or worse. As Rix LJ put it in *The Achilleas*, 'it is the actual loss suffered, rather than the conventional market loss, which can be claimed'.[131] The assessment of the claimant's breach position will include all the harms that would not have occurred but for the defendant's breach, subject to the remoteness limitation. For example, where the claimant is unaware of defects in goods supplied by the defendant,[132] it can recover damages for any personal injury,[133] property damage,[134] or lost profits[135] suffered through using the goods. It can also

[128] *SAAMCO* (n 46) 221.
[129] See further Dyson and Kramer (n 5) 272–73.
[130] *Bunge* (n 7) [22].
[131] *The Achilleas* (CA) (n 30) [109] (Rix LJ). See also *The New Flamenco (CA)* (n 39) [25] (Longmore LJ). For an earlier example of this reasoning, see *Simon v Pawson and Leafs Ltd* [1932] All ER Rep 72 (CA) 78 (Greer LJ), distinguishing *Grebert-Borgnis v J&W Nugent* (1885) 15 QBD 85 (CA) on the basis that in the latter case there was no available market and thus 'the buyer was unable to prevent the damages from arising'.
[132] In relation to extrication in a 'no transaction' case, see also *SAAMCO* (n 46) 221 (Lord Hoffmann): '[I]t seems to me impossible to say that the loss was caused by any decision of the lenders not to go into the market . . . They did not know until some time afterwards that the valuations were wrong.'
[133] *The Wren* (n 27); *Grant v Owners of the Egyptian (The Egyptian)* [1910] AC 400 (HL).
[134] *Wilson v Rickett Cockerell & Co Ltd* [1954] 1 QB 598; *Bacon v Cooper (Metals) Ltd* [1982] 1 All ER 397 (QB).
[135] Note 86.

recover the cost of settling claims with sub-buyers[136] or issuing a product recall[137] suffered through reselling the latently defective goods. The non-application of the market rule has the same effect in cases where the claimant cannot afford to have resort to the market,[138] or is otherwise unable to access it.[139]

On this analysis, the claimant's damages in *Bostock v Nicholson* appear to have been unduly restricted.[140] In that case, the claimants purchased sulphuric acid from the defendants, which was supplied in breach of the implied term of correspondence with description (as the acid contained arsenic). Before the breach was known, but at a point when the claimants could, with ordinary care, have discovered the breach, the claimants used the acid in the manufacture of brewing sugar. The resultant sugar was rendered poisonous, exposing them to claims by the brewers to whom the sugar was sold and causing harm to their reputation. The claimants claimed damages for: (1) the whole price paid for the acid; (2) the value of other goods that had been spoiled by mixing with the acid; (3) their liability to the brewers to whom they had sold the sugar; and (4) the loss of goodwill in their business.

Bruce J allowed the claim under the first two heads of damage. However, he held that the claimants could not recover for their liability to the brewers, as 'no liability is incurred in the ordinary case of a separate and distinct collateral contract with a third person uncommunicated to the original contractor or wrong-doer'.[141] He also denied the claim for loss of goodwill, on the basis that '[The loss] did not arise directly from the act of the defendants, but arose from the act of the plaintiffs in selling the poisonous glucose and invert.'[142] The problem with this causation reasoning is that the sub-sale was done without awareness of the defendant's breach. The claimants did not have choice to buy replacement acid to make the sugar before selling it on to the brewers, because at that time they were unaware of the contamination.

One interpretation of the decision, which I discussed but rejected in Chapter 7,[143] is that constructive knowledge of the breach suffices to trigger the replication rule.[144] However, if so, that would mean that the claimants should also have been denied damages for the value of the other goods that had been spoiled

[136] Note 87.

[137] Note 88.

[138] See eg *Dodd Properties (Kent) Ltd v Canterbury City Council* [1980] 1 WLR 433 (CA) 453 (Megaw LJ); *Alcoa Minerals of Jamaica Inc v Broderick* [2002] 1 AC 371 (PC) 382–83 (Lord Slynn).

[139] See eg *R&H Hall* (n 96); *Kwei Tek Chao* (n 34) 490 (Devlin J); *Louis Dreyfus* (n 95) [21] (Andrew Smith J); *M&J Marine Engineering Services Co Ltd v Shipshore Ltd* [2009] EWHC 2031 (Comm) [30] (Field J).

[140] *Bostock & Co Ltd v Nicholson & Sons Ltd* [1904] 1 KB 725.

[141] ibid 742.

[142] ibid 741. Curiously, Bruce J did not apply this causation reasoning to the claim in respect of liability to the brewers, instead holding that this liability 'may in one sense have resulted from the original wrongful act or breach of contract': ibid 742.

[143] See further Chapter 7, text to n 114.

[144] Given Bruce J's finding that the claimants could, with ordinary care, have discovered the breach.

by mixing with the acid (ie the second head of damage listed above). Either way, there is a clear inconsistency, at least in relation to mitigation, in allowing damages under head (2) but not under heads (3) and (4). Another explanation, which would be consistent with my account of mitigation, is that the claims under heads (3) and (4) for liability to the brewers and loss of goodwill, were instead rejected on remoteness grounds. Remoteness certainly appears to have been a factor in relation to liability to the brewers, since Bruce J referred expressly to collateral contracts that were 'uncommunicated' to the defendant.

Where the claimant did in fact resort to the market at the earliest opportunity, the actual loss incurred will be recoverable rather than any abstract market value. In *Hinde v Liddell*, Cockburn CJ allowed the claim for the actual cost of purchasing replacement goods on the basis that if '[t]he course the plaintiff pursued was right and reasonable ... He is, therefore entitled to the damages he claimed'.[145] More recently, in *Hooper v Oates*, Lloyd LJ held that in non-acceptance cases the actual resale price was used in assessing damages 'not because it represents the market value at the date of the breach, but because it shows what loss the seller has suffered, uncomplicated by issues of remoteness or failure to mitigate'.[146] Additional harms besides the actual 'market loss' will also be recoverable. In *Tattersalls v McMahon*, the defendant failed to pay for horses they had won at auction.[147] The claimant was unable to resell the horses immediately but did so eventually. In addition to the loss realized on resale, Carver J held that the claimants were also entitled to recover the actual costs of keeping the horses in the meantime.[148]

[145] *Hinde v Liddell* (1874–75) LR 10 QB 265 (QB) 268.
[146] *Hooper* (n 73) [38].
[147] *Tattersalls v McMahon* (n 32).
[148] ibid [31].

11
Relationship to Other Doctrines

1 Introduction

So far, my focus in this book has been on explaining and restating what might be termed the 'core' of mitigation, comprising the avoidable loss rule, the avoided loss rule and the market rule (as conventionally understood). I have argued that this body of law can be restated by two rules of mitigation: the replication rule and the exceptionality rule, both of which reflect the commonsense causal principles of choice and abnormality.[1] As I outlined in the Introduction, I identified this 'core' on the basis that it comprised the rules that judges themselves had typically labelled as part of the doctrine of 'mitigation'.[2] In this chapter, I now foray beyond that core to examine a series of other doctrines that have often been thought of as somehow *related to*, or at least overlapping with, mitigation. The aim is to ascertain which, if any, of these other doctrines are indeed related to mitigation as I have restated it (and if so, how), and which ones are better regarded as distinct.

I examine five doctrines in total, all of which have previously been linked in some way—either by judges or scholars—to mitigation.[3] These are: intervening acts by the claimant; betterment; remoteness; contributory negligence; and the so-called '*White & Carter* limitation'.[4] I argue that intervening acts by the claimant and betterment are *part of* the law of mitigation, properly understood, because they entail applications of the replication and/or exceptionality rules.[5] By contrast, remoteness is distinct from mitigation since it has major differences in scope and application, and—unlike mitigation—is a true limitation on damages. Contributory negligence and mitigation can overlap. Their effects are incompatible, and although there is a lack of direct authority, the better view is that mitigation will have primacy. Finally, the *White & Carter* limitation is also distinct from mitigation, because it serves to restrict the availability of the action for the agreed sum rather than as a tool for assessing damages.

[1] See further Chapter 6.
[2] See further Introduction, text to n 45.
[3] See also Chapter 9, Section 4, for discussion of the relationship between mitigation and the so-called insurance and benevolence rules.
[4] *White & Carter (Councils) Ltd v McGregor* [1962] AC 413 (HL).
[5] Specifically: intervening acts by the claimant can entail an application of either the replication rule or the exceptionality rule, depending on the context; betterment entails an application of the replication rule.

Mitigation in the Law of Damages. Andrew Summers, Oxford University Press. © Andy Summers 2025.
DOI: 10.1093/9780191864032.003.0011

2 Intervening Acts by the Claimant

The doctrine of intervening causation has often been linked with mitigation. For example, Burrows argues that 'both the duty to mitigate and intervening cause can be regarded as denying damages for exactly the same reason'.[6] This is correct, at least in relation to intervening acts by the claimant. Where the claimant chose not to replicate the no-breach position, its conduct has sometimes been expressed in terms of intervening causation.[7] The intervening act doctrine has also commonly been invoked where the claimant chose to act in an exceptional way.[8] Accordingly, intervening acts by the claimant can reflect an application of either the replication or the exceptionality rule. Where the claimant's conduct formed part of an attempt to replicate the no-breach position, it is more often referred to as mitigation, whereas outside this context it is instead conventionally classified as an intervening cause. However, this distinction has no legal significance, and all the cases invoking intervening acts by the claimant could equally be explained in terms of mitigation.

2.1 The replication rule

The claimant's choice not to seek repair has sometimes been regarded by the court as an intervening act that breaks the chain of causation. For example, in *Lambert v Lewis*, a farmer's trailer collided with the claimant after coming loose from a defective coupling.[9] The farmer, who was liable to the claimant in negligence, sought a contribution from the seller of the coupling for breach of warranty. The House of Lords rejected this claim on the basis that the farmer's conduct 'in failing, when he knew that the coupling was damaged, to have it repaired' broke the chain of causation.[10] However, as Tettenborn identifies, 'his claim for damages failed on causation grounds: but the result could equally well have been grounded on failure to mitigate'.[11] The underlying principle at play, whether expressed in terms of

[6] Andrew Burrows, *Remedies for Torts and Breach of Contract* (4th edn, OUP 2019) 84–85. See also Tettenborn, *The Law of Damages* (2nd edn, LexisNexis 2010) [5.62].

[7] See eg *Farr v Butters Bros* [1932] 2 KB 606 (CA); *Quinn v Burch Bros (Builders) Ltd* [1966] 2 QB 370 (CA); *Lambert v Lewis* [1982] AC 225 (HL).

[8] See eg *Adams v Lancashire & Yorkshire Railway Co* (1868-69) LR 4 CP 739 (CP); *Cutler v United Dairies Ltd* [1933] 2 KB 297 (CA); *McKew v Holland & Cubitts (Scotland) Ltd* [1969] 3 All ER 1621 (HL); *Arkin v Borchard Lines Ltd* [2003] EWHC 687 (Comm), [2004] 2 CLC 242. The claimant's conduct must also be voluntary: see eg *Corr v IBC Vehicles Ltd* [2008] UKHL 13, [2008] 1 AC 884 [16] (Lord Bingham), [42] (Lord Walker).

[9] *Lambert* (n 7). Intervening causation similarly applied in *Anderson (Commander of the Flying Fish) v Hoen (The Flying Fish)* (1865) 16 ER 29 (PC) 33 (Lord Chelmsford) on the basis that the claimant 'appears not to have been doing, or attempting, or suggesting, anything to save the vessel'. See also *Grant v Owners of the Egyptian (The Egyptian)* [1910] AC 400 (HL).

[10] *Lambert* (n 7) 277 (Lord Diplock).

[11] Tettenborn (n 6) [5.62].

mitigation or intervening causation, was a choice not to replicate the no-breach position by repairing the coupling.

The decision in *Parsons v Uttley* to hold the defendants liable for the dead pigs may be questioned on this basis.[12] The defendants defectively installed a food-hopper used by the claimant farmer to store nuts for pig-feed. Although the claimant knew that the food-hopper was defective and that the nuts had gone mouldy, he fed them to the pigs anyway and several pigs died.[13] In the Court of Appeal, Lord Denning held that: 'There is no problem here about causation. The closed ventilator was clearly the cause, or one of the causes, of the deaths of the pigs. There was an unbroken sequence all the way. There was no intervening human action . . . The only problem here is with remoteness of damage.'[14] The Court of Appeal therefore allowed the claimant to recover the cost of the dead pigs on the basis that it was a foreseeable consequence of the defendant's breach.

Lord Denning's assessment of the causation issue in *Parsons* is flawed. Although foreseeable, the claimant made a choice not to replicate the no-breach position; he could have sought to repair the food-hopper and purchased replacement nuts but chose not to do so. On this basis the replication rule, whether expressed in terms of mitigation or intervening causation, should have been applied. For example, in the earlier decision in *Dobell v Barber*,[15] the claimants purchased linseed cake to incorporate into cattle food, but the linseed was contaminated with castor. Greer LJ correctly commented that:

> If the buyers had before resale ascertained that the linseed cake contained castor and was therefore unfit for cattle food, and had then sold it for use as cattle food, it seems to me quite clear that they would not have been entitled to say to the sellers: "The damages I have to pay are the result of your breach of warranty, you are bound to pay them to me."[16]

On the facts, the claimants in *Dobell v Barber* were unaware of the contamination and thus the court held that they could recover the cost of claims by dissatisfied sub-buyers who had purchased the linseed for cattle food.[17] However, Greer LJ's

[12] *Parsons (Livestock) Ltd v Uttley Ingham & Co Ltd* [1978] QB 791 (CA). See also Adam Kramer, *The Law of Contract Damages* (3nd edn, Hart Publishing 2022) [16-13].

[13] *Parsons* (n 12) 799 (Lord Denning), 811 (Scarman LJ).

[14] ibid 801.

[15] *Dobell & Co Ltd v Barber & Garratt* [1931] 1 KB 219 (CA). See also *Biggin & Co Ltd v Permanite Ltd* [1951] 1 KB 422 (KB) 435 (Devlin J); *British Oil and Cake Co Ltd v Burstall & Co* (1923) 39 TLR 406 (KB) 407 (Rowlatt J).

[16] *Dobell* (n 15) 246. See also 238 (Lawrence LJ): '[The claimants] obviously could not after they had received notice that the cake was unfit for cattle food increase the damages by delivering any more of the cake.'

[17] Greer LJ dissented on the basis that (1) the defendants were not liable; and (2) the claimants could have made further attempts to discover the contamination (ibid 245–46). On the second issue, see further Chapter 7, Section 4.1.

obiter comments show the correct approach to the problem in *Parsons*. Irrespective of whether the death or illness of the pigs was foreseeable, the claimant's conduct amounted to a new cause for which the defendants were not legally responsible.

Another example focusing on the claimant's voluntary conduct is *Farr v Butters Bros*, in which a crane operator was killed when a crane fell on him.[18] Whilst assembling the crane, the operator had noticed that some of the components did not fit properly. As Lawrence LJ put it: 'The defect in certain of the parts was patent and discoverable, and was in fact discovered . . . yet he took his chance of operating it without remedying the defect'.[19] The Court of Appeal rejected a claim by the crane operator's widow under the Fatal Accidents Act 1846. More recently, the general proposition in relation to defective goods has been summarized as follows: 'if [the claimant] becomes aware of a defect in goods, but continues to use the goods notwithstanding this knowledge, there is a break in the chain of causation from that point on.'[20]

The claimant's choice not to obtain a replacement has also sometimes been treated as an intervening cause. In *Quinn v Burch Bros*, building contractors failed (in breach of contract) to supply a stepladder to the claimant plasterer.[21] The claimant was injured falling from a trestle that he had attempted to use instead. The Court of Appeal rejected the claim on the basis that the defendants' failure to provide the equipment 'was not the cause of the accident.'[22] Sellers LJ reasoned that 'the obvious way to minimize damage for the failure to supply a ladder would have been to acquire another ladder of a like kind'[23] but instead 'the plaintiff chose to do this work . . . from the trestle'.[24] Danckwerts LJ and Salmon LJ also reasoned that the claimant had made a voluntary choice to use the trestle instead of seeking a replacement stepladder.[25]

Similarly, in *Simon v Pawson* the defendants failed to supply material used by the claimant for making school blazers.[26] The claimant was unable to fulfil her orders and the school cancelled her appointment as their exclusive supplier. The Court of Appeal rejected the claim for loss of profits arising from cancellation of the appointment. Scrutton LJ held that the loss of appointment was too remote.[27] However, the other two judges both reasoned that even if the loss of appointment

[18] *Farr* (n 7).

[19] ibid 617.

[20] *Trac Time Control Ltd v Moss Plastic Parts Ltd* [2004] EWHC 3298 (TCC) [182] (Grenfell J).

[21] *Quinn* (n 7).

[22] ibid 391 (Danckwerts LJ). The other two judges also expressed their conclusions in terms of causation: see 389–90 (Sellers LJ); 394–95 (Salmon LJ).

[23] ibid 388–89.

[24] ibid 391. Sellers LJ noted that the choice was made 'conscientiously' with a view to completing the work. Again, this jars with a conclusion that the conduct was 'unreasonable' in the ordinary pejorative sense.

[25] ibid 391 (Danckwerts LJ) and 392 (Salmon LJ).

[26] *Simon v Pawson and Leafs Ltd* [1932] All ER Rep 72 (CA).

[27] ibid 76.

was foreseeable, it was not caused by the defendant's breach of contract.[28] Greer LJ held that the claimant 'had ample opportunity of preventing the defendants' breach from resulting in the loss of her appointment' by ordering replacement material,[29] but 'she failed to take those reasonable steps'.[30] Slesser LJ also decided on the basis that there was no evidence the claimant had 'even attempted to get the material elsewhere'.[31]

2.2 The exceptionality rule

It is well-established that 'human action does not per se sever the connected sequence of acts'.[32] For example, in *Summers v Salford Corporation*, the claimant was injured whilst cleaning a window when the sash cord broke.[33] Lord Wright held that 'if a plaintiff suffers damage by the defendant's default, the damage may be directly due to that default and recoverable even though the accident and damage would not have happened but for some action of the plaintiff, so long as his action was in the ordinary course of things'.[34] The claimant's window-cleaning was not an intervening cause because 'she was doing what any intelligent observer, knowing exactly how she was circumstanced, would have expected her to do'.[35] Since her conduct was, in Lord Wright's opinion 'in the ordinary course of events', it followed that 'her injury was thus the direct and natural consequence of the respondent's default'.[36]

By contrast, as I outlined in Chapter 6, and illustrated in the context of the avoidable loss rule in Chapter 8, if the claimant chooses to act in an exceptional (ie unusual) way, they will be held responsible for the consequences. Where the claimant acts unusually whilst seeking to replicate the no-breach position, this is conventionally expressed as an issue of mitigation. However, where the claimant's exceptional conduct was not part of an attempt to replicate the no-breach position, it has often been described as an intervening cause. The issue here concerns any acts or omissions that would not have occurred 'but for' the breach, but which were nevertheless not 'caused' by the breach—applying commonsense principles of causation—owing to their voluntariness and abnormality. The exceptionality rule applies only where the claimant acted abnormally given their own circumstances, characteristics, and preferences ie it is an essentially subjective test. It also

28 ibid 78 (Greer LJ); 80 (Slesser LJ).
29 ibid 79.
30 ibid 78.
31 ibid 80.
32 *The Oropesa* [1943] P 32 (CA) 37.
33 *Summers v Salford Corporation* [1943] AC 283.
34 ibid 296.
35 ibid 297.
36 ibid.

crucially depends on the claimant having acted voluntarily. Both these requirements are evident in the cases on intervening acts by the claimant.

The leading authority applying the exceptionality rule in the context of intervening causation is *McKew v Holland*.[37] The claimant was injured such that his leg was known occasionally to give way without warning. The claimant nevertheless attempted to descend some steep stairs without a handrail. His leg gave way, and he fractured his ankle in the fall. The House of Lords rejected the claim in respect of the fractured ankle. Lord Reid concluded the claimant's conduct was such that 'the chain of causation has been broken and what follows must be regarded as caused by his own conduct and not by the defender's fault'.[38] In particular, he dismissed the argument that the conduct may have been normal in the claimant's circumstances, noting that 'there is nothing in the evidence here to suggest that the appellant is abnormally stupid'.[39]

It may be that the exceptionality rule was too readily applied in *McKew*. More recently, in *Spencer v Wincanton Holdings*, the Court of Appeal reached a different conclusion on apparently similar facts.[40] The defendant negligently injured the claimant's leg, such that the claimant required a prosthetic limb. The claimant subsequently suffered further injury when he fell, after attempting to walk without first fitting the prosthesis. The Court of Appeal upheld the trial judge's conclusion that the further injury had been 'directly caused' by the defendant's original negligence.[41] However, the court also upheld a one-third reduction in damages for contributory negligence.[42] Burrows has argued that a reduction for contributory negligence should have similarly been considered (instead of intervening causation) in *McKew*.[43]

The threshold for establishing that the claimant acted exceptionally given its own circumstances, characteristics and preferences, appears to be quite high, although it has been met on various occasions.[44] In *Adams v Lancashire and Yorkshire Railway*, the claimant was a passenger aboard the defendants' railway.[45] The door of the train carriage flew open several times through the negligence of the defendants. Although there was room to sit away from the door, and the train would have stopped at a station in three minutes, the claimant attempted several

37 *McKew* (n 8).
38 ibid 25; see also 28 (Lord Guest).
39 ibid 25.
40 *Spencer v Wincanton Holdings Ltd* [2009] EWCA Civ 1404, [2010] PIQR P8.
41 ibid [21] (Sedley LJ), quoting Bullimore J at [93].
42 The reduction for contributory negligence had not been appealed: see ibid [22] (Sedley LJ).
43 Burrows, *Remedies* (4th edn) (n 6) 117. In *Spencer* (n 40) [45], Aikens LJ admitted that the line between intervening causation and contributory negligence was difficult to draw.
44 See eg *Arkin* (n 8), where the claimant, with knowledge of the defendant's infringement of competition rules, decided to continue trading in the market, having cut its prices to what witnesses described in evidence as 'suicide levels': [268] (Colman J). See also *Cutler* (n 8); *The Glendinning* (1943) 76 Ll L Rep 86 (PD); *The Spontaneity* [1962] 1 Lloyd's Rep 460 (PD).
45 *Adams* (n 8).

times to shut the door, and on the fourth attempt he fell out of the train and was injured. The court held that the claimant's conduct was unreasonable. Montague Smith J reasoned that 'if [the claimant] is only suffering some inconvenience, and, to avoid that, he voluntarily runs into danger, and injury ensues, that cannot be said to be the result of the company's negligence'.[46]

The importance of choice is also clearly evident in the cases.[47] For example, in *Corr v IBC Vehicles*, the House of Lords declined to hold that the claimant's suicide was an intervening cause where the claimant was suffering from depression. Lord Bingham based his decision on the fact that 'Mr Corr's suicide was not a voluntary, informed decision'.[48] However, as I outlined in Chapter 6,[49] the claimant will not be held to have acted voluntarily where they were forced to decide under extreme pressure.[50] In these circumstances, the exceptionality rule (and hence, intervening causation) will not apply merely because the claimant made 'an error of judgment in deciding on the best course in difficult circumstances'.[51] There may be some practical overlap here between the issue of choice and the question whether the claimant acted exceptionally in the circumstances. As Baron Martin put it in *Wilson v Newport Dock*, 'very often there is no "usual course of things" in the event of a breach'.[52]

2.3 The effect on damages

Just as with mitigation, it is tempting—but wrong—to apply the 'guillotine heuristic' when determining the effect of an intervening act by the claimant on damages. As I explained in Chapter 2, the guillotine heuristic assumes that the court simply 'chops off' recovery for any losses that were actually incurred as a result of the claimant's unreasonable conduct. Another way of conceiving of this effect (which is equally wrong) is that the court simply 'stops the clock' at the time of the claimant's unreasonable conduct and denies damages for any harms that were suffered afterwards. Instead, the better view, as I explained in the context of the avoidable loss rule, avoided loss rule and market rule in Chapters 8 to 10, is that the replication and exceptionality rules result in a counterfactual assessment of damages, as if the claimant had replicated its no-breach position in the usual way. This

[46] ibid 742. See also 741 (Byles J).

[47] See also, in relation to the mental capacity of children Edelman (ed), *McGregor on Damages* (21st edn, Sweet & Maxwell 2022) [8-099]–[8-100].

[48] *Corr* (n 8) [16]. See also [42] (Lord Walker).

[49] See further Chapter 6, text to n 63.

[50] See *Symrise AG v Baker & McKenzie* [2015] EWHC 912 (Comm), [2016] 1 All ER (Comm) 603 [80] (Burton J), rejecting an argument along these lines, on the basis that 'there was no time pressure'. See also *Jones v Boyce* (1816) 1 Stark 493, 171 ER 540; *United States Shipping Board v Laird Line Ltd* [1924] AC 286 (HL); *The Oropesa* (n 33); *Sayers v Harlow UDC* [1958] 1 WLR 623 (CA).

[51] *Baron Vernon v SS Metagama (The Metagama)* (1928) SC (HL) 21 (HL) 26 (Viscount Haldane).

[52] *Wilson v Newport Dock Co* (1865–66) LR 1 Ex 177 (Ex Ch) 184 (Baron Martin).

counterfactual assessment is similarly evident in the cases involving intervening acts by the claimant.

For example, in *Stacey v Autosleeper*, the Court of Appeal held that the claimant's unreasonable conduct when resolving a dispute with a third party (that had arisen as a result of the defendant's breach) amounted to an intervening cause.[53] But for this conduct, mediation with the third party would not have been necessary. However, Floyd LJ held that 'Nevertheless this did not mean that the judge was bound to disallow all costs after the mediation', because 'if the claimant had acted reasonably, the [other costs of resolving the dispute] would still have been incurred'.[54] Similarly, in *McKew v Holland*,[55] the House of Lords did not simply 'chop off' recovery for the consequences of the claimant's broken ankle, or 'stop the clock' at the time of their fall, which resulted from their own voluntary and abnormal conduct. Instead, the £200 damages award was calculated based on the costs that would have been incurred anyway as a result of the claimant's original injury for which the defendant was responsible, including loss of earnings following the fall.

There are other cases where the guillotine heuristic appears more plausible but still fails close inspection. In *The Egyptian*, the defendants collided with the claimant's ship. The claimants did not inspect or repair the damage, and the ship later sank. The defendant was held liable for the original damage but not the sinking.[56] On its face, the result could be consistent with the 'guillotine heuristic' because the claimant was denied recovery for the events that happened following their failure to inspect the initial damage. However, the better view is that the House of Lords undertook a counterfactual analysis and asked itself what would have happened if the ship had been repaired. As their Lordships put it, 'the mischief could have been remedied' and if it had been, the ship would not have sunk.[57] They also made clear that if the judge's finding had instead been that despite attempting repair the ship would still have sunk, they would have held the defendants responsible for the total loss of the ship.

Another example which at first seems to point towards the 'guillotine heuristic' is found in *Wandsworth LBC v Railtrack*.[58] In this case, the claimant council was denied full recovery for the costs incurred cleaning up pigeon excrement from its pavement where pigeons had roosted under the defendant's railway bridge (leading to an actionable private nuisance). It was held that following the defendant's offer to permit abatement, the claimant could have mitigated by taking

53 *Stacey v Autosleeper Group Ltd* [2014] EWCA Civ 1551.
54 ibid [25].
55 *McKew* (n 8).
56 *The Egyptian* (n 9).
57 ibid, 402 (Lord Atkinson) and 403 (Lord Shaw).
58 *Wandsworth London Borough Council v Railtrack plc* [2001] 1 WLR 368 (QB). Gibbs J's decision on damages was upheld in the Court of Appeal: [2001] EWCA Civ 1236, [2002] QB 756 [26] (Kennedy LJ).

steps to pigeon-proof the bridge. While the claimant was entitled to pavement-cleaning costs up to the date at which the defendants had given permission to abate the nuisance, they were not recoverable thereafter. This rested on a finding that the extra cleaning costs could have been avoided entirely if the claimants had proofed the bridge.[59]

Whilst again this result could be interpreted as 'chopping off' the additional cleaning costs, or 'stopping the clock' on damages once the defendant permitted abatement, instead it is better to view the damages as the product of a counter-factual assessment as if the claimant had taken the relevant mitigating steps. For example, Gibbs J correctly asked whether, had the claimants acted to pigeon-proof the bridge, further cleaning costs would still have been incurred. On the facts, the answer to that question was 'No'. But suppose the claimant had adduced evidence to the effect that the pigeon-proofing would only have been partially effective. If the judge had accepted that evidence, then it would have followed that some pavement-cleaning costs would still have been incurred even if the claimant had taken steps to replicate its no-breach position as nearly as possible. In those circumstances, these hypothetical costs ought still to have been recoverable.

3 Betterment

The doctrine conventionally known as 'betterment' is also an aspect of mitigation.[60] Specifically, betterment applies where the claimant chose to put itself in a *better* position than if the breach had not occurred, or in other words to *supersede* its no-breach position. It thus involves an application of the replication rule. In this regard, it is important to note that even if it was not possible to replicate the no-breach position exactly, betterment will nevertheless apply where the claimant made a choice to *supersede* the position that would have replicated the no-breach position as nearly as possible.[61] However, properly understood, betterment only applies where the claimant *could* have put itself in a position that was closer to the no-breach position but *chose* not to. This element of choice is crucial and reflects the application of the replication rule.[62]

Where betterment applies, damages are assessed counterfactually as if the claimant had replicated (rather than superseded) its no-breach position with a direct equivalent or, if a direct equivalent was unavailable, with goods or services

[59] See also *Howmet Ltd v Economy Devices Ltd* [2016] EWCA Civ 847.

[60] As Kramer puts it, 'The rule of betterment is the flip side of the principle of mitigation': Kramer, *Contract Damages* (3rd edn) (n 12) [4-212].

[61] For further discussion of this 'as nearly as possible' element, see Chapter 9, Section 2.4.

[62] *Lagden v O'Connor* [2003] UKHL 64, [2004] 1 AC 1067 [34] (Lord Hope); *Thai Airways International Public Co Ltd v KI Holdings Co Ltd (formerly Koito Industries Ltd)* [2015] EWHC 1250 (Comm) [71] (Leggatt J).

more closely matching the description of those that the claimant was originally entitled to.[63] This applies with respect to both the costs and benefits of the hypothetical replacement. By contrast, where the claimant had no choice but to supersede, because replication with a direct or closer equivalent to the no-breach position was unavailable, the betterment doctrine has no application and the claimant will recover for its factual loss, for better or worse.[64] This assessment of factual loss will include any expenses incurred in the attempt at replication, but it must also take into account any 'real pecuniary advantage' obtained as a result of superseding the no-breach position.[65]

3.1 Claimant chose to supersede

Where betterment is in issue, it must first be determined whether the claimant chose to go further than was necessary to replicate its no-breach position as nearly as possible. The importance of choice in this context was aptly captured by Leggatt J in *Thai Airways v KI Holdings*, where he held that 'there is a general expectation that, where more than one option is reasonably available, the claimant will adopt the one which is or is likely to be the least expensive. If the claimant in fact chooses a different option, the additional cost (or benefit) of doing so will again be treated as a consequence of the claimant's choice and not of the defendant's wrong.'[66] As Pearson LJ put it in the earlier decision of *Darbishire v Warran*, the claimant is not entitled to 'charge the defendant by way of damages with any greater sum than that which he reasonably needs to expand for the purpose of making good the loss. In short, he is fully entitled to be as extravagant as he pleases but not at the expense of the defendant.'[67]

A helpful illustration of a claimant choosing to go beyond what was necessary to replicate the no-breach position as nearly as possible is the case of *Sunlife Europe Properties v Tiger Aspect Holdings*.[68] There, the tenant failed to comply with a repair covenant by leaving several elements of the property in disrepair after it

[63] See eg *Dimond v Lovell* [2002] 1 AC 384 (HL) 402–03 (Lord Hoffmann); *Sunlife Europe Properties Ltd v Tiger Aspect Holdings Ltd* [2013] EWHC 463 (TCC), 147 Con LR 105 [37] (Edwards-Stuart J); *Stevens v Equity Syndicate Management Ltd* [2015] EWCA Civ 93, [2015] 4 All ER 458 [39] (Kitchin LJ).

[64] See eg *The Gazelle* (1844) 166 ER 759; *The Pactolus* (1856) 166 ER 1079; *Harbutt's Plasticine Ltd v Wayne Tank & Pump Co Ltd* [1970] 1 QB 447 (CA); *Dominion Mosaics & Tile Co v Trafalgar Trucking Co* [1990] 2 All ER 246 (CA); *Lagden* (n 62).

[65] *Voaden v Champion (The Baltic Surveyor)* [2002] EWCA Civ 89, [2002] 1 Lloyd's Rep 623 [85] (Rix LJ); *Thai Airways* (n 62) [81] (Leggatt J). See also the explanation of *British Westinghouse Electric & Manufacturing Co Ltd v Underground Electric Railways Co of London Ltd (No 2)* [1912] AC 673 (HL) on this basis in *Hussey v Eels* [1990] 2 QB 227 (CA) 236 (Mustill LJ) and *Thai Airways* (n 62) [76] (Leggatt J).

[66] *Thai Airways* (n 62) [36].

[67] *Darbishire v Warran* [1963] 1 WLR 1067 (CA) 1057 (Pearson LJ).

[68] *Sunlife* (n 63).

had vacated the property upon expiry of the lease. The landlord carried out and sought compensation for the total recovering of the roof. The judge held that this amounted to an unnecessary supersession and limited recovery on the basis of partial recovering or 'patch repairs'.[69] In other words, while the works carried out by the claimant were 'reasonable' in the ordinary sense, insofar as it may have been a sensible business decision to take the opportunity to upgrade and future-proof the property, this did not equate to the works being necessary to restore the building into the condition it would have been in had it not been for the defendant's breach of contract.[70]

In *Thai Airways*, the claimant airline sought damages for the breach of three contracts made with the defendant manufacturer of airplane seats.[71] Some seats were delivered late and others were never delivered. This meant that, among other things, the claimant was unable to make use of five brand new aircraft until it was able to procure seats from another supplier around 18 months later. In the meantime, the claimant leased replacement aircraft from another airline, under a three-year contract. One issue was whether the claimant could recover damages for the entirety of this leasing period. Leggatt J held that it could not. This was because the claimant had always expected the replacement seats to arrive within two years and the claimant could have entered into a two-year lease if it had wished.[72] The extra year on the leases was thus amounted to a choice by the claimants (even though driven by sensible commercial considerations) for which the defendant was not responsible.[73]

3.2 Claimant had no choice but to supersede

In cases where the claimant had no choice but to supersede its no-breach position, betterment does not apply, again reflecting the way the replication rule works. For the same reason, there is also an affinity here with the application of the market rule. For example, where the claimant has purchased replacement goods that are of higher value—because they are better quality—than the goods it had originally contracted for, its damages may nevertheless be measured by reference to the actual cost of this replacement. The outcome depends on whether goods that more closely matched the description of the original goods were available at the time when the claimant first had an opportunity to resort to the market.[74] If there was no available market for such goods, betterment will not apply because the claimant

[69] ibid [97] (Edwards Stuart J).
[70] ibid [45].
[71] *Thai Airways* (n 62).
[72] ibid [55].
[73] ibid [62].
[74] *Lagden* (n 62) [34].

had no choice but to supersede. Another way of framing this would be to say that in such circumstances, the claimant did in fact replicate its no-breach position as nearly as possible.

Thai Airways again provides a helpful illustration.[75] As part of its response to the defendant's late delivery and non-delivery of aircraft seats, the claimant airline purchased replacement seats that were lighter (and therefore better) than the original. Leggatt J held that the claimant could recover the actual cost of these seats. The implication—although Leggatt J did not make any express finding on this point—is that in the circumstances it was not open to the claimant to buy any other seats that were closer to the original specification. Accordingly, it seems that the claimant had no choice but to supersede.[76] As I explain further below,[77] although the claimant was able to recover for the actual cost of the replacement seats, it also had to give credit for the real pecuniary benefit obtained from flying with lighter seats. By contrast, if the claimant could have purchased seats closer to the original specification, then damages would instead have been assessed according to this hypothetical replacement, such that the actual costs and benefits of the lighter seats would have been irrelevant.

Another example of a claimant having no choice but to supersede its no-breach position is *The Gazelle*.[78] In this case, the claimant's ship was damaged in a collision with the defendant's ship due to the latter's negligence. As a result, the claimant had repaired the ship and replaced the items that were destroyed with new ones, effectively putting themself in a better position than if the breach had not occurred, since the replacements were in a better state and of greater longevity than the items that had been destroyed. The actual cost of the replacements were held to be recoverable (with no deduction for the additional benefit) on the basis that '. . . if that party derives incidentally a greater benefit than mere indemnification, it arises only from the impossibility of otherwise effecting such indemnification without exposing him to some loss or burden, which the law will not place upon him'.[79]

3.3 The effect on damages

Where betterment applies, because the claimant made a choice to supersede its no-breach position, the actual cost incurred by the claimant is not recoverable but nor are any of the benefits actually accruing to the claimant taken into account.

[75] *Thai Airways* (n 62). For a summary of the facts, see text to n 71 above.

[76] Again, one could alternatively say that the claimants did in fact replicate their no-breach position *as nearly as possible*. The effect of these alternative framings is the same: either way the replication rule does not apply.

[77] Text to n 89.

[78] Note 64. For other examples involving 'new for old' replacements, see also *Harbutt's Plasticine* (n 64); *Dominion Mosaics* (n 64); and *Bacon v Cooper (Metals) Ltd* [1982] 1 All ER 397 (QB).

[79] *The Gazelle* (n 64) 760 (Dr Lushington).

Instead, just as with the replication rule, damages are assessed on a counterfactual basis as if the claimant had replicated its no-breach position by obtaining a direct or more closely matching substitute.[80] Consequently, the fact that the claimant has chosen to carry out more extensive work than is needed does not prevent it from recovering the (hypothetical) costs that would have been necessary to replicate its no-breach position as nearly as possible.[81] Accordingly, in *Thai Airways*, Leggatt J correctly awarded damages as if the claimant had entered into two-year leases instead of three-year ones,[82] and expressly left out of account the value of the benefits that the claimant had actually obtained from the leases in the third year.[83]

Most of the complexity and confusion around so-called deductions for 'betterment' arises in cases where the claimant did *not* have any choice but to supersede its no-breach position, and hence the betterment rule as such does not apply. In these cases, just as with the (non-)application of the replication rule discussed in preceding chapters, there is no reason to displace assessment of the claimant's factual loss. This means that the claimant will be entitled to recover damages for the actual costs of the steps that they took but must—where these can be quantified—also give credit for the value of any benefits or savings that they derived compared with their no-breach position. The challenge is typically to determine whether there was in fact any net benefit from the steps that the claimant took, in circumstances where the benefits may be difficult to quantify. Here, the courts have consistently held that benefits are only deductible if they amount to a 'real pecuniary benefit'.[84]

The classic case where benefits were deducted in circumstances where the claimant had no choice but to supersede its no-breach position (and hence, the replication rule did not apply), is *British Westinghouse Electric v Underground Electric Railways*.[85] The facts and decision are discussed in detail in Chapter 1.[86] To give a very brief recap: the defendant delivered defective machines and the claimant purchased replacements that were more efficient; when the case reached the House of Lords, Viscount Haldane held that the claimant could recover for the cost of the replacement machines but must also give credit for the benefit obtained.[87]

[80] *Riyad Bank v Ahli United Bank (UK) Plc* [2006] 2 All ER (Comm) 777 [170] (CA) (Moore-Bick J); *Carmel Southend Ltd v Strachan & Henshaw Ltd* [2007] EWHC 1289 (TCC) [49] and [54] (Coulson J). In Australia, see *Tyco Australia Pty Ltd v Optus Networks Pty Ltd* [2004] NSWCA 333 [261].

[81] *Sunlife* (n 63) [46] (Edwards Stuart J).

[82] *Thai Airways* (n 62) [62] (Leggatt J).

[83] ibid [98].

[84] *The Baltic Surveyor* (n 65) [85] (Rix LJ). See also *Thai Airways* (n 62) [81] where Leggatt J referred to a 'monetary benefit', meaning 'a benefit which either takes the form of money or which the claimant could reasonably be expected to realise in terms of money'.

[85] Note 65.

[86] See further Chapter 1, Section 3.2. See also Andrew Dyson, 'British Westinghouse Revisited' [2012] Lloyd's Maritime and Commercial Law Quarterly 412.

[87] *British Westinghouse* (n 65). Also note Buckley LJ's dissent in the Court of Appeal, where he stated that the arbitrator should have asked whether machines of equivalent specification were available: [1912] 3 KB 128 (CA), 148.

The case has sometimes been misinterpreted as one in which the claimant chose to take steps that were not 'required' in mitigation.[88] However, the correct understanding is that the claimant did no more than replicate its no breach position as nearly as possible, such that there were no grounds for displacing an assessment of its factual loss. As Leggatt J put it in *Thai Airways*:

> what distinguishes the *British Westinghouse* case from [other cases in which benefits were ignored] is not that London Underground had a relevant choice but that the benefit which they obtained was pecuniary. Where a claimant as a result of a step reasonably taken to mitigate its loss receives money which it would not have received if the defendant had performed the contract, justice requires the sum received to be brought into account in the calculation of damages whether its receipt was an unavoidable consequence of mitigation or not. That is because money is entirely fungible.[89]

The facts of *Thai Airways* itself also provide a good example. As explained above, following the defendant's breach, the claimant airline purchased replacement seats that were lighter than those originally specified.[90] As Leggatt J reasoned: 'It is not in dispute that . . . installing lighter seats will save fuel. The issues are whether the amounts of money saved can be quantified and whether [the defendant] is entitled to claim the benefit of such savings as a matter of law.'[91] In relation to one batch of replacement seats (the 'ZIM' seats) he held that it could be.[92] Consequently, although the claimants were permitted to recover the additional cost of the seats,[93] they also had to give credit for the 'financial saving' that the claimant had obtained in the form of lower expected fuel costs.[94] Leggatt J's rationale, correctly, was that 'money is entirely fungible. Thus, there is generally no material difference between incurring a cost which results in the receipt of money back and simply incurring a lower cost.'[95]

These cases involving a real pecuniary benefit can be contrasted with examples where the benefit was non-pecuniary or otherwise not capable of quantification. In *British Westinghouse*, in the Court of Appeal, Buckley LJ gave the hypothetical example of a man having no choice but to purchase a first-class ticket as a result of

[88] See eg Harvey McGregor (ed), *Mayne and McGregor on Damages* (12th edn, Sweet & Maxwell 1961), and subsequent editions.

[89] *Thai Airways* (n 62) [76]. See also *Dimond* (n 63) 401–402 (Lord Hoffmann); and *Hussey* (n 65) 236 (Mustill LJ).

[90] Text to n 75.

[91] *Thai Airways* (n 62) [143].

[92] In relation to another batch of seats (the 'Recaro' seats), Leggatt J held that there was insufficient evidence of any financial saving: ibid [158]. On this issue, the burden of proof was on the defendant: [144].

[93] ibid [141]–[142].

[94] ibid [152].

[95] ibid [76].

a breach of contract where he was originally supposed to take a third-class ticket.[96] He concluded that in these circumstances damages should be awarded for the whole sum of the first-class ticket, notwithstanding the greater luxury of travel experienced as a result. In *Thai Airways*, Leggatt J expressly rationalized this kind of example on the basis that 'it is not a benefit which either takes the form of money or which [the traveller] could readily realise or be expected to realise in terms of money'.[97] As some commentators have criticized, this has the effect of leaving the claimant in a better position than if the breach had not occurred.[98] However, it is important to note that the law has this effect only where the benefit was not chosen by the claimant, because no closer substitute was available.

Finally, in some cases it may be unclear whether or not the claimant obtained a real pecuniary advantage from steps taken in mitigation, in circumstances where it had no choice but to supersede its no-breach position. For example, in *The Baltic Surveyor*, the defendant damaged the claimant's pontoon.[99] The original (undamaged) pontoon only had a remaining lifespan of eight years, whereas the replacement would last thirty years.[100] The Court of Appeal upheld the trial judge's award of 8/30ths of the cost of the new pontoon, which sought to account for this benefit. By contrast, in *Harbutt's Plasticine*, where the claimant's factory was destroyed and replaced with a new one, no deduction was given for the benefit.[101] In *The Baltic Surveyor*, Rix LJ explained the difference on the basis that 'buildings are such potentially long-lived objects that the mere newness of a building may be entirely by the way'.[102] In *Thai Airways*, Leggatt J concurred with Rix LJ's explanation, but added that 'The position would have been different if it had been shown, for example, that the new factory would cost less to run'.[103] Accordingly, this issue appears highly fact-sensitive, although the principle is tolerably clear.

4 Remoteness

It has been noted that 'the relationship between remoteness. . . and mitigation is somewhat obscure'.[104] In *Smith New Court Securities*, Lord Steyn stated that 'they

[96] *British Westinghouse (CA)* (n 87), 147. See also *Hinde v Liddell* (1874–75) LR 10 QB 265.
[97] *Thai Airways* (n 62) [80].
[98] See eg Ogus, *The Law of Damages* (Butterworths 1973) 134. cf Burrows, *Remedies* (4th edn) (n 6) 218.
[99] *The Baltic Surveyor* (n 65).
[100] ibid [62].
[101] Note 64. See also *Dominion Mosaics* (n 64) and *Bacon v Cooper* (n 78). Contrast the Australian case of *Hoad v Scone Motors Pty Ltd* [1977] 1 NSWLR 88.
[102] *The Baltic Surveyor* (n 65) [85].
[103] *Thai Airways* (n 62) [79].
[104] Kramer, *Contract Damages* (3rd edn) (n 12) [15-39]. See also David Winterton, *Money Awards in Contract Law* (Hart Publishing 2015) 253.

are distinct legal concepts',[105] but in *Platform Home Loans*, Lord Hobhouse considered that '[t]here is a close relationship . . . the same result can often be justified or formulated in any of these. . . ways'.[106] In my view, remoteness is distinct from mitigation, in that it reflects different (non-causal) principles and has different requirements and effects. At a practical level, remoteness differs in several respects from mitigation, including that the rules have a different scope and requirements, and remoteness (unlike mitigation) differs according to the cause of action, and can also apply to the claimant's no-breach position. At a more theoretical level, remoteness also differs from mitigation because it operates as a true limitation on damages, rather than a rule that defines the extent of the loss caused.

Despite these differences, remoteness and mitigation have often been conflated. The most direct example comes from Templeman LJ's judgment in *The Borag*, where he stated that 'in some circumstances different principles may require different tests and produce different results, but in the present case, if the interest charges were unreasonable—they were too remote; they were not caused by the breach; they were not part of a reasonable form of mitigation—all these matters hang together'.[107] It is true that the application of mitigation and remoteness can overlap.[108] This is especially true with the exceptionality rule, because very often a claimant who acts in an exceptional manner will also be acting unforeseeably. Overlap is also common in relation to sale of goods cases where sub-sales are concerned.[109] However, the fact that both doctrines can arise on the same set of facts does not necessarily mean that they share any common theoretical basis.

4.1 What is remoteness?

The nature and content of the rules on remoteness are, at least in contract, the subject of some controversy. The leading authority is the case of *Hadley v Baxendale*,[110] from which discussions of remoteness typically begin. In that case, Alderson B articulated the rule that damages for breaches of contract should compensate those losses 'as may fairly and reasonably be considered arising either naturally. . . from the breach of contract itself, or such as may reasonably be supposed to have been in

[105] *Smith New Court Securities Ltd v Scrimgeour Vickers* [1996] UKHL 3 (HL) 248. See also *The Borag* [1981] 1 WLR 274, 285 (Templeman LJ).

[106] *Platform Home Loans Ltd v Oyston Shipways Ltd* [2000] 2 AC 190 (HL) 208. Lord Hobhouse's speech in fact referred to causation (along with remoteness and contributory negligence), rather than mitigation. But, as this book has sought to argue, the latter is merely one aspect of the former. See also *County Ltd v Girozentrale Securities* [1996] 3 All ER 834 (CA) 857–58 (Hobhouse LJ); *Kuwait Airways Corp v Iraqi Airways Co (No 6)* [2002] UKHL 19, [2002] 2 AC 883 [70] (Lord Nicholls); *Schering Agrochemicals Ltd v Resibel NV SA* (1993) 109 LQR 175.

[107] *The Borag* (n 105) 285.

[108] Edelman (n 47) [6-019].

[109] See eg Chapter 10, text to n 98.

[110] *Hadley v Baxendale* (1854) 156 ER 145.

the contemplation of both parties at the time they made the contract as the probable result of the breach of it'.[111] This type of remoteness doctrine (which has seen considerable development in the case law)[112] can be considered remoteness in the strict sense. However, a looser label of 'remoteness' has also sometime been applied to describe the rules relating to intervening causes, as well as to the so-called 'scope of duty' inquiry. I have already addressed the former above,[113] and deal with the latter in a separate sub-section below.[114]

The basis of remoteness in contract is itself the subject of significant debate.[115] In *The Achilleas*, Lord Hoffmann argued that it was merely part of a broader enquiry into the kinds of losses that the parties had assumed responsibility for. The orthodox view now seems to be that only losses for which the defendant has assumed responsibility will be recoverable, but that '*Hadley v Baxendale* remains a standard rule . . .[,] rationalised on the basis that it reflects the expectation to be imputed to the parties in the ordinary case, i.e. that a contract breaker should ordinarily be liable to the other party for damage resulting from his breach if, but only if, at the time of making the contract a reasonable person in his shoes would have had damage of that kind in mind as not unlikely to result from a breach'.[116] This echoes Lord Hoffmann's view in *The Achilleas* that the rules in *Hadley v Baxendale* are 'intended to give effect to the presumed intentions of the parties and not to contradict them'.[117] Fortunately, I need not comment on this debate here, as what follows applies equally to all of the varying conceptions of remoteness.

In tort, the rules are more straightforward, albeit that the underlying basis is still debatable. A loss will be too remote (ie, the claimant will be unable to recover damages in respect of that head of loss) if it is of a kind that was not reasonably foreseeable at the time of commission of the tort.[118] Foresight of the magnitude of

[111] ibid 151.

[112] See eg *Transfield Shipping Inc v Mercator Shipping Inc (The Achilleas)* [2008] UKHL 48, [2009] 1 AC 61; *Supershield Ltd v Siemens Building Technologies* [2010] EWCA Civ 7, [2010] 1 Lloyd's Rep 349; *John Grimes v Gubbins* [2013] EWCA Civ 37, [2013] PNLR 17; and *AG of the Virgin Islands v Global Water Associates* [2020] UKPC 18.

[113] See further Section 2.

[114] See further Section 4.4.

[115] See eg A Kramer, 'An Agreement-centred Approach to Remoteness and Contract Damages' in N Cohen and E McKendrick (eds), *Comparative Remedies for Breach of Contract* (Hart 2005); A Robertson 'The Basis of the Remoteness Rule in Contract' (2008) 28 Legal Studies 172; Lord Hoffmann 'The Achilleas: Custom and Practice, or Foreseeability?' [2010] Edinburgh Law Review 47; A Burrows, 'Lord Hoffmann and Remoteness in Contract' in P Davies and J Pila (eds), *The Jurisprudence of Lord Hoffmann: A Festschrift in Honour of Lord Leonard Hoffmann* (Hart 2015); and N Venkatesan, 'The Contract Remoteness Rule: Exclusion, Not Assumption of Responsibility' in A Dyson, J Goudkamp, and F Wilmot-Smith (eds), *Defences in Contract* (Hart 2017).

[116] *Supershield* (n 112) [43]. See also *Gubbins* (n 112) [24].

[117] *The Achilleas* (n 112) [24].

[118] *Overseas Tankship (UK) Ltd v Miller Steamship Co Pty Ltd (The Wagon Mound (No 2))* [1967] 1 AC 617; *Cambridge Water Co Ltd v Eastern Counties Leather Plc* [1994] 2 AC 264. Note, however, that when liability—at least for negligence—lies concurrently with contractual liability in respect of the same breach of duty, the contract rules, rather than the tortious rules, will apply: *Wellesley Partners LLP v Withers LLP* [2015] EWCA Civ 1146.

the loss is irrelevant. Only the same kind of loss need be foreseeable, which can put significant pressure on the categorization of losses into types.[119] The remoteness limitation does not apply at all in the tort of deceit, in other words it is sufficient that the loss is a direct consequence of the tort (ie, that there are no breaks in the chain of causation).[120] There are obiter dicta suggesting that this limitation on the scope of remoteness is true of all torts that have been committed in bad faith.[121] The Supreme Court has recently emphasized that the remoteness inquiry, even in tort, is not identical to the '*SAAMCO*' inquiry, which is concerned instead with identifying the scope of the defendant's duty.[122]

4.2 Practical differences

Remoteness and mitigation differ in several practical respects. First, and most obviously, the tests are different in scope and have different requirements. Mitigation, as I have analysed it, exclusively concerns the claimant's post-breach conduct,[123] and applies where that conduct was both voluntary and abnormal. By contrast, remoteness can be triggered both by circumstances that are already extant at the time of the breach and by any kind of post-breach event, including natural events and the conduct of third parties, as well as the conduct of the claimant. Even in relation to the post-breach conduct of the claimant, where the scope of the two doctrines can overlap, remoteness—unlike mitigation—can apply to involuntary conduct. Whilst many cases that trigger the exceptionality rule of mitigation will also trigger the remoteness limitation, the claimant's choice not to replicate the no-breach position can trigger the replication rule without also triggering remoteness, because such conduct may be entirely foreseeable.

Second, unlike mitigation, the remoteness test varies between contract and tort, and does not apply at all in cases of fraud.[124] As I explained in Chapter 7, mitigation is striking in that it applies in exactly the same way across all causes of action, and irrespective of the defendant's fault.[125] This is not just an incidental or trivial distinction. It suggests that there is something more basic or fundamental about mitigation that explains its universal application. I have argued that mitigation's ubiquity is due to its causal nature. By contrast, the fact that remoteness is sensitive to the type of wrongdoing giving rise to the claim indicates that it is a more flexible tool for determining the extent of the defendant's liability. As such, remoteness

[119] See eg *Victoria Laundry (Windsor) v Newman Industries* [1949] 2 KB 528 (CA).
[120] *Smith New Court Securities* (n 105).
[121] *Kuwait Airways* (n 106).
[122] *BPE Solicitors v Hughes-Holland* [2015] UKSC 39, [2015] AC 1663; *Wellesley* (n 118). See further Section 4.4.
[123] See further Chapter 7, Section 4.
[124] See further Section 4.1.
[125] See further Chapter 7, Section 3.

appears to depend on a wider range of factors that go towards balancing the claimant's and defendant's interests, compared with mitigation which is essentially exclusively claimant-focused.

Third, although not commonly remarked upon, it is also worth highlighting that remoteness can apply to assessment of their claimant's no-breach position, as well as their breach position. For example, remoteness may be triggered by an unforeseeable event that actually happened, such as oil fire damage to a wharf.[126] In that case, the counterfactual assessment serves to modify the claimant's breach position by substituting a foreseeable harm instead. But remoteness can also apply to events that did not happen, but which would have happened if the breach had not occurred, such as where the claimant would have earned profits from an unusually lucrative contract.[127] In that case, the effect of remoteness is to modify the claimant's no-breach position. There is no equivalent in relation to mitigation, which only ever concerns the assessment of the claimant's breach position.

4.3 Remoteness as a limitation

At a more theoretical level, the most fundamental difference between remoteness and mitigation is that the former—unlike the latter—functions as a true limitation on damages. In other words, remoteness does not serve to define the extent of the claimant's loss; rather, it comes in only after the claimant's loss has been established (as a result of the application of mitigation, amongst other rules) in order to limit the extent of the defendant's liability.[128] There are several clues that remoteness has this status. First, semantically, judges almost invariably speak in terms of *losses* being too remote, which presupposes the identification of the losses caused. Second, as I discuss further below, remoteness operates asymmetrically: it can only ever restrict liability, never augment it. Third, at least in its modern incarnation, where the remoteness test depends on foreseeability or assumption of responsibility rather than any concept of 'directness', the doctrine is clearly separate from the kinds of causal enquiry used to determine the claimant's loss.

The distinction between remoteness and mitigation is complicated somewhat by the fact that remoteness—like mitigation—can result in a counterfactual assessment. In *Cory v Thames Ironworks*, the defendant was delayed by six months in delivering a hull to the claimant.[129] The hull would normally have been used for storing coal, but the claimant instead planned to install a crane on the hull to use

[126] See eg *Overseas Tankship (UK) Ltd v Morts Dock & Engineering Co (The Wagon Mound)* [1961] AC 388 (PC).
[127] See eg *Victoria Laundry* (n 119).
[128] See eg *John Grimes* (n 112) [17]. See eg Venkatesan (n 115) 189. cf Burrows, *Remedies* (4th edn) (n 6) 84, in which both remoteness and causation are treated together as comparable to 'limits on damages'.
[129] *Cory v Thames Ironworks & Shipbuilding Co Ltd* (1867–68) LR 3 QB 181 (QB).

it for shipping coal. The claimant accepted that this novel use of the hull was unforeseeable; the defendant was therefore not liable for the harm actually suffered by the claimant as a result of the delay. However, Cockburn J instead awarded damages for the hypothetical loss that *would have been* recoverable if the claimant had been planning to use the hull for storing coal (even though this was not in fact the claimant's intention, nor did the claimant suffer loss *on this basis*). Cockburn J justified this counterfactual assessment on the basis that:

> The buyer has lost the larger amount, and there can be no hardship or injustice in making the seller liable to compensate him in damages so far as the seller understood and believed that the article would be applied to the ordinary purposes ...[130]

Numerous other cases have applied this counterfactual element of the remoteness rule.[131] The counterfactual assessment was expressly approved by Lord Reid in *The Heron II*, who described the effect of the rule as 'conjectural'.[132] In *The Forum Craftsman*, Hobhouse J held that 'remoteness of damages in contract cases is not to be decided on an all or nothing basis'.[133] It appears that the same counterfactual approach applies where the claimant's loss, despite not being too remote, is excluded because the defendant did not assume responsibility for it.[134]

Although the remoteness rule can result in a counterfactual assessment, unlike mitigation, its effect is asymmetrical. Substitution of the (actual) unforeseeable event with the (counterfactual) foreseeable event *only* applies where the claimant's 'foreseeable loss' is *less than* its factual loss. Remoteness cannot ever enable the claimant to recover damages greater than its factual loss. This point was directly addressed in *Elbinger v Armstrong*, another case concerning the counterfactual element of remoteness.[135] Blackburn J held that the amount that the claimants 'actually' lost 'forms the extreme limit of the damage they can recover'.[136] This asymmetrical effect must not be confused with the 'inclusionary effect' of the assumption of responsibility test noted by Toulson LJ in *Siemens v Supershield*, which

[130] ibid 190.

[131] See eg *Victoria Laundry* (n 127); *Coastal International Trading v Maroil AG* [1988] 1 Lloyd's Rep 92 (QB) 96 (Leggatt J); *R&H Hall Ltd v WH Pim Junr & Co Ltd* (1928) 30 Ll L Rep 159 (HL) 767 (Viscount Dunedin); *Horne v Midland Railway Co* (1872) LR 7 CP 583 (CP); *Satef-Huttenes Alberns SpA v Paloma Tercera Shipping Co SA (The Pegase)* [1981] 1 Lloyd's Rep 175 (QB) (Goff J); *Islamic Republic of Iran Shipping Lines v Ierax Shipping Co of Panama (The Forum Craftsman)* [1991] 1 Lloyd's Rep 81 (QB) 85–86 (Hobhouse J).

[132] *Koufos v C Czarnikow Ltd (The Heron II)* [1969] 1 AC 350 (HL) 389. See also *Victoria Laundry* (n 127) 543 (Asquith LJ).

[133] *The Forum Craftsman* (n 131) 85.

[134] *The Achilleas* (n 112). The counterfactual element of the final award is explained by Kramer, *Contract Damages* (3rd edn) (n 12) [14-79].

[135] *Elbinger AG v Armstrong* (1874) LR 9 QB 473 (QB).

[136] ibid 479.

merely establishes that the amount of the loss for which the defendant has assumed responsibility may be greater or less than the amount that was foreseeable.[137]

4.4 The 'scope of duty' rule

The so-called 'scope of duty' rule also differs from mitigation. Established in *SAAMCO*, the rule provides that the claimant can only recover damages to the extent that 'the loss fell within the scope of the duty he was owed'.[138] In *Platform Home Loans*, Lord Hobhouse clarified that this principle 'involves an exercise of attribution in relation to the extent of the defendants' legal responsibility for the plaintiffs' basic loss'.[139] In other words, the rule applies at a subsequent stage *after* the assessment of loss.[140] The *SAAMCO* case concerned negligent overvaluation of property used as security for a loan. In this context, the court used the extent of the overvaluation to 'ascertain the maximum amount of loss capable of falling within the valuer's duty of care'.[141] The claimants' damages were limited to the extent of the overvaluation.

In *SAAMCO* itself, Lord Hoffmann held that 'the defendant should not be liable for loss which would have been a consequence of the transaction even if the representation had been true'.[142] On this basis it is sometimes said that the rule effectively limits the defendant's liability to the same extent as if it had warranted the valuation.[143] If this calculation was rigidly adopted, the rule would have counterfactual effect in that the assessment would depend on the position that the claimant *would have been* in if the property had really been worth the sum that the valuer had stated.[144] However, it appears that the test applied is simply the amount of the original overvaluation, which may not equate precisely with the warranty loss.[145] If so, the assessment demanded by the rule is not really counterfactual.

The scope of duty rule operates as a true limitation on damages. In SAAMCO, Lord Hoffmann referenced its 'asymmetry' explicitly.[146] The House of Lords rejected an argument by counsel that the claimant should be able to recover to the

[137] *Supershield* (n 112) [43].

[138] *South Australia Asset Management Corp v York Montague Ltd ('SAAMCO')* [1997] AC 191 (HL) 221, 220 (Lord Hoffmann).

[139] *Platform Home Loans* (n 106) 211–12. See also *SAAMCO* (n 138) 218 (Lord Hoffmann).

[140] *Platform Home Loans* (n 106) 207 (Lord Hobhouse); *SAAMCO* (n 138) 220 (Lord Hoffmann).

[141] *Platform Home Loans* (n 106) 213 (Lord Millett). *Nykredit Mortgage Bank plc v Edward Erdman Group Ltd* [1997] 1 WLR 1627 (HL) 1632 (Lord Nicholls).

[142] *SAAMCO* (n 138) 216.

[143] See eg Jane Stapleton, 'Negligent Valuers and Falls in the Property Market' (1997) 113 Law Quarterly Review 1, 3.

[144] See also Lord Hoffmann's mountaineer example, in which he relied on the events that '*would have occurred* even if the advice had been correct' (emphasis added): *SAAMCO* (n 138) 213.

[145] *Platform Home Loans* (n 106) 207 (Lord Hobhouse). See further Kramer, *Contract Damages* (3rd edn) (n 12) [14-114]–[14-120].

[146] *SAAMCO* (n 138) 218.

extent of the overvaluation regardless of whether the market subsequently went up or down.[147] In the first of the three appeals considered in *SAAMCO*, the claimant's factual loss was just below the overvaluation sum; the claimant recovered only its factual loss.[148] Subsequently, in *Nykredit*, Lord Hoffmann reiterated that although the rule may lead to recovery less than the claimant's factual loss, 'it is of course also the case that the lender cannot recover if he is, on balance, in a better or no worse position then if he had not entered into the transaction at all. He will have suffered no loss.'[149] Moreover, in *BPE Solicitors*, Lord Sumption stated that the *SAAMCO* cap, unlike the account of mitigation that I have put forward, 'has nothing to do with the causation of loss.'[150]

5 Contributory Negligence

Mitigation and contributory negligence both seem to respond to the same kinds of concern: they deal with questions about how the claimant's own conduct has affected the outcome in respect of which damages are sought. However, on the orthodox understanding of both doctrines, there are also some key differences. First, it is often claimed that mitigation and contributory negligence differ in their temporal applications: broadly, contributory negligence is thought to apply to the claimant's pre-breach conduct whereas mitigation applies post-breach. Second, it is acknowledged that mitigation can apply even though the claimant's conduct was not blameworthy, whereas contributory negligence is explicitly fault-based. Third, contributory negligence results in apportionment, whereas (on the orthodox account) mitigation serves to prevent recovery of discrete heads of loss.

I take a different view. Contributory negligence and mitigation can overlap, both in terms of their temporal application and the kinds of conduct to which they apply. However, their legal effects are mutually inconsistent because they rest on opposing models of causal responsibility for harm: whereas mitigation reflects a binary attribution of causal responsibility, contributory negligence under the Law Reform (Contributory Negligence) Act 1945 reflects a model of concurrent causal responsibility. Consequently, it is not possible to cumulate the legal effects of the two doctrines by applying both on the same facts. Instead, it is necessary to address head-on which doctrine should have primacy, where both apply. I argue that the answer to this question is uncertain as a matter of direct authority, but that the better view is mitigation.

[147] ibid 220.

[148] ibid 222–24.

[149] *Nykredit* (n 141) 1638 (Lord Hoffmann). See also *Platform Home Loans* (n 106) 213 (Lord Millett): 'The recoverable damages are limited to the lesser of the amounts produced by the two calculations.'

[150] *BPE Solicitors* (n 122) [36].

Before developing this analysis, it is important to highlight that whereas mitigation is of universal application in claims for damages regardless of the cause of action,[151] contributory negligence is much more limited in scope. Contributory negligence does not apply to contract claims unless the defendant has a concurrent duty of care in tort.[152] Furthermore, it is inapplicable to intentional torts such as deceit and trespass to the person,[153] and to claims for conversion under the Torts (Interference with Goods) Act 1977,[154] even where the conversion is unintentional.[155] Although it may be fruitful to explore these differences further, here I focus my analysis on causes of action where it is settled that both contributory negligence and mitigation are applicable, most importantly the tort of negligence.

5.1 Temporal scope

The most commonly cited difference between contributory negligence and mitigation concerns their temporal application: it is thought that contributory negligence (only) applies to pre-breach conduct, whereas mitigation (only) applies to post-breach conduct.[156] On this view, contributory negligence and mitigation have mutually exclusive applications, and the boundary is marked by the occurrence of the defendant's breach of duty, or arguably the time when the claimant becomes aware of the defendant's breach. Indeed, Glanville Williams concluded that the timing of the claimant's conduct was the *only* difference between contributory negligence and mitigation, and that apart from this distinction 'the conditions necessary to bring the two doctrines into operation are very similar, if not identical.'[157]

Even if this temporal distinction was once an accurate description of the law,[158] it is certainly not any longer. There is now extensive judicial authority that contributory negligence, like mitigation, can apply to the claimant's post-breach conduct.[159] One of the clearest examples is *Spencer v Wincanton Holdings*, the facts of

[151] See further Chapter 7, Section 3.

[152] *Forsikringsaktieselskapet Vesta v Butcher* [1988] 3 WLR 565 (CA), affirming the decision of Hobhouse J [1986] 2 All ER 488 (QB) 508; *Barclays Bank Plc v Fairclough Building Ltd* [1995] QB 214 (CA).

[153] *Standard Chartered Bank v Pakistan National Shipping Corp (No 2)* [2002] UKHL 43, [2003] 1 AC 959 (deceit); *Co-operative Group (CWS) Ltd v Pritchard* [2011] EWCA Civ 329, [2012] QB 320 (battery and assault).

[154] s 11.

[155] For criticism of this restriction, see Burrows, *Remedies* (4th edn) (n 6) 135.

[156] See eg Edelman (n 47) [4-018]. See also in Australia: *Ackland v Commonwealth of Australia* [2007] NSWCA 250 [142]–[145] (Ipp JA).

[157] Glanville Williams, *Joint Torts and Contributory Negligence: A Study of Concurrent Fault in Great Britain, Ireland and the Common-Law Dominions* (Stevens & Sons 1977) 282.

[158] WVH Rogers, *Winfield and Jolowicz on Tort* (18th edn, Sweet & Maxwell 2010) [6-46] fn 345: '[B]efore the [1945 Act], the courts seem to have regarded contributory negligence as something that related to the occurrence of the initial injury and mitigation as relating to the time after that occurrence.'

[159] In addition to the authorities discussed below, see eg *Owners of Swedish MS Carlsholm v Owners of Liberian Steamship Calliope (The Calliope)* [1970] P 172; *Barings Plc (In Liquidation) v Coopers &*

which were outlined above.[160] The focus of the Court of Appeal's decision was on the question whether (just as in *McKew v Holland*)[161] the claimant's conduct had constituted an intervening cause. The court unanimously held that it did not, but nevertheless upheld the trial judge's decision to reduce damages by one third for contributory negligence.[162] Aikens LJ stated that 'the judge's conclusion . . . that Wincanton is liable for the consequences of the second accident, subject to a reduction for Mr Spencer's contributory negligence, cannot be faulted'.[163] The claimant's decision to walk around the forecourt without his prosthesis occurred long after the defendant's breach, and hence the finding of contributory negligence clearly depended on the doctrine's application to post-breach fault.

Similarly, the House of Lords tacitly assumed that contributory negligence could apply to post-breach conduct in *Corr v IBC Vehicles*.[164] In that case the claimant committed suicide following depression caused by an injury that he had sustained at work as a result of his employer's negligence. Whilst their Lordships declined to reduce damages for contributory negligence because it had not been argued before them, they were unanimously prepared to assume that contributory negligence might apply to the claimant's suicide provided that his conduct could, on the facts, appropriately be characterized as blameworthy.[165] None of their Lordships raised any suggestion that contributory negligence might as a matter of principle be inapplicable to post-tort conduct.

5.2 Conduct

Williams concluded that the conduct necessary to trigger contributory negligence and mitigation was identical: 'Both presuppose negligent or unreasonable conduct on the part of the plaintiff; reasonable conduct amounts neither to contributory negligence nor to a breach of the duty to mitigate damages.'[166] However, this view assumes that 'reasonableness' has the same meaning in both contexts. I have argued that in mitigation, the so-called reasonableness test is better understood in

Lybrand (No 8) [2003] EWHC 2371 (Ch) [892]; *Sayers v Harlow UDC* [1958] 1 WLR 623 (CA); *Calvert v William Hill Credit Ltd* [2008] EWCA Civ 1427; [2009] Ch 330 [71]; *Smith v Badenoch* [1970] SASR 9 (SC).

160 *Spencer* (n 40). See further text to n 40.
161 *McKew* (n 8).
162 Sedley LJ recorded that the claimant's application to cross-appeal against the finding of contributory negligence had been rejected by Smith LJ on sight of the papers; however, none of the judges on the appellate panel expressed any reservations about this decision: *Spencer* (n 40) [8].
163 ibid [47].
164 *Corr* (n 8).
165 ibid [22] (Lord Bingham); [32] (Lord Scott); [44] (Lord Walker); [47] (Lord Mance); [58] (Lord Neuberger).
166 Williams (n 157) 282.

terms of 'choice' and 'abnormality'. Neither of these concepts are fault-based: mitigation does not prescribe that the claimant *should* replicate their no-breach position in the usual way, and choosing not to do so does not (of itself) imply any fault or 'failure' by the claimant. By contrast, contributory negligence is expressly fault-based. The 1945 Act provides that:

> Where any person suffers damage *as the result partly of his own fault* and partly of the fault of any other person or persons . . . the damages recoverable in respect thereof shall be reduced to such extent as the court thinks just and equitable having regard to the claimant's share in the responsibility for the damage.[167]

However, it is important to note that whilst fault forms the gateway to the 1945 Act, the resulting apportionment depends on 'the claimant's share in responsibility for damage', which subsequent cases have held requires consideration of both the 'blameworthiness' of the claimant's conduct (meaning fault)[168] and also its 'causal potency'.[169] Historically, contributory negligence has had a close affinity with causation. In *Caswell v Powell Duffryn Associated Collieries*, Lord Atkin stated that he found it 'impossible to divorce any theory of contributory negligence from the concept of causation'.[170] In his account of the process leading up to the 1945 Act, Mitchell argues that 'if we are aiming to interpret the 1945 Act in the light of what can be discerned as Parliament's intentions, we should be thinking in terms of broad causal responsibility for damage'.[171]

If mitigation and contributory negligence are both ultimately concerned with the attribution of causal responsibility for harm, as well as temporally overlapping, this brings into even sharper focus the question of whether they apply to the same kinds of conduct. In *Spencer v Wincanton Holdings*, Aikens LJ held that 'the line between a set of facts which results in a finding of contributory negligence and a set of facts which results in a finding that the "unreasonable conduct" of the claimant constitutes a novus actus interveniens is not, in my view, capable of precise definition'.[172] In turn, given that (as I have argued) mitigation and intervening acts by the claimant are part of the same doctrine, it follows to ask whether the application of mitigation will necessarily coincide with the application of contributory negligence, and vice versa.

[167] s 1(1), Law Reform (Contributory Negligence) Act 1945. Section 4 provides that 'negligence, breach of statutory duty or other act or omission which gives rise to a liability in tort or would, apart from this Act, give rise to the defence of contributory negligence'. Accordingly, 'fault' appears to include failures to take reasonable care according to the negligence standard.

[168] *Corr* (n 8) [21] (Lord Bingham).

[169] *Davies v Swan Motor Co (Swansea) Ltd* [1949] 2 KB 291 (CA) 326 (Denning LJ); *Stapley v Gypsum Mines Ltd* [1953] AC 663 (HL) 682.

[170] *Caswell v Powell Duffryn Associated Collieries Ltd* [1940] AC 152 (HL) 165. See also J Charlesworth and RA Percy, *Charlesworth & Percy on Negligence* (12th edn, Sweet & Maxwell 2010) [4-19].

[171] Paul Mitchell, *A History of Tort Law 1900–1950* (CUP 2015) ch 13.

[172] *Spencer* (n 40) [45].

In *Corr v IBC Vehicles*, Lord Bingham held that 'consistently with my rejection of arguments based on novus actus and unreasonable conduct, I would similarly absolve the deceased from any causal responsibility for his own tragic death. I would accordingly assess his contributory negligence at 0%.'[173] This implies that at least in relation to post-breach conduct, if the claimant's conduct is not sufficiently exceptional to count as an intervening act, then it will also not be contributorily negligent. However, in *Spencer v Wincanton Holdings*, the Court of Appeal expressly held that the reverse is not true: ie a finding of contributory negligence does not dictate that the claimant's conduct amounted to an intervening act.[174] This stands to reason, since contributory negligence requires a finding of fault, which the exceptionality rule (and replication rule) does not.

Finally, one might think that contributory negligence only applies to conduct which contributes to the occurrence of the accident, rather than to the extent of the claimant's damage.[175] However, it is clear that the doctrine is not so limited. For example, in *Davies v Swan Motor Co*, there was a collision between an omnibus and a dust-cart.[176] The claimant's husband, who had been negligently standing on the dust-cart's steps, was crushed and killed. Although his conduct in no way contributed to the accident (it merely exacerbated his resulting injuries), contributory negligence was applied and the damages payable to his widow were reduced by one-fifth.[177] Furthermore, the archetypal instances of contributory negligence such as failure to wear a seatbelt or crash-helmet both involve contribution only to the damage, not to the initial accident.[178]

5.3 Legal effect

Burrows has distinguished contributory negligence and mitigation on the basis that the former yields a 'partial' reduction in damages whereas the latter is an 'all-or-nothing' rule:

[173] *Corr* (n 8) [22].

[174] *Spencer* (n 40) [46].

[175] In an illuminating article, Field suggests a subtly different distinction, that contributory negligence applies to conduct contributing to the claimant's 'damage', but not to conduct contributing to the indirect losses that flow from that damage: Iain Field, 'Contributory Negligence and the Rule of Avoidable Losses' (2018) 38(3) Oxford Journal of Legal Studies 475–99. However, on my account of mitigation, there is no distinction between direct and indirect losses.

[176] *Davies* (n 169).

[177] See also *Jones v Livox Quarries Ltd* [1952] 2 QB 608 (CA), where the claimant's decision to ride on the back of a traxcavator contributed to his injuries but not to the occurrence of the accident.

[178] In *Capps v Miller* [1989] 1 WLR 839 (CA), the trial judge's decision to make no reduction for a motorcyclist's failure to secure his helmet was overturned on the basis that the judge had erroneously focused on responsibility for the occurrence rather than the injury.

> the essential distinction between contributory negligence on the one hand, and intervening cause and the duty to mitigate on the other, is that the former is a partial defence while the latter two are total defences; i.e. if a claimant has broken the chain of causation to the loss, or has failed in its duty to mitigate that loss, it cannot recover any damages for that loss, whereas if it has been contributorily negligent in relation to that loss, its damages are merely reduced to the extent that this is thought just and equitable.[179]

It is inapt to describe mitigation as a 'total defence' because, as I have argued, the doctrine results in a counterfactual assessment of damages as if the claimant had taken steps to replicate its no-breach position as nearly as possible and in the usual way. This means that mitigation will very rarely reduce the claimant's damages to nil. However, there is an element of truth to Burrows' distinction. The effect of mitigation is *binary* in the sense that it attributes responsibility for the consequences of the claimant's conduct to either entirely to the claimant (where mitigation applies) or entirely to the defendant (where it does not). By contrast, contributory negligence *apportions* responsibility for the consequences of the claimant's conduct between the claimant and defendant.

Simplifying for now, when contributory negligence applies, the court must start with an assessment of the claimant's loss,[180] and then reduce this by a percentage that reflects the claimant's contributory negligence. As I outlined above, the latter process of apportionment requires consideration of both the 'blameworthiness' of the claimant's conduct and its 'causal potency'.[181] One may ask how it is possible to assess 'degrees' of causal potency, because as a matter of factual (ie 'but for') causation, something is either a cause or it is not. However, in *Causation in the Law*, Hart and Honoré demonstrated that a scalar assessment of causal responsibility is possible via an assessment of the ex-ante riskiness of the relevant conduct.[182] Whether or not this is how judges actually approach making a percentage deduction in contributory negligence,[183] the upshot is still that the doctrine's effect is to divide responsibility for the relevant conduct—in some proportion—between the claimant and defendant.

Spencer v Wincanton Holdings can be used to illustrate the contrasting effects of contributory negligence and mitigation (or equivalently, intervening causation).[184]

[179] Burrows, *Remedies* (4th edn) (n 6) 75. Here the term 'defence' is being used loosely not to refer to a liability rule, but to a limitation on compensatory damages.

[180] For now, I am being deliberately ambiguous as to whether 'loss' here means factual loss or the assessment of loss post the application of mitigation. See further text to n 190.

[181] Text to n 169.

[182] HLA Hart and Tony Honoré, *Causation in the Law* (2nd edn, Clarendon 1985) 233.

[183] In practice, reductions are often applied by reference to standard tariffs: see eg *Froom v Butcher* [1976] QB 286 (CA), in relation to failures to wear a seatbelt. They must otherwise be 'dealt with in a broad, jury-like and common sense way': *Badger v Ministry of Defence* [2005] EWHC 2941 (QB), [2006] 3 All ER 173 [16] (Stanley Burnton J).

[184] *Spencer* (n 40).

To recap the facts,[185] the claimant lost his right leg due to his employer's negligence. Some years later, the claimant tried to walk without his prosthesis and fell and injured his other leg, such that he subsequently lost the use of both legs. The trial judge awarded damages for the claimant's loss of use of both legs, reduced by one third for contributory negligence.[186] The Court of Appeal upheld this decision, rejecting the defendant's argument that the claimant's conduct amounted to an intervening act.[187] On my analysis, this is equivalent to holding that the claimant's conduct was not sufficiently voluntary and/or abnormal to trigger the exceptionality rule of mitigation.[188] However, had that rule applied, its effect would have been to assess damages on the counterfactual basis as if the claimant had used his prosthesis appropriately, not fallen, and therefore retained the use of his left leg.

It should be apparent from this example that the effects of contributory negligence and mitigation are incompatible.[189] Where both doctrines apply on a given set of facts, it is not inappropriate to cumulate their effects. Contributory negligence involves applying a percentage reduction to the claimant's *factual loss*,[190] whereas mitigation involves applying a counterfactual assessment to construct a *hypothetical loss*. The latter approach already achieves the effect of holding the claimant fully responsible for the consequences of their relevant conduct, by awarding damages for the loss that would have been suffered if they had not conducted themselves in that way. Applying a further percentage reduction to this amount would clearly be excessive, since it would leave the claimant in worse position than if they had not engaged in the relevant conduct. If the doctrines cannot both be applied on the same set of facts, then the obvious question is: which should have primacy?

5.4 The primacy of mitigation

The tension between contributory negligence and mitigation arises because the two doctrines reflect fundamentally different models of causal responsibility. As Hart and Honoré put it, 'When the law is faced with two or more wrongful acts ... it may regard them as concurrent causes instead of holding that one of them negatives causal connection between the other and the harm suffered.'[191] Contributory negligence, under the 1945 Act, is an example of the concurrent causes model.

[185] See further text to n 40.

[186] *Spencer* (n 40) [7] (Sedley LJ).

[187] ibid [23] (Sedley LJ), [46]–[47] (Aikens LJ).

[188] See further Section 2.2.

[189] This was expressly recognized by Aikens LJ in *Spencer* (n 40) [44], although referring to intervening causation rather than mitigation.

[190] *Platform Home Loans* (n 106) 212 (Lord Hobhouse).

[191] Hart and Honoré (n 182) 205. Mitigation is not a 'wrongful act' but the general point, regarding the attribution of responsibility for events, still stands.

It seeks to identify two operative legal causes of the claimant's eventual harm and then apportions damages in proportion to each of them. By contrast, mitigation is an example of Hart and Honoré's second model. It negatives the causal connection between the defendant's initial wrongdoing and the claimant's eventual harm, such that the defendant is not responsible at all for the consequences of the claimant's conduct. To isolate these consequences (distinct from the consequences of the original wrong), the defendant is held responsible for the consequences that would have followed from its wrongdoing in the normal course of events.

The historic origins of this tension between contributory negligence and mitigation are easy to trace. Pre-1945, the common law developed consistently according to the model of negativing causal connection, rather than of recognizing concurrent causes. The common law doctrine of contributory negligence, which operated as a 'total bar' to damages, followed this pattern.[192] The 1945 Act uprooted this internal consistency, and imported what was conceptually a completely new model of causal responsibility into the assessment of damages. Whilst the instrumentalist advantages of apportionment featured prominently in the reform process,[193] there appears to have been very little in the way of consideration—either then or since—as to how the relationship between the statutory regime and the subsisting common law doctrines was to work. Although this issue has been addressed in a handful cases,[194] there remains no direct authority on the relationship between contributory negligence and mitigation in a case where they both apply.

From a policy perspective, it has sometimes been argued that contributory negligence *should* have primacy over mitigation, owing to the relative 'inflexibility' and 'harshness' of mitigation.[195] This view often rests on the misapprehension that mitigation is all-or-nothing rather than yielding a counterfactual assessment.[196] However, the Law Commission also took the view that: 'although [counterfactual assessment] is more equitable than an "all or nothing" result, it has less flexibility as a means of achieving justice than an apportionment of liability'.[197] On the other hand, the flexible nature of apportionment also has downsides. The risk of increasing the uncertainty of litigation was what sunk the Law Commission's initial proposals to extend the application of the 1945 Act to breach of contract claims.[198]

[192] However, since there was no question of recovery for the hypothetical loss that the claimant would have suffered if it had not acted negligently, the effect of contributory negligence at common law was much harsher than mitigation.

[193] Mitchell, *A History of Tort Law 1900–1950* (n 171).

[194] See eg *Spencer* (n 40) [44] (Aikens LJ) in relation to intervening causation; and *Platform Home Loans* (n 106) in relation to the 'scope of duty' rule.

[195] See eg Law Commission, *Contributory Negligence as a Defence in Contract* (No 219, 1993) [3.21]. See also Burrows, *Remedies* (4th edn) (n 6) 122 fn 9, who seems to suggest that contributory negligence should (if applicable) displace mitigation, but notes that 'no case has been found allowing contributory negligence as a mid-position alternative to the duty to mitigate'.

[196] See further Chapter 2, Section 3.

[197] Law Commission, *Contributory Negligence as a Defence in Contract* (n 195) [3.21].

[198] Burrows, *Remedies* (4th edn) (n 6) 143; Law Commission, *Contributory Negligence as a Defence in Contract* (n 195) [3.39]–[3.40].

Although the counterfactual assessment required by mitigation is not entirely free of uncertainty, it is surely more readily ascertainable than apportionment, which the courts have acknowledged 'must inevitably be somewhat rough and ready'.[199]

Whilst acknowledging the lack of direct authority, I think that once the ubiquity of mitigation is fully appreciated, it becomes apparent that supplanting it with apportionment is not tenable.[200] Even within the relatively narrow set of cases where contributory negligence and mitigation can overlap—namely, the claimant's post-breach conduct following a tort (excluding intentional torts)—it hard to see how apportionment could replace, for example, the application of the market rule, which I have argued is an aspect of mitigation. Where the victim of a tort chooses not to resort to the market for repair, replacement or extrication, and the market subsequently turns against them, there is nothing on the face of the 1945 Act to prevent the defendant from raising contributory negligence. The fact that this point is never taken suggests a strong convention that counterfactual assessment (as if the claimant had resorted to the market), rather than apportionment, has primacy in such cases. Once this is accepted, it becomes difficult to see how one could draw a line to take a different approach for other mitigation cases.

6 The *White & Carter* Limitation

The so-called '*White & Carter* limitation', which derives from obiter dicta in Lord Reid's speech in that case, provides—in neutral language—that a claimant will not succeed in an action for the agreed sum if they lacked any 'legitimate interest' in performing the contract after the defendant's repudiation, rather than claiming damages.[201] Some cases have described this as a question of whether or not the claimant has 'an election [following their counterparty's breach] to keep the contract alive'.[202] Similarly, in *White & Carter* itself, Lord Keith claimed that a party who suffered a breach of contract 'must take steps to minimise the cost sustained by the breach'.[203] These comments have led some scholars to argue that the rule in *White & Carter* is,[204] or should be,[205] a part of the law of mitigation, or to criticize

[199] *Corr* (n 8) [70] (Lord Neuberger).

[200] See also James Goudkamp, 'Rethinking Contributory Negligence' in JWA Neyers, SG Pitel, and E Chamberlain (eds), *Tort Law: Challenging Orthodoxy* (Bloomsbury Publishing 2013) 334–6, who similarly favours the primacy of mitigation over contributory negligence, but for different reasons.

[201] *White & Carter* (n 4) 431. For reference, the exact quote is: 'It may well be that, if it can be shown that a person has no legitimate interest, financial or otherwise, in performing the contract rather than claiming damages, he ought not to be allowed to saddle the other party with an additional burden with no benefit to himself.'

[202] See eg *The Odenfeld* [1978] 2 Lloyd's Rep 357 (QB) 374.

[203] *White v Carter* (n 4) 442.

[204] Qiao Liu, 'The White & Carter Principle: A Restatement' (2011) 74 Modern Law Review 171.

[205] Jonathan Morgan, 'Smuggling Mitigation into *White & Carter v McGregor*: Time to Come Clean?' [2015] Lloyd's Maritime and Commercial Law Quarterly 575.

the rule on the basis of its inconsistency with the law of mitigation (suggesting that the doctrines are fundamentally comparable).[206]

The limitation imposed by Lord Reid's dictum in *White & Carter* is best viewed as a restriction on the availability of the action for the agreed sum, rather than a restriction on the claimant's right to keep the contract alive following a repudiatory breach. As Lloyd J noted in *The Alaskan Trader*,[207] 'Although the point is sometimes put in terms of the innocent party being obliged to accept the repudiation... It is... the range of remedies which is limited, not the right to elect'.[208] This was confirmed by a majority of the Supreme Court in *Geys v Société Générale*,[209] and also supported by obiter dicta in *Makdessi v Cavendish Square Holdings*, where Lord Neuberger and Lord Sumption stated—in reliance upon *White & Carter*—that 'the law will not generally make a *remedy* available to a party, the adverse impact of which on the defaulter significantly exceeds any legitimate interest of the innocent party'.[210]

Consequently, in a direct sense, the *White & Carter* limitation differs from mitigation simply in that the former doctrine affects the claimant's right to the agreed sum (ie the price promised by the defendant) whereas the latter affects their right to damages. These are, conceptually, quite distinct remedies and in this respect, there is no reason why a doctrine applying to one should be related to—or have any bearing on—a doctrine applying to the other. However, in practice, things are somewhat more complicated, because the availability and quantum of damages affects the importance of being able to claim the agreed sum. In particular, if, but for the defendant's breach, the claimant would have been able to earn the agreed sum, then it is very likely that—unless mitigation applies—the claimant's loss (for which damages are recoverable) would include loss of the agreed sum less any expenses that the claimant would have incurred in earning it.

For this reason, in circumstances where the *White & Carter* limitation might apply, it is important know whether mitigation (ie the replication or exceptionality rule) might also apply to reduce the claimant's damages on account of their insistence on performing the contract against the wishes of the defendant. The first observation, from the perspective of the *White & Carter* limitation itself, is that there seems to be some circularity here. Lord Reid referred to a legitimate interest in 'performing the contract rather than claiming damages'.[211] But if the claimant's damages would be reduced by mitigation, this correspondingly increases the

[206] Burrows, *Remedies* (4th edn) (n 6) 387.

[207] *Clea Shipping Corpn v Bulk Oil International Ltd (The Alaskan Trader)* [1984] 1 All ER 129 (QB).

[208] ibid 137.

[209] *Societe Generale, London Branch v Geys* [2012] UKSC 63, [2013] 1 AC 523 [87], where Lord Wilson approved remarks in *Decro-Wall International v Practitioners in Marketing* [1971] 1 WLR 361, 375, which are similar to those of Lloyd J's in *The Alaskan Trader* (n 207).

[210] *El Makdessi v Cavendish Square Holdings BV* [2015] UKSC 67, [2016] AC 1172 [29] (emphasis added).

[211] *White & Carter* (n 4) 431.

claimant's incentive (if not legitimate interest) to seek the agreed sum. However, pressing to perform the contract also poses a major risk for the claimant. If they are held to have acted 'unreasonably' they might fail in their action for the agreed sum (applying the *White & Carter* limitation) *and* receive a substantially reduced damages award (applying mitigation).

My account of mitigation can help make sense of this conundrum, by clarifying how the doctrine would apply in a *White & Carter* type case. Here I consider two alternative analyses, depending on the view taken about when mitigation applies in relation to anticipatory repudiations. In Chapter 7, I argued that although the law is not entirely clear, the better view is that mitigation does not arise until the claimant has accepted the repudiation.[212] This depends on the view that there is no actual breach until acceptance.[213] If this is correct, then in a *White & Carter* type case, mitigation will usually be irrelevant. That is because if the claimant rejects the defendant's anticipatory repudiation and continues with their own performance, mitigation will typically not apply until the price has become due and is not paid, since only then will there be an actual breach.[214] It follows that mitigation can have no application to the claimant's earlier 'unreasonable' decision to perform.

If on the other hand the courts were to conclude that an anticipatory repudiation *did* amount to an actual breach of contract, even prior to acceptance, then the analysis would be different.[215] In that case, it would be necessary to apply mitigation to the claimant's decision to perform the contract with the defendant against their wishes. As I have argued, the test is not one of reasonableness per se.[216] Instead, mitigation applies where the claimant chose not to replicate its no-breach position (the replication rule), or chose to do so in an unusual way (the exceptionality rule). Where the claimant has promised to provide goods or services and the defendant has promised to pay the price but is now refusing to do so, the claimant can replicate either by performing for the defendant and pressing them to pay the price, or by selling the same goods or services to someone else. Whether performing for the defendant amounts to a 'failure to mitigate' therefore depends on whether selling to a third party would replicate the claimant's no-breach position as nearly as selling to the defendant.

The answer to this depends on whether the claimant could have sold to a third party in addition to the defendant. If the claimant could only have satisfied one

[212] Chapter 7, text to n 131.

[213] Chapter 7, text to n 147.

[214] In most contracts, the price only becomes due once the corresponding performance has been completed, although this depends on the terms of the contract. See further Andrew Summers, 'Termination and the Agreed Sum' in Graham Virgo and Sarah Worthington (eds), *Commercial Remedies: Resolving Controversies* (CUP 2017).

[215] Burrows argues that 'the duty to mitigate should arise once there has been an anticipatory repudiation', although he grounds this on reasons of economic efficiency: Burrows, *Remedies* (4th edn) (n 6) 132; see further Chapter 7, text to n 141. For a critique of the economic efficiency explanation of mitigation, see Chapter 4, Section 3.

[216] See further Chapter 8, Section 2.

contract, and if they could have sold their goods or services to a third party instead, then performing for the defendant in circumstances where the defendant has already said that they will not pay, is likely to be an exceptional mode of replication. In that case, damages will be assessed as if the claimant had sold its goods or services to a third party instead. By contrast, if the claimant had excess capacity and could have sold to the defendant in addition to any other customers, it is not obvious that they can replicate their no-breach position any other way than by performing for the defendant and then pressing them to pay the price. One caveat may be if pressing the defendant to pay the price is very likely to be futile (for example, if the defendant is insolvent).[217] Subject to this, mitigation seems unlikely to apply and so the claimant would be entitled to recover for its factual loss, which would include the price owed by the defendant.

[217] See further Chapter 8, Section 2.1.5.

12
Conclusion

1 Introduction

My aim in this chapter is not to rehearse the main arguments of the book: for that, the reader can refer to the Introduction, or to Chapter 6 for further details. Instead, I want to draw out some implications and open questions raised by my account of mitigation, taking a broader perspective that I hope will be of interest to private law theorists—including those who have not previously thought much (or had reason to care) about mitigation. As I have argued, mitigation is far more ubiquitous and deep-rooted within the law of damages than private law theorists have hitherto given credit. If I am right in my central claim that mitigation is an aspect of causation, and that its effect forms *part of* the legal concept of loss, then the doctrine deserves a much more prominent place in theories of private law, or at least within theories of damages.

I organize my reflections below according to four key concepts that are touched upon by my account of mitigation: causation; choice; rights; and loss. This list is not intended to suggest separate lines of enquiry; as will be evident, many of the underlying issues overlap, and I am unsure of the relationship between them. The implications that I raise are tentative, since they involve taking on much 'bigger' questions—about the nature of causation, choice, etc—which can be approached from a variety of disciplinary perspectives, and about which I do not claim to be an expert. My aim is merely to flag some debates that I am aware of, and to suggest where I think my account of mitigation fits within these. Others may disagree and wish to characterize my account differently. That is fine; I do not think that my contribution rests on being right about which existing theory (if any) my account supports.

Where I am confident—since this is where most of the book focuses—is on my explanation and restatement of the (English) law of mitigation as it stands. Accordingly, I think that theoretical debates within private law that are descriptive or explanatory in nature,[1] will mostly need to 'bend' to my account, rather than the other way around. Having said that, I recognize that there are some areas where English law—as a matter of judicial authority—currently remains uncertain. Some examples include the precise criteria for determining whether the claimant had a 'choice',[2] and relatedly, how to decide what amounts to replication 'as nearly as

[1] As opposed to justificatory or prescriptive: see further Chapter 4, Section 2.
[2] See further Chapter 6, Section 3.3.

Mitigation in the Law of Damages. Andrew Summers, Oxford University Press. © Andy Summers 2025.
DOI: 10.1093/9780191864032.003.0012

possible'.[3] Here, perhaps in line with how an 'interpretivist' sees their task, I think there is scope to invoke wider theories (whether descriptive or normative) to help point judges in a coherent direction. This suggests a practical reason why doctrinal scholars or practitioners should also care about the discussion in this chapter.

2 Causation

I have argued that mitigation is an aspect of causation. Judges have always been strongly supportive of this explanation, but legal scholars have tended to resist it.[4] This scepticism reflects a widely-held view amongst private law theorists that the 'but-for' test (ie counterfactual necessity) is the only meaningful concept of causation.[5] The process of selecting 'the' cause from amongst multiple counterfactually necessary causes has conventionally been treated as a matter of pure legal policy rather than causation.[6] Hart and Honoré were exceptions in arguing that this process rests on causal principles used outside the law.[7] To a large extent, their view remains marginalized by legal philosophers.[8] In this book, I have sought to revive and develop Hart and Honoré's commonsense theory of causation in the law, drawing on recent experimental evidence into how ordinary people make causal judgements that corroborates and refines the principles they originally identified.[9]

My focus in this book has been on the application of commonsense principles of causation to the law of mitigation. However, Hart and Honoré's project was originally much broader; indeed, mitigation hardly featured.[10] In their view, the ambit of commonsense causal reasoning extended to the criminal law,[11] as well as to other areas of private law.[12] In relation to the criminal law doctrine of 'novus actus interveniens', Hart and Honoré's theory has subsequently received direct approval from the courts and been relied upon expressly in the leading cases.[13]

[3] See further Chapter 9, Section 2.4.

[4] See further Chapter 5, Sections 2 and 3.

[5] See eg James Edelman (ed), *McGregor on Damages* (21st edn, Sweet & Maxwell 2022) ch 8. In philosophy, this approach is traceable to David Hume (London 1739) 171. See also John Stuart Mill, *A System of Logic: Raciocentive and Inductive* (Longmans 1843) 360–61; David Lewis, *Counterfactuals* (Blackwell 1973) 558–59.

[6] See eg Wright, 'Causation in Tort Law' (1985) 73 California Law Review 1735; Stapleton, 'Cause in Fact and the Scope of Liability for Consequences' (2003) 119 LQR 388; Edelman, *McGregor on Damages* (21st edn) (n 5) ch 8.

[7] HLA Hart and Tony Honoré, *Causation in the Law* (2nd edn, Clarendon 1985).

[8] See eg Jane Stapleton, 'Causation in the Law' in Helen Beebee, Christopher Hitchcock, and Peter Menzies (eds), *The Oxford Handbook of Causation* (OUP 2009) 753.

[9] See further Chapter 5, Section 4; and Andrew Summers, 'Common-Sense Causation in the Law' (2018) 38 Oxford Journal of Legal Studies 793.

[10] Across the whole book, there are only two passing references to mitigation: Hart and Honoré (n 7) 230, 312.

[11] ibid ch 12.

[12] ibid ch 6 (tort) and ch 11 (contract).

[13] See eg *R v Latif* [1996] 1 WLR 104, 115 (Lord Steyn); *R v Kennedy (No 2)* [2007] UKHL 38, [2008] 1 AC 269 [14] (Lord Bingham); *R v Wallace* [2018] EWCA Crim 690 [47] (Sharp LJ).

And yet, in this domain, both judicial and scholarly analysis has still not grappled at all with the corresponding experimental evidence on causal reasoning.[14] As I have urged elsewhere,[15] although this evidence should not be treated prescriptively in legal enquiries, I think it can serve a useful purpose by helping to pinpoint latent distinctions in the case law. I hope my analysis of mitigation illustrates the potential utility of this approach.

There are at least two open questions left by my 'mitigation as causation' thesis. First, what kind of principles are the choice and abnormality principles that I say underpin the law of mitigation? Towards the end of Chapter 5, I suggested that debating whether these principles are properly described as 'causal' is potentially a distraction.[16] We could describe them more neutrally as cognitive principles used to attribute responsibility outside the law. Alternatively, we could call them principles of counterfactual reasoning. Counterfactuals appear to be the common thread between 'causal' judgments (as recognized by philosophers) and attributions of responsibility (as tested by experimental psychologists).[17] As Gerstenberg and Lagnado summarize, 'how responsible for an outcome a person is seen to be depends not only on what the person actually did but also on what would have happened if the person had acted differently'.[18]

This link between attributions of responsibility and counterfactual reasoning—whether expressed in terms of 'causation' or not—seems to underlie both the 'standard' application of the compensatory principle, and the application of mitigation. The defendant's responsibility for the consequences of their breach depends on what would have happened if they had not breached the relevant legal obligation: this is the compensatory principle, as we all recognize it. Similarly, on my account of mitigation, the defendant's responsibility for the consequences of the claimant's post-breach conduct depends on what would have happened if the claimant had replicated the no-breach position in the usual way. The no-breach counterfactual that underpins the compensatory principle self-evidently derives from the defendant's primary obligation. In relation to mitigation, the source of the 'normal replication' counterfactual (as one might call it) is less obvious. But the structure of the enquiry is, I think, essentially the same.

The second, and closely related, open question is whether the law is justified in adopting the choice and abnormality principles that I have identified, for the purpose of determining the defendant's responsibility for the consequences of the

[14] See eg Antje du Bois-Pedain, 'Novus Actus and Beyond: Attributing Causal Responsibility in the Criminal Courts' [2018] 80 CLJ 61.

[15] Summers, 'Common-Sense Causation in the Law' (n 9) 816–19.

[16] See further Chapter 5, Section 5.

[17] See further Chapter 5, text to n 164.

[18] Tobias Gerstenberg and David Lagnado, 'Attributing Responsibility: Actual and Counterfactual Worlds' in Joshua Knobe, Tania Lombrozo, and Shaun Nichols (eds), *Oxford Studies in Experimental Philosophy: Volume 1* (OUP 2014) 94. See also Tobias Gerstenberg, 'Beyond the Here and Now: Counterfactual Simulation in Causal Cognition' (2024) PsyArXiv, preprint.

claimant's post-breach conduct. In Chapter 6, I sketched two possible justifications.[19] The first was if consistency between ordinary (ie non-legal) and legal attributions of responsibility is itself an important value, for example if it was necessary to achieve institutional or democratic 'buy-in' to the law's approach to assessing damages. The second, which I suggested was more promising, was if we can identify normative reasons in favour of the choice and abnormality principles in their ordinary usage outside the law, and then further argue that the same reasons have force for the purpose of attributing legal responsibility. Along these lines, in the following section I discuss the normative significance of choice.

3 Choice

The concept of choice plays an important role in my account of mitigation because it serves as a precondition of the claimant's responsibility for the consequences of their post-breach conduct, under both the replication and exceptionality rules. In short, mitigation applies only where the claimant *chose* not to replicate their no-breach position as nearly as possible, or *chose* to take steps (including steps towards replication) that were descriptively abnormal. In Chapters 8 to 10, I demonstrated that in the cases on avoidable loss, avoided loss, and the market rule, the notion of choice more accurately reflects judicial reasoning than does the conventional emphasis on the 'reasonableness' or 'directness' of the claimant's conduct. Perhaps the best illustration of this emphasis on choice, and its relation to responsibility, comes from Lord Toulson's articulation of the market rule in *Bunge v Nidera*:

> The *option* to re-enter or stay out of the market arises from the breach, but it does not follow that there is a causal connection between the breach and [the claimant's] *decision* whether to re-enter or to stay out of the market, so as to make the guilty party responsible for that decision and its consequences. The guilty party is not liable to the innocent party for the adverse effect of market changes after the innocent party has had a free choice whether to re-enter the market, nor is the innocent party required to give credit to the guilty party for any subsequent market movement in favour of the innocent party. The speculation which way the market will go is the speculation of the claimant.[20]

As I have emphasized throughout, my aim in this book has been primarily to describe and explain the law of mitigation as it stands.[21] It is from this standpoint

[19] See further Chapter 6, Section 4.
[20] *Bunge SA v Nidera BV* [2015] UKSC 43, [2015] 3 All ER 1082 [80] (emphasis in original). See also, in relation to avoidable loss, *Downs v Chappell* [1997] 1 WLR 426 (CA) 437 (Hobhouse LJ); and in relation to avoided loss *Blue Circle Industries plc v Ministry of Defence* [1999] Ch 289 (CA) 315 (Chadwick LJ), 321 (Simon Brown LJ).
[21] See further the Introduction, and Chapter 4, Section 2.

that I alighted on the concept of choice, because it is so plain to see in the cases on mitigation. However, there is also an extensive literature, both in legal philosophy and moral philosophy more generally, on the normative significance of choice.[22] As Scanlon has put it, 'Choice has obvious and immediate moral significance'.[23] A number of theories have been developed for why choice has moral significance: I will not attempt to summarize all of them, let alone adjudicate between them.[24] However, I do want to highlight one distinction that emerges from this literature, that I think could be important in the context of mitigation (even though I have skirted over it up until now): between and 'making' and 'having' a choice.

Roughly speaking, 'making' a choice requires that a person consciously turned their mind to the relevant options, whereas 'having' a choice merely requires that those options were available to them, whether or not they thought about it. Scanlon has referred to these as the 'Forfeiture' and 'Value of Choice' theories respectively.[25] They reflect quite different visions of why choice matters morally.[26] The Forfeiture theory (which rests on *making* a choice), relies on the idea that an individual has an inherent moral power to legitimate outcomes by giving consent.[27] This power is treated as morally basic ie it is not capable of explanation in terms of any further moral argument. By contrast, the Value of Choice theory (which rests on *having* a choice) is instrumental. As Scanlon puts it 'This theory starts from the idea that it is often a good thing for a person to have what will happen depend upon how he or she responds when presented with the alternatives under the right conditions.'[28]

This raises the question: is it 'making' or 'having' a choice that matters for mitigation? The most obvious place to look for an answer is in relation to the temporal scope of mitigation. In Chapter 7, I showed that as a matter of current English law, mitigation appear to apply only once the claimant has *actual* knowledge of the breach.[29] This position seems most consistent with the requirement of *making* a choice. If having a choice was sufficient, then one would expect mitigation to apply from the point at which the claimant could reasonably have uncovered the breach

[22] For a small sample, see eg HLA Hart, *Punishment and Responsibility* (OUP, 1968), Ch 2 'Legal Responsibility and Excuses'; Thomas Scanlon, 'The Significance of Choice' in *The Tanner Lectures on Human Values VIII* (1988, University of Utah Press) 149–216; Tony Honoré, 'Responsibility and Luck: The Moral Basis of Strict Liability' (1988) 104 LQR 530; Serena Olsaretti, 'Scanlon on Responsibility and the Value of Choice' (2013) 10 Journal of Moral Philosophy 465–83; Emmanuel Voyiakis, *Private Law and the Value of Choice* (Hart, 2017).

[23] Scanlon, 'The Significance of Choice' (n 22) 151.

[24] For a short overview, see Thomas Scanlon, 'Responsibility and the Value of Choice' (2013) 12 Think 9.

[25] Scanlon, 'The Significance of Choice' (n 22) 151. cf Olsaretti, 'Scanlon on Responsibility and the Value of Choice' (n 22), who casts some doubt on the distinction.

[26] See further Voyiakis (n 22) 77–86. It is also important to note that, even on the Forfeiture theory, fault is irrelevant: Scanlon, 'The Significance of Choice' (n 22) 193.

[27] Hence, they 'forfeit' rights that they may otherwise have had to object. However, in later work, Scanlon reframes this as the 'Will-Based' theory, thereby focusing on the exercise of will directly: Scanlon, 'Responsibility and the Value of Choice' (n 24).

[28] Scanlon, 'The Significance of Choice' (n 22) 178.

[29] See further Chapter 7, text to n 111.

(ie constructive knowledge).[30] However, it is fair to say that there is currently no clear authority on this point. Given this, it seems to me an area where there would be room for express moral argument in the development of the law, should an appropriate case arise. I do not express any view on this myself, but Scanlon concludes in favour of the Value of Choice theory (ie *having* a choice),[31] and Voyiakis has since applied this view to justify the institutions of private law specifically.[32]

Finally, I am sure that there are other aspects of my exposition of mitigation and choice that could also benefit from distinctions drawn by legal and moral philosophers. To take three examples: first, in some cases, the question for the judge is effectively whether the claimant had a choice in a context where all the available options looked objectively like 'bad' ones;[33] second, there could also be cases in which the claimant's apparent lack of choice stems from their own specific preferences, such that options look bad to them that would likely be acceptable to others;[34] third, in some cases the claimant was making a choice under pressure, whether a time constraint or other external influence.[35] In each of these cases, it is not entirely clear where to draw the line. In the scheme of things, these are all relatively minor edge cases around a substantial and well-settled core, so I do not think that they undermine the overall utility of my restatement of the law in terms of choice. Nevertheless, there seems to be scope to refine my account here.

4 Rights

Very broadly, existing general theories of damages are of three types.[36] First, are conventional 'loss-based' theories, which hold that damages serve exclusively to compensate the claimant for the (actual) consequences of the defendant's breach. I address this type of theory in the next section. Second, arguably at the opposite end of a spectrum along which consequences matter more or less, are 'rights-based' theories. These hold that at least some damages awards are designed to vindicate the claimant's right, and hence are calculated exclusively by reference

[30] Adam Kramer, *The Law of Contract Damages* (3rd edn, Hart 2022) [15-61].

[31] Scanlon, 'The Significance of Choice' (n 22) 196: 'the fact that an outcome resulted from a person's choice under good conditions shows that he was given the choice and provided with good conditions for making it, and it is these facts which make it the case that he alone is responsible. A conscious decision to "take the risk" is not necessary.'

[32] Voyiakis (n 22). Voyiakis touches on mitigation only briefly, in the context of 'protection against the burden of repair': 121–22.

[33] See further Chapter 11, Section 3.4.

[34] The classic example in criminal law is *R v Blaue* [1975] 1 WLR 1411, involving a Jehovah's witness who refused a blood transfusion. However, one should not necessarily assume that the meaning of choice for intervening causation will be identical in criminal and civil cases.

[35] See further Chapter 6, text to n 64.

[36] My focus here is on theories within the corrective justice tradition. Another kind of theory—based on the law and economics tradition—plays a much quieter role in relation to English law than it does elsewhere, such as the United States.

to the value of that right, irrespective of the actual consequences of the breach. Third, are 'performance-based' theories. These hold that some damages awards are substitutes for *performance of* the primary right. On this view, the actual consequences of the breach matter to some extent, but only insofar as they affect the cost of obtaining substitute performance.

The foremost proponent of a pure rights-based theory of damages is Stevens.[37] Stevens seeks to 'distinguish between damages awarded as a substitute for the right infringed and consequential damages as compensation for loss.'[38] Consequential damages follow the conventional loss-based model, but so-called 'substitutive damages' are 'available even where the claimant is not factually worse off at all.'[39] Initially, Stevens suggested that substitutive damages were measured by the value of the right that was infringed (taken to mean the full value of the indivisible right),[40] but in later work he clarified that the aim was to measure the value of the *infringement* of the right.[41] Stevens asserts that the *actual* consequences of the breach are strictly irrelevant, since 'the time for the assessment of the value of the right is the moment of infringement.'[42]

The performance-based theory has a more disparate set of advocates, and accordingly comes in multiple variants. Some pre-date Stevens' substitutive damages thesis,[43] whereas others have evolved contemporaneously with or in response to it.[44] The gist is that the claimant can—always or sometimes—recover damages substituting for their right to performance, even where they have not suffered any consequential loss on the conventional (loss-based) measure. Unlike Stevens' substitutive damages, performance-based damages are quantified by the cost of obtaining substitute performance (ie the 'cost of cure' measure) rather than the difference in market value between the original right and the right as infringed.[45]

[37] Robert Stevens, *Torts and Rights* (OUP 2007) ch 4; Robert Stevens, 'Damages and the Right to Performance: A *Golden Victory* or Not?' in Neyers, Bronaugh, and Pitel (eds), *Exploring Contract Law* (Hart 2009); Robert Stevens, 'Rights and Other Things' (2014) in Robertson and Nolan (eds), *Rights and Private Law* (Hart 2011).

[38] Stevens, *Torts and Rights* (n 37) 60. Stevens argues that the failure to distinguish between these two types of damages 'leads to confusion and muddle': Stevens, 'Damages and the Right to Performance' (n 37) 172.

[39] Stevens, *Torts and Rights* (n 37) 78.

[40] ibid ch 4. See further James Edelman, 'The Meaning of Loss and Enrichment' in Chambers and others (eds), Philosophical Foundations of the Law of Unjust Enrichment (OUP 2009), 218–21.

[41] Stevens, *Damages and the Right to Performance* (n 37) 171, 195. Stevens has emphasized that what is valued is the *infringement* of the right, not the right itself: Stevens, *Rights and Other Things* (n 37) 126–27.

[42] ibid 60. See also 69, 138. Nevertheless, to determine the severity of the infringement, it must surely be necessary to refer to some kind of consequences, even if these are the 'normal' or 'expected' consequences as at the date of breach.

[43] See eg Brian Coote, 'Contract Damages, Ruxley, and the Performance Interest' [1997] 56 CLJ 537; Charlie Webb, 'Performance and Compensation: An Analysis of Contract Damages and Contractual Obligation' (2006) 26 Oxford Journal of Legal Studies 41.

[44] Steven Smith, 'Substitutionary Damages' in Charles Rickett (ed), *Justifying Private Law Remedies* (Hart 2008); James Edelman, 'Money Awards of the Cost of Performance' (2010) 4 Journal of Equity 122; David Winterton, *Money Awards in Contract Law* (Hart 2017).

[45] Winterton, *Money Awards in Contract Law* (n 44) 10.

Winterton highlights two further differences compared with Stevens' theory.[46] First, performance-based damages are not universally available: they depend on a test of reasonableness. Second, some events occurring after the breach *are* relevant, because—for Winterton—such damages are assessed based on the cost of cure at the date of trial.[47]

What are the implications of my account of mitigation, for each of these theories? The original appeal of the rights-based theory of damages was its ability to account for the slew of cases in which claimants have been awarded damages greater than their factual loss. But to do this, the theory used a sledgehammer to crack a nut: it argued that (for substitutive damages) post-breach events, of *all* kinds, are *always* irrelevant. My account of mitigation explains a large subset of the cases to which the rights-based theory was originally directed,[48] but in a more parsimonious way. Specifically, the actual post-breach conduct of the *claimant* is irrelevant *in circumstances where they chose to depart from the normal response to breach*. But other types of post-breach event, including other conduct by the claimant, remain relevant to the assessment of damages unless some other rule (such as remoteness) applies. In this way, I think my account of mitigation removes one of the pillars used to support the rights-based theory.[49]

In relation to the performance-based theory advocated by Winterton and others, my account of mitigation seems more complimentary. To recap, I argue that when the claimant chooses not to replicate their no-breach position (or does so in an exceptional way), damages are nevertheless assessed as if they had taken usual steps to replicate the no-breach position as nearly as possible. This 'replication' measure is effectively the cost of obtaining substitute performance (ie 'cost of cure'), and similarly does not depend on the claimant having actually incurred that cost or showing that they intend to do so. Winterton argues that mitigation does not apply to performance-based damages,[50] but I think this is a mistake based on the orthodox understanding of mitigation. It is true that performance-based damages—as Winterton understands them—are not further cut back by mitigation, but in my view, they involve an *application* of mitigation properly understood.

[46] See further, highlighting the distinction between two types of substitutionary account, David Winterton, 'Two Conceptions of the "Performance Interest" in Contract Damages', in Roger Halson and David Campbell (eds), *Research Handbook on Remedies in Private Law*, (Edward Elgar 2019).

[47] Winterton originally eschewed the 'rights-based' label: Winterton, *Money Awards in Contract Law* (n 44) 9. However, in more recent work, his position on the nature of substitutionary awards has moved closer to Stevens: see David Winterton, 'Claims for the Value of the Lost Contractual Performance' (2019) 45 University of Western Australia Law Review 75.

[48] See eg all of the cases on sale of goods and carriage of goods cited in sections 3 and 4 of Stevens, *Damages and the Right to Performance* (n 37) 176–86.

[49] This does not preclude there being other sets of cases that the rights-based theory explains, which my account of mitigation does not. For example, Stevens also relies on vindicatory damages, negotiating damages, and damages in lieu of specific performance, as pillars of his theory.

[50] Winterton, *Money Awards in Contract Law* (n 44).

Just as the so-called market rule (which awards difference in value) is best understood as 'built-in mitigation',[51] so is the cost of cure.

The main difficulty I have with the performance-based theory is the sharp distinction that it draws between damages for the 'cost of cure' and damages for 'difference in value'. Winterton identifies this as the key dividing line between his account and Stevens' substitutive damages thesis: crudely, cost of cure is performance-based whereas difference in value is rights-based.[52] However, on my account of mitigation, there is no substantive difference between these two measures. They are both just ways—in different circumstances—that the claimant can replicate its no-breach position as nearly as possible. As Leggatt LJ correctly noted, assessing the difference in market value 'is not an exercise in valuing the contract considered as an *asset* but an inquiry into the *loss* actually sustained by the claimant as a result of non-performance'.[53] The same can be said about damages for cost of cure. The mistake, leading to identification of a distinct 'performance-based' measure, lies in thinking that the legal concept of *loss* can be constituted only by the actual consequences of the breach.

5 Loss

In Chapter 1, I started by setting out the orthodox account of mitigation in the context of the 'conventional' account of the law of damages.[54] On this account, assessing compensatory damages comprises two main stages: first, the court must apply the compensatory principle to determine the claimant's factual loss; and second, the court must apply various limitations on damages (including mitigation), which serve to cut down recovery. Here, the concept of 'factual loss' involves assessing the claimant's breach and no-breach positions by taking into account *all* post-breach events up to the date of trial.[55] As I pointed out, a more accurate term would strictly be 'single counterfactual loss',[56] because even (so-called) factual loss still involves a counterfactual assessment of the claimant's no-breach position.[57] Still, whatever the precise terminology, it is this concept of loss—taking

[51] See further Chapter 11, Section 2.1.
[52] ibid 10.
[53] *Nagel v Pluczenik Diamond Company NV* [2018] EWCA Civ 2640 [41] (emphasis added).
[54] See further Chapter 1, Section 2.
[55] This term appears to derive originally from *Parry v Cleaver* [1970] AC 1 (HL) 17, where Lord Pearce held that 'in claiming that he has lost something a plaintiff must prove a genuine factual loss'. Various similar terms have also been used: see eg ibid 7, 10, and 22 (Lord Morris) ('actual loss'); *Smith New Court Securities Ltd v Citibank NA* [1997] AC 254 (HL) 268 (Lord Browne-Wilkinson) (the 'loss actually suffered'); *Koufos v C Czarnikow Ltd (The Heron II)* [1969] 1 AC 350 (HL) 395 (Lord Reid) (the loss 'in fact suffered').
[56] On this approach, 'compound counterfactual loss' would describe the application of additional counterfactual processes in the assessment of the breach and/or no-breach positions.
[57] See further Chapter 1, text to n 32.

into account all of the actual consequences of the breach evident up to the date of trial—that forms the basis for the conventional 'loss-based' theory of damages.

The conventional loss-based theory must perform some contortions to account for the numerous cases in which claimants have recovered (compensatory) damages greater than their factual loss. These include, amongst others, the cases applying the so-called insurance and benevolence rules, many of the cases applying the market rule, and all of the cases that I discussed in Chapter 9 in the context of the so-called avoided loss rule.[58] Structurally, none of these cases can be accommodated by the two-stage assessment outlined above, because this framework contemplates starting with the claimant's factual loss and then cutting it back. The most prominent proponent of the conventional loss-based theory is Professor, now Lord, Burrows.[59] In his book on *Remedies*, Burrows accepts the insurance and benevolence rules as limited exceptions to the cap on factual loss, justified on specific policy grounds.[60] However, he rejects almost all of the other cases in which claimants have recovered more than their factual loss as wrongly decided,[61] on grounds that they amount to 'overcompensation'.[62]

As a descriptive account of the law, this position is not sustainable. As I demonstrate in Chapters 9 and 10, there are simply too many cases—including of the highest authority—where claimants have recovered damages greater than their factual loss under the so-called avoided loss and market rules, to dismiss them all as wrongly decided. Recall that this was the original appeal of Stevens' substitutive damages thesis, since it provided a unified explanation of these cases, together with others that the loss-based theory struggled to explain. Stevens' theory has scored some hits, not least in prompting the development of the latest iteration of the performance-based view, as articulated by Winterton. However, it has also been subjected to forceful criticisms.[63] Burrows urges that 'it would be a fundamental

[58] For a short exposition of each of these, see Chapter 1, text to n 55 and following. See further Chapters 9 and 10.

[59] Andrew Burrows, *Remedies for Torts, Breach of Contract, and Equitable Wrongs* (4th edn, OUP 2019).

[60] ibid 147–62.

[61] Comparing closely, one can detect a slight softening of Burrows' position on these cases between the 3rd edition (2004) and 4th edition (2019) of *Remedies*. Without wishing to overclaim my influence, my doctoral thesis, which Burrows examined in 2016 and on which this book is based, is cited—with tentative and conditional approval—in the 4th edition, at 50.

[62] See eg Burrows, *Remedies* (4th edn) (n 2) 190–92; David McLauchlan, 'Expectation Damages: Avoided Loss, Offsetting Gains and Subsequent Events' in Djakhongir Saidov and Ralph Cunnington (eds), *Contract Damages: Domestic and International Perspectives* (Hart 2008); Samuel Beswick, '"Losses in Any Event" in the Case of Damage to Property' (2015) 35 Oxford Journal of Legal Studies 755, 773.

[63] See eg Edelman, 'The Meaning of Loss and Enrichment' (n 40) 218–21; Burrows, 'Damages and Rights' in Donal Nolan and Andrew Robertson (eds), *Rights and Private Law* (Hart 2011) 277–80. It appears to have been Edelman's critique that precipitated the adaptation (one might say 'retreat') of the original substitutive damages thesis, from a focus on the 'value of the right' to the 'value of the *infringement* of the right'. See text to n 40.

mistake to give up on working through [the loss-based theory] in favour of the superficially attractive, but ultimately flawed, substitutive damages analysis'.[64]

I agree. I think that my account of mitigation can be read as a rehabilitation of the loss-based theory of damages, in a new form. The conventional loss-based theory rests on the view that post-breach events, of *all* kinds, are *always* taken into account in the assessment of damages. In this respect, it is the precise opposite of Stevens' rights-based theory. As I pointed out above,[65] my account of mitigation shows that the actual post-breach conduct of the claimant is sometimes 'ignored' (more accurately, replaced) in circumstances where they chose to depart from the normal response to breach. But otherwise, and unless any other relevant doctrine applies, the claimant's factual loss is left undisturbed. In this way, my account effectively charts a path between the 'extreme' versions of the loss-based and rights-based theories. However, it differs from the performance-based theory (which could also be said to occupy a mid-position) in that it unifies the cost of cure and difference-in-value measures, both as instances of counterfactual assessment in circumstances where the claimant chose not to replicate their no-breach position as nearly as possible, and in the usual way.

The crux of this new loss-based theory, then, is that the legal concept of loss does not only depend on *actual* consequences (as the conventional loss-based theory supposes), but also sometimes on *counterfactual* consequences. In one respect, this is trivially true: as I have said, 'factual loss' is really 'single counterfactual loss', since the standard application of the compensatory principle requires an assessment not only of the claimant's 'actual' breach position, but also their counterfactual no-breach position. The move that I make in the new loss-based theory, is to argue that the legal concept of loss can also encompass *additional* counterfactuals, besides the standard no-breach counterfactual. Specifically, where mitigation applies, it entails a counterfactual assessment *within* the claimant's breach position.[66] It is for this reason that I describe mitigation as *part of* the legal concept of loss rather than a limitation on damages.

But is my account of mitigation really 'loss-based'? There is a risk of getting too much into semantics here, but my instinct is to say that it is. Judges routinely refer to the product of applying mitigation as damages for 'loss', even when the award exceeds the claimant's factual loss (on the conventional loss-based view). They have used a variety of terms including 'direct loss',[67] 'immediate

[64] Burrows, *Damages and Rights* (n 63) 290.

[65] Text to n 48.

[66] This does not preclude that other doctrines could impose other counterfactual assessments (within the breach and/or no-breach position) as well, but mitigation seems to be by the far the most common instance of this phenomenon.

[67] See eg *Burdis v Livsey* [2003] QB 36 (CA) [85] (Aldous LJ); *Uzinterimpex JSC v Standard Bank plc* [2008] EWCA Civ 819, [2008] 2 CLC 80 (n 69) [54] (Moore-Bick LJ); *Parabola Investments Ltd v Browallia Cal Ltd* [2010] EWCA Civ 486, [2011] QB 477 [55] (Toulson LJ); *Coles v Hetherton* [2013] EWCA Civ 1704, [2015] 1 WLR 160 [29] (Aikens LJ).

loss',[68] 'prima facie loss',[69] and 'notional loss',[70] but *loss* is common to all. Legal scholars too—even those who favour a factual loss cap—frequently slip into loss-based language: McGregor's own invention of the term 'avoided loss' is a prime example.[71] It is hard to maintain that loss must depend only on actual consequences when the conventional concept of factual loss itself rests on counterfactual consequences. Finally, as I noted above,[72] the relation between counterfactuals and causation is deep and complex, but I suspect it holds the key to explaining both the standard application of the compensatory principle and the doctrine of mitigation.

[68] See eg *Primavera v Allied Dunbar Assurance plc* [2002] EWCA Civ 1327, [2003] Lloyd's Rep PN 14 (CA) [27] (Simon Brown LJ); *AKAS Jamal v Moolla Dawood Sons & Co* [1916] 1 AC 175 (PC) 180 (Lord Wrenbury); *Nykredit Mortgage Bank plc v Edward Erdman Group Ltd* [1997] 1 WLR 1627 (HL) 1639 (Lord Hoffmann).

[69] See eg *Primavera* (n 68) [37] (Mance LJ); *Blamire v South Cumbria HA* [1993] PIQR Q1 (CA) Q4 (Steyn LJ).

[70] See eg *Biggin & Co Ltd v Permanite Ltd* [1951] 1 KB 422 (KB) 436 (Devlin J); *Hussey v Eels* [1990] 2 QB 227 (CA) 241 (Mustill LJ); *Lowe v Guise* [2002] EWCA Civ 197, [2002] QB 1369 [53] (Potter LJ).

[71] See further Chapter 1, text to n 125.

[72] Text to n 18.

Index

For the benefit of digital users, indexed terms that span two pages (e.g., 52–53) may, on occasion, appear on only one of those pages.